CHOREOGRAPHIC MUSIC

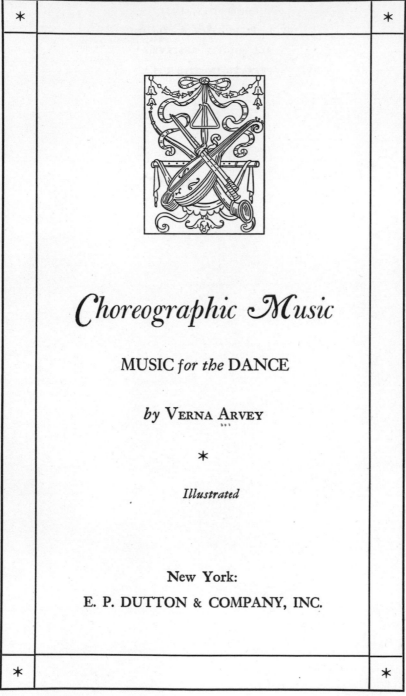

Choreographic Music

MUSIC *for the* DANCE

by VERNA ARVEY

*

Illustrated

New York:

E. P. DUTTON & COMPANY, INC.

FIRST EDITION

To

NORMA GOULD,

in recognition of her
service to all arts
allied with the Dance

FOREWORD

*

The art of the Dance is as yet recordless, as fleeting as the life of the artist who interprets it. Once Pavlowa's dancing was supreme artistry. Now it is mere memory and many descriptive, written words; but the music to which she danced still lives. Mozart danced the Minuet faultlessly. His dancing has passed on with him but the Minuets he wrote remain to charm us with their exquisite perfection.

Composers of all times have created a *living* body of musical literature for the Dance. For those who scorn the writing of such music, and deem it light and unworthy, let it be said that most great composers have been guilty of the crime. We now call their dances classics, simply because they wrote them. This book is therefore occupied equally with the classics of the past and of the future.

Then, if music be the spine of Dance, write on, ye composers great and small! The small will add to the luster of the great, and the great will re-create in their music the ephemeral Dance and its disappearing forms.

TABLE OF CONTENTS

*

LIST OF ILLUSTRATIONS

*

CHOREOGRAPHIC MUSIC

*

*

THE FUNCTION OF MUSIC IN PRIMITIVE DANCE CEREMONIALS

Choreographic music and music are one in primitive life. Whoever sings, dances. Whoever dances, sings. It is inconceivable otherwise (1).* This dance music has varied functions among scattered people, and for different dances. It has various external forms. The fact that all such music sounds monotonous to sophisticated ears does not imply that it is all similar.

The mental capacity of the primitive man is not so limited as one has been led to suppose. Some of his dance-songs, therefore, are truly great, speaking from literary and musical standpoints. Nor is the native as simple as his civilized brother wishes to believe. Were tourists in Africa to understand the words of certain modern dance-songs performed for their delighted eyes and ears, their smug dignity would be highly affronted, for the native dances gaily, while in the accompanying songs he aptly satirizes his audiences. The tourists are delighted with the show. So is the native.

There may be a reversion to the primitive among groups of people after a civilization has passed them by. Africa is known to have had a highly developed civilization in the unchronicled past. Today, that continent is a stronghold of

* See notes at the end of each Chapter.

contemporary primitives. Its music is reputed to be merely two
or three simple, oft-repeated measures; its tunes small in compass and therefore monotonous; its tone intervals weird. Yet
the entire religious, social and economic life of the African
people is embedded in their song and dance.

The dances may be secular or religious. In the latter (sup-
posing there is a catastrophe which must be averted) the witch
doctor first goes into a state of prayer, then begins the song for
the dance. Drummers pick up his rhythm, improvising as they
go along. The song usually presents the facts of the case, states
the tribe's innocence of crime and ends with a plea for forgive-
ness. Thus, the witch doctor is able, through the music, to bind
the people together in a common cause, to focus their minds
on one thing alone, so that their concentrated thought will be
able to achieve a result. The ritual dancer senses the intensity
of the mass: the dance becomes a visual expression of its plea.
In some cases, the witch doctor himself performs the ritual
dance as he sings. The people dance with him, taking up the
song as he finishes a phrase. The movement grows stronger
with the song(2).

Gorer(3) has described a Dahomey ritual when, at a signal
from one of the medicine men, the natives began to sing a
canticle—one of the most impressive of all African tunes—
while they performed a rhythmic and ritualist brushing of the
ground: a curious, solemn ceremony.

Abyssinians accompany their religious ceremonies with song
and movement, beating the earth with sticks and emphasizing
the strokes with movements, which increase in speed with
the increasing sound until at length all melody and meter
are lost.

Still another phase of the religious is offered by the Sene-
galese (Wolof) people in their m'Deup dances, when psychic
revelations are obtained by clairvoyants in the tribe. The
sound of the tom-tom is the signal for the m'Deup to fall into
a trance. There are special m'Deup songs and special drums.
For clairvoyants whose guiding spirits live in water a small
calabash, floating upside down in a larger, water-filled calabash,

is used. For other spirits the drum is used. The dance and its accompanying songs continue until the seer speaks (4).

African secular dances are entirely different. In place of the witch doctor, there may be professional dancers and drummers, all hired from families traditionally engaged in that occupation, just as families of professional mourners are hired for funerals. (In West Africa, a funeral song is danced, sung and clapped by a score of women, circling around a male soloist. Hired mourners continue the song for days.) On the other hand, the usual secular dances that happen nightly because there is nowhere to go, nothing else to do, are performed by those in the tribes who wish to dance or sing (5).

For these dances, the music is gay, vivacious, often irregular. Someone may begin a song on the subject of one girl, which will inspire a tribal colloquy on her merits, demerits, appearance or characteristics. The m'Goiyu m'Gomas are said to have a popular dance song with these words repeated many times: "In England the rupees are as stones on the ground." The variations in tune and in rhythm are so many that for at least half an hour of word repetition, the listener's interest may be sustained.

The function of music in these secular dances is a simple one. Where the dance has no profound meaning, the music will also be light. Both may be spontaneous outbursts for the display of virtuosity, whether it be in the quality of musical or poetic invention or in the extent of the dancers' technique.

African festival dances depend on what is then being commemorated. They work from the secular into the religious, from religious to secular. Language controls the rhythmic figures; costumes govern movements which are, nevertheless, spontaneous results of the singing. The steps themselves correspond to the drum rhythms. African drummers are thus conductors of the dance. Their rhythms are successive and varied. Often many different counter-rhythms are heard at once. The song may stop for many pulsing moments while the drums play alone.

The differences in song and dance in separated African

tribes lie in rhythmic and melodic variations, but underlying
motifs and methods are identical throughout the dark continent.   Of all the dance-songs, Nicholas J. Ballanta (6) places in
the highest class the artistic songs of the Yorubas with
". . . cross rhythms in abundance.   In these dances are characteristic rhythms which have meanings ascribed to them in directing the dancers how to proceed."

A tremendous emotional force is generated by the songs
for war dances, most of which have the same general form
among primitives : rising to a thrilling climax of speed and
sound.   Zulu tribes, for instance, have a very old war song,
dating back to the time before the coming of the white man.   As
a prelude to battle, it is sung to rouse a fighting frenzy in the
warriors and is accompanied by a fierce, defiant war dance.
The song increases in speed as the dancers advance with a
rhythmic thud of feet, above which anklets clank and add to
the general rhythmic effect, as do the sounds of many primitive
costume ornaments.

Seabrook (7) quotes a Gueré song, sung by the youths just
admitted to the war dances :

> "Our fathers were men
> Now do we do as they taught us
> We follow their steps
> And shout as they do—
> So as not to forget."

An ecstatic, expansive music, obviously meant to whet sensu-
ality in the dancers, may accompany a fertility dance.   Appropriate whistles, carried by the dancers themselves, are often
utilized to further characterize various birds or animals in
dances descriptive of their habits.

Another use for the whistle occurs in the Shangaan (a
South African dance) when it is blown in a code of long and
short blasts at pauses by the ballet masters, as a means of
instructing the corps de ballet.   This dance is also accompanied
by singing and wooden clappers.

Legends of the different tribes are often put into dance

songs, though some legends have dance-songs embodied within them. Natalie Curtis(8) mentions, also, laboring tunes which have been converted into dance songs by the natives.

Zulu dance-songs are said to be largely clever, spontaneous improvisations. If, for instance, a dance pantomimes a certain illness, the accompanying song speaks of the misfortunes of that illness. It has been said that many Zulu dance-songs are native imitations of "white" tunes which assume an African sound when accompanied by rhythmic handclapping, colored with the varied tonal effects produced by striking the hands together in different ways: a percussion orchestra of human palms(9). This often has the precision and sound-quality of a man-made percussion instrument, such as a pair of giant castanets. Though these tunes may be sung steadily for an hour and a half, no one person claps the same way throughout. Rhythms are interchangeable.

A surprising function of some African dance accompanists is mentioned by Gorer(10). It is their duty, declares he, to sing and dance grotesquely, parodying the dancers they accompany!

When the Negroes were forced out of Africa, they took with them their arts, so that today much of what we regard as native to other countries is really African. In some spots, African arts have remained primitive and untouched and have superseded the arts of other inhabitants. In other places, they have been fused with alien cultures.

The United States, Cuba and various South American countries have been the recipients of many Africans. Those in Brazil have had a powerful influence on the nation's art. Travelers never tire of describing the savage songs and dances on which the more sophisticated product is based: sounds of tom-toms coming faintly through the wilderness, shrill cries, the wailing of women. A central Brazilian death dance has for its musical accompaniment a song designed to be a communication with the dead person. The words address him endearingly, as if he were present. The erotic Colombian Cumbia, danced by Indians as well as Negroes, is designed to create desire in the dancers. The music, passionate and everchanging, helps to intensify the original meaning and purpose of the dance: it creates mood, inflames the senses and finally forms a faraway accompaniment to the intimate, personal rites that the dance precedes.

Melville J. Herskovits (11) has written that in the Haitian ritual of possession by the gods, the dance plays a prominent part. Certain gods are associated with particular drum rhythms, and specific dances are for specific deities. Songs are important in calling the spirits. In the dance itself the use of iron to sound basic rhythms for the drums, the outer form and function of the rattle and the fact that a circle of participants always rotates in a counter-clockwise direction, are equally African.

The Nigerian Prince, Modupe(12), has observed in modern North American Negro churches the feeling of African dance-songs. The prayer of one man becomes a chant, others join in the chant, the chant becomes a shout and the shout becomes movement. A splendid safety valve. The old "ring-shout" was pure African movement and sound. The Spiritual, accompanied by handclapping, became a shout and the monotonous repetition of single phrases induced ecstatic trances in those who participated.

The music of the North American Indian is almost entirely choreographic. Moreover, it greatly differs from that of other primitives. For example, Indians on the Morongo Reservation hold a yearly ceremony for the dead. The motive is to relinquish all earthly hold on the departed spirits. To that end, the accompanying song tells of events liable to distract the minds in the tribe from personal grief. Arthur Farwell's translation(13) of another "Song of the Ghost Dance" reveals the Indian's consciousness that his race is doomed: "Have pity on me! There is nothing here to satisfy me. . . ." In other tribes, dances are done to songs invoking the aid or approval of the spirits. Great chorales alternate with individual pleas from different soloists. During the Sun Dance in Taos, a Pueblo anthem is sung. It is a repetition of simple syllables, a prayer of praise and of thanksgiving and a supplication for the continuance of the Sun-Father's favor. In a part of the Arapahoe Sun Dance, whistles made from the wing bone of an eagle are blown during the dance-song. These are said to symbolize the breath of life and to represent the cry of the thunderbird(14).

The Pawnee Hako has a final dance of thanksgiving on the fifth day of the ceremony: a prayer for children, so that the tribe may increase and be strong. There are two special dance-songs for this: songs in which everyone joins. The Hako ceremony was originally given to the fathers of the tribe in a vision(15).

"One has to study the Indian dance music (rather, their music) from the nature and variety of the dancing," declares Farwell(16), "And from the inner ritualistic or legendary significance of the dance. One must know the exact meaning of the ritual, and the particular thought-of-the-moment in it that is being danced. Then the different rhythms have an occult significance. The drum tremolo among the Plains Indians, for instance, means the Great Spirit (Great Mystery)."

Indian songs for dancing form a running accompaniment for the movement, or they may consist merely of vocables. They usually have to do with the earth: plants growing, people aging, and so on. There are solemn songs and happy songs, but the dance patterns conform to the general pattern of the music(17).

The Pawnees have many dance-songs in honor of young warriors. A war dance-song may also be a vivacious call to action to an individual, or to tribesmen.

Still another type of song derives from animals. An Iroquois Buffalo Dance is derived from the actions of the buffalo, its songs from what the Iroquois heard at a Kentucky salt lick (when they warred against the Cherokees) when the buffalo were singing their favorite songs, bellowing and grumbling. Frances Densmore tells of seeing an Indian warrior who had dreamed of a bear and believed that he was therefore victorious, performing a war dance to acknowledge the aid of his spirit-helper, while the drummer sang the song given him by the bear.

The primitive Veddahs of Ceylon have many songs invoking success in the hunt, accompanied by pantomimic ceremonial dances. Those who are invoked are the spirits of dead relatives. There are also songs and dances to invoke success in the collecting of honey—an important item of Veddah fare. Here, the dances pantomime the occupation while the song tells the story.

In primitive Australian dance-representations of hunted animals, the music reproduces feelings appropriate to the hunt: suspense, excitement. Another type of Australian dance-song, sung by the wives of seal-hunters, is a prayer for protection for their men.

According to one writer, music for the Maori war dances acts as a regulator or coördinator, for (in his opinion) their Haka is a disciplinary measure. His opinion, however, is disapproved by many who believe the Haka, with its savage, barked accompanying chorus, is intended to whip the Maoris into a blood frenzy before they close with their enemies. The fierce gestures and grimaces in this dance are to distract the enemy's thoughts from the difficulties at hand.

By far the most gruesome function of all primitive dance music is that of the head-hunting dance songs of the Ibalaos in the Philippine jungle. The ceremony is held after the heads have been taken. Song and dance crescendo rapidly and become hysterical. Praises of the killer are shouted. At that precise moment, the chief administers the oath of allegiance to all young men from puberty up who have not yet killed. The orgiastic ceremony is intended to inspire them!

If a Greenlander has a grievance against another, he composes an ironic poem to which he sets dance movements. Then he and his family compete with the other for satirical supremacy. The group that evokes the loudest laughter is victorious.

The Hawaiian Hula offers an example of primitive *absolute* music derived from dance-songs, for there are several different kinds of Hula. Under the designation of Mele Hula fall those less-formal chants adapted to dance purposes. Plain Hula chants are in the style of those usually accompanied by dancing, though the dance itself is lacking. In olden times there were no plain Hulas, and the Mele Hulas were chanted only by trained performers. The older the Hula, the smaller its tonal compass. The older the dance, the less foot-movement it contains. Thus, from a stark, utterly simple, primitive beginning, pure music has arisen from dance music in Hawaii!

The Hula is a legendary matter. It began at the instigation of Pele, Goddess of Volcanoes, and it means nothing more nor less than to dance to the sound of music. Thus "Hula" has as wide a scope as our word "dance," and it embraces everything from the buffoonery of dancing marionettes to descriptive or sacred dancing. The chants have functions allied to those of the Hula they accompany. The Pu-Niu, a cocoanut shell rattle containing dry seeds, is a Hawaiian musical instrument used in the accompaniment for ancient Hulas.

It is possible to describe hundreds of native ceremonials, to speak of strange musical instruments and curious ways to accompany the dance. In essence, it would mean no more nor less than the examples already given. Dance and song prepare for war and the hunt. They promote skill and strength in peaceful times. They amuse, they form the cultural background of many tribes. They are essential elements in primitive drama. They regulate labor, stimulate the body organs. They are religious—that is to say, they have an occult significance in many cases.

The dances and their songs have the same end in view. They are sometimes spontaneous, sometimes carefully designed and rehearsed beforehand. Each has its particular function, each accomplishes its end. Without dance, there would be no song. Without song (or rhythmic accompaniment) the dance would not exist. Each is equally important.

Is it too much to say that dance and song constitute the very life of primitive people the world over?

CHAPTER 1

NOTES

(1) However, Dr. A. N. Tucker (in his book, *Tribal Music and Dancing in the Southern Sudan,* p. 54) declares that it is a mistake to suppose that there is no singing without dancing. He has often seen natives crooning to themselves by the hour, without moving a finger. But, he admits, the songs they croon are usually dance-songs, or fragments of dance-songs which, when he later heard them at dances, with the added drum and body rhythms, changed their characters so completely that he scarcely recognized them. More, Joseph Schillinger found in his investigations of dance music of Georgia's forty-four tribes that the dance and music in general were derived from pagan ceremonials, and that the tribes with the most primitive musical forms *do not dance at all!* (taken from a letter to the author from Joseph Schillinger in New York City, dated March 5, 1936). So that there are, in every case, exceptions to the general rule.

(2) In an interview with Prince Modupe of Nigeria in Los Angeles on November 24, 1935

(3) Gorer: *Africa Dances,* p. 172

(4) Gorer: *Africa Dances,* p. 46

(5) Prince Modupe

(6) Maud Cuney-Hare, *Negro Musicians and Their Music,* p. 28

(7) Seabrook, *Jungle Ways,* p. 182

(8) Curtis, *Songs and Tales from the Dark Continent,* p. 107

(9) Curtis, *Songs and Tales from the Dark Continent,* p. xxi

(10) Gorer, *Africa Dances,* p. 304

(11) Herskovits, *Life in a Haitian Valley,* pp. 177, 182, 183

(12) Prince Modupe

(13) Farwell, Preface to *American Indian Melodies,* p. 6

(14) Havemeyer, *The Drama of Savage People,* pp. 88-89

(15) Fletcher, *The Pawnee Hako,* pp. 26, 253

(16) In a letter to the author from Arthur Farwell in East Lansing, Michigan, March 4, 1936

(17) In an interview with Tom Youngplant, Hopi dancer, in Los Angeles on April 4, 1936

ANCIENT CHOREOGRAPHIC MUSIC AND ITS SURVIVAL

There was a distinction between pure music and dance music in ancient civilizations, but the one (in most cases) was as highly esteemed as the other. Very little of the ancient music has been preserved, though it has been amply pictured and described. Nevertheless, in the opinion of close observers (travelers and musicologists) this music survives today in many lands. It is kept alive through choreographic music!

Ancient music itself was based upon the primitive variety. Rhythmic variations, regarded as ultra-modern today, were natural in primitive and ancient music. José Iturbi(1) volunteers the information that music was created first; afterward the professors came along to divide it into regular counts. Cecil Sharp(2) tells us that the ancients (i.e., the Greeks) did not invent their modes. They merely explained them. Presumably, it was from the folk that they derived the material which they analyzed and from which they deduced their theories. Sharp also believes that Greek dancing was based on the indigenous dances of the common people scattered throughout the country.

If these premises are correct, it is probable that ancient music has survived—in the very form in which it originally existed. And what more natural than that it should survive in dance tunes, bound up with music as dance has always been? This is no mere superficial observation, although it is a difficult thing to prove, since there were intervening years when so much was lost. More, when it has been possible to trace certain songs back to certain centuries, impulsive people are always apt to forget that they must have been based on what went before, musically speaking, since no new creation is entirely devoid of dependence on the old—folk music least of all.

The Emperor Shun (China, 2255 B.C.) was first to introduce the dance into Chinese religious ceremonies. Thereafter, the Chinese dancing master was also director of music. Confucius described the Emperor Yu-Yang (1100 B.C.) as being the originator of many dances and their accompanying music. Among his many ballets was a great historical spectacle, beginning with the creation and ending with what was then contemporary history. The music was of a peculiar symphonic form, melodious and dramatic. It was preserved in Pekin in fragmentary form for many years, but vanished during political disturbances.

Old Chinese fairy tales speak of dance music so graphic in its description of a story that "the hair of the guest, as he listened, rose in his head with terror!" (3) They speak of strings, flutes, little golden bells, pipes and cymbals as dance accompaniments.

When Emperor She Huang-Ti (246 B.C.) destroyed the greater part of the existing books (including music books) the music that remained was almost entirely choreographic. We are told that at the rise of the Han dynasty, the great music master, Chi, scarcely remembered anything about music but the noise of tinkling bells and dancers' drums. It was not until A.D. 485 that an imperial decree gave dancing a place in the Confucian ceremonies.

Chao Mei-Pa (4) says: The voice forms the foundation of Chinese music, the instruments accompany it and later, the dances animate the whole. Indeed, Chinese dances must express to the eye what the voice and instruments convey to the ear.

There are several outstanding differences in the music for the classic Chinese drama (which includes dance) and the modern. Speaking generally, the music for the classic drama is a single tune, underlying and underscoring the actors' voices without a variation in intensity, though the voices themselves are most expressive. That is to say that the melodic line of the voice follows that of the leading instrument, with a soft, rhythmic percussion accompaniment underneath. The music for the modern drama is more dramatic, more like incidental music as we know it. The voice does not adhere so closely to the melodic lines of the instruments. It often goes contrapuntally, or enters a bit off-rhythm, in the manner of a modern crooner. These subtle changes may be due to foreign influences, and may not.

A modern Chinese composer of ballets, Dr. Y.M. Hsiao (5), utters this sage observation on China's music, ancient and modern: "For China's choreographic music, I should say very complicated, and have no system too." Nevertheless, that the ancient forms of Chinese dance music (theatrical and sacred) exist today as they did in ancient days, there seems to be no doubt. They are as traditional and as exact as any of the dramas presented in the Chinese theater. The two classifications today: Bugaku (classic) or Sangaku (leisure dance) are the same as of yore. Sōgaku, Chinese orchestral music, includes the accompaniments to these two forms of dancing.

There is another method by which ancient Chinese culture has been preserved and, in most cases, amplified. Japan dances the Chinese Bugaku and Sangaku (and these are the names accorded them in Japan) though she has added her own Dengaku and Sarugaku, (for which only thirteen pieces of accompanying music had been approved up until the middle of the thirteenth century) as done in the Nō plays beginning at the close of the fourteenth century. In these dramas, a singing chorus sits at one side. Occasionally, the dance postures are clarified by abbreviated words. The Chinese stringed biwa (used so often in the Bugaku dance that it was called the Bugaku-biwa) was also imported into Japan, and exerted a profound influence on modern Japanese dance music for the samisen. The Chinese koto was brought into Japan at the same time as the biwa, to replace the crude Japanese yamato koto.

The first record of Japanese dance-song comes in the form of a legend. Amaterasu, the Sun Goddess, withdrew into a tree-trunk in anger, whence the beautiful Amé-no-Uzumé danced and sang before her hiding place to lure her out, so that the world would again be bright. This legend was oral until A.D. 712, when the Kojiki (Record of Ancient Matters) was compiled.

It is the Imperial Household of Japan that has preserved the nation's most ancient music, known as Gagaku, or Graceful Music, and divided into two kinds, one of which is that which accompanies the dance in the entertainments of the Imperial Household. This music is performed today as an accompaniment to the solemn dance called Kagura, in order to console the spirits of ancestors with their own special music and dancing, since this is the primitive Japanese music that existed long before the introduction of Chinese culture.

Japanese drama and music grew out of the dance: all of Japan's music is indebted to the need for accompanying the dance, in the opinion of Mme. Kimiyo Ito(6). A.D. 901-922 was the Golden Age of old Japan, an entire epoch of Japanese musical history based equally on song and dance, when all the arts and sciences flourished under the genial encouragement of the court. Success for a new dance or musical composition was determined only by a court performance by an imperial band of female artists. In the contemporary Japanese theater, a female orchestra still accompanies the dancing. It was in A.D. 901 that the famous national Saiba-gaku (or Saibara) was invented. It was based on a song sung by the peasants as they trudged over the mountains to bring tribute to the Emperor. This dance finally had fifty-three accompanying songs, and was performed annually at the palace after it had obtained royal favor. This often happened. For instance, the song and dance of the rice-planters was imperially ordered to be established as music. Many other daily occupations were given dance and musical form, such as the Bon-odori-uta, the moonlight dance of the fishermen in July.

In fact, inspiration for most of the dances was then sought in common, everyday incidents. Characteristic features of each occurrence were reduced to rhythmic form and amplified with symbolic gestures, just as a composer makes a motif the subject of a musical composition and thereafter develops it. The musical accompaniment to each such Japanese dance outlined the action of that dance. Thus the Japanese made a perfect blend of poetry, dance, and music. They considered the human voice—not the musical instrument—as giving the true and balanced rhythm of the dance and of drama, however. The voice was used as a conductor uses his baton. It also was made to fill the musical pauses. It was in these pauses—crucial moments—that the art and ingenuity of the dancer were judged: by what he was able to do with little support from the music. Thus the voice and the instrument became as melody and accompaniment carried out through the medium of the dancer's body.

The famous Kabuki incantations and dances, accompanied by flute and drums, were begun by Okumi of Izumo, a young temple dancer. She danced in the attire of a nun, meanwhile beating a drum and reciting Buddhist prayers. She had been taught to play and sing by her lover, Sanzaburo Nagoya, who had composed songs for her.

The Nō drama, mentioned in a previous paragraph, was originally meant for the nobility. Its music arose from the Gagaku music of the Imperial Household, according to some authorities. To this day, the Nō drama remains rather exclusive. The bringing of the stringed samisen from the southern island of Ryukyu several hundred years ago marked the beginning of popular music and dance for commoners. It also marked the beginning of notated music for the dance in Japan.

Today, there is no change in the native, traditional dance music Japan has always enjoyed, though with her acceptance of the outside world she has also developed an affection for foreign music and instruments. This makes no difference what-

soever in her love for traditional arts. There is even a sort
of native Japanese jazz for dancing, but no one considers it
really important (7).

Some Japanese composers have disappeared from time to
time into faraway lands and have begun to write a different
sort of music. Sooner or later they are expected to find their
own individual idiom, based on their native temperaments and
aided by their special training. The contemporary Japanese
soprano, Toshiko Sekiya, has made an interesting venture
along these lines. She has written a song after a Japanese folk
tale which had long before been dramatized as one of the
Kabuki dramas. Her music follows the line of the drama, in
which the episodes are shown in dance-form, while the vocal
score is adapted to the dramatic moments of the dance. Though
the accompaniment is scored for piano, it resembles the music
of the koto, samisen and shakuhachi. Other modern Japanese
composers are: Hidemaro Konoe, Yamada, Michio Miyagi,
Sawada, Itow, Ohono, Nakayama. Some write in occidental
forms and for occidental instruments, others follow the examples of their musical ancestors.

Ancient Japanese arts also owed something to Korea,
though occidental travelers have described Korean dance music
as being so weird that, by contrast, all other oriental music is
completely harmonious.

The modern musical accompaniment to the Royal Cambodian Ballet, which makes periodic appearances on festival days
or in state ceremonials, is based on ancient musical modes, the
heritage of Angkor-Vat legends. In some cases, this music
begins slowly and accelerates to a frenzied climax. There is also
martial music for warlike dances and humorous music for the
dance of Hanuman, the monkey-general. According to George
Groslier (8), the instruments used are tiny viols and the thin-
toned Cambodian tom-tom, as well as flutes and the exotic,
sonorous instruments imported from Siam "dominating and
chiseling into relief the musical motif."

The Siamese Lakhon, or classic dance, is also dramatic and
vocal. In olden times, it was given only by royalty. That it is

traditional in all respects is evidenced by the fact that five choristers chant the long history, or assist the dancers in their own chanting of verses, timing the chants by striking two pieces of wood together. There is a small orchestra in which the flute is the leading instrument. Drums accompany. In the larger orchestras there are instruments enough to provide for a fugal device, when different instruments take the melody, while others play variants on it. Each musical theme belongs to a well-defined dance posture. Both theme and posture are conventional and traditional. There are action themes: walking, marching, laughing, weeping, anger tunes. All express corresponding actions.

The Philippine Malays, living north of Manila in the Ilocano provinces, had a highly developed culture in ancient times. Their alphabet was related to Sanskrit. Their handiwork, literature, dancing and music were superb. The ancient Philippine dance was said to be largely pantomimic, the dance-songs monotonous. When the Spaniards came, they fused their culture with ancient Philippine arts, so that Filipino folk dances and music today bear the stamp of Spain.

Ancient Chinese music was similar, technically speaking, to the music of the old Greeks. Notation and style were similar too. It has even been said that the three types of Chinese music: religious, grotesque and dance music, were also found in Greek music. In Greece, the composers of music, of dance and of poetry worked closely together. Thus unity was achieved. Often these three creative qualities were vested in a single person. In 630 B.C. Alcman composed and directed a ballet. In it, the story underlying the dance was clarified by a prologue or a vocal accompaniment, so that the dancer was left free to express the mood of the composition. Aeschylus and Sophocles were both noted dance authorities and musicians. They improved both music and choreography of the Bibasis. Aeschylus composed the music, rehearsed the chorus and designed the scenery and costumes for all his plays.

Music and dance were indispensable to the education of cultured Greeks. The Arcadians were one of the backwoods peoples of Greece even in Polybius' time, yet he avers that their sons were forced to learn music and dance, to practice a military step to the music of the pipe, and to produce, in regular order of battle, elaborate dances in theaters. *They did not hire their musicians, but did their own singing.*

It must be remembered that these particular arts of the Greeks reached their highest perfection—not singly—but in the theater where all were combined. No one of them was regarded as a separate art. Sometimes a flautist or harpist in the orchestra furnished the accompaniment for the dancing of the chorus. But it was just as common for the dancers to sing *a cappella* as they moved, or to accompany themselves on some instrument. This gives rise to the modern theory: that the rhythm of ancient music corresponded to that of verse and the dance step. Dalcroze(9) says that to have composed the music which the Greeks appear to have realized, musicians must surely have acquired experience with physical movements.

Plato pictured an ideal republic with music important for the regulation of the voice, and dancing for the acquisition of noble, harmonious and graceful attitudes. He refused the title of musician to everyone who was not perfectly versed in rhythm. Aristophanes (445-385 B.C.) speaks in a poem of "the music of thy feet." The authors known as Museus and Orpheus desired that the hymns they composed in honor of the gods should be accompanied by dancing. Plutarch, in his *Symposiaca*, describes the dance as the handmaiden of poetry: its purpose to emphasize the poet's creation. When Aristides (died 468 B.C.) spoke of Greek music he said, "Meter is not a thing which concerns the ear alone, for in the dance it is to be *seen*." Sophocles was famed as a skillful musician and dancer.

The Curetes, young single men, were initiated into the secret rites of a society for the worship of Zeus Kouros with ecstatic dances in armor. That courage might predominate, they used in their musical accompaniment the loud tones of the Cretan measures, invented by Thales. In Homer's time, the Cretans had six kinds of ⁵⁄₄ time to which they danced. These were

FIJI ISLANDERS IN A DRUM RITUAL
Photograph courtesy of Columbia Films

A WAYANG BEBER

Javanese Picture-Theater banner, showing in the upper left-hand corner a shadow puppet show with orchestra

From the collection of Hubert Stowitts

called Paeans, as was the hymn to Apollo, since the singers danced in Cretan rhythms as they chanted. Many Greek dances had their own characteristic rhythms. The Ionian characteristic was two long and two short steps, corresponding to Ionic feet in verse. Others had their individual forms. As these steps were known by certain names, so were the melodies or modes to which the steps were danced, declared Edward MacDowell(10).

It was MacDowell's opinion(11), also, that the voice was used to accompany the flute in early Greek dances to prevent their appealing directly to the senses. Nevertheless, Xenophon described a Greek Mysian war dance to the sound of the flute alone. The Hormos, reputed to be invented by Lycurgus, was a graceful and lively war dance in which a leader, playing the lyre, regulated the dancers' movements. All dances and sacrifices in honor of Apollo were performed to the sound of flutes, wrote Plutarch. The armed Hyporchemes, or military dance, was sung by the dancers themselves to the sound of flutes and citharas. Pindar was the first poet-musician to compose for this dance.

Military dances were termed "Pyrrhic." A contemporary Albanian dance called the Arnaöut is usually danced in armor and is supposed to be the ancient Pyrrhic dance.

A traveler describes another modern Greek Pyrrhic dance in a different place, done to the squealing of a clarinet and the beating of a large drum. This music was described as being a wild, monotonous chant, with several ornaments on high notes, running down to a long drone at the end. The phrases are not more than two or three bars long, and are repeated again and again. Modern Athenians insist that this music is Turkish. Their long slavery, they say, has completely destroyed ancient Greek musical traditions. This, of course, is doubted by many. On the other hand, Hoyt Rawlings(12) has described a modern Turkish dance, when the "inevitable piper and drummer furnish the inevitable rhythm to which the men dance: a slow, leisurely, oriental clog. The monotony of both music and dance is varied only by the addition of more dancers." So, that if (as the Athenians insist) modern Greek dance music is really of Turkish origin, the Greeks have added something of their own to it. It is not entirely Turkish.

Ethel H. Thomson(13) declares that the inhabitants of Epidaurus in Greece still dance the dances of their pre-Christian ancestors. Today, a choral dance, relic of the fourth century B.C., is done by men with linked hands. The vocal accompaniment bears similarities to the Gregorian chant. Both music and dance are rhythmic. "There is no doubt that in Crete especially," declares yet another writer, "the ancient dances are still popular. All the old customs prevail there."

A modern dance of Casos, near the Aegean Sea, is described as being accompanied by a youth who plays the lyre, sings and dances at the same time. Modern Greece has also its klephtic songs, some dating back to the seventeenth century, which tell stories of events and which are now used as they may have been used originally: as an accompaniment to the dance. The refrain is always an emphatic dance rhythm, while the verse is an ornate recitative. A historic Greek event is commemorated in a song called the Dance of Zalonghos when Greek women, preferring death to enslavement by the Turks, joined hands and began to dance and sing their favorite song. As they went around, at the end of each measure the last woman in the line flung herself into a chasm. The song of those Suliote women is still popular. There are three principal modern Greek dance rhythms: tsamikos (slow ¾); syrtos or kalamatianos (⅞); and chasapikos (quick ⅖). Usually a recitative is followed by the danceable refrain. But since the dance nowadays is the principal object of the song, the recitative is often eliminated entirely.

Today at Delphi, the music of the composer Constantine Psachos is used for dancing in the festival. It harks back to archaic motifs, yet is modern and is suited to express a pastoral atmosphere. An enlarged orchestra (woodwinds, harps and percussion) is used, rather than the classic flutes.

The ancient Romans, who still labor under the stigma of having borrowed Greek art and having allowed it to deteriorate rather than having advanced it, preferred pantomime to dancing. They liked unaccompanied pantomime telling a story; pantomime accompanied by an orchestra; and pantomime with both chorus and orchestra on the stage, playing, acting and singing the narrative.

Numa, legendary king of Rome, chose twelve handsome, patrician young men to be dancers and singers of hymns in praise of the god of war. This was a religious institution. The young men danced through the city, singing assamenta and beating time on their sacred shields. Because of their violent motions, the Romans called them Salii (leapers). Because other dancers imitated the Salii, they were termed Saltatori. In the time of Burney (latter part of the eighteenth century) Italian operas were still employing Saltatori.

In 1927, choral dancing was revived in Rome. The setting was the Domitian theater on the Palatine Hill. A chorus of three hundred and a ballet interpreted music of the sixteenth century, brought from the museums or extracted from the recent Turin discoveries.

In Hindu literature, the Anugita (a later portion of the Bhagavad Gita) condemns Sangit (dancing, singing and playing) altogether. Nor is the Anugita the only form of Hindu literature which adopts such a condemnatory attitude.

Yet, the arts of dancing, singing and playing are said to be of divine origin in India. They are also ancient, and are said to have originated simultaneously. One tradition as to their origin revolves around the phoenix, that strange, ancient bird called the Dipak-Lata. When the Dipak-Lata approaches one thousand years of age, it falls into a state of ecstasy and dances around a fire of combustibles which ignite when the seven apertures in its beak play the Dipak Rága. (A Rága, in Hindu music, is a male theme.) The bird then disappears into the fire. From the warm ashes which remain, an egg is created—an egg that later becomes a Dipak-Lata. This has been going on since the beginning of time. The bird is thus perpetuated, and music and dance created.

It is known that the Hindus, at the beginning of the Aryan

invasion (about 2000 B.C.) had already developed their music and dance. Because of its divine origin, it played a significant part in all ceremonials. In the old days, there were in existence sixteen thousand themes (rágas or ráginis) and three hundred and sixty talas (rhythms). Music was divided into seven parts of which the fifth was, and still is, Nirt-Adhaya: that which treats of dancing.

Brahma, the Creator, is the first person in the Hindu triad. He it was who invented the drum, made from the bloody earth of a demon enemy-god whom he had killed in battle. The earliest Indian drums (myrdangas) were clay-bodied. Later came wooden drums. The flute came second in the evolution of musical instruments. Krishna, the pastoral God, fashioned the first flute from a section of bamboo. He was also a gifted dancer. Today no dance is ever given in India without either drum or flute, or both. The talan (a disc of copper against one of polished steel) and the oboe may be added. An anonymous Hindu poem (1500-1000 B.C.) called "Dance of a Nautch Girl" describes her as dancing to "Music's five-fold sound."

It was, however, Brahma who added six ráginis (female themes) to the principal musical rágas, and at the same time taught Rambha the art of dancing. This celestial female imparted, in turn, her knowledge to mankind. Some Sanskrit authorities are nevertheless inclined to the opinion that Brahma taught the art of dancing to the sage Bharata, who imparted his knowledge to other rashís, and thus dancing was handed down to humans. The accompaniment to ancient Vedic dances was provided by lutes, flutes and drums.

Indra's heaven, on Mount Meru, was said to be filled with dancers and musicians. Today the Deva-Dasis, or Hindu dancing girls, claim their descent from the Apsaras, celestial dancers of Indra's court, while the strolling musician claims a like descent from the Ghandarvas, or male singers of Indra's court.

The continuous rhythm of music for Hindu dance leads the hearer into himself. From the Indian point of view, the aesthetic experience is purely of the spectator. The artist can only provide the conditions. This is perhaps best explained by Coomaraswamy and Duggirala (14) : "The song should be sustained by the throat; its meaning must be shown by the hands; the mood must be shown by the glances; rhythm is marked by the feet. For wherever the hand moves, there the glances follow; where the glances go, the mind follows: where the mind goes, the mood follows; where the mood goes, there is the flavour."

No liberties with rhythm are taken in Hindu music. Nothing breaks the flow. Within its compass, the time may be doubled or taken twice as slowly; or a four-beat measure may change to a six without altering the main accents of the rhythm. The understanding between dancers and musicians is therefore perfect. They are always in unison. The drummer, no matter what his rhythmic innovations, will always meet the dancer, singer or instrumentalist on the climax of the beat. There is no need for a choreographic interpretation of a composer's intention, for there are no notes to be played. However, the rágas, ráginís and talas have been mastered so thoroughly that the instrumentalists are able to create an infinite variety of patterns within the prescribed forms. The ancient rules governing the moods of the melodies today also govern their visible representation in dance form. "But when the Indian prophet speaks of inspiration, it is to say that the Vedas are eternal . . . it is then Sarasvati or Narada or Krishna, whose flute is forever calling to us to leave the duties of the world and follow Him—it is these, rather than any human individual, who speak through the singer's voice and are seen in the movements of the dancer," declares Ananda Coomaraswamy (15).

Thus, the music and dance of contemporary India are practically the same as they were five thousand years ago. Every important festival is celebrated with special music and dance. The Spring Dances of Vasant worship the gods with music and movement: the symbols of Nature's resurrection and fructifying. Every notable Hindu temple has its attendant bands of musicians and dancers. Tradition has decreed their songs and movements. Some travelers maintain that modern

rural dancing in India, accompanied by emphatic and characteristic music, greatly surpasses the professional variety in
point of interest.

An Afghan military dance is described as being more varied
in step and in accompanying music than the monotonous Nautch.
The drumbeat accompanied handclapping, the dancers sang a
falsetto chant, and the pipes wailed shrilly.

Bali and Java were at one time part of the same kingdom.
That their theatrical arts are allied to those of India is common
knowledge.   In the words of Gorer(16) : It is almost certain
that in present-day Balinese art and ritual we have a highly
individual version of the arts of Hindu Java as they existed
before the drying wind of Allah blasted them.   Hickman
Powell(17) tells us further that the gamelans of Bali and Java
are related also to the musical instruments of Siam and Cam-
bodia, though he was told that the music of these continental
countries is quite inferior.   The civilization of all these lands,
of course, came from a common root; and kinship may be seen
especially in the dancing.   The Balinese fled to the island of
Bali for freedom, just as the Puritans fled to America.   At the
same time, they freed themselves from certain conventions, and
this spirit of freedom is shown today in their music and dance.
The priests, however, still practice old Buddhist and Hindu
rituals of mudras (hand and arm postures) and their accompanying mantrams (chants).   Often the old Hindu epics, the
Ramayana and the *Mahabharata*, are the subjects for their
dance-dramas.   Balinese dance and music, nevertheless, have
never been formalized(18).   Every day something new is
composed.   A piece of music is written on or around a dramatic
idea, and on that structure a dance will be built.   There is great
rivalry as to who will write the next great music.   Javanese
dance and music, on the other hand, is classic and rigidly prescribed, though it is preserved by means of human memory
rather than by notation.   There are thirty-four different themes
handed down from one generation to another.

Strangely enough, in spite of the fact that Javanese dance
music is traditional and that in Bali constantly changing, the

latter is truer to the ancient spirit than the former, due to the disturbing effect Chinese traders have had on Javanese arts. The Balinese people are inclined to incorporate foreign elements into their own art in such a way that those elements lose their foreign identity. The Javanese are apt to adopt bodily what comes into their land.

In Java and Bali, the dance movements correspond to the tones of the gamelan, which is the finest type of percussion orchestra in the world. Everything that takes place on the stage or the dancing floor follows the music, beat by beat. Raden Adjeng Kartini(19) wrote of this music: "The gamelan never rejoices. Even at the most extravagant festivals, it is mournful." Some dances tell a story in a language of postures. The tale is clarified orally by the dalang (master of ceremonies), and emphasized by the music of the gamelan, certain notes of which correspond to particular postures. In the Javanese Serimpi dance, ascribed to sacred legend and danced by princesses, the deep-toned gongs sound as the dancers pause at the end of a phrase which, according to their philosophy, is also the beginning of the next phrase. The final pose is accompanied by the striking of the lowest, deepest gong. The vibrations of the tone continue long after the movement has finished.

The dance of the Bedoyoes, feminine Javanese court dancers, is considered so holy that its accompanying poem must not be chanted publicly (this poem speaks of a goddess who assumed mortal form to chant her passion for the reigning potentate and to dance for him) nor must rehearsals occur on any but propitious holy days. Today this dance is performed while the holy poem is played and chanted by a concealed orchestra.

Javanese music for dances, says Hendrik de Leeuw (20), must be in true harmony with the stage effects and nature. These, for the Javanese artist, must be absolutely one. And so there exists for them in the atmosphere a certain vibration in every hour of day or night, which is so effectively expressed in the tempi and rhythms of the different periods which mark the performance.   In the first period (from 9 until 12 P.M.) the music is heavy and dull as an exponent of mysterious, hidden forces; in the second (until 3 A.M.) indifferently loud; in the third (until 6 A.M.) very clear. . . . These colorful descriptions are dismissed lightly by Gorer, who bids fair to become the principal de-bunker of the travel world.   Of Javanese theatricals, he declares(21): They are stylized out of all relation with life; and the musical accompaniment seems to me to be without interest or invention.

Covarrubias(22) has written at length of the dance music in Bali.   The strong melodies for masculine dances are called bapang and gilak, he asserts.   The accompaniment for the famous Legong (a delicate, feminine dance) is called pelegongan: a large ensemble playing classic Balinese music.   This same style of music is used to accompany other dances (such as the Barong, Djauk and Tjalonarang) while still other dances, lighter in character, are accompanied by a smaller, more simple orchestra.   Bali has purely demonstrative dances interpreting the music, as well as the Kebiyar, a popular dance clarifying epic poems chanted in the archaic language.   In this case, the dancer merely translates the episodes of the poems into rhythmic movement and abstract gesture.   It is usually danced by a boy. Its accompanying music has long and short musical phrases, like expectant questions and answers, as well as many unexpected pauses.   Some parts are fast, some slow.   Some moods are mystic, with high bell traceries more exquisite and delicate than any produced by the woodwind choir in a modern occidental symphony orchestra.

A contrast to the precise Legong is the new Djanger dance in Bali, with its continually new songs played on fiddles, sung nasally and accompanied by drums and cymbals.   It is a popular, rollicking dance and an exciting syncopated music.   Sometimes there are rhythmic lines shouted by men above a rather oriental melody played on a weird wind instrument.   Then girls' voices rise in a unison song, with percussion accompaniment, only to be joined by men's voices.   Strangely, the melody finishes a phrase, there is a pause, then the end of the phrase is repeated and the melody continued from that point. The Djanger music steadily accelerates as it progresses and ends after a burst of speed.

Music for the Balinese Djogèd, a purely "demonstrative flirtatious dance without a story" is light (doubtless due to its character and to the fact that the instruments are said to be made of bamboo) and capricious, with sudden stops. There are a few recurring mellow notes on leading tones in the scale which give a feeling of underlying permanence or stability.

Powell describes(23) the Balinese dance dramas. Each dancer has a different tune, always the same. Each time the dancer speaks, that same short, plaintive, peculiar minor tune is used to characterize him or her. There is a cameo precision about the little themes, used during the movement, or as the dancer "freezes in a weird pose of expectation." Like the dancing, they form a set, disciplined art-form.

Balinese music for the dance, on the whole, is infinitely varied in mood, rhythm and nuance, and thematically more unified and more closely knit than other music of its kind. Further, the themes of different compositions have very little obvious similarity, as is the case with the music of other ancient peoples.

The Singhalese also learned to dance from their compatriots in India when King Gaja Bahu (109-131) brought twelve thousand Cholian captives, including many dancers, to Ceylon. The Singhalese had danced a little before, but the new, foreign dance fascinated all the people. It has come down through the centuries to be known today as the Kandyan dance, accompanied mainly by the tabor. As time passed, vocal music was added to this accompaniment, and finally the music of other instruments. In the reign of Parakrama Bahu the Great (A.D. 1153-86) when dancing and music received a great impetus, groups of women carrying tabors "danced and sang songs sweet and melodious as the music of heaven." This monarch and his wife were accomplished dancers and musicians. With the decline of the Singhalese monarchy, dancing and music were relegated to the background. They became the sole property of the Berawa caste in Ceylon's interior. Today the ancient Kandyan dance is returning, especially at Buddhist festivals.

Musicians in ancient Assyrian sculptures are shown dancing to their own music. The Ashkurakhbal bas-relief pictures an orchestra in a procession to welcome some conquerors. In the orchestra are three male harpists, two of whom are dancing as they play.

In ancient Egypt, too, dancing and music were united. These artists must have been on the same social plane, for the sculptures portray musicians dancing as they play, or mingling with the dancers. The two arts formed the accepted mode of Egyptian entertainment. Sometimes the dancers played a sort of castanet, formed by cylindrical maces surmounted by small balls in the form of human or animal heads. These heads, when struck together, produced a clang which was sometimes used without other accompaniment—as was the tambourine— to guide the performers. Handclapping and finger-snapping were also Egyptian dance accompaniments, though soft instruments were sometimes used. The astronomic dance was accompanied by flute, lyre and syrinx.

Dancing as a religious ceremony exists today in Egypt in many forms: even as it did in the time of the Pharaohs. Modern village folk dances are devotional and are danced at the time of the full moon, to the sound of the word "Allah," intoned deeply and monotonously and at an accelerating pace. One voice is heard in a solo, then the entire male chorus enters on one of the "Allahs." This is similar to whirling dervish music. Modern Egyptians regulate their work and play by songs. In Nubia, a dance at graves is accompanied by a long, well-defined musical phrase descending from a very high note. This phrase is said to be as ancient as the tombs of the Pharaohs.

Machol, or dance, was considered an integral part of religious ceremonies in ancient Israel. The little drum (tof) was popular among Semites as a rhythm-indicator. David used it at the installation of the Ark in Jerusalem. The Bible speaks often of praising His Name in the dance, and with the timbrel and the harp. It was always, also, considered of merit to sing and dance before the bride in Israel. However, Israel associated all secular music with dance and wine. This music was similar to the other oriental music which is of two types: unrhythmic (a solo voice and accompaniment) or rhythmic (used for bodily movements). The latter was considered inferior to the former.

In Chassidic song, certain melodies (as those for "awakening") are built on vigorous, syncopated, dancing rhythms and are meant to be sung in unison. The Yemenite Jews today have many inspired melodies in strict rhythm, accompanied by drums, handclapping and dancing. A folk song of contemporary Jews of Babylonian origin is sung in praise of a saint and induces an ecstasy which merges into a whirling dance.

No one can affirm or deny that Hebraic dance music today is the same as in Biblical times. The fact that (in the era of captivity of the Babylonian Jewry) dance and instrumental music were prohibited so that they would not menace the purity of sacred song has resulted in the borrowing of much folk dance music from other countries by the Jews. Several earnest authorities have set themselves to discover which dance songs are really Hebraic and which are not. Saminsky mentions some songs that are direct borrowings from other people (mainly Slavs) and claims that they weren't in the least transformed by the "Jewish melodic folk-genius." When the Arabs developed a secular rhythmic music for their poems which were accompanied by body motions, both poetry and music made a great impression on the Jews and influenced among them a similar development of rhythmic song. After the Jews were expelled from Spain in 1492, they developed popular literature and songs in Ladino (Spanish-Yiddish). These were, of course, based on what they had taken with them from Spain. Idelsohn, however, finds one of the Ladino songs to be in the Dorian mode, and to bear characteristics of Greek music!

The dances mentioned in the Iliad are said to have been ancient Iberian dances. In the days of Imperial Rome, the finest ballet dancers came from Cadiz. The Moors' invasion of Spain in 711 A.D. brought an African tone to Iberian music and dance. Their influence has been felt largely in southern Spain. But, in the mountainous regions of the north, some of the ancient dances and music have been preserved, declare modern musicians! From the characters of the northern Basque Zortzico and the Gallegan dances today, and in view of Homer's graphic descriptions, the belief has grown that they are the same dances and music that existed in the time of Homer.

Indeed, the history of music in Spain begins with dancing. However, later on, florid Arabian music was adopted (apparently) bodily. This music was classified as "sorrowful" and "joyful" songs, as well as ballads, or "danceable" songs. All Arabian rhythms were danceable, since tradition claims that Arab meter itself comes from the rhythm of bodily motion. Every dance approximated a certain rhythmic form, and the movements of the dancer had to coincide with the rhythmic beats. Even the Spanish Baile Clásico is a combination of Arabic and ballet, while Gypsy dancing and deep song (canto hondo) combine the Arabic and the Hindu. Certainly, the Arabian dance music, in its modern Spanish form, is far superior to that remaining in Arabia, where Western influence has popularized the clarinet, which squeals and squawks a dance accompaniment lasting several hours.

In spite of the fact that Spain was a very bad stepmother to her children, the Latin-Americans adopted many of her songs and dances and allowed them to transform, or to obscure entirely their own ancient heritage.

Before the conquerors came, music, dance and the drama had become very highly developed in the highlands of South America. The mystic element was often present in those ceremonies. Peruvian circular dances, done around a central group of musicians, were often used as invocations to ward off evils or illnesses. Most Incan melodies were in the nature of regular, symmetrical choreographic songs. The Incan Harawi was a song of love and sorrow. Its structure has survived in contemporary Peruvian dance music, such as the Marinera and Pampeñas (heel-tapping dances) and the northern Resbalosa and Tendero, though there are Negroid influences in the two latter dances. The modern Peruvian Indian has a strong leaning toward the pentatonic scale, once used by his Incan ancestors. One writer insists that Incan dance music was always monotonous, because it was achieved by percussion instruments and by the clapping and stamping of the spectators, and was inspired by sacred chants.

Strangers in Peru today cannot distinguish between different types of music, though students have no such difficulties. Some of the Danzas and Bainuman (Indian popular dances) are ancient, (that is, pre-Incan), some Incan and some colonial. The modern Quechua orchestra, according to Winthrop Sergeant(24), has an incredible endurance. It plays repetitious melodies for several days at a time, accompanied by the rhythmic stamping of the dancers' feet. The rhythms themselves are curious and intricate, sometimes forming strange units by means of several simultaneous or alternating meters. "There is in the dance and music a total absence of voluptuousness. It is surprisingly austere and formal; haunting and sad in its joyful moments. The passionate Spaniard has been unable to eradicate the Inca spirit."

The Araucanians in Chile had a musical system unlike the European, unlike the Incan. Often three-quarters of a tone was sung. More, the Araucanian instruments produced the seven tones of the major scale, a decided dissimilarity to the Incan pentatonic scale. Since the Araucanians had no metrical system, all their songs were in prose. The dance-songs, then, were brief, and were simply repeated until the dancers were weary. This music exists among Chilean Indians today, in remote spots. It has not been entirely extinguished by the Spaniards and has been made the object of intensive study by leading musicians in Chile, such as Humberto Allende.

Six different types of ancient Guatemalan music have been discovered by Jesús Castillo during forty years of investigation. Some of these melodies are based on the intervals sung by the cenzontles (birds found in Central America) and are subjected to foreign musical forms only with the greatest of difficulty. When Castillo wrote of Guatemalan autochthonous music in general, he said: With the tun (a hollow wooden cylindrical instrument with rectangular incisions) and two trumpets, the indigenes were wont to accompany the ballet in *Rabinal Achí*, the music of which has been put in written form by Brasseur de Bourbourg. Castillo has written an opera (*Queche Vinac*) in which some of these autochthonous themes appear, and of which a certain section is often termed the "Mayan Minuet." Ancient Guatemalans used drums, cane and deer bone pipes to accompany their dances. The old Baile del Venado (Dance of the Hunt, or Deer Dance) survives yet. The accompaniment to the modern Dance of the Young Bulls in Guatemala embodies a strange combination of native and Spanish music: the melody is indigenous, while the rhythmic accompaniment is thoroughly Spanish.

Historic Mayan ballets were accompanied by songs, founded on local legendary tales. Songs and instruments, beginning on low tones and gradually accelerating and rising in pitch, accompanied all ancient Mexican dances. The great Montezuma kept for his own amusement many dancers, a "whole district of people who had no other occupation," according to Bernal Diaz de Castillo. One of the most popular of Aztec dances was that in celebration of Macuilxochitl, the god of music, *and therefore* of the dance.

Clavigero says that the dances of the old Mexicans were accompanied by singing, and that both song and dance movements were adjusted by the beating of the instruments. Some of the singing was antiphonal. The dancing was circular, with the huehuetl and the teponaxtle (short and tall drums) in the center of each circle. On some occasions, the owners of those prisoners who were to be sacrificed in the festival passed the night within the temple singing and dancing with them. Clavigero also describes a sacred dance accompanied by unseen musicians.

It is evident that in the times of Clavigero and Mendieta

(end of the sixteenth century) Mexican dance and dance-songs were as they were in ancient days. There is, however, an intriguing description (from a traveler's point of view) by Mendieta: "Each chief has in his house a chapel with its dancers and singers who seek to compose songs in their own modes, or coplas. When they have won a victory, elected a new chief, or for any other reason, the musicians compose new songs, besides those that have come to them from their composers of ancient times. Some days before the fiesta, the singers are provided with the songs they have to sing. In new songs or dances they help each other, so there will be no defects on the fiesta day. When they begin to dance, several Indians raise very lively whistles, then play the atabales (kettledrums) in a low tone, gradually growing louder. By the very tone of the atabales, the dancers recognize the song and dance, and they begin. The musicians sing the songs, repeating each verse three or four times and enunciating very clearly. Neither the atabales, song nor dance are separated from each other. When the song is finished, the singers rest and the atabales are muted, the dance goes on. Then the musicians begin another song a little higher, and with a quicker measure, and thus the songs climb. . . . Always the songs and dance become livelier, higher in tone and more graceful, till they sound like gladsome hymns. The atabales also climb. . . ." Thus their dances were a series of crescendi in every possible way: tone, tempo, dynamics.

There still exists in Mexico a wealth of melodic themes indicative of ancient dance-songs. The flageolet has replaced the tlapitzalli, while a drum and an ayacachtli (rattle) are used to mark the rhythm. Some of the rhythms are said to be uninfluenced by European music; the melodies to be distinctly Aztec in their melancholy. All over Mexico, in the smaller fiestas, there are survivals of ancient dances and songs. One such survival is in the dance at Tatlahuamaca in the state of San Luis Potosí. The musical introduction to this dance lasts a day in itself. The dance occupies from two to ten days, and is a part of the original worship of Huitzilopochtli in the rites of the Nahua tribe.

Other modern Mexican dance music will be discussed in the chapter on folk dance music, because the influence of Spain is so clearly apparent in it.

In few countries is it possible to determine definitely just how much or how little of the ancient dance music has survived despite the influence of alien elements. But it becomes increasingly evident that *if* any ancient music exists today as it did in ancient times, it is indebted to choreographic music—to the need of folk the world over for accompanying the dance—for its preservation!

CHAPTER 2

NOTES

(1) *The Étude,* April 1930, p. 239

(2) Sharp, *English Folksong: Some Conclusions,* p. 36

(3) *Musical Quarterly,* October, 1922, p. 533

(4) Chao-Mei-Pa, *The Yellow Bell,* p. 41

(5) In a letter to the author from Shanghai, China, dated January 27, 1936

(6) In an interview with Mme. Kimiyo Ito, exponent of the classic dance of Japan, in Los Angeles on December 17, 1934

(7) Mme. Kimiyo Ito

(8) *Asia Magazine,* January, 1922

(9) Dalcroze, *Eurhythmics, Art and Education,* p. 60

(10) MacDowell, *Critical and Historical Essays,* pp. 82-83

(11) MacDowell, *Critical and Historical Essays,* pp. 13, 31, 82

(12) *Travel,* January, 1933

(13) *The Dancing Times,* November 1933, p. 147

(14) Coomaraswany and Duggirala, *Mirror of Gesture,* p. 17

(15) *Musical Quarterly,* April 1917, p. 170

(16) Gorer, *Bali and Angkor,* pp. 43-44

(17) Powell, *The Last Paradise,* p. 279

(18) In an interview with Hubert Stowitts in Los Angeles on November 16, 1935

(19) Kartini, *Letters of a Javanese Princess,* p. 213

(20) *The Dance Magazine,* September, 1929

(21) Gorer, *Bali and Angkor,* p. 29

(22) *Theatre Arts Monthly,* August, 1936, p. 599

(23) Powell, *The Last Paradise,* p. 243

(24) *Travel* for January, 1933, p. 55

DANCE MUSIC IN THE MIDDLE AGES

While Europe passed through the turbulent Middle Ages, the more ancient civilizations calmly continued their music-dance, as did the primitives, with the difference that the primitives were making a continually renewed music in the old tradition, rather than adhering to set nuances. So it is of Europe that we must speak now.

The ban of the Christian Church on dancing naturally damned the flow of dance music for a time—at least, that which was performed publicly. As early as the fourth century, Athanasius was upset because he found the congregation in Miletus accompanying song in the church with handclapping, theatrical gestures and bodily rhythms. Thus we are made to realize that such "heathen" practices had vanished before his time.

However, dancing must also have been done in the churches as late as 589, when the third Council of Toledo forbade it. It must have persisted, in some measure, until the twelfth century when Obo, Bishop of Paris, forbade it entirely in his parish; and until 1209, else why should the Council of Avignon place further restrictions upon it? Yet, a woodcut of 1493 pictures dancers in the Church of St. Magnus, accompanied by flautist and drummer. In the time of Arbeau, churchgoers danced while singing the hymns of the faith, and in 1683 Père Ménestrier wrote that in Paris the senior canon lead the choir-boys in a circular dance while singing hymns of praise. Even Dante says the singing and dancing of carols occurs in Paradise, while Fra Angelico represents the Christmas angels singing and dancing in a painting. In this sense, it is interesting to note that the word "carol" (now a holy Christmas song) originally meant a song accompanied by dancing, in which sense it was often used by the old poets. The name was first given by the trouvères to a circular, singing dance. (Nevertheless, some authorities claim that it is of the same derivation as "choir," or that its medieval form was "cordula," derived from the Celtic.) The circular Danse au Virlet, in which each dancer sang a verse and everyone joined in the chorus while a few in-struments marked the rhythm, may have been just such a *carole*, in the parlance of the trouvères. In France, these caroles (or the primitive danse chantée) were the sources of French lyric poetry. Eventually French rhymed verse was victorious over the alliterate versification of the ancient Germans, Anglo-Saxons and Scandinavians. This, avers M. Yves Lacroix-Novaro(1), was due to its ancestor, the carole.

From the beginning, the Iberian peninsula was the chosen land of the troubadours. Before the time of Alfonso the Wise, juglares came to Spain. Early miniatures show the troubadour as master of ceremonies, the juglar playing a viol and the juglaresa dancing with castanets. Since no one knows where their musical knowledge was acquired, it is presumed that they must have had some reason for hiding it—or else that they made wide use of Spanish music. Supporting the latter con-tention is the fact that the few existing examples of their music are similar to contemporary or to early Andalusian poetic forms.

Troubadours, jongleurs (one of whose main duties was "to set the jig going to brighten the tune of the psaltery") and Gypsies did much to spread rhythmic popular dance tunes. Even early organ music was derived from folk dance-songs.

(These the Council of Trent later forbade, so that organists were forced to find other music to use in church, thus occasioning a gradual trend toward virtuosity.) With greater popularity, the dance rhythms became definite—in fact, so definite that Franco, a monk of Cologne in the middle ages, put forth in a treatise his system of time notation. This found its way into the Church: the first victory of dance rhythm! During the Inquisition, Friar Marti of Alicante found time to write a treatise on dancing.

These men, however, were the exception rather than the rule. To holy men our scanty knowledge of medieval dance music is due, for the reason that then they were almost the only people who knew how to write, and that they were the very men who (probably because of restrictions placed upon them) were not given to violent enthusiasms over the choreographic art. Nevertheless, Lucrezia Bori(2) tells us that the early Franciscans sang and danced and called themselves the "singing servants of Christ."

The famous Echternach procession every Tuesday in Whitsun week when clergy, choir and congregation dance to the church and around the altar, singing carols, is a survival of medieval dancing. It is in commemoration of St. Willibord, who lived around A.D. 690. Both dance and music are traditional.

Christianity modified the German dance, but because the leaders of the new faith were broad, the same dances were done at Christian festivals as at pagan ones, and the only change in the musical accompaniment was in some of the words to the dance-songs. The folklore of this country tells us that though giants dance, their dance-songs are weird and sad, since they themselves are never merry. The Middle Ages in Germany found the *Vortänzer* holding a post of great honor among the people. He was the leader of the song as well as of the dance. There were then two types of dance: circular (jumping) and the measure (gliding). Their accompanying music corresponded, in general, to the character of the dances, and a dance-song was termed *leiche*.

In old Wales, when the lord of a castle called for music
and dance, his own bard would come running to him, or he
might be obliged by a traveling band that had stopped for the
night.   There were sometimes orchestras composed of four
or five harps, sometimes there was a single harp.   One air
(with intermittent instrumental variations) would continue for
about fifteen minutes, while the bard would sing and the dancers
would dance.   Sometimes they, too, joined in the chorus.

Brian Ború March, with its strong, clear dance rhythm, is
the answer of the Irish to those who claim that the Irish jig
is an imitation of the Gigas of Corelli and Geminiani, for this
march is a very ancient Irish tune.   Tradition has it that the
Dalcassian clans played it on war pipes and marched to it to
the Battle of Clontarf in A.D. 1014.   Irish dance tunes of the
fifth century are known, and the Irish corn-pipes (mentioned
in twelfth century manuscripts) are believed to be the inspiration for the hornpipe, though the instruments survived only
until the seventeenth century.

Old Scottish Satanic conventions, at which men paid nocturnal homage to Satan, always featured dancing to instrumental
and vocal music.   Scotland, too, had her wandering medieval
musicians, among whom were many men from other countries.
These men brought in fresh song and dance forms and changed
the entire aspect of Scotch music.   After this period, dancing
and its fluted and piped music were mentioned in many Scotch
literary works.   The Medieval was the Golden Age in Scotland,
as far as music was concerned.   Musicians were employed at
court, castles and boroughs, and *sang schoils* were cultivated.

Scandinavian countries were the sources of some of the
dance-songs introduced into cultured Iceland in the twelfth
century.   These were all romantic folksongs, or ballads, which
were accompanied by rhythmic steps.   In earlier centuries the
Icelandic dance seems to have been non-existent and even music
was seldom practiced, except in magic incantations.

At times during the Middle Ages, the joy in the dance
became a mania and resulted in dance plagues that swept entire
districts.   The dance-songs dealt with anything and everything,

and derived their names from the first words of their ditties. Tilts were fought with clever song and retort on the dance floor (3). Dancing was a daily occurrence, for it was usual for most English households to dance after dinner. The accompaniments were provided by minstrels, or by the singing of the ladies themselves. The musicians, until their banishment to a higher "music gallery" were on the same floor with the dancers.

In 1347-8, the Black Death gave rise to the Danse Macabre. This dance was sometimes done to the chanting of the *Miserere*, sometimes to the *Ad Mortem Festinamus*, in triple time.

European folk and nobles both danced Chain Dances, Rounds and Heys, in the twelfth and thirteenth centuries. During the latter period, music and poetry were again brought into the Church by means of Mystery and Miracle plays, which were dramatic representations of Biblical scenes, and which were sometimes given in the ballatoria (dancing floor) an awninged space in front of the church. There was, asserts Guillaume Paradin, but one difference between momerie and ballet: the former was given in fancy costume. "Mummings" or "disguisings" were the old English words for the Masques that were to come to England in the sixteenth century. In them, women and men danced Morris dances to Morris music, slow and stately "Base daunces," Rounds, lively Gaillards and Corantos.

This Base Daunce was a dance suited to the needs of court life (fourteenth and fifteenth centuries) and influenced, both in music and movement, by the heavy court costumes then in vogue. When music for this dance was written in duple time, it was necessary to play it in triple time when it was used for dancing. It was played on oboe and tambour. Chansons Regulières for the Basse Danse, according to Thoinet Arbeau, were composed of sixteen bars repeated, a middle part of sixteen bars and a close of sixteen bars, repeated, making eighty in all. If the air of the song was longer, it was termed irregular. The dance was said to be so named because it was played in Major Perfect and because "when one dances it one goes quietly without bearing oneself as graciously as one is able." From the sequence of steps in the Basse Danse finally evolved the Pavane, written in duple time; the Courante; Branle; Menuet and Volta, ancestor of the Waltz.

The French and Italian forms of the Basse Danse were totally different. France, in the fifteenth century, was yet medieval, while Italy was at the peak of the Renaissance. The five steps of the French Basse Danse (Réverence, Branle, two singles, doubles, reprise) each required an equal amount of music: about four bars of triple time. Italy's four steps were Bassa Danza, Quardernia, Saltarello, Piva. Each of these steps, danced to a "measure" of music, was in a different rhythm, yet was related to what had preceded it. The dancers had not only to master the elements proper in every mode, but to be able to dance the step of one against the music of any other.

While the nobility danced the Basse Danse, the common people had their Danse Haute, or Baladine, consisting of Rondes, Farandoles and Bourrés. The latter, written in duple rhythm, was marked on the third beat of each measure by the stamping of sabots.

Next appeared Morality plays and pompous, glorious Masques, with song and dance enlivening intermissions. The Masque (a development of earlier mummings) was, in effect, a ballet. It was also a forerunner of later opera-ballets. It made an ingenuous story weld dialogue, song, and dance into a harmonious whole. Celebrated masters wrote the music and songs. Princes participated in and patronized it. At the entrances and exits of various characters, all English Masques had appropriate music. For instance: "Soft music. Enter Fancy," or "Exit, waving his wand. Music," appear in some of the preserved scripts. Each Masque had an anti-Masque, a dance which was exactly opposite in character to the entry dance which was to follow it. The anti-Masque dance airs were faster in tempo and more irregular in form and rhythm than the music for the intermixed dance (done by actors and spectators: the social dances of the day) and for the masquers' own dances, in three formal entries. Nearly all the formal

Masque dance tunes approximate two separate airs, the first in even measure and the second in triple. It is thought that the men who composed these songs also gave musical performances, acrobatic displays and dances.

King René of Provence in 1462 organized a religious Masque, or strolling ballet called *Lou Gué* for the eve of Corpus Christi. He composed all the details: decorations, dances and music. The score included the "Air Lou Gué" (a sort of theme song), the "March of the Princess of Love" (later the inspiration for various Noëls), the "Menuet of the Queen of Sheba," the "Vie de Noué" and the "Air des luttes." The dancers performed to the sounds of fife, drum and castanets.

A Ducal wedding was the inspiration for the fête given in 1489 by Bergonzio di Botta of Tortona. In this, Jason and the Argonauts entered to martial music, a fanfare of horns preceded Diana's entrance, lyric lutes and flutes announced Orpheus (who entered singing and playing the lyre), percussion accompanied the spirited dancing of Atalanta and Theseus, while notorious queens like Cleopatra and Phaedra sang of their own prowess. Thus the musical instruments were changed according to the character of the people they were to accompany. Each dancer had his own little orchestra to assist him in conveying his meaning to the audience.

In 1583, Master Stubbs in England published a book called *The Anatomy of Abuses*, among which was "the horrible vice of pestiferous dancing." In his fervent denunciation he managed unwittingly to convey a splendid description of the combination of music and movement in medieval English Morris dances: "Their hobby horses, together with their pipes and thundering drummers . . . then march this heathen company toward the church, their pipers playing, their drummers thundering, their stumps dancing, the bells jingling, their handkerchiefs thundering about their heads like madde men, dancing and swinging their handkerchiefs over their heads . . . like devils incarnate."

All this dance music, in its varied medieval forms, was a

means to an entirely different end, as well as being an end in itself.   It was (along with vocal polyphony) the direct cause of the new absolute or pure music, written for instruments alone.   This was practically non-existent before the second half of the sixteenth century, though there was a great deal of vocal dance music.   The dance of this period was responsible (in the history of music as a whole) for the element of measured time, as distinct from contrapuntal music where the emphasis is laid on the interweaving of voices, since in dance music one voice or instrument predominates.

We find that Fabritio Caroso, in 1581, wrote dance pieces for lute and treble and called them *Il Bailarino*.   They stood alone as music and did not have to be accompanied by movement to be understood.   It is supposed that Tom d'Urfey wrote his songs to dance tunes to please Charles II (1649-1685) who was fond of easily-grasped rhythms.   The English John Dowland (1562-1626) wrote *Five Pieces for String Music*: three Pavans, a Gaillard and an Allemande.   These were first published for lute, viols or violins in five parts and were termed *Lachrimae or seaven Teares—Figured in Seaven Passionate Pavans*.   Gian Giacomo Gastoldi, in 1581 musical director at the Ducal chapel at Santa Barbara, had composed some dancing songs to be sung by four or five voices or by a soloist accompanied by lute, or to be played by instruments for dancing.   They won for him an enormous success all over Europe. Monteverdi ended his *Scherzi Musicali* with a Balletto, a suite of dance-songs in different keys and rhythms preceded by an instrumental introduction.   When John Cooper (English) went to Italy in the seventeenth century, he became José Coperario.   Under that name he wrote Masques and songs and taught the art of composition to Henry and William Lawes, who in Queen Elizabeth's time wrote music to a Masque of which it was said to be "so well performed in the dances, scenes, clothing and music that the Queen was pleased to observe at her going away that she liked it very well. . . ."

The musical content of the English madrigals definitely arose from folk songs and dances.   Indeed, so similar were the madrigals of most countries to church music that it was only the inclusion of dance rhythms that lent variety! Many were the musicians who protested vigorously against the serious madrigal. The Canzonets imitated with voices the effects of popular instruments and led eventually to the vocal Balletts of Morley (1595) and Weelkes (1598). The latter is said to be the greatest of the Tudor madrigalists. He wrote, incidentally, two delightful madrigals dealing with Morris dancing, as well as his Balletts. Morley, however, was the man who excelled as a writer of Balletts, and who gave the form more variety than would be expected by its limited scope, according to E.H. Fellowes(4).

Balletts were known as far back as the fourteenth century. A colloquial name for them was Fa-la, since these syllables were attached to a florid, vocalized refrain—not part of the lyric, but added as a sort of interlude, between sharply defined sections of the words. Ballets corresponded to the Italian Ballata, and the French Chanson Balladée. The English Ballett, in its early form, was actually a combination of song and dance. Although it was not danced by Elizabethan singers, the dance rhythms were ever present in their minds, and in the minds of the composers.

Shakespeare, known to have been a good singer and dancer, influenced the music of his day strongly. In one of his plays (*Much Ado About Nothing*) occurs an allusion which suggests that burthens (or burdens, or Hey, Nonny, Nonnies) usually regarded as meaningless refrains, were in his time accompanied by dancing. According to Shakespeare, the music of the celebrated court dance known as the Dompe, or Dump, might be merry or sad. Before his time, it was always stately, as befitted court dance music. (Another authority classes the Dumpe as the music of a small Irish instrument akin to the harp, popular in England during the fifteenth and sixteenth centuries.) Shakespeare's *Winter's Tale* mentions "With a fading"—the old Irish dance tune called *Rinnce Fada*. He also alludes to the medieval corn-pipe in this play: "There is but one Puritan among them, and he sings psalms to hornpipes."

His plays serve to acquaint us with the fact that in his day, not only did dance and music play a highly important part in any fine stage production, but they served him as a means of sharpening his points, making clearer his meanings. At one time, during the first part of the eighteenth century, it was customary to have entertainments of singing and dancing between the acts of Shakespeare's plays, so that the actors and actresses had also to be fine dancers and vocalists.

Byrd, founder of the Elizabethan School of Music, took the dance tunes of the streets, added to them his technical knowledge, embellished them with appropriate variations, and started a new vogue. The mixture of absurdly simple little dance tunes with a contrapuntal setting is little short of amazing, and one feels that no one but Byrd could have done it and survived, asserts Margaret Glyn(5). In time, no dance composition was considered complete without variants of each strain. Naturally, dancing did not benefit by these additions, but the object of the composers was music. Occasionally they wrote long, abstruse musical compositions—and still gave them dance titles! That is the reason that so little actual dance music of that period survives. What remains is purely a musical development which has retained only the name, but is far removed from dancing. The Pavan is said to be the highest achievement of the Elizabethan school, while the greatest examples in this form are those of Gibbons and Bull.

Since 1508, the *seises* (choirboys) have danced in the Cathedral of Seville to commemorate a dance of children who unconsciously delayed the Moors' plundering, but the music for the dance has been constantly re-composed by each succeeding choirmaster as the dance changed. The music is thus as modern as any other Spanish dance music—sometimes almost popular in quality. Musicians like Guerrero and Eslava have held the post of choirmaster. In 1544 one of the dancers "kept the time" with a rebeck. In 1577 one of the boys played cymbals and bells, and in 1677 they all sang and played castanets. These were introduced by the church authorities themselves, who wished to discover a different device with the same effect of the little Moorish finger cymbals, used in religious dances.

The vein of Arab music was still to be found in the music of Christian Spaniards of the Middle Ages, though popular Spanish dances of that time corresponded to those of other nations: Pavanes, Chaconnes, Gaillardes, Sarabandes. These gave way to Boleros, Jotas and Seguidillas, which evidently did not exist in Spain during the Middle Ages.

These ages bridged the gap between the dance music of the ancients and of the classic era. Medieval dance-songs, widely disseminated, made various nations aware of the arts in neighboring countries. Most important of all: during this epoch, abstract music was born of dance-song!

CHAPTER 3

NOTES

(1) *Archives Internationales de la Danse,* April 15, 1935, "La Danse Carole," p. 58
(2) *The Étude,* September, 1923, p. 587
(3) Elizabeth Selden, *The Dancer's Quest,* p. 17
(4) Fellowes, *English Madrigal Composers,* p. 182
(5) Glyn, *Elizabethan Virginal Music and Its Composers,* p. 67

FOLK DANCE MUSIC

What European dance tunes are native to which regions? No one knows. Sometimes a town or province regards a song as its own, when in reality it has come to them spontaneously, from another group of people, through a passing traveler. Assimilation of the melody and of the rhythm may have been entirely unconscious. There are, however, certain characteristics of folk dance-songs that are universal.

One thing is certain. Had there not been a folk music and dance of different peoples, there would not today be a music and dance created by individuals. More, it is the individual art that is imperfect, not the folk. When Raoul Laparra (1) said, "Only trained composers commit errors of style. Such faults are never found in folk music" he explained the reason for the increasing return of creative artists to the folk for their inspiration. The folk dance-song is always modern: never old. It is always growing, never completed. It exists always in many forms. Did not Chaliapin say that "Folk song is that which moves the hearts of those in whose country it was written hundreds of years after it was composed"?

One of the best ways to gain an insight into the lives of different people is to learn the forms of their music and dance, which are always racial. Indeed, some modern dancers have discovered that the dance music of different nations is so suggestive of the accompanying dance that an unusually sensitive choreographer could construct a typical "national" dance merely by following the musical curves and accents peculiar to that country. Complete accuracy might be lacking, but the spirit would be present. In all folk dances, music and movement are true to the prevailing mood. In ritual dances they are solemn, purposeful, significant. In recreational and harvest dances they are joyous, full of laughter.

Some folk dance tunes have come down to us in an incomplete form, shorn of their proper endings. These are circular tunes, repeated as often as the dancers require it. For this purpose false cadences were invented to dovetail into the beginning of the pieces so that there would not be too many full-stops in the music. Perfect cadences were played only at the close of the dance. Consequently, declares Cecil Sharp(2), they tended to fall into disuse and to be forgotten.

Rhythm is fundamentally related to the lives and work of all folk. Most tradesmen have a song or rhythm peculiar to their trade. If rhythm is not inherent in their occupations, an appropriate one is invented. Actual folk labor songs (not those celebrating the completion of labor) have always been rhythmic, and often the very actions of work assume a dance-like quality in response to that in the music. Those who sing are skillful enough to vary the songs, the variations largely occurring in the verses of a leader, while the refrains are taken up by everyone. Their repetitive intensity and excitement help the work along. Abstractions of the movements of work have become occupational dances in all lands, and doubtless the songs that are sung during the work itself form the accompanying music for these dances.

Bela Bartok(3) feels that the shortness of many folk tunes and their strict rhythms arose from the rhythmical body motions that first accompanied them, and that no complicated rhythmic pattern could evolve from such primitive elements. It is his opinion that the dance-like rigor of the original terse rhythm relaxed only when the tunes became independent of the body's motion, and when the rhythm of the tune adapted itself to the rhythm of the words. Today it is difficult to notate the rhythms in folk dance music since they are not conventional. Some writers solve the problem by using alternate meters. Some, like Chavez, write in metrical fractions, in an effort to clarify the strange, unconventional, rhythmic folk impulse.

The range of folk dance music (much of which is choral) is small. "Folk who live in congested districts," declares Percy Grainger(4), "Connot be expected to write melodies with wide melodic range. Their melodies are restricted by the group. The group can sing just so high or so low. It has a narrow range. The compass is short. On the other hand, men who are solitary in their music-making will give a wider range to their melodic lines."

Singing games are a natural outgrowth of folk dancing, since in almost all cases the music for the games is sung by onlookers, or by the dancers themselves, as in "London Bridge is Falling Down" or "All Around the Mulberry Bush."

Folk dance music is largely modal—not, as some people would have us believe, because of the influence of the Church, but spontaneously so. Cecil Sharp who (according to Rutland Boughton(5) went to life, not to documents, for his data, is authority for the latter statement.

Strong accents mark most folk dancing, due to the importance of the first step and to the beat of the sabot on the floor, as in the Lithuanian Klumpakojis, a wooden shoe dance. When many people dance together, the tendency is toward a heaviness which is reflected in the tempo and dynamics of the music, rather than in its character. Some folk dances (usually those in which there is a soloist) are quick and light, the dancers leaping high into the air. In these cases, the stamps serve only to accentuate the rhythm and to make it more piquant. Education and sophisticated dance forms have placed the emphasis on arms and hands. The folk tendency was downward, the classic upward. So with the music. The gradual discarding of the heavy accent placed the emphasis on harmony, form, and on purely musical developments which were later "interpreted" in the dance.

Tschaikowsky (6) wrote to Count Tolstoi : Only the Russian choral dances of the folk have a regularly accented measure; the legends (Bylini) have nothing in common with the dances. Whereas some folk dance music increases in speed and pulls the dancers along with it, the Slavic people are noted for their dances which are done completely, then repeated in double time, with the music remaining as before. With the increased tempo among the Russians comes a stamping, a whistling and lusty singing to the music of balalaika and concertina. Songs of the Russian folk are often minor and melancholy, yet those for dancing rise to amazing heights of intensity and hilarity. The music is usually characterized by an irregular structure, changing time values and phrases of unequal length.

Folk songs of the Ukraine are divided into Dumki (Little Thoughts, often in the minor mode) and Shumki (Little Noises, suitable for dancing). Ukrainian Spring Songs (Vesnianky) were originally an accompaniment to ritual dances, so that the rhythm of body movements is preserved in them. They express man's communion with all the powers of Nature, since man is not a separate being to the Ukrainians. He is a part of universal life.

Several dance rhythms that became universal were really of Polish origin. One was the Krakowiak, which took its name (and possibly its origin) from the city of Cracow in Poland. Its chief musical characteristic is a strong bass accent on the second half-beat of the measure. It is written in ¾ meter. The Mazurka is also acknowledged to be of Polish origin, one of the folksongs in that rhythmic pattern being Pozegnanie. The Varsovienne, though it originated in France, had many musical similarities to the Mazurka and the Redowa. Its movement was slow, in triple time, and pauses in its steps coincided with long, accented notes at the beginning of alternate measures in the music. It was a favorite of Empress Eugénie.

Near the year 1835, a Czecho-Slovakian village held openair festivities at which a young girl was inspired to sing and to introduce some dance steps of her own invention. The village schoolmaster recorded both her song and dance and later took them to the capitol of what was then Bohemia. They became the Polka (probably from pulka, or half-step) and spread like wildfire over the world. A special, very graceful Berlin Polka was developed in Germany. The Schottische, first introduced into England in 1848, was really only a form of the Polka, but was the cause of much discussion by people who assumed that it was a libel on Scotland! The Polka also became very popular in the United States when James K. Polk was running for president (1844). Obviously, the name was merely a curious coincidence.

Polka music is spritely, and has an aggressive accent on the third half-beat. The meter is always ¾. It might be presumed, from the formal origin of the Polka, that it was an individual creation, not a folk expression. However, the young girl's outburst was entirely in accord with the musical traditions of her people, since their folk songs usually have a dance-like quality, the exuberance and gaiety of pure animal spirits and many of the Polka's rhythmic characteristics.

Rumania has an ancient Epiphany ritual dance called "The Hobby Horse and the Caliesari," the latter being the dancing attendants who wear jangling bells which from one end of Europe to another denote magic-making at the seasonal feasts and which form an additional accompaniment to the dance. When the Rumanian youth dances the Hora, he is accompanied by the long-drawn notes of the bagpipe. He may also be accompanied by the village flautists, or by peasant fiddlers, but his ecstatic shouts and those of his companions, along with the heavy tread of his feet, completely drown out the music.

The Czardas, national dance of Hungary, has two alternating movements. When the music is slow the couples promenade and converse: Lassán. Then they command the orchestra to play the rapid Friska, which they dance vigorously. Sometimes the music of the two movements is identical. Only the tempi are varied. There are sudden, breathtaking pauses. The Czardas is said to have originated in the Hungarian

DRUMMER BOYS WHO ACCOMPANY THE DANCE IN CEYLON
(Note the double drum with cymbal attached)
Photographed by John Herat, o.m.i.

EGYPTIAN DANCER AND ACCOMPANISTS

Published in "Ancient Egyptian Paintings" by Davies and Gardiner and reproduced here by
courtesy of the publishers, The Oriental Institute of the University of Chicago

palotás dance, popular in the sixteenth century. This was, in turn, allied to the Lantosok, a dance accompanied by lyre artists in the Middle Ages. The form of the dance changed with the centuries, but the rhythm in the three was identical, believes Professor Herrimann. Hungarian music, with its sudden changes from lassitude to vigor, is not Gypsy music, though the Gypsies who find themselves in Hungary naturally assume some of Hungary's musical characteristics. Liszt(7) spoke of Gypsy dance tunes that no one could imitate.

Some Gypsies dance to melancholy oriental music full of startling pauses, and to handclapping, which is developed into amazingly complex and varied rhythmic patterns. Some (in other parts of Europe) dance to the sound of little bells (which they first wore to entice country people to flock around them), to drums or tambourines. Gypsy dance-song usually rises in pitch and in dynamics, and modulates strangely. Song is the chief accompaniment to the dance of the Spanish Gypsies, among whom improvisation is a favorite sport. Thus, their dance music is freer than that which does not bear the Romany stamp.

Each of Spain's forty-nine provinces, as well as each section of every province, has its own music and dance, and each dance has its own special prelude, with rhythmic and harmonic effects varied infinitely by good guitarists. It has been said that only the opposing rhythms of guitarist, dancer and singer can produce the appealing, passionate effect of Spanish folk music, as a whole.

In some Spanish dances, movement and dance music alternate with the singing of florid rhymed verses. In others, there are musical pauses during which the dancers also stop, only to resume when the melody again crashes forth. The dances are punctuated by yells, finger-snapping, castanets, heel-tapping. Many Spanish dancers, possessors of active hands and feet, even create their own accompaniments. Some clap a duple rhythm while stepping a triple rhythm. They may chant, or add intricate castanet or fingernail variants on the rhythm.

The Sevillanas, which has been declared to contain the

basic elements of all Spanish dances, has been described at length by José Otero(8). "For foreigners the Sevillanas is very difficult," opines Spain's celebrated dancer, "Because they say the steps and the castanets go against the music. But this never occurs to us Sevillanos since we know *how* to fit the feet and castanets to the measure of the music. When a person has a bad ear in this respect, we note it immediately. There are many kinds of Sevillanas, but all have the same form. The introduction will sometimes be shorter or longer, but after it there are a few measures of dance and a few measures of song for the dance. These are both repeated twice, in order, and then the final chord."

The earliest known Basque tune, *Une Musique de Biscaye,* was called a dance tune by Rabelais. Its words are a satire on the Basques! It was printed in 1502 in an extremely rare volume, now said to be in the Biblioteca Columbina in Seville. The Basques' isolation has inspired the development of a unique music. Their dances and songs have peculiar, complicated rhythms and irregular phrases. They are marked by 5/8 and 7/4 meters, frequently alternating. The Basque dance orchestra consists of a fife and drum, played by a single musician: fife in left hand, right hand beating the drums suspended about his neck. He is a salaried musician called Tambilero (drummer) and his function in every village is to have an accurate memory for ancient airs.

Portugal is famous for its Ballets Ambulatoires (religious processions with dances) as is Italy. Portugal's folk songs are divided into two sections, with two contrasting rhythms: a narrative, and a lively choreographic section. Some authorities are of the belief that at one time the slower section may also have had a connection with the dance. Therefore, Portuguese folk songs are allied to dances bearing the same name. There is the Carrasquinha or Chamarrita, and there is the famed Fado, a story told to guitar accompaniment, with another instrument playing the melody. There is a running Fado, and there are sad Fados, as well as hilarious Fados, bearing the names of prominent convivial men. The Fado is simply harmonized. Its rude texts are often vehicles for political satire and mockery.

Portuguese dance-songs travelled to other parts of the world, as did those of other nations. In some sections of the Azores, embellishments were added to the melodies. In Cuba the songs acquired an oriental feeling. In other sections, the Moorish quality is emphasized. Portuguese dance-songs from Provincetown, Cape Cod, Massachusetts, are mostly fishing ditties called Fados Maritimos.

Most Italian dance music—on first hearing—appears to be a succession of triplets. Indeed, that is the form in which modern music for the Tarantella, the Saltarello and the Forlana is written. Nevertheless, Saltarello music, though rhythmically similar, is utterly unlike Tarantella music. The Saltarello is still danced in Italy in the Campagna Romana (the Campo Paso) at feast days. It is, however, rapidly disappearing, and the dance itself varies in different communities. The ancient Saltarello is danced only in Piedmont. It was originally intended to be an exaltation of the harvest season, done to the music of accordion, or organetto. Musical examples of the Saltarello—especially those for lute—were printed in the earliest editions of instrumental music.

The Tarantella, born in Naples, did not always have the musical form it has today. In 1654, it was written in ¼ time. The measure began with two groups of notes, each comprising an eighth note and two sixteenths; and concluded with a dotted quarter and two sixteenths. In 1680, an example of the rhythm was a dotted quarter note and an eighth, followed by a quarter and two eighth notes. The meter was, of course, ¼. It was much later that the successive triplets came into vogue. Mme. de Staël's(9) account of the Tarantella informs us that "the character of the music was expressed alternately by exactness or softness of movement."

The Forlana rhythm too, (⅝) closely resembles the modern Tarantella rhythm, but its character differs. It hails from Venice, and has been termed a little love-poem without words. The Villanella was a dance of the Italian folk of the sixteenth century.   It was rustic, humorous, and was accompanied by singing.   Today the girls of the Puglie and Calabria dance a choral scene representing the ancient legend of the labyrinth.

The Siciliana is danced, as the name implies, in Sicily.   It is of a tender nature, and is frequently done at weddings to the sound of flute, or of a tambourine equipped with bells.   Many of the old Sicilian folk dance-songs are reminiscent of minor, oriental Moorish melodies, probably because Sicily was once part of Africa, opines an investigator.

All of France's traditional folk songs, even the gravest, are said to be old dance tunes, though they have long since ceased to fill that purpose.   The refrains of these songs (which have their counterparts in other countries) represent the rhythm and movements of the dance: la-la; oh! oh!; lon-lan-la; etc. Many French nursery rhymes are really old Branles, such as "Marlbrough s'en va-t-en guerre," "Carillon de Dunkerque" and "Chevalier du guet."   French dance music resolves itself into two types: the Round (a binary rhythm) and the Bourrée (a ternary rhythm).   The choreographic types are, fortunately, more varied.   There is, for instance, the Farandole of southern France, a quick step danced by a procession in single file headed by a musician who plays the fife and drum at once, as does the Basque tambilero.   He skips along without losing a beat.

The words of Breton dance-songs are often limited to vocables.   M. Bourgault-Ducoudray(10) has observed that it is customary, in Brittany, to join with the dance tunes any poetry having a similar rhythm.

At least one English historian has chillingly declared that the great attention paid to English dance music has obscured other, more "worthy" music.   Very well, then, Mr. Historian, let us devote more time to your despised dance music, for it is apparent that it is largely the basis of your more worthy English product.   Also, Margaret Glyn has declared that "No national music can exist long without national dance and it is evident that the Puritan movement in England, by killing the dance, dealt a heavy blow at the national music."

English Morris dancing will always be, to the student, an aid to musical understanding and interpretation, considering that each tiny section of England has its own dances and music. Together they amount to more than five hundred, of which no one dance can be done to the music of any other dance. The archaic form of the Morris dance is thought to be the traditional sword dance of northern England. The tunes for this are in the order of rhythmic and spirited jigs, all with a strong accent on the first beat of the measure, a characteristic of most Morris dance music.

The Morris dance was first done to an ancient instrumental combination of pipe and tabor, a distinctive sound to which the dancers became so accustomed that they were satisfied with no other. The music was enlivened by the sound of the bells worn on the dancers' ankles. Some of the dance music was sung. Later woodwinds and strings replaced the singers. One of the Morris tunes is Sellenger's Round (St. Leger's Round, or "The Beginning of the World"), a melody of great antiquity. It was seen danced in Ireland in 1540 by Sir Anthony St. Leger, who brought it to England with him. There it was popular during the sixteenth and seventeenth centuries and was arranged by Byrd for his music-pupil, Queen Elizabeth. "Greensleeves" is an exquisite dance-song, perfect enough rhythmically to serve as a dance accompaniment and fine enough musically to be a favorite with many concert artists.

In the seventeenth century in England there were dances such as the Cushion Dance, started by one person who declared "This dance it will no further go," to which the musician replied "I pray you, good sir, why say you so?" More byplay between musician and dancer led the dancer to kiss a woman who thus became his partner, after which both danced and sang together. In parts of England today, the kissing custom still prevails, a certain two notes on the fiddle meaning "Kiss her" at the end of certain dances. Perhaps that was the inspiration for Wordsworth's lines:

> "They hear when every dance is done,
> They hear when every fit is o'er,

> The fiddle's squeak, that call to bliss,
> Ever followed by a kiss."

The words "ballad" and "ballet" were once akin in England—meaning a song to be danced. When they were later differentiated, the latter was applied to dance only, the former to song. Curiously, among the folk (since the primitive ballad was communal in performance as well as in authorship) their synonymous use still survives. The English peasant will often say he has learned a song "off a ballet," meaning a ballad-sheet. Or, as a singer once remarked, "Never had no ballet to it." Cecil Sharp(11) tells us also that "Fiddlers associate the tune with the dance in precisely the same way that singers connect the air of a song with its words. I have often heard them say that if only they could recall the form and figures of the dance to which it belongs they would also remember the tune. On one occasion, a concertina player, from whom I had just noted down a Morris tune, innocently remarked, 'Now, sir, you know all about the dance.' He really believed that a knowledge of the tune carried with it the knowledge of the figures of the dance also."

That folk dance music is quite different from social dance music is evidenced by a letter from Haydn(12) describing a formal English entertainment in the latter part of the eighteenth century. He was unable to stay in the salon where only Minuets were danced, partly because of the bad music made by the two violins and a single 'cello. The Minuets, he said, were done in the Polish style, rather than in the Viennese or the Italian. In another hall English dances were being danced. Haydn was more favorably disposed toward that music, because one of the violinists played a drum!

The renowned Neil Gow (1727-1807) was said to be "one of Nature's own musicians" who did much to promote the use of the violin in playing Scotch dance music. He was a famed player for dancing, and was much in demand at dance parties of the English aristocracy. His up-bow never failed to charm and electrify by its strength and certainty. (In playing Highland reels, much depends on bowing.) A blind musician once declared that the stroke of Gow's bow could be distinguished among one hundred players.

In parts of Scotland, people sing for the dances. The Strathspey, mentioned in the works of Sir Walter Scott, is a Scotch dance somewhat slower than the reel. Its name was taken from the place in which it was first danced. Its meter is 4/4, and a single rhythmic figure (a dotted eighth and sixteenth) characterizes both movement and music. The Scotch Snap, peculiar to most Scottish melodies, reverses the aforementioned rhythmic figure and places the accent on its final note.

Welsh dances were accompanied by harp and crwth. The Welsh people have their own Hornpipes (in common time) and Jigs (in 6/8). One of the Welsh Jigs, printed for harp about a century ago, was marked in this fashion: "The dancers drum it, as they call it, with their feet, that is beat time very loud." This applied only to the last section of the tune.

During the first half of the eighteenth century Irish bagpipes were used a great deal for country festive dances. The country fiddler was also in vogue. Walker's account of Handel's friend Dubourg (last half of the eighteenth century), as quoted by Grattan Flood(13), gives us indirectly an idea of the Irish fiddler's playing for dances: He often wished to enjoy unobserved, the sports of an Irish fair. An opportunity occurred in the town of Dunboyne, near Dublin. Having disguised himself as a country fiddler, he (Dubourg) sallied forth among the tents. He was soon engaged and a company of dancers stood up. But though he exerted himself to play in character, that is, discordantly, there was still a sweet charm in his playing that fixed his audience with rapture. At length the crowd pressed and gazed so upon him that he thought it but wise to retire.

Irish music, in general, is classified as Weeping Music, Sleeping Music, Laughing Music. Under the latter heading comes all dance music. Irish peasants have a distinct feeling for rhythm. Seldom does one dance out of time. Perhaps the best known of all Irish dances is the Jig, of which there are several different varieties, the music of each possessing strong Celtic characteristics. The Double Jig consists of two parts of eight bars each in ⅝ meter, a succession of triplets. The Single Jig differs in that the triplets give place to a succession of dotted eighths and sixteenths which change the character of both tune and step. The Hop Jig, written in ⅝ time, is the most Irish of them all. The Irish Hopping Dance (Espring-gall) belongs to the twelfth century, the melody being sung by one person while the dancers join in the chorus. The refrain of this dance-song is said to be like that of the Fer Gigaoila, a humorous kind of giggling, in short catches of the breath, accompanied by sudden starts of the body.

A popular Swedish folksong is called the "Nack's Dance" (Nackens Polska). Nacks are water-sprites believed to be enchanted humans. It is significant that music dealing with them should be in the form of dance-song. Sweden also dances the Fyramannadans (Swinging Reel) and the Skordedans (Harvest Dance).

Norwegian dances and music are more formal. These are performed by small groups of people in their own homes. Most famous are the Hallings and the Spring Dances. The former is peculiar to Scandinavian countries. It is danced to heavily accented ¾ music, played on a fiddle. The music becomes fiery and more animated and boisterous as the dancer rises from a crouching position to an upright, whirling one. Edvard Grieg once held a neighborhood moving bee to move his little music-house away from the road and its curious sight-seers. When the work was finished and the piano in place, Grieg started to play a Halling, whence all the neighbors danced and threw pine cones at one another. Spring Dances are round dances in ¾ meter, for both men and women. Their chief characteristics are the lovely and unusual modulations from minor to major, as well as a striking combination of binary and ternary rhythms.

Grieg's(14) preface to seventeen peasant dances as played by an old Norwegian fiddler and notated by John Halvorsen aptly describes the Norwegian dance music: "Those who can appreciate this kind of music will be delighted at the extraordinary originality of these tunes, their blending of delicacy and grace with rough power and untamed wildness as regards the melody and more particularly, the rhythm. These traditional tunes, handed down from an age when Norwegian peasantry was isolated from the world in its solitary mountain valleys, all bear the stamp of an imagination equally daring and bizarre."

Finck(15) finds that many European dance tunes, dances and instruments found their last refuge in the North, which preserved them, altered by the imprint of Northern characteristics. The remoteness of the North made this possible.

There are places on the Faroe Islands where custom decrees that the same song must not be sung in the dance rooms more than once a year. Their traditional dance-songs, or ballads, tell of heroes, giants and magic. Some are ironic. The clasped hands of the dancers move up and down rhythmically while their feet take the simplest of steps to the right, and to the left. The Faroe dance-songs, which number more than two hundred, are so long that one often fills an entire evening.

The country dance is the social recreation of the peasantry in many countries. Each nation has its own distinctive music and a different name (or simply a translation of the original word into the common tongue) for the dance. The English quickstep in a 6/8 marching rhythm is said to have reached Germany at the time of Frederick the Great and then to have found its way into the works of Beethoven. Schubert and Weber were also said to have been somewhat influenced by the "military ball-room style."

To her folksong "Ach, du Lieber Augustin," Germany is said to owe the typically racial German Waltz. The song was used in a ballet by Gardel called *La Dansomanie,* produced in Paris in 1793. From it the German Waltz developed.

Switzerland enhances her folk dances with the yodel. The Bavarian Schuhplattletanz has a joyous and sparkling Waltz rhythm played on zithers as its accompaniment. Bulgarian dances (sometimes accompanied by singing) are said to be of the Horo type, descendant of the ancient Greek chorus or chain dance.

When Cecil Sharp came to the Appalachian Mountains and to eastern Kentucky in the United States to investigate American survivals of old English folk dances, he gathered a great deal of material from the backwoodsmen who are descendants of early English settlers. The American composer, Charles E. Ives, derived his early musical ideas from such diversions as hearing these men fiddling for a dance, when they played slightly off-pitch, slipped and slid and dipped and pulled the tones. American folk dance-songs have unwritten variations, but their spontaneity is rapidly being lost. As Cecil Sharp discovered, not all of the country fiddler's dance tunes are indigenous to America, but his style and his accents are unique. He has rhythm and gaiety. Sometimes he arises and dances while he plays. He stamps out the time with his heavy boots and plays without accompaniment, as his forefathers did when the country was sparsely settled, instruments were rare, and eight-piece jazz orchestras weren't available from nearby towns. Therefore, to imitate an orchestra and to vary his monotonous and limited repertoire, the fiddler adds chords and double stops and somehow, manages to accomplish the impossible. He also holds his fiddle loosely on his chest. In many characteristics, then, he is similar to his European contemporaries. Carleton S. Smith(16) therefore presumes that they are all bearers of an age-old tradition.

Another type of folk dance tune is found in North America. It is that which relates to the Negro. One of the principal Afro-American folk dances is the Juba, the stamping on the ground with the foot and following it with two staccato pats of the hands in ¾ time, according to Dr. Dett(17). This rhythmic figure is similar to the leading figure in the Bamboula, a dance which appears everywhere there are Negroes and which has always kept its own name. It is said to have taken that name from an African drum which accompanied it.

A Calinda is also an African dance-song known in all Creole countries.

The influence of Negro music is strong in all the Americas. There are, in fact, three origins of modern Cuban dance music: Indian, Spanish and African; within which there exist as many sub-origins as there were African tribes arriving in Cuba since 1514 (the date of the arrival of the first Negro slaver) and today those are forming a curious mixture which constitutes the base of the best Cuban music. Caturla(18) finds that the music for the two native Cuban dance forms (the Danza and the Rhumba) offers great possibilities for symphonic development. The famous "Son," prominent throughout the Tropics, originated in Cuba. It was adopted to fit the peculiar movements of a native dance.

All the dances of Cuba and South America are irrevocably bound up with their accompanying music. And the influence of Spain is noticeable.

The music for the Zamba, the most typical of Brazilian dances, is as popular as the dance itself: nervous, warm, joyous. This dance may be a descendant of the Moorish Zambra, as danced in Spain, a night revel at which there was dancing, singing and the playing of musical instruments.

The Pericon, one of Argentina's many group dances, is done to the accompaniment of guitars and the singing of the dancers. The Zamacueca, or Cueca, is Chile's leading folk dance. The music for this is largely in major mode. It follows the verse scheme, for the most part. Both words and music are capricious since they accompany in mood the elusiveness and pursuit expressed by the dance. They echo what is in the hearts of the participants.

Modern Mexican dance music (classified by Chavez as sacred and profane) displays a Spanish influence, but has no Negroid tendencies whatsoever. All of these dances are flexible. Each dancer, by his instinctive knowledge of rhythm, is able to lend his own interpretation to every dance. Just so does the Mexican dance accompanist, or member of the Mariachi orchestra, treat the dance music. Write it down for him, compel him to play it to order, and he will stifle and lose his spontaneity. Mariachi music is wild. Eight or ten men play in different meters simultaneously: complex, earthy, fascinating rhythmic and tonal combinations.

Mexico's most famous folk dance, the Jarabe Tapatio, has had its music, costume and movement conventionalized in the cities. This official Jarabe music consists of nine gay melodies. However, when this dance is done in the villages, it varies in every region and is danced to a great variety of Sones, many of which have been utilized as a basis for the nine "official" Jarabe tunes. There are more than thirty different Jarabes, in varied meters.

The Sandunga is danced on the Isthmus of Tehuantepec. The minor music is haunting and graceful for the women; faster and more vigorous for the men who dance around them. The Jarana is danced in Yucatan, to music without words. During this dance there are pauses when the man must invent verses (bombas) complimenting his partner. The Huapango is danced by the villages of the three Huastecas in Vera Cruz, Hidalgo, Potosí. In singing Huapango Sones to guitar accompaniment, the player comes down with his fist on the last note of the measure, producing a peculiar Huapango rhythm. These Sones define customs and relate events in simple melodies. (In some places this dance is called Fandango after what might have been its Spanish ancestor.) In Michoacán exists a series of traditional dances and songs in Tarasco (the ancient language) called Canacuas (Crowns). These Canacuas were formerly more beautiful than they are now, since some of their loveliest melodies have been lost. The only transcription in existence (as far as the writer knows) is that made by Francisco Dominguez(19). His harmonization, because of its conventionality, does much to rob the melodies of their native character.

Today, upon the distinctive, racial foundation of their own folk music (which is largely dance music) modern composers of every nation in the world are constructing their art! And by its similarity to the folk, the creative product is known and judged!

CHAPTER 4

NOTES

(1) *The Étude,* November, 1924, p. 736
(2) Sharp, *English Folksong: Some Conclusions,* p. 62
(3) Bartok, *Hungarian Folk Music,* p. 9
(4) *The Étude,* September, 1924, p. 593
(5) Boughton, *The Reality of Music,* p. 97
(6) *Life and Letters of Peter Ilyich Tschaikowsky,* p. 197
(7) Liszt, *The Gypsies and Their Music,* p. 130
(8) Otero, *Tratado de Bailes,* p. 126
(9) Kinncy, *The Dance,* p. 161
(10) *The Musical Quarterly,* January, 1930, p. 129
(11) Sharp, *English Folksong: Some Conclusions,* p. 21
(12) Hadden, *Haydn,* pp. 95-96
(13) Flood, *History of Irish Music,* pp. 298-299
(14) Finck, *Grieg and His Music,* p. 99
(15) Finck, *Grieg and His Music,* p. 89
(16) *The New York Times*
(17) Preface to his *Juba Dance,* Clayton F. Summy Company, Chicago, 1913
(18) In a memorandum to the author from Los Remedios, Cuba, dated February 9, 1935
(19) *Mexican Folkways,* Volume VI, 1930

＊

FORMAL FRENCH BALLET MUSIC

In almost all histories of dancing, the French ballet is mentioned first, later to be coupled with the Italian ballet, and still later to be acknowledged as the parent of the Russian ballet. But students of ancient lore cannot fail to recollect photographs of Tibetan art, hundreds of years before Christ, depicting people in stylized ballet attitudes. The Japanese dancer falls into a second position plié, and so on. One cannot say definitely that the formal ballet originated in the Orient, but it is certain that its beginnings elsewhere antedated its appearance in France by many years. Spain, and the dancers of Cadiz who were popular in Rome for so many years, influenced its development. One authority informs us that the Rome of several hundred years ago gave us the Italian ballet technique, based on lines somewhat removed from the Greek ideal. It was a highly finished, decorative technique, colored to a certain extent by pantomime. It sprang into popularity and, perfected by France, took root in the dancing world. All the current ballet terms derive from the French. This does not mean that the ballet was born in France, any more than the use of Italian musical terms implies that music itself was born in Italy.

We are told that formal ballet began in France after the

fifteenth century, and that some of the greatest composers of the day wrote its music. Cecil Sharp(1) informs us that the ballet-mascarade made its appearance in France after the discontinuance of the royal ballet on a large scale, that the ballet-mélodramatique (when recitative displaced spoken dialogue) followed and gave way, in the third decade of the seventeenth century, to opera. Thus, one of the most grandiose of all theatrical productions arose from the ballet.

Indeed, Castil-Blaze, in chronicling the history of the French Opéra, said that the productions of the seventeenth century, commonly called at the time "ballets," were usually nothing less than operas treated in such a way as to give a little more freedom for the introduction of dances, the singing being nevertheless the main object. The function of singer and dancer were usually well separated, but one actress managed, in the opera *Perseus*, to score a double success as singer and dancer, an "unusual combination, as it is seldom that a dancer is good for much as a vocalist."

Since the operas of that period included much dancing and the ballets much singing, one might presume that the two types of performance were identical. This presumption is not entirely correct. The difference was that the operas had plots and were tragedies, while the ballets were a series of *entrées* which might even be interchanged, with no appreciable lack of interest resulting, since they were merely several repeated lines of melody.

When Catherine de Medici came to France in the sixteenth century, she brought with her a taste for Italian dancing, and introduced the lively Gaillarde, Volte and Courante to replace the stately Pavane and Branle. For a time, there was chaos in dancing. Masked dances were done to an accompaniment of psalms, and Diane de Poitiers actually danced a Volte to the air of *De Profundis*.

On October 15, 1581 occurred the famous *Ballet comique de la Reine Louise* by the violinist Beaujoyeux, or Baltazarini. (This musician must have changed his name from Baltazarini to Beaujoyeux upon his arrival in France.) The music of this ballet is said to be the product of Lambert de Beaulieu, to whom Baltazarini had a last-minute recourse when all the rest of the court artists were found to be engaged in other projects and therefore unavailable, in spite of the fact that the ballet was to honor the marriage of Catherine de Medici's sister. It represented twelve geometrical figures and included poetry to be recited, music to be sung and a variety of things which should be represented by painting and dancing. This spectacle, costing over 3,500,000 francs, was considered (along with Lully's *Le Triomphe de l'amour*) one of the greatest of all court ballets. Burney thought the music very poor. It contained no solos, but was similar in style to Italian madrigals. There was an overture of oboes, horns and sackbut. Its first part contained *Le Son de la Clochette* (the Sound of the Little Bell) eight measures of which were later included in No. 2 of Henry Ghys' piano pieces, Op. 10, under the name *Air de Louis XIII*. Later it was known as a *Gavotte de Louis XIII* and, still later, as *Amaryllis*. The music following Baltazarini's opening eight measures was composed by Ghys. Some authorities say that Louis XIII himself composed a good four-part song entitled *Amaryllis*, thus giving rise to the belief that he also composed Baltazarini's (or Beaulieu's) melody.

In 1581 there was also produced in France a ballet called *Circé* with music of that same Beaulieu, in collaboration with another court musician named Salmon. *Circé* utilized, besides the orchestra, ten violinists in costume on the stage in Act I. Then a troupe of swimming tritons played lutes, harps and flutes on the stage. Jupiter's appearance was accompanied by forty musicians.

Certain subjects were popular with many ballet composers. The French ballet, *Le Balet des Douze Mois de l'Année* (about 1636) dealt with the twelve months of the year. The same subject was used for at least two English masques, one earlier and one later.

The time of Louis XIV was the favored epoch for ballets and ballet music in France. In 1661 he established L'Académie Royale de la Danse. At the ripe age of forty-six he yet danced and was seen in Lully's ballet "Eclogue de Versailles." Basque peasants of today still dance to music of the Louis XIV period, especially the Gavotte by Gardel, who also wrote the ballets, *Psyché* and *Achille à Scyros*, and who invented new dances and steps. In Louis XIV's time, we find the composer enjoying the lion's share of the remuneration for each performance. An old article in *Comœdia* says that at the Académie Nationale de Musique, where the performers were of the best and most expressive of the day, the principal singers were paid sixty-five to ninety cents per performance, the chorus members forty cents each, the priemière danseuse fifty cents. The King himself regulated the author's rights. An opera composer received forty dollars for each of the first ten performances, twenty dollars apiece for following ones. A ballet composer received twenty-four dollars for the first ten days and twelve dollars afterward. How different from the present day, when performers are richly remunerated and composers are lucky when someone even recalls that there is a royalty fee!

During the reign of Louis XIV, the Duchesse du Maine was celebrated for her entertaining *Nuits de Sceaux* or *Nuits Blanches*. She had determined to realize on her own stage something like one of the antique pantomimes. Therefore, she took the fourth act of *Les Horaces*, had it set to music by Mouret just as if it were to be sung, then had it played by orchestra alone, while two celebrated dancers mimed the action.

Lully, too, was said to have made efforts to imitate the mute play of the chorus of antique tragedy. He was thus able to turn the thoughts of the audience to the *music* of the ballets they were seeing. Efforts like his made Théophile Gautier say, one later day: "The Ballet is music that one can see."

Jean Baptiste de Lully! What can one not say of this remarkable man, the "monarch of the French Opera," the more-than-Wagner of his day?

While he was heading the French Opéra, no works but his own were allowed to be given. Because he wanted his creations to be presented just as he wrote them, he taught the singers to sing, the musicians to play, the dancers to dance. He was everything at the Opéra: stage manager, conductor, composer, machinist and ballet manager. His compositions occupy thirty-six large volumes, so prolific was he as a creator!

Lully originated in Florence. In his early childhood, he was known to have had an ear for music. He danced, sang and played in the streets and in the booths at fairs instead of attending to his father's business. Here it was that he absorbed all he saw of strolling Italian players—a knowledge that greatly aided him in his later work as producer. And here it was that a French nobleman saw him and invited him to come to Paris, where his mistress, impressed by the spontaneity of his music, decided to give the boy lessons.

When he finally entered Louis' royal ballet, it was as a dancer. Then he persuaded the conductor to include some of his airs in the ballet music. Three months later he was appointed Composer of Instrumental Music to the Court. His airs were played everywhere then. The King took dancing lessons from him and made him sole director of the court ballets. In this position he remained until the ballet was transferred from court to theater.

At one time, the French Basse Danses were called "Danses Nobles," because of the dignity they required. These were replaced by what was termed a "Baladinage" from the medieval peasant Baladine. This became, in its turn, the sole Danse Noble. Later, declares Cahusac, there was substituted for it an animated dance *in bad taste*. It then happened that Lully saw his dances treated as Baladinage because of their speed! Lully was first, in 1653, to give the Minuet in France a musical form. The dance itself had been introduced into the country in 1650. Moreover, Lully retained and enriched signified dances such as the Pavane, and employed new orchestral elements to enhance them. When he produced his own *Cupid and Bacchus*, he had the orchestra members costumed in the period of the ballet. His *Ballet du Roy* (1659) contained a beautiful Gavotte in *d* minor. His *Ballet royal de l'impatience* (1661) included an interlude praising tobacco, The Snufftaker's Tale. For the *Ballet des saisons* in 1695, Lully had as his collaborator Pascal Colasse whose musical style, in general, was so close to that of Lully that he is often termed a plagiarist. Whether it was Lully's *Le Triomphe de l'Amour* that set the style of all the ballets in the Louis XIV period, or whether Lully's work merely partook of the accepted style is something that is yet to be decided. The fact remains, however, that it was the most perfect work of its kind. Indeed, M. Louis Lievin is of the opinion that all the Louis XIV ballets had identical scenes: that they all might have been rightly entitled *Le Triomphe de l'Amour*.

Quinault was librettist for *Le Triomphe de l'Amour*. When it was first performed on January 21, 1681, at the court of Saint-Germain-en-laye, female dancers appeared for the first time on the French operatic stage. The score of this ballet was not at first orchestrated by its composer. He merely set down the part for the clavichord with instrumental indications written in for violins, flutes, etc. Following the *Prélude de l'Amour*, Lully had a melancholy episode, played by four transverse flutes alone.

Rameau declared that "Lully . . . in a manner forgot his country, and by his performances made France triumph even over Italy by the charms of these very sights which Rome and Venice had invented. Not satisfied with setting them off with all the lustre music was capable of, as he was obliged to represent Triumphs, Sacrifices, Enchantments and Noble Banquets, which required dances in character, he made choice of the most able dancers in France." In one of the ballets on the Venetian Feasts, described Rameau further, there was a singular scene in which a dancing master in a song boasts of all the advantages of his art; and at the same time performed the difficult characters of dancing in the ballets.

When Lully's *Le Triomphe de l'Amour* was revived in Paris in 1925, the music became boring as it progressed, due to the limited musical idiom of the day in which it was composed and the consequent lack of variety. Nevertheless, near Lully's own time, there were discussions and conflicting opinions about his music. There were then reversed opinions and so on, until today, Wanda Landowska(2) is able to state emphatically that out of a thousand musicians you will now find scarcely ten capable of telling apart compositions by Lully, Rameau and Gluck. This, in spite of the tremendous advance each made over the other!

Noverre considered Lully's dance music cold, tedious and devoid of character. This he said despite Lully's admirers, and added that it was composed at a time when dancing was restrained and dancers were expressionless. Noverre deplored the fact that new, voluble dances had been set to the taciturnity of Lully's music. On the other hand, he considered Rameau's music witty and full of expression. He considered that it had improved dancing and awakened it from its lethargy. In Noverre's opinion, Rameau was a man of vast genius, combining everything beautiful, grand and harmonious in his work.

In the eighteenth century, the style of Lully's Danse Noble had again reached an extreme of refined splendor, and it was then that a violent reaction began to stir against the pure dance in its fixed and meaningless rhythms. People then dubbed Rameau's ballets a "mere collection of dance suites," strung together on an allegorical pretext. They searched Lully's works for charming bits which were then set end to end, with a bit of re-scoring. Adds J. G. Prod'homme(3) : "In a word, the ballet of the eighteenth century was a species of variety show."

A lesser known composer of the earlier period was Colin de Blâmont. His *Les Fêtes Grecques et Romaines* was a ballet in three acts (Jeux Olympiques, Bacchanals, Saturnals) and Prologue. Michel Pignolet de Montéclair was also a composer of ballets (1666-1737) between the times of Lully and Rameau. He, a member of the Opéra orchestra in Paris, was one of the earliest players on the modern double bass. His ballet *La Tentacion de la Bergère* was reconstructed many years later by the Ballet Russe, when critics praised the attractive score because it avoided conflicts between the movement and the orchestra! Montéclair in 1716 wrote a ballet-opera called *Les Fêtes de l'été.* This was, of course, produced at the Opéra.

Jean Phillippe Rameau, whose music was compared to that of Lully first to the advantage of the one, and then to that of the other, was an energetic person. In the words of Kirstein(4): France provided dance music for the continent, and a good part of the airs were written by Rameau. By a curious co-incidence, the author of one of the earliest authoritative books on dancing bore the same surname of this composer. Pierre Rameau was the author of the book called *The Dancing Master*. In the preface he wrote that he had "spent all my time in studying and teaching the Dance" and had written the book simply because no other dancing master had thought to communicate the rules in writing. His energy compelled him to fill such a void. The book deals with the five positions, manner of bowing, taking off the hat, etc. There are also descriptions of the various steps we know today, including details of foot and arm movements in dances like the Minuet, as well as descriptions of the positions of every part of the arm: elbow, wrist, shoulder and oppositions of arms and legs. There is even a set of rules for conducting oneself at a court ball.

The composer did, however, write a book: a treatise on music, containing the principles of composition. In the chapter on Remarks Touching the Discord, he explained what is probably the secret of his startling, new music, which even today retains its charm: "A discord, instead of being troublesome to a composer, on the contrary, it gives him greater liberty . . ." and accounts for his advance over earlier, more academic composers. There is also a chapter on how one and the same discord may be used in several chords successively following upon different notes, and how it may be resolved by notes that seem to be foreign to that purpose. He believed that "chromatick is chiefly used in flat keys and is more difficult to comprehend when the parts descend than when they ascend." The former has more "sorrowfulness" than the latter.

J. P. Rameau wrote a heroic ballet, *Les Indes Galantes* (1735) based on the Peruvian Incas. He even went so far as to write for clavecin a dance for the Caribs who had been imported from South America for exhibition in Paris. He titled it *Les Sauvages*. In such ballets as *Zais*, however, he returned to the typically French scene and composed music descriptive of a jinn, renouncing his magical powers for love of a shepherdess.

Dupré (about 1697-1774), who was known as King of the Dance at the Paris Opéra, was first a violinist, though doubtless a very bad one. He once accompanied a dancer's rehearsal, sitting in the pit of the Théâtre de Rouen. The dancer said, "Your scrapings are driving me mad." The violinist responded with some haughty aspersions on the dancer's art and then invited him to play the violin in his stead. The dancer accepted the invitation, learned the violin and actually became head of the French school of violin playing, while the unmusical fiddler turned out to be the great Dupré!

Grétry's *Céphale et Procris*, based on the Greek tale of Cephalus, ardent devotee of the chase, was styled an heroic ballet. This composer had a thorough acquaintance with the stage, though he never studied the more profound branches of the musical art. He was primarily a melodist, and therefore invaluable to the world of dance. One of his critics remarked that "You might drive a coach and four between his bass and his first fiddle."

In 1778, on May 14th, Mozart wrote from Paris that Jean Georges Noverre was about to design a new ballet for which he would compose the music. This project, outcome of Mozart's modest desire to write a work for the French stage, developed into *Les petits Riens* (The Little Nothings) which was nothing more nor less than "love in a cage delivered by cupids, and shepherds playing blindman's buff to Gavottes." It was described by a contemporary as being a semi-serious ballet. It was, at any rate, a great favorite with Noverre. He presented three versions of it in succession at Vienna, Paris and London. Despite the charm of Mozart's music, the press praised the dancers most highly, while receiving the musical accompaniment indifferently. The music was put away. In

1873 it was re-discovered. Now, bits of the score are heard often, not as dance music, but as music for the concert stage.

Noverre, French ballet master, born in Paris in 1727, is said to have introduced in dancing the same reforms that Gluck brought to music. His views on the ballet were as far-reaching in their effects as were those of Diaghileff in a later day. Naturally, his reforms were concerned also with music. Was not music an integral part of the ballet of his day? Said he, "A good ballet is Nature itself, ennobled by all the charms of art. The music is to the dance what a libretto is to the opera. In training, it is well to begin with the natural instincts and to permit the pupil to interpret the sounds of music as fancy dictates during the earlier stages of schooling." How very far the formal ballet went from this early precept can only be realized by careful observation of students trained solely on strict ballet principles, since their regard for music is more or less that of automatons.

Another of Noverre's thoughts regarding music is evidenced in his description of *La Toilette de Vénus, ou Les Ruses de l'Amour*. In this ballet, he "had thought of introducing pauses into the music, and these produced the most flattering effect. The spectator's ear suddenly ceasing to be struck by the harmony, his eye took in with more attention all the details of the pictures. These pauses in the music showed up to greater advantage the pieces which followed. But the skill consists in employing them sparingly; they become fatal to dancing if they be abused."

Noverre found complete understanding in the Viennese audiences of 1767 to 1774, the best years of his artistic life. With this new public, his heroic ballet-pantomimes found great favor. More, he was able to work with composers like Gluck (who was apparently undisturbed by the controversy between Noverre and that other choreographer, Gaspare Angiolini, born in Milan in 1723), Starzer and Aspelmayer. Starzer supplied music for Noverre's comic ballet *Don Quichotte*, while Rudolph furnished the musical background for the ballets

La Morte d'Hercule (tragic), *Renaud et Armide* (heroic), and *Psyché et l'Amour* (heroic).

Since at the Viennese Court(5) a strict line was drawn between vocal and instrumental composers, Italians wrote the operas while the ballet music within the operas, as well as music for court festivities and dances, was written by Germans. Johann Heinrich Schmelzer, a Viennese, was the most renowned in this field. He was the first to write real Viennese popular peasant dance tunes into his ballets, thus distinguishing them from the Italian music of his time. He wrote an equestrian ballet, *The Contest between Air and Water*. Much of his music is preserved in the National Library in Vienna. His son, Anton Andreas Schmelzer, succeeded him in this field, as did Wolfgang Ebner, Johann Joseph Hoffer and Nicola Matteis. The latter was called in court archives "The English Violinist." He was violinist and composer of ballets at the Court from 1700 until his death in 1737. All the Viennese opera scores between 1714 and 1740 are said to contain his incidental dances to be done between acts and at the end of the operas.

But, to return to Gluck, Noverre and Angiolini: Noverre directed Gluck's opera-ballets, while the Italian dancer choreographed Gluck's efforts in the realm of pure dance music. To him was entrusted Gluck's ballet, *Don Juan*, with its well-known Gavotte. This ballet was said to have subordinated both music and dance to the plot and to have omitted many of the irrelevancies with which Gluck had hitherto (following the fashion of the day) filled his operas. Its main quality was directness. There was no unnecessary detail. Its music suggested dancing to such an extent that one writer believes it possible to gather from it something of Angiolini's style as a dancer: simplicity, vigor, severity and dignity in slow passages, and a lack of ornamentation suggesting movements as stiff but as expressive as a Greek statue. There were no emotional complexities in the music, since the story itself contained only the elements necessary to a successful unfoldment. Gluck also wrote a ballet called *L'Orfano della China* after a Voltaire story concerning Genghis Khan. In the music, the composer obviously tried to contrast the savage Tartar followers of Genghis Khan with the gentle, civilized Chinese. Voltaire's tragic *Sémiramide* furnished the subject for a short pantomime-ballet by Gluck and Angiolini in 1765. It lasted about thirty minutes. Gluck's three-act ballet, *Cythère Assiégée* was produced in 1775. The ballet, *Festin de Pierre*, after Molière, is today said to be full of vitality, though it was first danced in 1761. It, too, was a product of the Gluck-Angiolini collaboration.

The father of Adolphe Adam was professor of piano playing at the Paris Conservatoire. He was also an operatic composer. Consequently, he refused to allow his son to write for the French stage. What more natural than that? Doubtless, he thought he was doing his son a favor. At long last, he permitted the boy to enter the Conservatory, at the same time exacting from him a promise that he would never write for the French stage. And, what more natural than that the promise should be broken? Forbidden fruits are always the most tempting. As it happened, he was successful. The approbation accorded his operas and ballets justified his faith in his own ability, and doubtless proved the injustice of the early promise he had been forced to make to his father. The younger Adam was known as the "lesser Auber." (Auber was also known as a writer of dance music, though his field was really comic opera. For example, his opéra comique, *Marco Spada*, written in 1852, was expanded into a ballet in 1857. Of him it has been said that "In Auber's comic operas the dance, a mere accessory to French Opéra thus far, became its nerve.") Adam wrote music for many ballets danced by Maria Taglioni. (It is interesting to note that the glamor surrounding this dancer persisted many years after her death, and in 1902 Meyer-Helmund wrote an opera called *Taglioni*, glorifying her.) Perhaps the most famous of all Adam's ballets is *Giselle* (1841). Gautier said "The blue rays of German moonlight glide mysteriously over the silvery notes of its music" but, of course, Gautier may have been prejudiced in its favor. He wrote the scenario. Another contemporary critic called it "truly captivating," but a modern critic dubs it "one of the most wretched works of a

mediocre musician" and Arnold Haskell(6) declares that this
banal, tuneful music, composed of slightly syncopated French-
Italian melodies, has nothing whatever to do with the subject,
and is a definite emotional handicap. (And this was the composer from whom Delibes is said to have learned much!) The
ballet was and is popular. After Taglioni, Carlotta Grisi and
then every other famous ballerina starred in it.

For Taglioni, Adam also wrote *La Fille du Danube* (1836)
abounding in simple melodies and dances for mortals and water
nymphs. Other of his ballets were *Le Diable à Quatre* (1845),
Le Corsaire (1856); *L'Écumeur de la Mer* (1840), *Faust*,
La Jolie Fille de Gand, and *Les Mohicans* in two acts (1837)
after James Fenimore Cooper's novel. Martens(7) quotes a
contemporary critic who subtly disparages the music and text
of the latter ballet.

The search for the name of the composer of *La Sylphide*,
first of the romantic ballets, occupied many months, since so
many writers have praised Taglioni (for whom it was written)
meanwhile conveniently forgetting that it was danced to music.
The composer's name is practically unknown today but the
ballet he created has made history. What sort of music was
it, for such an epoch-making ballet? It was, at any rate, the
best work of its composer whose name—at length unearthed—
was Jean Madeleine Schneitzhoeffer, a talented musician who
had previously written such ballets as *Les Filets de Vulcain*.
La Sylphide was based on the short fairy story, *Trilby* and was
first performed at the Paris Opéra in 1832. It proved to be a
departure from the pure technicalities of the old ballet. No
dance production before had so expressed spiritual beauty. In
it, Taglioni was delicate, virginal, ethereal. Now the names
Taglioni and *La Sylphide* seem inseparable. They have merged
into a legend.

In London, 1833, Sir Michael Costa wrote the ballet
Sir Huon for Taglioni, while F. Taglioni composed (1830)
a ballet termed *Brésilia* in which a Brazilian princess wrote two
love letters on plantain leaves and a savage ballet was dressed
in coy ballet costumes. Also in 1830, Halévy wrote the grand

ballet, *Manon Lescaut* in Paris, two years after Hérold's
romantic, rococo *La Fille Mal Gardée*. (*La Fille Mal Gardée*
was recently revived in New York, with music credited to
Hertel.) Casimir Gide composed in 1836 in Paris *Le Diable
Boiteux* (The Limping Devil) a pantomime-ballet. It was
described as being brilliant, facile music with Andalusian and
Flamenco dances. It followed by exactly one year his *L'Ile des
Pirates*.

Without a doubt, the pinnacle of ballet music in the formal
French style was attained by Delibes who, all his life, cherished
longings to write a "higher type of music." When at last he
attempted this dream in the incomplete drama, *Kassya*, it was
discovered that his success had been indeed more secure in the
more facile music. Delibes (born 1836) wrote music that
was perfectly adapted to the medium for which he was composing. To expect it to satisfy the demands of the modern dance
is absurd. One writer classes his *Sylvia* as an excellent specimen
of French ballet, "the music full of grace and charm and especially suitable for dancing," but Dalcroze (8) insists that Delibes
was careless in much of his music, especially when the text
says "Sylvia takes flight." In this spot, Delibes wrote a very
short, light chromatic scale which suggested to Dalcroze a
scurrying mouse, not an active ballerina. Surely Delibes' reason-
ing was illogical, though it is evident that if dancing had been
anything but the formal expression it was at the time, Delibes
and other composers would have written different music for it.
Nevertheless, modern composers would do well to emulate
Delibes in a study of the particular medium for which they
compose.

It was Delibes who revolutionized the silly ideas of ballet
music, declares Van Vechten (9), introducing in his scores a
symphonic element, a wealth of graceful melody and a richness
of harmonic fiber based, it is safe to hazard, on a healthy distaste for routine. Beyond any manner of doubt, Delibes is the
father of the modern Ballet—even, we presume he means, over
such men as Stravinsky. He adds, Delibes, aware of his limitations, or governed purely by his taste, deliberately excludes the

barbaric and the savage from his work; everything is gracious and refined. At any rate, Delibes was almost the first to write ballet music which held its own on the concert stage of its own day. His ballets brought the past to light in a modern manner, and anticipated the succeeding period when the French ballet came to its full glory.

Adolphe Adam taught Delibes much. When Adam's ballet, *Le Corsaire* was revived in 1867, Delibes was invited to supply a divertissement, *Le Pas de Fleurs*, such was the impression made by his music for *La Source*. Of this latter ballet, Saint-Saëns (10) has spoken at length. He, Bizet, Delibes and Massenet were invited to the Opéra Comique, where Massenet proposed the *Rat-Catcher* from an old German tale, as a subject for a ballet, while Saint-Saëns suggested *Une Nuit de Cléopâtra* on Gautier's text. "They refused us the honor and, when they consented to order a ballet from Delibes, didn't dare to trust him with the whole work. They let him do only one act and the other was given to a Hungarian composer. As the experiment succeeded, they allowed Delibes to write, without assistance, his marvelous *Coppélia*." Doubtless the Hungarian composer he mentions was Minkus. Perrin, the Paris Opéra Stage Director, commissioned *La Source*. (In Vienna, this was called *Naila, die Quellenfee* or "Naila, the Water-Nymph.") Although the second and third tableaux were the only ones composed by Delibes, the audiences liked his music better than Minkus'. Naturally, their preference had a corresponding effect on the opera management.

The request for *Coppélia* followed shortly after. This story is taken from the tales of E. A. T. Hoffman, is in two acts, and is a mere thread to introduce such charming dances as the Waltz of the Hours. Coppelius is a toymaker and magician. The ballet was written in 1870. An amusing incident is related of its music and its composer. Budapest invited both Delibes and Massenet to conduct an act from one of their works. When Massenet reached the orchestra, amid enthusiastic hurrahs from the audience, he found on his desk the score of the first act of *Coppélia* instead of the third act of *Herodiade* that he was scheduled to conduct. There was no way out of the situation. He had to conduct from memory. Delibes, in his turn, saw the third act of *Herodiade* on his desk. He mopped his brow, turned this way and that, drew long breaths and begged the Hungarian musicians (who didn't understand a word he said) to give him the right score. His efforts were in vain. He was exasperated at having to beat time from memory, but managed to get through well enough. At the banquet later, Massenet suggested that they collaborate on their speeches as they had with their scores. Massenet thus spoke for Delibes, Delibes for Massenet. Result: a succession of incoherent sentences which were received with the utmost delight by the Hungarians!

Delibes' ballet *Sylvia* was also called *The Nymph of Diana* and was based on Tasso's poem, *Aminta*, the scenario of the pastoral variety, picturing a land where nymphs, shepherdesses, fauns, satyrs and goddesses mingle. Tschaikowsky(11) wrote to a friend: "Lately I have heard Delibes' very clever music in its own style, to the ballet *Sylvia*. The performance fascinated me, especially the first part. *Swan Lake* is poor stuff compared to *Sylvia*. Nothing during the last few years has charmed me so greatly as this ballet of Delibes', and *Carmen*."

In 1880 Delibes became Professor of Advanced Composition at the Conservatory and later was made a Chevalier of the Legion of Honor. Immediately following him, as French ballet composers, were: Widor, Wurmser, Messager, Vidal, Saint-Saëns, Lalo, Maréchal, Busser and Dubois.

Théodore Dubois was the composer of the ballet *La Farandole*, on the theme of a dance so fascinating that no one can escape from its clutches. It was in three acts, and was presented at the Paris Opéra in 1883. The music was said to be light and animated, but also well written and well scored. It included the Divertissement of the Tambourinaires, La Provençale, an Adagio and the Valse des Olivettes. Dubois, born in 1837, was Delibes' successor as Professor of Harmony and

Composition at the Paris Conservatory before he became its Director in 1896. He wrote operas and oratorios in addition to ballets.

There was another Dubois in this same field of musical endeavor, but this was Léon Dubois, born in Brussels in 1849 and later the second Conductor at the Théâtre de la Monnaie. To his credit is the one-act ballet *Smylis* (1891) and the mimo-drama, *Le Mort* (1894).

André Messager, opera composer and conductor, born in 1853, composed music for an allegorical ballet in two acts and three tableaux called *The Two Pigeons* (1886). The plot of this ballet is rather vague, no decision having been reached as to whether it was the male or the female pigeon who left the nest in search of adventure. Surely it was a fanciful ballet! The scene was laid in Hungary. Messager also wrote the ballets *Fleur d'Oranger* (1878), *Les Vins de France* (1879), *Mignons et Vilains* (1879), *Scaramouche* (1891), *Amants Eternels* (1893), *Le Chevalier aux Fleurs* (1897), *Le Procès des Roses* (1897), and *Une Aventure de la Guimard* (1900).

In studying dance music of the formal French ballet, one finds in it little variation. One might compare it to an existing book of dance tunes dedicated to the famous ballerina, Fanny Ellsler, by different composers, but all in undeviating, regular rhythms. Jessmin Howarth, after intimate work at the Paris Opéra, discovered that the ballet members had to be rehearsed every morning in each tiny detail of the ballets they were to perform that night, else they were liable to do an entirely different ballet to the scheduled music. The reason was that the limited ballet form makes all the steps alike. The sole problem was to remember how many of which steps came when. Thus, the music contributed to this precarious memory, since it was so regular, so *similar*, metrically. Little of it was different from any other part of it. Miss Howarth once wished to have her ballet dance and sing at once, but the traditions with which she had to cope were too strong to break so quickly.

Tradition! It is what modern composers for the dance have had to fight every step of the way. Yet, if they but knew, they have even older traditions (those of the Ancients) that would justify the things they believe to be artistically right. Stravinsky may be unconscious of his affinity with the ancients. All the same, it exists.

CHAPTER 5

NOTES

(1) Sharp, *The Dance, an Historical Survey of Dancing in Europe*, p. 37
(2) Landowska, *Music of the Past*, p. 10
(3) *Musical Quarterly*, October, 1919, p. 521
(4) Kirstein, *Dance*, p. 206
(5) *Musical Quarterly*, January, 1933, p. 79
(6) Haskell, *Balletomania*, pp. 53-54
(7) Martens, *A Thousand and One Nights at the Opera*, p. 236
(8) Dalcroze, *Eurhythmics, Art and Education*, p. 207
(9) *Musical Quarterly*, October, 1922, p. 607
(10) Saint-Saëns, *Musical Memories*, p. 37
(11) *Life and Letters of Peter Ilyich Tschaikowsky*, p. 241

BALLET MUSIC IN EARLY OPERAS

The age when the writing of dance music was regarded as a diversion rather than a serious occupation began with what we know as the classic era. Into the minds of the pre-classicists also, some such idea had crept, though they did much to further the custom of dancing in all theatrical productions, no matter how serious. Ironically enough, their greatest fame is based on their simple, appealing dance tunes, no matter what the zealous investigator may discover to the contrary. "Rameau's *Airs de Danse* will live eternally," it was said(1), "For while he composed many operas, he was there at his best."

When the first oratorio appeared in 1600 in the oratory of the church itself, it was evidently thought best to treat it as a theatrical production, for it was acted, sung, danced and costumed elaborately. Its name: *The Representation of Soul and Body*. The oratorio has now come far from that, indeed! Nevertheless, Sir Hubert Parry(2) is of the opinion that in oratorio the dance influence maintained its place, though not so openly as in opera: "In oratorio the importance of dance rhythm is shown by negative as well as positive evidence. In the parts in which the composers arrive at pure declamatory

MEXICAN MARIACHI ORCHESTRA
with Folk Dancers in the Fo·eground
Photograph courtesy of *Mexican Folkways*

ÉCOLE DE DANSE

By François Dequevauviller, after N. Lavrience, from an impression in the possession of Messrs. F. B. Daniell and Son. Plate 16 in *Old French Line Engravings*
by Ralph Nevill. Published in London by Halton and Truscott Smith, Ltd., 1924

music, the result, though often expressive, is hopelessly and inextricably indefinite in form. But in most cases they submitted either openly or covertly to dance rhythm in some part or other of their works."

In the field of purely secular endeavor, Torquato Tasso's play, *Aminta* (1573), many years later the basis for Delibes' *Sylvia*, had an episode in which a dance was done to the music of a concealed chorus. In 1635 a Roman opera gave ample opportunity for divertissements in song and dance, but purely for the delight of the senses, with no appeal to the mind or heart. Again, in 1639, the Florentine opera, *Galatea*, by Vittori, had airs, choruses and ballet only as a diversion. Many of these early operas had intermissions during which music and dancing took place. Later this intermission entertainment became a thing of itself: *Opéra Comique* and *Opéra Buffa*. Much later, it was known as vaudeville.

In comic opera, it was customary for the duets and other vocal ensembles to have musical interludes to which the singers danced. Therefore, they had to be adapted to movement. In its use of dancing, the French Opéra Comique (which produced Grétry's works) outdid the Italian Opera Buffa. When the French ballet gave way to Grand Opera, the ballet itself was treated as a series of episodes more or less divorced from the main action of the drama. It had a place of great importance, however. The same development in Italy saw a greater emphasis placed on the opera than on the ballet divertissement, though composers such as Monteverdi wisely utilized all possible resources to achieve a coherent whole.

Monteverdi (1567-1642) was one of the first to recognize the importance of ballet music as a contrast to his more serious melodies. In one case, he requested the inclusion of a final canzonetta which could serve as a general ballet in a work he had previously rejected. A ballet in each act was his plan for *La Finta Pazza Licori*, each ballet to be different and extraordinary, with its music imitating the actions of the separate characters. Monteverdi's opera, *Orfeo*, when the protagonist's apotheosis occurs, concludes with a choral song and dance to the accompaniment of instruments. The first act is given over to joyous, dancing shepherd choruses, with little or no dramatic action. In one instance, the composer has made a vocal canon supply the entrée for the ballet, and has followed it with a lively ¾ meter, a 6/4 ritornello and again the ¾.

"The most characteristic part of the French Opera is the choruses and the dances," observes Quantz (3). "We have the impression that the recitatives and airs are there merely to give greater relief to the choruses and ballets. It is undeniable that French music lends itself better than any other to the perfection of the dance."

Lully (1632-1687) played a very great part in the development of the ballet in French opera. In his day, each act of the opera, as well as the Prologue, had to have a divertissement, including a ballet. (A definition formed by one of Lully's contemporaries aptly describes the situation: "An opera is a spectacle in which all the joy and sorrow of the personages consists in watching the dances going on around him!") While other composers were struggling to bring their operas closer to the realm of concert music, Lully was making his ballets more dramatic. As we have seen, the ballet was always uppermost in his mind. For a long time he rated it as more important than opera. Naturally, this belief was apparent in the structure of the operas he wrote.

He was father to many innovations. He established the French type of overture, which includes a prelude, a fugue and then, as its third section, a slow movement or a Minuet. To him is also due the introduction of the rapid style of dancing, for he insisted upon writing lively dance tunes, against the wishes of Louis XIV who had a notorious aversion to brilliant music and who preferred the heavy monotonies of Lully's operatic music. Lully introduced his gay music, which automatically demanded rapid movement, simultaneously with the introduction of the country dance from England (supposed to have been taken to England originally from Normandy, by William the Conqueror), and with England's adoption of the Minuet.

Lully's dances in the formal entrées (though not so named

in the scores, according to Sharp (4)) were Gavottes, Minuets, Chaconnes, Bourrées, Gigues and Canaries. In 1686 he composed the opera *Armide et Renaud* (the scene laid in the Crusades) in which appeared several Minuets, a Rondeau, a Passacaglia of the Spirits. In this opera (Act II) Renaud was asleep at the water's edge to muted strings, when a ballet of water nymphs surrounded him. The composer found further occasion for ballet maneuvers in Act III, when Armide discovered that she was in love with her captive, and summoned to her aid the passions of rage, hatred, vengeance and cruelty. Lully was also the composer of imtermezzi for the interludes in Molière's plays.

Song and dance began to be combined in operatic presentations all over Europe. In 1666 the dancing master, de la Chausée, himself wrote music for a play called *The Victory of Love over Misfortune*. Reinhard Keiser, German, (1674-1739) wrote an opera called *Crösus*, with a *Ballett von Bauern und Bauernkindern* (Ballet of Peasants and Peasants' Children) with an Entrance of the Harlequins, as well as rustic music. Cambert (later with the London court of Charles II) wrote the first opera-ballet, *Pomone*, to Perrin's libretto in 1671. *L'Europe Galante* was an opera-ballet in four acts with music by Campra, performed in France in 1697. Even Lacoste's tragic opera, *Philomèle* (performed in 1705) contained a Sarabande.

Soon, in France at least, the succession of various dance-forms in operas became set. This was due, avers Noverre, to the insistence of certain danseurs and danseuses on dancing to certain airs in certain spots in every opera. A Passepied therefore occurred in the Prologue; Musette in the first act; Tambourine in the second act; alternating Chaconnes and Passepieds in the following acts. The dancing was limited to slow, measured movements on a horizontal plane because of the cumbersome court dresses worn as costumes. These costumes affected the tunes as well as the dances, for the accompanying music then had to be solemn and to pause frequently. This troublesome state of affairs continued until 1721, when the dancer Camargo was bold enough to shorten the costumes by a few inches.

In Henry Purcell's day (1658-1695), it was the custom to supply plays with interludes of dance and music. Therefore Purcell was called upon to do much of that sort of thing. For Dryden's *King Arthur*, his music was so fulsome that it needed only a few links to make it an opera, in the opinion of Fullerton Waldo. A great deal of this incidental music was dance airs, and many of these were afterward made into suites. For example, from the music to d'Urfev's play, *The Virtuous Wife*, a suite for string orchestra was taken: Overture, Slow Air, Hornpipe, two Minuets and an Allegro. *The Fairy Queen*, performed in London in 1692, contained Hornpipe, Rondeau, Air in D Minor, Jig, Entry Dance, Dance for the Fairies, Dance for the Green Men, Dance for the Haymakers, Air in C Major and Monkey's Dance. Purcell's dance music for *The Gordian Knot Untied* was the basis for two suites. He also wrote dances in his music to *The Moor's Revenge* and to *The Married Beau*—later included in instrumental suites.

Purcell was also the composer of one of England's first opera-ballets. He called it *Dido and Aeneas*, and wrote it for a performance by young lady students in a school in Chelsea.

Handel's operas (1685-1759) are rich in dance music. Most of his overtures were planned to end with some kind of dance, after an introduction and a contrapuntal section. In the opera *Rodrigo* (probably first performed in Florence in 1707) were a Gigue, Sarabande, Matelot, two Menuets, Bourrée, Passacaille. The opera *Almira* (1704) contained Rigaudons, Gigues, a Courante, a Bourrée, a Chaconne, Minuet and several Sarabandes. The first period of one of these instrumental Sarabandes (eight measures) later became the famous "Lascia ch'io pianga" in Handel's opera, *Rinaldo*. Thus Handel stole his own dance melody, though there are those who claim that the melody was old long before Handel made it into a Sarabande.

In the opera *Samson*, Handel inserted a Minuet in ⅜ time, in which sweet voices, each phrased differently, sang together with great charm. *Acis and Galatea* was the recipient of an Irish Jig from its renowned composer. The opera *Ariadne* contained a Gavotte, while *Pastor Fido* was introduced by a Prologo and a ballet with singing entitled *Terpsichore*, in which were a Chaconne, Sarabande, Gigue and Ballo. There was a Minuet in *Tamerlano*, and a three-sectional choral and instrumental Gavotte in *Atlanta*. *Alcina* had a Musette, Minuet, Tamburino (featuring the piccolo) and a complete ballet scene, with the Entry of Pleasant Thoughts, Entry of Unpleasant Thoughts, Entry of Frightened Pleasant Thoughts and Fight Between Pleasant and Unpleasant Thoughts. This ballet music has been termed "superb" by critics. It has been said to show Handel in his richest moods. The Minuet in the opera *Bérénice* was termed "divine."

Handel concluded each act of his *Ariodante* with a ballet in order to accommodate a group of French dancers which he desperately needed to recoup his waning fortunes. There is said to remain from this opera a Ballo and Musette. The music of the rest of the production was slight, however. When the French dancers returned to Paris, one writer said that though their loss was in many ways a good thing for Handel, they had nevertheless inspired some of his greatest ballet music.

The *Beggars' Opera* in England, a mere collection of broadly marked ballad and dance tunes (most of them taken from Playford's *Dancing Master*, published in 1650) struck a blow at formal opera, in spite of the overabundance of dancing then included in formal opera to make it more acceptable as entertainment. It is significant that those rhythmic tunes, redolent of the folk, have kept the *Beggars' Opera* alive when more austere theatrical works have sunk into oblivion.

Rameau, who gave new life to old forms, appeared on the French scene a few years before Lully's death. His harmonies were said to be more novel, his rhythms more skilful, his orchestrations more brilliant than Lully's. He lived from 1683 to 1764, a long life, and, in many ways, a controversial one. Said he, "I try to conceal art by that same art(5)."

No sooner did he write a dance piece for the clavecin than

he turned it to good account as part of a ballet in an opera. He instrumentated all of these former solo compositions in such a way as to emphasize their clear-cut rhythms. But writing ballets into his opera was not enough for Rameau. Very little time elapsed before he managed to create much discussion by writing his serious operatic airs in dance meters. Was that the proper thing to do? Arguments on the subject were the order of the day. Rameau also made use of traditional measures, though he treated them contrapuntally.

The Contre-dance had been neglected in France until, in 1745, Rameau wrote one into the fifth act of an opera-ballet. Again, the dance spread like wildfire over Paris. Rameau's *Castor et Pollux*, a lyric tragedy in five acts and prologue, contained the first ballet to be performed without a mask on the operatic stage of that day. At a performance on January 21, 1772, the leading dancer was unable to appear. The substitute danced only on condition that he be allowed to relinquish the traditional mask and wig. Public approval greeted the innovation: thenceforth all the dancers appeared minus masks.

Rameau's most popular Tambourin occurs in his opera, *Fêtes d'Hébé*, along with other charming dances. It has been said that the rhythms of his infernal dances and chants for *Hippolyte et Aricie* and *Castor et Pollux* have an amazing dynamic energy and great power. He also wrote airs de ballet for *Dardanus, Acante et Céphisse, Zoroaster, Platée*. The airs from *Hippolyte et Aricie* and *Les Indes Galantes* are published in suites.

Debussy(6), in *Monsieur Croche, the Dilettante-Hater*, tells us that Gluck (1714-1787) was only able to supplant Rameau on the French stage by assimilating Rameau's finest creations and making them his own. Gluck is known now as the first great reformer of opera. His feud with Piccini was historic, but seldom remembered today, whereas Gluck's various reforms are often mentioned. Now, in more or less vehement fashion, all of the opera reformers in history have concerned themselves with the ballet in opera. Gluck was no exception to that rule. In his operas, for the first time dramatic power began to take precedence over formal toe dancing and vocal artifices. Mozart was later to further this ideal. Nevertheless, both wrote ballets into their operas, although the dancing was more of an incidental episode than a *raison d'être* for the entire score.

Gluck tried hard to be true to facts. When he composed his *Iphigenie en Aulide* in 1774 Gaetan Vestris asked him to write in a Chaconne for his son Auguste, who was to dance in the opera. Gluck refused. The Greeks, he explained, didn't dance the Chaconne. "Didn't they?" asked Vestris. "Then I'm sorry for them. But you must write a Chaconne for my son because I am '*le diou de la danse*.'" (This was indeed the name by which Gaetan Vestris was popularly known, but he always pronounced it badly because French was not his native tongue.)

Gluck was irritated. "Well, if you are that," he roared, "Go and dance in your heaven—*not* in my opera!" It is significant that the Chaconne was finally written.

Gluck's judgment must have been unusually accurate, though, for on one occasion, when dancers overruled his decision and interpolated a ballet between the second and third acts of *Alceste*, it was hissed from the stage. That Gluck handled the ballet adroitly in his operas is agreed even by modern critics. In writing of *Armide*, Van Vechten(7) says: "He made the art of the dance an essential part of his scheme, giving the ballet as much attention as the orchestra or singers and making it an essential part of the action." Of the same opera, H.T. Parker(8) wrote: In five of the eight scenes a ballet appears, not for ornamental dances or showy spectacle, but for intimate and delicate illustration of the situation and the music. Berlioz spoke of a performance of the same work, "The Hatred Scene had admirable dances composed by Paul Taglioni, had verve and a pervading infernal harmony. The dance air in A Major ⅜ (usually played) was suppressed and instead there was introduced the great, well-constructed, striking and fiery Chaconne in B Flat, unknown in Paris."

When, in 1796, Gluck wrote the ballet called *Don Juan* or

The Stone Banquet it was known as the first ballet on a tragic subject. Later he used its Ballet of Furies, when Don Juan descended into Hell, in Act II of his opera, *Orfeo ed Euridice*, when the Furies dance in the underworld. In his *Armide* also, the Dance of the Furies and the Sicilienne were taken from the ballet *Don Juan*, for all of Gluck's later works were enriched by many numbers which had done service in operas he had written in earlier days, which were quickly forgotten then and have been entirely forgotten today, except by the compilers of musical biographies and the makers of thematic catalogues, according to Van Vechten(9).

Indeed, Gluck had no intention of letting good material go to waste. The same dance tunes appear in many of his operas. Moreover, he added dance tunes or took them out at will, as he deemed it advisable. Thus, both music and text of *Alceste* in the French version differed from the Italian. Gluck added more airs de ballet—unnecessary, perhaps, but pleasing to a frivolous public that might not have received as graciously a more serious, dramatic work. The composer carefully weighed his audiences. In *Alceste*, two types of dancing were demanded: the Balli Pantomimi and the Balli Ballat. This ballet music is said to be lost today.

Each of Gluck's ballets were in character. The opera *Paride ed Elena* (1769) had a martial ballet in Menelaus' palace in Act III, and a ballet attending the protagonists' embarkation for Troy in Act V. The opera *Iphigenia en Tauride* has a ballet of Scythian dances. *Écho et Narcisse* contains a short, charming pantomime and Minuet.

The actual form of Gluck's ballets in operas is perhaps best illustrated in his *Orfeo ed Euridice*. Act II has no less than three ballets. The first is a mere trifle of twenty-nine measures, consisting of a series of long runs. The second is the famous Ballet of the Happy Spirits dancing in the Elysian Fields, while the third is similar to the second in character. Just before the Finale in Act IV appears a long ballet. It begins in majestic fashion, breaks into a graceful ¾, continues to a brisk Gavotte with maggiore and minore sections, is fol-

lowed by a slow ¾ and an allegro ¾—all of which lead into the
final chorus which opens on the ¾ theme belonging to the preceding ballet, though it is here, for the sake of contrast, treated
in more robust fashion, and taken at a faster tempo.

As time went on, the famous operas of that period all had
their own ballet versions, danced by leading dancers. Whether
or not the original opera music was adapted to these choreographic translations is yet a matter of study. It is certain, however, that whenever the music was entrusted to different composers, it was at least similar to the original opera in style and
treatment. Vigano had a ballet version of Grétry's (1741-
1813) *Richard, Cœur de Lion* in Vienna in 1794, in which the
Viennese applauded a procession so well regulated that the
"iron shoes of the horses struck the stage in perfect rhythm."
La Vestale, an Italian ballet of 1818, was a pantomime version
of Spontini's opera of 1807. It was Vigano's most perfect
ballet, and it featured a sacred Bacchanale.

Haydn (1732-1809) fell a victim to the inviting subject
of *Don Juan, or the Stone Banquet* five years before his death.
On it he wrote an allegoric pantomime that was presented in
Leibach. Gluck's *Don Juan* ballet had been produced in Vienna
many years before—1761. The setting of *Don Juan* that was
destined to win the greatest fame was that of Mozart.

Mozart (1756-1791) had much charming dance music in
his operas, though—significant fact—he never interpolated a
dance air unless there was a good reason for it. His innate
artistry led him to do everything with finesse and with simple
perfection. The *Marriage of Figaro* has a Fandango in Act
III (of the slower nature characteristic of Basque provinces)
as well as a Siciliana, or wedding dance. *Don Juan* has a
simultaneous Minuet and Alemana. In *Idomeneo*, composed
in 1780 for the Munich Carnival of 1781, there are two Chaconnes and a Gavotte. Mozart also wrote an opera buffa,
La Finta Semplice, when he was twelve years of age. Reckon-
ing with the custom of the day and the age of the composer, we
may safely assume that it contained many dance airs.

Cherubini (1760-1842), whom many writers consider more

French than Italian despite his Italian birth, had ballet music in his *Anacréon*. He was also (1804) the composer of a ballet inspired by the piquant picture of heroic Achilles sporting with the girls on the isle of Scyros. Its name: *Achille à Scyros*.

It may have been Vigano's great reputation as a choreographer that helped Rossini, the opera composer, to reach La Scala in the late eighteenth century, for none other than Vigano's sister was librettist for a Rossini opera. Rossini valued the dance as much as anyone. A contemporary review of one of his operas was to the effect that "it contained fewer Valses and Contredanses than Rossini's other serious operas, which is a loss for the festivities of the next carnival and a gain for us" and accused it of being "a monotonous string of formless airs." Rossini once wrote an opera divided, as it were, by a ballet. It was termed *A Journey to Rheims* and was not so good as his usual music, since it was "official" music. He realized, himself, that he had no flair for that sort of thing. For different presentations, he evidently revised the ballets in his operas to suit the audiences. There was an entirely new ballet in the revised French version of his *Mosè en Egitto*. In the third act of *William Tell* is a ballet with a Tyrolienne, music to which Taglioni danced years later, as a sort of homage to Rossini during his last years. The overture to *William Tell* has an Alpine Dance as its third section, while village dances open the opera itself. An analysis of the Soldiers' Dance in *William Tell* (preceded by a soldiers' chorus and passo a tre) shows that it is most usual music. It is in ²/₄ meter for the most part, alternating with complete sections in other usual rhythms. No startling ideas for ballet music here!

On the other hand, the ballet music in Donizetti's *La Favorita* is just as attractive as is any other part of the opera. This music comes in Act II, and consists of an Introduction, Pas de trois, Pas de six, and Finale. Each section is characterized by a slow beginning and a gradual accelerando.

The romantic period brought few changes to operatic dance melodies. It did bring to the dancers themselves a sense of added importance and the will to maltreat music if they wished. This has, unfortunately, continued to the present day in all but a few enlightened cases.

Berlioz (10) gives us a graphic description of a performance of Weber's opera, *Der Freischütz* (which already contained a Bohemian Waltz written into Act I by the composer and librettist. This served only to have the other characters waltz into the inn by couples and leave Max alone on the stage) many years later: ". . . of course the producers wanted to introduce a ballet, and as all my efforts to prevent it were useless, I proposed to compose a choreographic scene, indicated by Weber himself, in his Rondo for the piano, *Invitation à la Valse*, and I instrumentated that charming piece for orchestra. But the ballet master, instead of following the plan traced in the music, could invent nothing better than commonplace figures. . . . To replace, therefore, quality by quantity, an addition of three other dances was insisted upon. Well, there were the dancers, who took it into their heads that I had some pieces in my symphonies very well suited for dancing, which would finish off the ballet beautifully . . . and asked me to introduce into Weber's score the ball scene from my *Symphonie Fantastique* and the Fête from *Roméo and Juliette*."

On this subject, Berlioz was wary. He asked the opinion of the German composer Dessauer, who said immediately, "Oh, Berlioz, don't do that." The director heard this admonition and nothing more was said on the subject. Instead, the ballet was finished off with Weber's own compositions, the dance tunes in *Oberon* and *Preciosa*—probably the three Spanish dances (one of them an old Spanish Bolero) that Weber wrote in his incidental music to the latter play. Later these gave way to a short version of *Invitation à la Valse*, while other parts of the opera were omitted. At this, Berlioz wrote: "This masterpiece of poetry, originality and passion serves merely to introduce the most wretched ballets, and has to be mutilated to make room for them. If some new choreographic work should arise, more developed than its predecessors, they will, without hesitation, clip the *Freischütz* afresh."

In the first French version of Weber's *Oberon* in 1859, thirty-three years after Weber's death, there were but seven scenes, enriched in the last act by a ballet called *The Butterfly and the Demoiselles*. The music for this was written by Justamant, and apparently was well received. (It was not uncommon for the ballet music in many an opera to be written by an entirely different—often a third-rate—composer. The supposition was, doubtless, that every man should be a specialist in his line. This was the usual thing in Vienna, as indicated in the preceding chapter.) Nevertheless, twenty years afterward, Justamant's ballet music in *Oberon* was replaced by a ballet in which the airs had been written by Weber himself. Tschaikowsky then wrote that *Oberon* had a ballet which falls flat on its face and writhes at the sound of the magic horn!

Weber's opera, *Silvana* (The Forest Maiden) contains dances of the Willis, or "ogresses of the Waltz," who nightly dance on highways to lure men to their death. The subject, taken from a medieval legend, was later utilized by Puccini in *Le Villi*. Weber's *Euryanthe* has an earnest round in Act I, while Acts II and III contain heavily-accented peasant dances. *Die Drei Pintos*, a Weber opera completed by Mahler, contains a vocal Seguidilla.

Grandiose Meyerbeer (1791-1864) had many dance scenes in his operas. In most of them, he combined the voice with dancing and in most cases, his ballet music is very little more than ordinary. *L'Africaine* has in Act IV a graceful dancing chorus in ¾ meter, more or less antiphonal. *Les Huguenots* has a chorus and ballet *delle bagnanti* in Act II, while Act III boasts a Danza Boema and a coro con ballo, and Act V is opened by a dance scene. *Roberto il Diavolo* has four dance airs and one chorus with dance at the end of Act III. One of these ballets is that of the phantom nuns, often termed the first serious manifestation of musical romanticism on the French lyric stage. It is often presented as an independent divertissement, when dissolute dead nuns try to tempt Robert with unholy dances to the chuckling of bassoons, according to Martens (11). There are several Waltzes in *Le Prophète*, also a last act chorus with dance, a Bacchanale in ¾ called "Glory to the Prophet!"

Widely celebrated and often danced independently of its opera is the Dance of the Hours, from Ponchielli's *La Gioconda*. This occurs during a splendid entertainment on the stage, with two dozen dancers representing the different hours. The music before dawn is slow and dreamlike. It breaks into a sparkling allegro as light comes, increasing in speed and strength until a forte tells of the full-fledged new day. Ponchielli's Biblical opera, *The Prodigal Son*, has a Babylonian ballet.

In 1832, Chopin (12) wrote to Hiller that Halévy's opera-ballet, *La Tentación* had "tempted no one of good taste, for it is as little interesting as your Germanic diet is in unison with the spirit of this country." This ballet was described by a critic as being a musical description of Hell in a series of grotesque but tiresome tableaux. A contemporary critic also described the Bolero in Halévy's *La Juive*, as well as the ballet at the Emperor's feast, to be antiquated. It would appear that public opinion scarcely approved of Halévy as a composer for the dance!

In 1823, Schubert wrote such delightful ballet music to the opera *Rosamunde* that it has survived long after the opera itself was forgotten. And in 1822-23, Mendelssohn devoted part of his time to the writing of a comic opera in three acts, *Der Onkol aus Boston*, with an overture and fourteen numbers, including much ballet music. This went unpublished until his letters were given to the world, in 1863. In 1852, a Bayadère Ballet marked Adolphe Adam's opera, *If I Were King (Si j'Étais Roi)*.

The libretto of Michael William Balfe's *Bohemian Girl* was founded on a three-act ballet by St. George entitled *La Gypsy* which had appeared in 1839 at the Paris Opéra with music for each act created by a different composer: Benoist, Ambroise Thomas and Marliani. The subject was the same as that of Weber's *Preciosa* and came originally from Cervantes' *Novelas Exemplares*. The *Bohemian Girl* contained many Gypsy marches, dances and songs, all in the accepted salon style of the moment. Balfe himself owed his whole musical career to a piece of dance music. Before he reached seven years of age, he had composed and scored for his teacher's band a *Polacca*, which the performers refused to believe came from his infant hands. This proved his vocation beyond a doubt, and led his father (a dancing master) to allow him to complete his studies. Some of his first musical experiences were as a violinist in his father's dancing classes.

Debussy (13) tells us, through the inimitable Monsieur Croche, that Berlioz was unsuccessful on the stage because he had not that particular experience. "What interest can you expect people to take in your *Marche Hongroise* if they do not see soldiers exercising at the back of the stage? As for your *Ballet des Sylphes*, it is most charming music. But you will never make me believe that a mere symphony orchestra can ever take the place of an attractive ballet dancer!" A double-edged remark, my dear Monsieur Croche. Surely you do not wish to make us believe that opera-goers prefer visual delights to audible ones?

The light, smooth, lovely Dance of the Sylphs occurs in Berlioz's *Damnation of Faust* as does the famous *Rakóczy March*, which was composed to please the Hungarian people. In this opera, peasanty music characterizes the dance of the countryfolk. There is also a piquantly rhythmic *Dance of the Will-o'-the-Wisps* preceding Mefistofeles' imitation of a Hurdy-Gurdy. Berlioz had a ballet of dancing satyrs in his *Les Troyens à Carthage*. This composer had a truly Wagnerian idea in regard to opera. He felt that he could not give full scope to his thoughts unless he were as completely master of a great theater as of his orchestra when conducting. He would require everyone to be under his orders: singers, musicians, dancers and supernumeraries. "A lyrical theater is first and foremost a vast musical instrument."

One fact cannot be denied. The romanticists' dance music was more apt to be inspired by the dance, and by gay carnivals and balls, than to be written directly for it, though folk dance tunes often found their way into the most serious compositions. They were more imbued with the spirit of writing music than with the desire to write for the theater. Perhaps that is why so many of their large dramatic compositions died an early death, while the dance episodes in them still live and enjoy great popularity!

CHAPTER 6

NOTES

(1) *Musical Quarterly*, January, 1928, p. 103
(2) Grove's *Dictionary of Music and Musicians*, Vol. I, pp. 658, 659
(3) Landowska, *Music of the Past*, p. 89
(4) Sharp, *The Dance, an Historical Survey of Dancing in Europe*, p. 41
(5) *Musical Quarterly*, January, 1928, p. 104
(6) Debussy, *Monsieur Croche, the Dilettante-Hater*, p. 81
(7) *Musical Quarterly*, October, 1917, p. 541
(8) *Musical Quarterly*, October, 1917, p. 542
(9) *Musical Quarterly*, October, 1917, p. 546
(10) Berlioz, *Autobiography*, pp. 150, 151, 152
(11) Martens, *Thousand and One Nights at the Opera*, p. 152
(12) Chopin, *Letters*, p. 167
(13) Debussy, *Monsieur Croche, the Dilettante-Hater*, p. 152

*

FORMAL ITALIAN BALLET MUSIC

Early Italian dramas had intermezzi, consisting of dance and music. These accessories were more important than the actual dramas! There was, for instance, a choral dance by youths, done to the music of a ringing orchestra. In the Commedia dell'Arte, song and dance alternated with improvised jests. The Florentines, like the French, tried to revive old Greek drama and to alternate declamatory scenes with songs and dances by the chorus. These classic fantasies, performed at court fêtes, were one of the sources of dramatic ballets.

La Scala's School of the Dance dates from before the construction of the theater itself. From the sixteenth century on, a choreographic tradition existed at Milan. Dancing was cultivated by the nobility as a cultural asset, as well as by professionals. For many years, the majority of celebrated dancers and ballet composers in other lands were really Italian. Some of them have been mentioned in previous chapters. Perhaps the renown they won made them reluctant to return to Italy where, like the prophet who is not without honor save in his own country, their talents were taken as a matter of course. Indeed, in Italy, a musician's efforts were said never to be occupied with dance unless the musician found himself in sad circumstances.   Nonetheless, the history of the early French, English, Viennese and Russian ballets owes much to individual Italians.

Once this process was reversed, when Michael William Balfe came to Italy from his native land.   Glossop, the impressario, commissioned from him a grand ballet on the subject of *La Pérouse*.   Balfe wrote piece after piece of the new opus with astonishing speed.   The music was all that could be desired in its adaptability to the dramatic and chorcographic needs of author and ballet master.   Two pieces were singled out for especial praise : the overture, and the music descriptive of a storm at sea and a shipwreck.   It greatly pleased the La Scala audience and thus won great fame for an unknown, foreign composer.

But we are advancing far ahead of our story.   Many years before Balfe, in Monteverdi's time, there were continual concerts, dances and ballets for the amusement of the bathers at Spa, in Flanders.   It was there, on one of his journies, that Monteverdi first saw the *Ballet du Cour* which, having been created in Paris in 1581, was popular over Europe.   The poet Ottavio Rinuccini first introduced it to Italy, after which Monteverdi composed a dramatic ballet.   This may have been the propagandist *Ballet of the Ungrateful One* to Rinuccini's libretto.   Monteverdi was attracted by the rhythms resulting from dotted notes, used by French instrumentalists.   (Evidently this music was on the point of decadence in France.   However, Monteverdi profitted by what he heard, and Italy gained thereby.)   He was also interested in antique meters, and thought the pyrrhic foot would be a good means of expressing agitation, since the Greeks had used it in warlike dances.   He managed to make an entirely individual use of it.

Monteverdi's *Ballo delle Ingrato* (performed June 4, 1608) is now the only ballet in the French style that exists today in its entirety.   Monteverdi created it at the same time that Marco da Gagliano and Striggio were working on another ballet, *Il Sagrificio di Ifigenia* which gave rise to mutual accusations of plagiarism.   Because the *Ballo delle Ingrato* serves as the only record of the ballet style of that epoch, it may be wise to describe it here, much as Prunières(1) has done in his biography of Monteverdi.

It opens with a long scene in recitative, outlining the story of the ballet. The figures were danced to a single melodic theme. The Entrée was in common time. At the end of a figure the rhythm was changed, though the melody remained the same. Sometimes the rhythmic variations weren't even notated. Pluto sang a long narrative in five stanzas, followed by the second part of the ballet, to the same air as before. In this ballet, as in Monteverdi's operas, each character was accompanied by the instrument best suited to him. The orchestra for the voices was hidden backstage, while a separate orchestra for the dances was on a platform in the auditorium.

Monteverdi wrote, in December of 1604, a choreographic divertissement on the subject of *Diana and Endymion*. All the stars danced successively in pairs in this ballet; then, to avoid monotony, came an ensemble of all the characters. This was accompanied by a brief, lively tune played by all the instruments, alternating with pas de deux done to an air played by five stringed instruments.

At the request of the Duke of Parma, Monteverdi wrote the ballet *La Vittoria d'Amore*. Though only the libretto survives, it is thought now that he must have treated the entire scene in the manner of a vast cantata, with dances both played and sung. He also wrote a ballet, *Movete al mio bel Suon* for five voices and two violins. It opens with a scene in recitative between the Poet and a Nymph. Then there is dance music, including a certain number of meter-changes corresponding to the different figures of the ballet. He even provided for the insertion (near the end) of some instrumental dances to be composed by the ballet master!

Book VII of the Madrigals preserves Monteverdi's ballet, *Tirsi e Clori*. Whether this ballet was or was not performed is not known today. It was composed in 1615 for the Court of Mantua. A gay ⁶⁄₄ opening tune, sung by Thyrsis, invites Chloris to dance. The ballet proper begins after a romantic vocal duet.

It is a Madrigal for five voices, accompanied by violins, spinet, small lutes; and consists of eight movements, with reprises. The dance, after a short introduction, begins in ¾ meter, but continues with varied melodies and rhythms until it finally ends in common time. Monteverdi gave minute instructions for its performance: the instrumentalists to be arranged in a crescent at one point of which is a harpsichord (to accompany Chloris) and at the other a theorbo (to accompany Thyrsis).

In 1615, a ballet-tourney called *La Guerra d'Amore* was enacted in Florence to music of Signorini, Turco and Jacopo Peri. During the seventeenth century, marionette shows became increasingly popular in Italy. Music for the puppet theater was constructed along the same lines as that for dancing, so it may be classed as dance music of a sort, even though it was interpreted by automatons, not humans. Composers in this medium were A. Stradella, Francesco Antonio Pistochini, Marc' Antonio Ziani, and K. Antonio dal Gaudio. It was also during the seventeenth century that Caroso wrote his books on dancing.

During the eighteenth century, many composers supplied ballets for the Italian theater. Among these were Giuseppe Scarlatti (1712-1777) of the famous Neopolitan musical family. Angiolini choreographed his ballet, *Les Aventures du Serail* after G. Scarlatti went to Vienna in 1757. Giuseppe is said by some to be the grandson and by others to be the nephew of Alessandro Scarlatti. At any rate, his works were widely produced on Italian stages and he was known, at one time, as Maestro di Capella at Naples. Three years before the passing of Giuseppe Scarlatti, Jean Georges Noverre arrived in Milan to spread his revolutionary doctrines of the proper relationship between music and dance. Angiolini first admired, then rivalled him. He next became his bitter enemy and finally, while appropriating some of Noverre's ideas, hurled at him the accusation that he was making the dance less artistic.

A little-known but prominent Italian ballet master of the eighteenth century was Gregorio Lambranzi, who in 1716 published a book in Nuremberg on *New and Curious Schools of Theatrical Dancing*, really a book of popular dances, those in-

spired by work or play.   On each plate the theme and costume
of the dance are given, as well as notes on the music and style.

Ballet versions of various popular operas have already
been mentioned.   Since the Italians were prominent in the
operatic field, it follows that their works were frequently subjected to this process.   Salvator Vigano produced many of
these.   He was at his height in the year 1812, when the Imperial
Academy of Dance was founded at La Scala, giving official
recognition to the choreographic tradition that had begun there
so many years before.   La Scala had an undisputed supremacy
in the field of Italian ballets.   In the school itself, an old violinist, seated in a corner, drew plaintive notes from his instrument
to give the rhythm for the pupils' steps.

Carlo Blasis (born 1803) is also said to have been a composer of ballets.   Like Adolphe Adam, he had a father who
composed operas and who instructed him in all the fine arts,
including the theory and practice of music.   Young Blasis early
showed great talent in musical composition, but chose dancing
as a profession, for the simple reason that he thought he could
make his mark more quickly there.   Nevertheless, his knowledge of all the arts gave him an advantage over most of his
fellows, and he produced an almost endless list of ballets.   Like
Rameau, he wrote a book on dancing.   His was called the
Code of Terpsichore and was published when he was but
twenty-two years of age.   In it, he gave his views on the relationship of the arts: "Poetry, music, painting and dancing bear
a strong affinity to each other and the enjoyment we derive
from them merit an equal gratitude and homage."

Cesare Pugni, born in Genoa in 1805, was one of the first
Italians to go to Russia.   He died in St. Petersburg in 1870.
His musical study was accomplished at the Milan Conservatory.   He made his debut in music by writing airs which were
introduced into operas of other composers such as Donizetti.
Then, he also wrote operas.   He may, however, have found
the Italian theatrical horizon a little too confining, for it was
not long before he found himself in Paris.   From there he was
sent to London to compose music for the ballets at Her

Majesty's Theatre.   He was there always in evidence, always on the alert for new musical or theatrical ideas.   His style of composition was eminently suited to the ballet.   From London, he went to Russia, where he successfully wrote music for the Imperial Russian Army.   In 1851, he was appointed ballet composer at the Imperial Theater in St. Petersburg, where he wrote music to order.

One authority says that he wrote twenty-one ballets for Milan, Paris and St. Petersburg.   Another credits him with the creation of more than three hundred ballets.   If the latter be true, he must have turned them out like a machine!   (In the words of Eleanore Flaig: "Three hundred! Hang yourself, Delibes!")   Among his ballets were *Esmeralda, The Magic Steed, The Daughter of Pharaoh, La Bayadère, Ondine* (danced by Fanny Cerito) and *Eoline.*   The latter ballet was in a prologue and six tableaux: *Palais du Gnome, La Vision, La Chêne de la Dryade,* and *Les Jardins du Chateau; La Chambre de la Fiancée* and *La Metamorphose, La Forêt de la Dryade; Les Noces Interrompus* and *La Vengeance du Gnome, La Forêt Embrassée.*   A contemporary English critic said this music had charming contrasts of liveliness and pensive melancholy well adapted to the wild, fantastic character of the legend. The young Moussorgsky(2) once went to see a certain ballet by Pugni and received from the music such a frightful impression that not even the strongest nerves could stand the strain. He called Pugni a "Scythian" and wrote: "Nevertheless the ballet made a remarkable impression on me.   I was very nearly ill in the theater."

Pugni must, however, have had some talent, although known to be careless, and rarely sober.   His duties as a ballet conductor included the writing of whatever dances or marches the ballet master needed, but he was so irresponsible and dilatory, according to Olga Racster, that often someone would have to accompany him home and stay close beside him until the necessary music was completed.

Another ballet composer of this period was St. Leon, violinist, ballet master and husband of Fanny Cerito (born in

1821). He composed for his talented wife the ballet *La Fille de Marbre*.

Schneitzhoeffer's *La Sylphide* was not the first ballet of its kind, despite its being hailed as the first of the romantic ballets. Four years before it was created, the Italian Luigi Carlini composed *La Sylphide de Louis Henry* and had it produced at La Scala on May 28, 1828. Years later, it was repeated at Florence and again at La Scala.

Sir Michael (Michele) Costa was another expatriated Italian ballet composer. He was born at Naples in 1808, and died at Brighton in 1884. After he had brought out four successful operas in Naples, he went to England for a single engagement. He liked the country so well that he stayed! First he was *maestro al cembalo* at the King's Theatre in London, then Musical Director, and finally composer and conductor. After he was knighted he took to the writing of more serious music, such as cantatas, symphonies, and a mass. Nevertheless, he has several ballets to his credit: *Kenilworth* (1831), *Une Heure à Naples* (1832), *Sir Huon* (1833) for Taglioni, and *Alma* (1842) for Cerito. He was noted as a dynamic, vigorous conductor. Perhaps the fact that his ballet music is not heard today may be attributed to an arbitrary judgment of his contemporaries: that a man can never be as good a composer as he is a conductor.

Riccardo Drigo (born in Italy in 1846) advanced from the directorship of Italian operas in the Imperial Theater at St. Petersburg to the post of ballet director at the same theater in 1886. He remained in Russia for forty-one years. In his youth, he had been gay enough to compose many dances in the styles of those of other nations, but all bearing the imprint of his Italian temperament. A combination of circumstances caused him to leave Italy. He resented the fact that the music in a ballet was not considered an important element in its success; he resented the mediocre musicians who were specialists in danceable music. He did not wish to be classed as one of them. In Russia, he felt that the ballet had become a work of art. No more unrelated Polkas and Mazurkas, but complete organisms in several acts: mimed operas, in which instruments were substituted for solo voices!

Surely, he found an appreciative audience in Russia, for to those people he was a genius, even when he merely accompanied their dancing. If they did not realize it then, they did later, as evidenced by a remark made by Anna Pavlowa: "I used to scream at Drigo, 'It is too fast! Do it again, Drigo! Again, I say! Slower!' And then after roaming all over the world I have worked with musicians who didn't know how to sit at the piano, and I have been afraid to ask them to repeat a phrase! I beg these people with my prettiest smile, 'Please, please repeat it!' And how I treated the splendid Drigo!"

Among Drigo's ballets were *La Forêt Enchantée*, *La Flûte Magique*, *Il Talismano* (widely performed), *Le Reveil de Flore*, *La Perle*, *Les Millions d'Arlequin* (most famous), *Le Porte Bonheur Côte d'Azur*, *Le Roman d'un Bouton de Rose*. The subjects of these ballets range from Hungarian legends to pastoral scenes and undersea fantasies. Some of them were choreographed by Petipa, and several of them have survived the Russian Revolution and are yet performed. Only a few have been produced in Drigo's native land.

Paolo Giorza (who worked with the librettist Rota) was born in Milan in 1838, had ballets produced on Italian stages, went to New York, thence to London, San Francisco and (in 1906) to Seattle, Washington, where he died in 1914. He was a pupil of his father, an organist and singer, and of Lacroix in counterpoint. The Royal Conservatory of Music at Milan accepted him when he was but eleven years of age, and graduated him at seventeen. Then for eight years he was assistant musical director of the Royal Theater at La Scala. He was famous for his ballet music. When he made brief departure from it (as when his opera was presented at Milan) he was a dismal failure. During the war of 1866 he wrote a martial hymn at Garibaldi's request. Among his more than forty ballets, the most famous were those presented at La Scala: *Un Fallo* (1853), *I Bianchi ed i Negri* (1853), *Il Giucatore* (1854), *Il Conte di Monte Cristo* (1857), *Rodolfo* (1858),

Cleopatra and *La Contessa d'Egmont* (both in 18;9), *Leonilda* (1865) and *Fiammella* (1866).

Another ballet composer-librettist combination well known in Italy was that of I. Montplaisir and C. Dall'Argine. The latter wrote *Brahma*, a ballet in seven scenes after the scenario by the former. It consisted of the Dance-March of the Sacred Dragon, Birth and Ecstasy, several pantomimic scenes and dances, Galop of the Renaissance, Tartar and Mongolian Dances, Funeral March, Finale and Apotheosis.

Because Amilcare Ponchielli (1834-1886) had written several successful operas, the management of La Scala commissioned from him a ballet, *Le Due Gemelle*, in prologue and six acts on a scenario by A.P. Pallerini. It was received with such great enthusiasm on its production there in 1873 that he was encouraged to write still another ballet, *Clarina*, in the same year.

Romualdo Marenco (born Novi Ligure in 1841, died Milan in 1907) was one of the few prominent Italian ballet composers who stayed at home to do his best work. He became Director of La Scala in 1873. There he produced operas as well as ballets, many of them in collaboration with the librettist, Manzotti. Though he did not settle in a foreign country, some of his music was produced elsewhere, as when his operetta was performed in Paris in 1884. This, of course, was the source of great satisfaction to him. His very first ballet, *Lo Sbarco di Garibaldi a Marsala* was written for the Doris Theater in Genoa, where he was second bassoonist. It was produced there in 1841. In all, he wrote more than a score of ballets, including *Sieba*, *Sport* (1896) and the famed *Excelsior* (1881). The latter used many massed dancers, performing dances of Fame, Valor, Love, Union. It pictured the appearance of the first steamboat, and utilized Egyptian dancers in a great scene picturing the completion of the Suez Canal. The music was described as being "tuneful but negligible."

Raoul Pugno (1852-1914), son of an Italian father, was known as a successful composer of ballets and operettas, though he was equally famed as an ensemble player, especially on the occasions of his recitals with Ysaÿe. He wrote the ballets *La Fée Cocotte* (1881), *Papillons* (1881), *Viviane* (1886), *La Danseuse de Corde* (1892), *Le Chevalier aux Fleurs* (1897), and a work he described as a mimodrame, *Pour le Drapeau* (1895).

Richard Wagner (3) described a nineteenth century performance at La Scala in no uncertain terms: "Although the Italian public was passionately fond of song, it was the ballet which they regarded as the main item; obviously the dreary opera at the beginning was only intended to prepare the way for a great choreographic performance on a subject no less pretentious than that of Antony and Cleopatra. . . ." Indeed, the success of the first performance of Rossini's *Barber of Seville* was doubted, since (owing to lack of finances) the opera could not be followed by a ballet. How then, they wondered, could it draw the crowds? At a performance of *La Gazza Ladra* in Rossini's later years, the opera was followed by a grand ballet, *The Return of Ulysses* which lasted until dawn. It had a score of dancers, eighty figurants and a band on the stage. Success greeted the venture, and Rossini was delighted!

Messalina, grand spectacular historical ballet in three acts and seven scenes, though produced in Paris in 1885, nevertheless was composed by the Neopolitan Giaquinto, a fellow-student of Rossini, who lived modestly in the town of his birth and was averse to travel. He died in 1882 at a considerable age, and was credited with the composition of a hundred and fifty ballet scores. Danesi, choreographer for *Messalina,* was known as the rival of Manzotti, choreographer of Marenco's *Excelsior.*

The ballet *Flik et Flok* with choreography by Paul Taglioni and music by Hertel was most enthusiastically received on its forty-seven presentations during the season of 1862. Milan sent entire ballets to Cairo and to Paris, so proud was she of her dancers. The idols of the Milanese public at one time were Verdi, Elssler, Taglioni and Cerito. Three dancers to one composer! The proportion was surely small. Moreover, if popularity is judged by applause, one must admit that Verdi was far less popular than the dancers!

Perhaps this explains the lack of acclaim given to Italian ballet composers in their own country, since their creations were deemed relatively unimportant. Perhaps it also explains the migration of so many of them to foreign lands, although Stravinsky(4) tells us that the same situation prevailed in Russia, in pre-Tschaikowsky days! What creator worthy of the name would wish to have his art entirely subordinated to the caprices of a ballerina? And why stay, when honors await elsewhere? (Modeste Altschuler(5) made an amusing remark in connection with just such situations: "In New York I had a big success, *because I was not local!*")

That modern Italy is not sparing in her praise is evidenced by the fact that her contemporary ballet composers are as famed and as esteemed in their own land as they are in the outside world!

CHAPTER 7

NOTES

(1) Prunières, *Monteverdi,* pp. 83-86
(2) Riesemann, *Moussorgsky,* p. 36
(3) Wagner, *My Life,* p. 704
(4) Stravinsky, *An Autobiography,* p. 40
(5) In a speech before the Society for the Advancement of American Music in Los Angeles on January 9, 1937

*

FORMAL RUSSIAN BALLET MUSIC

"The Russian ballet school is the French school that the French themselves had forgotten." So says Nicholas Legat(1). Nevertheless, in Russia the ballet really began with the nobles' own troupes, brought from Western Europe or composed of their own serfs. These danced only for the amusement of their masters, or for their guests—not for profit. Because the noblemen, on returning from the cities where ballets were performed, felt keenly their isolation in the midst of vast properties, they sometimes had a complete theater on each estate, with the attendant dancers, musicians and actors.

In 1735, Empress Anne founded a ballet school in Russia, though not till 1779 did the National School of choreography, favored by Catherine the Great, begin. Investigation reveals that what is usually regarded as the Russian classical school occurred during the "reign" of Marius Petipa, famous ballet master. His death in 1910 climaxed many years of service, for it was in 1847 that he went to St. Petersburg as premier danseur after he had perfected his dancing in Paris under Vestris.

Since the Russian ballet is often referred to as the synthesis of all ballets and since its music is spoken of in a more or less universal sense, it may be as well to describe this music here.

Actually, there is no reason to suppose that the music for the early Russian ballet was any better or worse than that for any other school of ballet, but when the glorified Russian ballet set Western Europe agog, conversations naturally centered upon it, while other ballet schools were largely forgotten. This has given rise to the popular theory that every element connected with the Russian ballet was the epitome of perfection. As a matter of fact, while a good deal of the music for early ballets in other countries has survived and has become classic, that for the very early Russian ballet is rarely heard. After all, it is quality, not age, that counts in music.

Anatole Chujoy(2) offered a résumé of the creation of Imperial Russian Ballet music: "Someone would write a libretto. It would be accepted and a composer would be commissioned to write the score. In very few cases the composer would be an outstanding or even moderately talented man; generally he would be just another musician in the employ of the state. He would execute his job in a routine manner, without particular knowledge of music, without taste or inspiration."

Henry Cowell(3) clarifies the foregoing in this way: "The problem of music and the dance was solved by taking very obvious music built in eight measure periods and constructing on it a similarly stereotyped dance. It is perfect from the dancer's standpoint, because the music is too uninteresting to detract from the dance." Adrian Stokes(4) adds that "The most naïve kind of music often serves ballet best, though, at the same time, some kind of wit must be induced from this naïvete." It is his belief also(5) that the fact that classical ballet music was composed to order at the choreographer's direction is not necessarily anything against it as music, since the requirements of particular dances have inspired the best composers at all periods.

To continue with Chujoy's description: "Next on the scene was a ballet master who would get ready-made music written to a ready-made libretto and it was his job to fit to the libretto and music, as it were, ready-made dances. The composer had a bowing acquaintance with the decorator; the costumer had no consideration for the ballet master; and the ballerina had little regard for anyone or anything. Outside of satisfying the ballerina, the composition of the rest of the ballet was easy, due to an accepted formula: pas de deux with variation and coda and a pas d'action. Between the spectacular dances of the ballerina the male dancer needed a variation, or there had to be a ballabile for the corps de ballet. It was considered best to have the corps de ballet dance to waltz time; for that would occupy many people and much time. And, Waltzes could be varied easily. With flowers, it is a Valse des Bouquets, with ribbons it is a Valse aux Rubans, with sheaves it is Valse Champêtre, etc. . . . The dances followed each other mechanically, their only logic being to give the soloists and corps de ballet alternate periods of work and rest, time to change costumes, and so forth." Moreover, into every Russian ballet (no matter what the subject, the scene or the action) a Russian dance was inserted. The high spot of all the classical ballets was the adagio, when the ballerina was assisted by her partner in displaying her virtuosity and grace. The word "variation" was used in the sense of the dance, not of the music. Often the two terms were entirely dissociated.

Despite the fact that most Russian classical ballet music is often decried, special attention was paid to the pupils' musical training in the Imperial Ballet School. More, Karsavina's revealing *Theatre Street*(6) informs us that in the Russian ballet a favorite method of reviving forgotten dance steps was to recall the dance by memory while the music was being played. "Music prompts," they used to say.

But what of the men who wrote this music? Pugni and Drigo have already been discussed. Gerber also composed ballets. Minkus, the Hungarian, was renowned as a truly talented ballet composer, though Haskell now terms his music "cheap." He wrote *Don Quichotte*, a ballet of which the music was praised by some and termed inferior by others. He also wrote *Fiammetta* and many other ballets. Rimsky-Korsakow referred to him as the official ballet composer of the Russian Imperial Theaters.

The origin of all the ballets, however, is said to have been in Petipa, known as a superb dancer, mime, teacher, choreographer; and as the greatest artistic force of the old Russian ballet. Music was composed to fit Petipa's requirements and, just as a bad dance can be composed to good music, so may indifferent music be written to good choreography. Mme. Rambert goes so far as to call even Tschaikowsky's delightful ballet music a mere accompaniment to Petipa's inspirations!

Rubinstein once wrote a ballet called *The Vine*. It was produced by the Russian Ballet, but later shelved because its music was considered too symphonic, too austere and too heavy, though artistic. Certainly, said Karsavina (7), it differed from the favored type of ballet music, which was a string of obvious tunes squared up in thirty-two or sixty-four bars to fit the dancer's endurance.

Tschaikowsky's three ballets were undoubtedly the finest of all formal Russian dance music. Before he began to write in this idiom, the Russians considered ballet music unworthy of a serious composer. His *Sleeping Beauty* first altered that impression, though even it was considered too symphonic. In fact, though Tschaikowsky himself complained (1881) that the mounting of his opera, *Maid of Orleans,* would be beggarly because the Direction refused to sacrifice a kopek for it, having just spent 10,000 rubles on a new ballet, formal Russian ballet music was entirely subservient to Russian opera music in the sense that the operatic music was good.

The fact that Tschaikowsky (like Delibes) wrote only three ballets is significant, since the music of exceedingly prolific ballet composers is now considered so commonplace. Tschaikowsky's wisdom in limiting his output doubtless had much to do with its fine musical quality. Stravinsky (8) tells us that Tschaikowsky's music is often more profoundly Russian than that so often labelled Russian by outsiders. If, as has been said, all Russian composers since the time of Tschaikowsky have owed something to him, then so does all Russian music for the dance written after his time. Not by his music alone did he try to revolutionize the Russian Ballet, but also by his insistence on the engagement of native dancers.

Cultured, aristocratic Ivan Vselvolojsky has been given the credit for urging composers like Tschaikowsky and Glazounow to write ballet music. However, it is also said that this, in Tschaikowsky's case at least, was begun at the instigation of Alexander II, admirer of the composer's artistry. That the ballet, as an outlet for his creative mind, had long intrigued Tschaikowsky is evident from this statement(9) of his: "The opera direction has commissioned me to write music for the ballet, *The Swan Lake*. I accepted the work, partly because I want the money, but also because I have long wished to try my hand at this kind of music." He was to receive a fee of eight hundred rubles, about eighty English pounds. He waited to compose the ballet until he had finished his *Third Symphony in D Major*. Then the first two acts were ready within two weeks!

Swan Lake was composed between August, 1875 and March of the following year. It was first produced in Moscow in 1877 and was, later, one of the first ballets the young Diaghileff saw. Merely moderate success greeted it on its first perform-ance. Scenery and costumes were poor, and the orchestra was conducted by someone who had never before been confronted with so complicated a score.

Kashkin declares(10) that an adagio in this ballet was originally the love duet in the opera, *Undine*, mostly destroyed by Tschaikowsky in 1873. On the other hand, his op. 40 for piano, besides including two Mazurkas and two Valses, con-tains also a Danse Russe, originally intended for *Swan Lake*! Thus Tschaikowsky expended as much care on his ballet music as on a work that would actually be considered serious by its hearers: eliminating, adding, altering, etc. This may have been due, of course, to the exacting Petipa with his demands for changes. If so, then it is possible for Tschaikowsky to have taken out more good music than he left in. That would not be so great a loss as one might suppose, for fine composers are notoriously economical and it is safe to presume that Tschai-kowsky utilized his unwanted material in some other work.

But it was his painstaking work that led Irving Deakin to remark(11), many years later, "Listen, one begs, to the Tschaikowsky music for the *Swan Lake*, how essentially right it is, how it fits Petipa's choreography."

In *Swan Lake* appears for the first time in ballet music a leit-motif to depict situations. It is the most romantic of all his ballets, and the memorable theme characterizing the Swan Queen, Odette, is one of the loveliest, most haunting, in all musical literature. The ballet is in two acts (Prologue, the feast; First Act, the swans; Second Act in two scenes, the Hall in Rotbart's Castle and The Lake; Apotheosis) and deals with a princess and her companions who were bewitched and who relinquished their swan-shapes only from midnight until dawn. When the ballet is performed, the Swan Lake theme is taken by oboe, with strings playing a hushed counter melody and with an arpeggiated harp accompaniment. Petipa had the corps de ballet making gestures in unison on the main musical accents as the soloists danced. In the musical pauses, while each dance was being applauded, the corps de ballet walked matter-of-factly to its places for the next dance. The dance of the four little swans was done to almost Oriental music in regular meter, with conventional ballet steps done in unison. This was laughed at by a 1936 audience, but widely applauded at its close. It had precision and vitality. Petipa and Tschaikowsky had a grand finale with everyone dancing, despite the sad ending. First came the corps de ballet, then two swans, then the Swan Queen, a beautiful diminuendo of forces before the grand ensemble.

About the beginning of November, in 1890, Tschai-kowsky(12) wrote to Anatol Tschaikowsky, "I have foolishly undertaken to write music for a ballet *Cinderella*, at a very small fee. The ballet has to be performed in December and I have only just begun it; but I cannot get out of the work, for the contract is already signed." *Cinderella* seems not to be mentioned again. It may have disappeared, may never have

JEAN PHILIPPE RAMEAU
Organiste et musicien celebre né à Dÿon le
25-7 br 1683
(After Carmontelle)

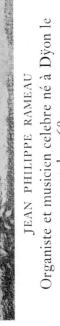

C. W. GLUCK
in his sixty-second year, from the painting by
J. S. Duplessis, Paris, 1776

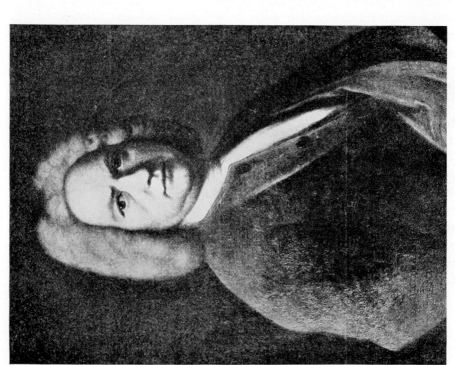

JOHANN SEBASTIAN BACH

WOLFGANG AMADEUS MOZART
From the painting by Lorenz Vogel 1887

been written after all, or may have been transformed into other works.

The subject of the *Sleeping Beauty*, taken from Perrault's fairy tale of the same name, and given to Tschaikowsky for a ballet by none other than the director of the Imperial Opera, pleased the composer very much. He worked at the first four tableaux with ease, enthusiasm and inspiration. The sketch was completed within four months. He wrote, "My ballet will be published in November or December. Siloti is making the pianoforte arrangement. I think it will be one of my best works. The subject is so poetic, so grateful for musical setting, that I have worked at it with all the enthusiasm and good will upon which the value of a composition depends. The instrumentation gives me far more trouble than it used to do; consequently the work goes slowly, but perhaps all the better. Many of my earlier compositions show traces of hurry and lack of due reflection."

Legat declares (13) that during the creation of the *Sleeping Beauty*, Petipa tried the patient Tschaikowsky to the utmost with his capricious exactions. He was accustomed to the orthodox forms of Pugni and Minkus and found it difficult to adapt himself to Tschaikowsky's novel arrangements (indeed, the subject itself differed greatly from the conventional ballet programme!) and demanded that tempi should be altered and cuts and additions made, to all of which the composer obligingly agreed. After hearing the music through several times, Petipa composed his dances in pieces of eight bars at a time.

This ballet was not enthusiastically received on its first performance. The delicate beauty of its music was not at once apparent. Critics said it was too heavy for ballet, and recommended it for the concert hall. Even the Imperial family was lukewarm. "Very nice," said the Emperor abstractedly, which scanty praise greatly mortified the composer. Was not the *Sleeping Beauty* second only to the opera, *Eugene Onegin* in his affections? Fortunately, the public was far from lukewarm, and provided a series of crowded houses for the ballet. Then said Tschaikowsky(14), "I only work quickly. I took my time over the *Enchantress* and the *Fifth Symphony*, and they were failures, whereas I finished the ballet in three weeks. The chief thing is to love the work." That later musicians agreed with his estimate of this ballet (which contains such episodes as Puss in Boots, the White Kitten and Panorama) is evidenced by Stravinsky, who considers it the "convincing example of Tschaikowsky's great power" and described it as being a work of direct character, simple and spontaneous. When it was produced at the Paris Opéra, however, Valerian Svetloff reported that a musician in the orchestra said, "We don't want to play this music. It is good for the Folies Bergères, but impossible for opera." The same treatment Stravinsky's music was destined to receive later!

Le Mariage d'Aurore, danced today, is an episode from the *Sleeping Beauty*, the scene of the nuptial feast. Chaliapin has spoken of Tschaikowsky's *Eugene Onegin* and his ballet music alike as "impersonal work" and has declared that "the late Tzar, Nicholas II, loved Tschaikowsky's wonderful ballets better than anything."

The composer thought his *Nutcracker Ballet* far weaker than the *Sleeping Beauty*: "No doubt about it," he wrote. The subject of the *Nutcracker*, commissioned by the Imperial Opera, did not please him. There was no joy in the creation. After he had begun to work with all his might on it, he became more reconciled to the subject. When he received news of his sister's death in the midst of his work, he wrote: "Today, even more than yesterday, I feel the absolute impossibility of depicting in music the Sugar-Plum Fairy."

This ballet is in two acts and three scenes. The subject was borrowed from Dumas' version of Hoffman's fairy tale. At the outset, Petipa made detailed suggestions for the program, and because they give a splendid idea of the conventions and requirements of the Russian Ballet, it will be interesting to reprint them here:

1. Soft music. . . . 64 bars.
2. The tree is lit up. Sparkling music. 8 bars.
3. Enter the children. Animated and joyous music. 24 bars.
4. A moment of surprise and admiration. A few bars of tremolo.
5. A march. 64 bars.
6. Entrée des Incroyables. 16 bars, rococo (tempo Menuet)
7. Galop.
8. Enter Drosselmeyer. Awe-inspiring but comic music. A broad movement, 16 to 24 bars.
   The music gradually changes character: 24 bars. It becomes less serious, lighter, and finally gay in tone.
   Grave music for 8 bars, then pause.
   Repeat the 8 bars—pause.
   Four bars which express astonishment.
9. 8 bars in Mazurka rhythm. 8 more. 16 still in Mazurka rhythm.
10. A piquant, spicy valse, strongly rhythmic. 48 bars.

It is not far-fetched to assert that this music, wrung from its unwilling composer, has lived longer and has been more popular than the music of his other ballets, which he enjoyed writing more.

When Saint-Saëns (then forty-five years of age) visited Moscow, he and Tschaikowsky (then thirty-five) discovered that in their youth they had both been enthusiastic admirers of the ballet and had often tried to dance. This suggested the idea of dancing together, and they brought out a little ballet, *Pygmalion and Galatea* on the stage of the Conservatory. Saint-Saëns was Galatea and Tschaikowsky Pygmalion. Nicholas Rubinstein was the orchestra and (significant fact!) there were no spectators.

Tschaikowsky was followed by Glazounow and Tcherepnine, who allied classicism with pageantry. Nicolai Tcherepnine's *Pavillon d'Armide* was the last of the ballets of the old Petipa school, with its ensembles, pas d'actions, ballabile. It was the composer's opus 29 and it contained *Courantes, Dance of the*

Hours, Animation of the Gobelin; Grand Waltz, Armide's Complaint, Dance of the Boys, Bacchanale, Entrance of Magicians and *Dance of the Shadows, Dance of the Buffoons.* It was first composed merely as a series of dances. Then the pantomime story was added. Still later, Tcherepnine changed it into its present symphonic form. He also wrote *Narcisse,* a ballet antique in one act which was (unlike the old ballets) a true collaboration of musician, scenarist and choreographer, with the incentive being supplied by the musician. Tcherepnine's *Masque of the Red Death* was published but never performed. (The number of musicians of all nations who have been intrigued by this subject as the theme of a ballet is rivalled only by those who have set Oscar Wilde's tale of the Dwarf and the Infanta in ballet form.) Tcherepnine also wrote *Russian Fairy Tale* and *Romance of a Mummy,* dedicated to Pavlowa. The latter two ballets were later combined in one. Pavlowa's first public performance of the ballet intended for her occurred with Tcherepnine himself conducting, on the exact twenty-fifth anniversary of his debut as a composer.

Alexandre, son of Nicolai Tcherepnine, considers that his father advanced further than Tschaikowsky. The latter was a bridge between the old and new in ballet music, whereas the elder Tcherepnine leaped toward the new: the creation of good symphonic music for ballets. In his time, the discarding of traditions was important. In the time of his son, it is a more practical theory, that of re-valorizing the old forms and of perfecting both old and new, to make a coherent fusion.

Not one man alone was concerned in this. History credits Diaghileff with the greatest of musical reforms in the ballet. But what of Fokine?

Many years before Fokine, Noverre, the "Shakespeare of the Dance," visualized a ballet so perfect that dancing, music, pantomime and poetry would be combined in a rhapsody of eloquent and harmonious expression. Fokine was the Noverre of his day, also one of ballet's greatest reformers. But, because he still lives, his accomplishments have often been minimized. His own outline for his reforms (in regard to music)

as published in the London *Times* on July 6, 1914, is as
follows: "Dance and mime shall be employed only in expression
of the theme (the subject-matter) and not as mere visual entertainment. In the arts associated with ballet, perfect freedom
shall be allowed to composer and decorator. The music need
not be a simple accompaniment to the dancers' movements;
every kind of music shall be permissible so long as it is good
and expressive."

Thus, the Russian stage is set for Diaghileff who (according to Goossens(15) never produced a ballet whose score did
not entitle it to be listened to as pure music!

CHAPTER 8

NOTES

(1) Haskell, *Balletomania,* p. 9
(2) *The American Dancer Magazine,* November, 1935, p. 7
(3) *The Dance Observer,* Vol. I, No. 5, June-July, 1934
(4) Stokes, *Tonight the Ballet!,* p. 17
(5) Stokes, *Tonight the Ballet!,* p. 97
(6) Karsavina, *Theatre Street,* p. 204
(7) Karsavina, *Theatre Street,* p. 207
(8) Haskell, *Balletomania,* p. 39
(9) *The Life and Letters of Peter Ilyich Tschaikowsky,* p. 173
(10) *Life and Letters of Peter Ilyich Tschaikowsky,* p. 728
(11) Deakin, *To the Ballet,* p. 61
(12) *Life and Letters of Peter Ilyich Tschaikowsky,* p. 122
(13) *The Dancing Times,* April, 1931, p. 11
(14) *Life and Letters of Peter Ilyich Tschaikowsky,* p. 603
(15) Propert, *The Russian Ballet in Western Europe,* p. 110

INSTRUMENTAL DANCE SUITES

Classicism lent its precision even to dance music, the writing of which had, by then, become a lighter pastime. Many a perplexed modern teacher has been known to stimulate the pupil's interest in good music and, at the same time, to salve her own conscience by teaching the dance pieces of the masters. The system seldom fails! There is, of course, no truth in the supposition that *all* dance music by famed composers is good just because they are its creators, although it has a better chance to be good, in such circumstances.

François Couperin, a court clavier and organ player, was the link between the operatic ballet and keyboard dance suites. He belonged to the Rococo period, which one writer says is essentially the same, whether given to the eye by a Watteau or to the ear by a Couperin. Dances for keyboard instruments were written by such composers as Daquin, Dandrieu, Galuppi, Frescobaldi. Rameau's first published book of *Pieces de Clavecin* (written when he was twenty) was simply another dance suite in the style of earlier French composers. The dances were all in the identical key and were preceded by a free prelude.

Small wonder, then, that the classical suite of dances (to be played by instruments) spread over Europe! In different countries, it was called by different names: ordres, leçons, partitas, sonata da camera.

Some are of the opinion that composers sought to picture every nationality in their suites, for the sake of contrast: German in the Allemande; Italian in the Coranto; Spanish in the Sarabande; French in the Gavotte, Bourrée and Minuet; English in the Jig. However, all of these dances were done—not in one country—but in many. They spread far from the lands of their origin and in every case both music and movement were adapted to the different nations' temperaments. This is proved by Mozart's letters. When he was but fourteen years of age, he wrote to his sister (1770) that a certain Minuet which everyone danced at the Feste di Ballo in Milan came from Vienna because it had so many notes, was a theatrical Minuet and moved slowly. Lest she misunderstand, he added that the Italian, or Milanese Minuets also had many notes and moved slowly through many bars, the first part containing sixteen bars, the second perhaps twenty or even twenty-four bars. In a later letter, Mozart wished he might introduce the German *gusto* in Minuets into Italy, because their Minuets often lasted as long as a whole symphony.

When the suite reached its highest development (under Bach) most of the dance forms contained in it were obsolete. Their musical counterparts in the suites were in themselves sufficient contrast to each other, though it was usually thought good, avers Fuller-Maitland(1), to have uniformity of key throughout, with occasional excursions into related keys. There were always three main movements in suites that were treated as fixed points: Allemande, Courante and Sarabande. The other dances were placed at the composer's discretion. These were sometimes: Pavane, Gigue, Minuet, Passepied, Gavotte, Bourrée, Loure, Air, Chaconne, Passacaglia, Polonaise. Several composers added unusual dance forms. Bach used "Balletto" as the name of a movement, and wrote Forlanes, Rounds, Badineries, a Rejouissance. Rameau added a lively Venitienne to the classic forms on one occasion. The Rigaudon and Tordion were occasionally used, and of course, suites of idealized music for national dance forms have often been composed throughout the centuries.

In spite of Bernard Shaw's(2) exceedingly apt statement: "If you want to explain a dance form to me, there is only one way of doing it, and that is to show me the dance for which the music was required. Until I see that, no information about sections and variations and ground basses can interest me in the least, because nothing that is arbitrary and unrelated to any artistic purpose can interest any human being unless he has taken a musical degree," it may be just as well to discuss here a few salient facts about the various dance forms included in suites, since composers have been and are writing suites constantly. The suite surely belongs to the classic era, but it is today as popular a form as it ever was. For most of the technical details, the writer suggests that the reader consult his musical dictionary. Only unusual facts will be mentioned here.

The Allemande, for example (usually not included in orchestral suites, since it was exclusively a keyboard piece) was described by many old writers. Says Arbeau: "In dancing the Allemande, when the musicians finish the first part, each dancer stops and converses with his damsel before the second part begins." Another writer says the Alman was sometimes similar to the Pavan, but often a light piece with two beats to the bar, in eight-bar strains, for the dance.

In passing, we must stress again the fact that these dances changed their names, spellings and characters, not only with the countries in which they were written, but with the epoch. The study of their evolution, both as music and as dance, would make a complete book in itself. Moreover, we find existing authorities to be wallowing in a maze of contradictions, a fact which makes truth most difficult for the contemporary investigator. The only possible method is to select from many facts those that seem most logical.

Catherine de Medici brought the Courante from Italy (where it was known as Corrente, a sort of country dance) to France, where Rameau described it as a "very solemn dance"

that "gives a more grand and noble air than other dances."
The music had running passages of eighth notes in quick ¾ or
⅝ time in phrases of eight bars each. The word is probably
derived from the Italian "correre," to run. Early Courantes
were written by Couperin, Bach, Rameau, Rosenmüller, Forchheim and others, while Cyril Scott, Niemann, von Dohnanyi
are modernists who have written in the form.

When the Sarabande was first danced in Spain in the sixteenth century, it had Moorish tendencies and was exotic and
suggestive. Francesco Corbetti, born in Pavia, Italy, in 1612,
composed a famous Sarabande for guitar which so charmed its
hearers that everyone wanted to learn it, and several delicious
anecdotes are related of the jealousies it occasioned at court
in England.

In 1597, Thomas Morley described a Pavane as a "kind
of musicke made without a ditty," a "fantasie," a "kind of
staid musicke ordained for grave dauncing, and most commonlie
made of three straines, whereof every straine is plaid or sung
twice . . . yet fewer than eight semibreves I have not seene
in any Pavan. After every Pavan was usually set a Gaillard
(that is, a kind of musicke made out of the other). This is
a lighter and more stirring kind of dauncing than the Pavan
consisting of the same number of straines. . . . The Italians
make their Galliards (which they term Saltarelli) plaine, and
frame ditties to them which in their mascaradoes they sing
and daunce and many times without any instrument at all, but
instead of instruments they have Curtisans disguised in men's
apparell, who sing and daunce to their own songs." The
French Pavane was a grand, solemn and majestic dance, accompanied by a song and hautboys, while drums accentuated the
rhythm.

Germany was said to have originated the *geige*, or *fidil*, a
musical instrument with three strings, the handle being a pro-
longation of the sounding board, not an independent part of
the instrument. This instrument was also said to have been
used in Ireland in pre-Norman days. Adenès, the trouvère,
spoke with admiration of the "gigueours of Germany" who

worked such wonders in performance. By the fifteenth century, the Gigue had disappeared in France, but was recalled by the dance, which for so long it had accompanied(3).

The Minuet is the most famous of classic dance forms today, doubtless due to the place it has won in the Symphony. Scarcely a composer has forgotten to write a Minuet, at some time in his life. Lully started the custom by writing the first good music for it in 1653. Writers of suites and Symphonies followed his example: Schubert wrote a trio to be regarded as the lost son of a Minuet. Modern composers write Minuets in the ancient style. The name Minuet came from the Latin minimus, or smallest, since it was danced with such tiny steps and such precision. It fully expressed the artificiality of the eighteenth century and therefore won great popularity as a dance. There were four famed Minuets at that time: *Le Menuet du Dauphin*, *Le Menuet de la Reine*, *Le Menuet d'Exaudet*, *Le Menuet de la Cour*. The dance itself was supposed to have originated in Poitou.

The legend concerning Haydn's *Oxen Minuet* is amusing: before the time of this composer's fame, he was asked by a butcher to compose something for his daughter's wedding. Haydn complied. Soon, much to his amazement, he heard this Minuet played under his own window! When he looked out, he beheld a street-band surrounding a huge ox, garlanded and gold-horned. The butcher had repaid the compliment in his own currency! Haydn had to keep the ox, though he had no use for it, and thus the Minuet was christened.

Another Minuet anecdote is that relating to the famous castrato, Farinelli, or Carlo Broschi, who was engaged to sing every night for four years the same four tunes for Philip V. One of these was a Minuet, on the theme of which the singer used to embroider at will.

The Polonaise common when the suites were at their height was the Serene Polonaise, in contrast to the military form adopted by Chopin. Bach wrote one in his French Suite, no. 6, and his son (W.F. Bach) also wrote Polonaises of this type.

The Passepied was said to have originated among the sailors of Basse Bretagne and to have been first danced by street dancers in Paris in 1587. After that, it was introduced into the French ballet and from there found its way into the suite. It is faster, more frivolous and more sprightly than the Minuet, though usually written in ⅜. Old descriptions for dancing it were to "run a Passepied." Couperin elaborated on its original plan by writing a Passepied with variations. Several modern Passepieds, by Debussy, Delibes and Lachaume, have so far departed from the traditional form of the dance as to have adopted another meter.

The name Gavotte is derived from the natives (Gavots) of the Gap country (Dauphiné, France). The dance began on the half-measure and was in a stately duple rhythm, though the beats were so divided as to make it seem like lively quadruple time. It first consisted of two alternating eight-measure strains (ABA). Later a second Gavotte was alternated with the first and, still later, this second Gavotte was played over a drone bass and named a Musette, due to its similarity to the sound of the ancient hurdy-gurdy, or Musette, once known as a serious instrument for which Sonatas were composed. Several of its strings were drones, and played the same pitch throughout an entire composition. It received its name from Henri and Charles Baton, who improved it as an instrument. Similar to the Gavotte, but quicker, was the Cebell, an English dance whose derivation is unknown. Lully's compositions for the Gavotte, and for the Cebell, as seen in an English book of *Lessons for the Harpsichord and Spinet* are similar in style.

The Bourrée is sometimes attributed to the Auvergne Province in France, sometimes to the Basque district in Spain, where it is known as the Borea. It is known to have been introduced into the feasts of Paris about 1890, and to be mentioned by Praetorius. The music for the dance is constructed somewhat like that of the Gavotte, though it may begin on the first beat of the measure, or on the anacrusis.

The Passacaglia and the Chaconne are both elaborations on a ground bass. The latter was originally a Spanish dance, adopted by the French people. The movement was in slow, triple time. Rousseau, in his dictionary of music, says that its beauty consists in the choice of songs which indicate the movements.

Many dance compositions, attributed to Bach, are of doubtful authenticity. Known to be authentic are his many suites, such as the three for violin without accompaniment, the one in A for violin and clavier, the one in B minor for strings and flute, the one in D for trumpet, as well as the six great (English) suites and the six little (French) suites. The former were written for a titled Englishman, while the latter were called so simply because they were written according to the French taste. Evidently, they were not named by the composer himself. The French suites are said to have a "lighthearted grace," while the English suites have "grandeur and depth of emotional power," their vivacity being reserved for their intermezzi. In all, Bach wrote twenty-three suites for harpsichord.

The earliest known of the Bach clan were Veit Bach and his son Hans, who occupied themselves with playing for village dances and attending Gypsy revels. Perhaps their affection for such Bohemian entertainment showed itself many years afterward, in Johann Sebastian Bach's creation of dance music. It is interesting to note the reactions of various modern musicians to these diversions of Bach. They are divided between their sincere admiration for Bach and their scorn of dance music. Put their opinions together: conflict results.

Says Sir Thomas Beecham(4): "Bach is not austere. He is very jolly; it is simple to listen to him. Of course, not the good Bach—I mean the jigging Bach, what must have passed in the eighteenth century for jazz." Another writer counters with the statement that the suites were merely a small part of Bach's creative power, and yet they are rich in thematic material, imagination and technical mastery. MacDowell(5) told us that the material at Bach's disposal was a poor set of dance forms, with the one exception of the fugue. It precluded spontaneity and limited emotional design. But as it was, Bach's innovations were considerable. Ezra Pound(6) opines that "Music begins to atrophy when it departs too far from the dance; poetry begins to atrophy when it gets too far from music; but this must not be taken as implying that all good music is dance music or all poetry lyrical. Bach and Mozart are never too far from physical movement."

Why, asks Wanda Landowska(7), play a Bach Gigue like a prayer because the belief is current that Bach is profound and colossal, even in his slighter things? Some of his Divertimenti for harpsichord were dedicated to amateurs for the delight of their minds, according to his own statement. Fuller-Maitland(8) declares that in one English suite, Bach told us that "Life has its sorrows as well as its joys, but the wise man will accept what comes, and a sense of humor never did anybody harm." Victor Herbert(9) agreed by saying: Look through the works of classic and modern composers and you will find dozens of dance tunes, and mighty good dance tunes they are. Did these masters lower themselves by looking out at the sunshine and the flowers for a little while instead of everlastingly poking about in musical crypts?

A Partita is usually the exact equivalent of a suite. Bach wrote six Partitas, slighter in texture than the English suites, though both the latter and the Partitas have beginnings in the nature of preludes. Some believe that the Partitas were thrown together from separated pieces, arranged without logical connection or sequence of movements.

Handel wrote dance suites for piano and for orchestra. Many of his Concerti Grossi are really nothing more than dance suites. These include the *Water Music in F Major* (No. 25) which in turn includes a Tempo di Menuetto, Alla Hornpipe, Loure and airs. It was composed in 1717 for a celebration on the Thames in honor of King George I. No. 25 of the Concerti Grossi is the *Fireworks Music in D Major*, composed in 1794 for the Royal Fireworks in Greene Park, London. This music contains two Menuets, a Bourrée and a Largo alla Siciliana.

There is yet another way in which suites of dance may be

compiled, and some of the most famous of them all are due to this process. When composers wrote operas, ballets, or incidental music to plays, much dance music was included. This was, of course, largely instrumental. Therefore, when conductors wished to present excerpts from theatrical music in concert, they simply took the instrumental dance episodes, arranged them in suites and played them.

Today, when composers like the ultra-modern Schönberg write dance suites, they will write (as he did) a Minuet, a Gavotte, and a Gigue, or other forms. In Schönberg's case, the dance suite was not atonal, as might be expected from him, nor was it based on an unusual scale. There were simple melodies with understandable counterpoint, harmonies and rhythms. A clever orchestration only served to enhance the composer's adoption of an older musical style. Many other such cases might be cited, such as Grieg's *From Holberg's Times* for piano, op. 40, or Mme. Roesgen-Champion's *Danceries* for piano and orchestra; Ravel's *Tombeau de Couperin* or Chausson's *Concert*. All of these were suites in the old style.

On the other hand, a composer like Hindemith will write a *Tanzsuite* based on rhythms resulting from a different, modern school of dance movement. Someone like Serge Youferoff or Max Reger will write a ballet suite with music reminiscent of the artificialities of ballet movement. And there is yet to be mentioned the sort of thing accomplished by Emerson Whithorne in his *Saturday's Child*, written in 1926, whose ever-changing rhythms and the fact that dancing is mentioned in the text caused ohn Tasker Howard(10) to call it "really a dance suite." It is scored for tenor and mezzo-soprano (the words are by Countee Cullen) and accompanied by chamber orchestra.

These unusual forms (among many that might be mentioned) arose from the classic dance suite. But this gave birth to yet another child—a child that was to gain a greater amount of fame in the musical world (the Sonata) and that was to produce a grandchild that won the greatest fame of all: the Symphony.

CHAPTER 9

NOTES

(1) Fuller-Maitland, *Bach's Keyboard Suites*, p. 6
(2) Shaw, *Music in London*, Vol. II, p. 252
(3) Lacroix, *The Arts in the Middle Ages and at the Period of the Renaissance*, p. 221
(4) *Musical Courier*, January 11, 1936, p. 17
(5) MacDowell, *Critical and Historical Essays*, p. 186
(6) Kirstein, *Dance*, p. 157
(7) Landowska, *Music of the Past*, p. 79
(8) Fuller-Maitland, *Bach's Keyboard Suites*, p. 36
(9) Cooke, *Great Men and Famous Musicians on the Art of Music*, pp. 240-241
(10) Howard, *Studies of Contemporary Composers, pamphlet devoted to Emerson Whithorne*, p. 26

✳

DANCE MOVEMENTS IN SYMPHONIES

After Bach's death, the Sonata gave way to the Symphony. Bach himself had written Sonatas, containing dance movements, for various instruments, as well as Concerti. Many of the Sonatas of Domenico Scarlatti contain sprightly rhythms deriving from the dance measures of the period. The "Symphony" to one of his father's operas was composed of three movements played without pause: Grave, Allegro, Minuet.

In 1685, when Corelli's Sonatas for Strings appeared, there began the custom of decreasing the movements in a Sonata to three. A century later, this custom was universal, only a few departures being made from it. The first movement in the seventeenth century Sonatas was usually an Allemande, the second a Sarabande, the third a Gigue. Really, the early Sonatas were miniature suites! Even when the dance titles were no longer used, the characteristics of the different dance movements were retained. Corelli had also many dance movements in his Concerti Grossi.

What, after all, is a Symphony or a Concerto if not a Sonata, expressed a little differently to the ear? Therefore, it is as well to discuss at once all compositions in Sonata form, in addition to those latterday compositions, termed "Symphonies," which have retained the name, but have departed far from the original plan. They are called so merely because they are scored for full Symphony orchestra.

To Haydn goes the credit for the perfection of the Sonata form. Rockstro(1) is assured that this was the great work of Haydn's life: "Though the details of this were entirely dictated by the bold originality of his genius, the main lines of the design were based upon the already existent dance tunes, whether Gavotte, Bourrée, Minuet, Branle or Allemande." MacDowell(2) tells us that Haydn, the bridge between idealized dance and independent music, always preserved a tinge of the actual dance. Beethoven retained the mere form and on it wrote great poems.

An explanation of the rustic, tuneful charm and sincerity of Haydn's music is found in the fact that he often built upon the popular folk dance-songs of his native land. These, in the matter of construction, were of the same order as Symphonies and Sonatas. Sir Hubert Parry(3) is sure that Haydn merely wanted to discover how this sort of music could be written on a grander scale. Few harmonies are used in national dance music; their combinations are similar to those in a Symphony or Sonata and "what had to be found out in order to make grand instrumental works was how to arrange more harmonies with the same effect of unity as is obtained on a small scale in dances and national songs."

Since Haydn was first to write the Menuet into the Symphony, his own Menuets may be mentioned here briefly. His experience with the *Oxen Menuet* has already been mentioned. On another occasion, he was the perpetrator, not the victim, of the joke. He and Dittersdorf heard a fiddle scraping out a Menuet as they strolled down a back street. They asked the fiddler whose Menuet he was playing. "Haydn's," replied the man.

"Well, it's a d . . . bad Menuet," responded Haydn, who only escaped being hit with the fiddle when Dittersdorf dragged him away.

Posterity has disagreed with Haydn—if, indeed, he thought

his Menuets were bad—for most of them have become classics, while many are as popular as folk music and as widely used.

Even with Haydn, however, the Menuet was not always obligatory in the Symphony. He disliked pedantry, as well as hard and fast rules, and would thus have been the last person on earth to have been arbitrary on such a matter. Of pedantry, he remarked, "Such trifling is absurd. I wish instead that someone would try to compose a really new Menuet." Sometimes, in the same work, Haydn would include two Menuets, each with trio, one before and one after the slow movement. There are examples of this in Haydn's first twelve quartettes, as well as in some of Mozart's "Serenades" and "Divertimenti." In general, Haydn retained the old form of the Minuet, though he changed its character. The old Minuet was stately. Haydn made it laugh and romp. Small wonder that Beethoven later found in it elements that could be developed into the Scherzo of a Symphony! As Haydn progressed, he wrote his trios in more remote keys from the Menuet proper. In some of his Sonatas, the Menuet and trio completely replace the slow movement.

Haydn's Menuets in the Symphonies lean now toward, now away from the dance form. They contain delightful contrasts and are more fully developed musically than a Menuet is wont to be. Some are graceful. Others, like that in the *London Symphony in D Major*, are spirited and strongly accented, with the trio alone supplying the smooth, lyric grace. (What would Haydn have thought of Vaughan-Williams' modern *London Symphony*, depicting the sounds, sights and life of London and alternating between moods of grim despair and folk gaiety? But then, as Holbrooke so aptly remarked, everyone will see and express London differently. Haydn could express it in but one musical manner: that to which he was accustomed.) Haydn also wrote scores of marches, and German dances. His string quartet no. 68 op. 64 no. 5 in D Major is called *Hornpipe* or *The Lark*. Victor Herbert classed the second subject of the first movement of Haydn's *E Flat Symphony* as a "capital waltz."

Leopold Mozart(4) wrote that his son, Wolfgang, when seven years old, challenged the incredulous to write down a Minuet and then, without touching the clavier, set down the bass and sometimes the second violin parts besides. The young Wolfgang himself often wrote of his having written variations on the Minuets of others. In later life, Mozart was said to have thought more of his dancing than of his music, and to have danced the Minuet beautifully. Truly, he would rather have danced than worked, was impractical and finally ended in a pauper's grave. Perhaps Mozart's dancing added to the charm of his dance music, for musicians who write for the dance and dance themselves have the same advantage as Shakespeare, who wrote for the theater and was of the theater, thereby understanding it from a practical point of view. Ezra Pound(5) has told us that the charm of Mozart, if one can analyze it, seems often to lie in a rare combination of notes which have musical structure, musical line, but which suggest, beyond these and simultaneously, dance steps and language.

Mozart composed what he called Dance Music for Orchestra: twelve Minuets. Most of his Minuets are suave and tender. In each of his Symphonies except one, a Minuet appears. That one, no. 38 in D Major, is known as the Symphony without a Minuet! Nevertheless, during the time that he was creating the Symphonies—some of the finest of all symphonic music—he was in financial straits and for his necessities was forced to earn money on the side, by composing Minuets, Waltzes and other dance music for the court balls at Vienna. In all, he wrote about one hundred and fifty dances for orchestra, band or chamber music, and six for piano solo. Outside of the Menuets, there are German dances and Contredanses.

Beethoven, lauded as one of the greatest composers of serious music of all time, descended far enough into the so-called "depths" to write about fifty-five dances for ensembles and about thirty-six for piano solo: Minuets, Ländlers, Ecossaises, Waltzes—not to mention his attempts at ballet. Then, of course, there is his development of the Minuet. In his hands it became a Scherzo, to be used as a contrasting movement in

the Symphony. This was, in the opinion of some, an attempt
to impress his individuality on a form so strongly defined by
his predecessors and which, as the representative of the dance
Minuet, seemed to have been almost exhausted by Haydn and
Mozart. Beethoven never entirely abandoned the Minuet.
He wrote many of them into his larger works, such as the *I*, *IV*
and *VIII Symphonies*. Movements in his early Sonatas were
described by critics as being dance-like. Often, he added a
Minuet to make a fourth movement in these early Sonatas.
Later, he too returned to the three movement structure established by Corelli. The fourth movement in his B Flat Quartet
op. 130 is said to be based on a popular German dance. Actually, Beethoven liked some of his Minuet themes so well that
he repeated them in other compositions!

Movement III of Beethoven's *Pastoral Symphony* (*VI*)
represents the peasants' merrymaking. Grainger(6) hears in
it a satirical picturization of a European peasant band unsuc-
cessfully attempting to play the same melody at the same time.
Upton(7) sees in it a veritable dance scene: "The first eight
measures usher in the good country people tripping briskly
along. But what a woeful failure the clumsy peasants make at
the end of the phrase, with their attempt at gracefulness, and
how they stumble over their wooden shoes! In the next phrase
the fair damsels carry their part of the programme quite gracefully. Then we strike the dance proper with its 'band accompaniment.' The Menuet-like movement is interrupted by a
short Tempo d'Allegro ¾, which seems like the change to another dance. Though being more boisterous it comes to a close
by two short pauses, as if to give the dancers a chance to catch
their breaths before returning to the triple time of the Menuet
at the close." Berlioz's(8) description of this movement is a
good explanation of how music can dance without being accompanied by dance movements, or even being titled a dance composition: "They dance and laugh, at first with moderation.
The bagpipes play a gay tune, accompanied by the bassoon
which can play but two notes. . . . The dance becomes noisy
and furious. The rhythm changes: a coarse phrase in two

beats announces the arrival of mountaineers with their heavy wooden shoes. . . . The women's hair begins to fly and flutter over their shoulders, for the mountaineers have brought in their noisy gaiety; they clap their hands, they yell, they run and rush furiously . . . when a muttering of thunder in the distance causes a sudden fright in the middle of the dance. Surprise and consternation seize the dancers and they seek safety in flight." Of course, different interpretations of this music came from each of these observers, but then that always occurs when the composer is not thoughtful enough to give us his own.

The Symphony has become such a symbol of abstract music that, despite historic evidence to the contrary, most people refuse to believe that even a part of it had its origin in the dance. Perhaps some day people will listen to Stravinsky's idealizations of jazz as to masterpieces, forgetting that dance inspired them. Thus, in the face of facts, it is difficult to listen to those who say today, "When the Symphony approaches the dance it is in itself a presage of death" (why should such an expression be made, when originally, it was the dance that approached the Symphony?) and who declare, when suggestions of dance are found in a Symphony, that "This makes the musical development retrograde to its physical origin." Such statements are absurd. A suggestion of dance in any piece of music cannot alter its worth, nor lessen its value. The *use* to which the music is put, as regards dance, may be questioned, but not its worth as music. A zealous investigator might find serious music that is far worse than any dance music ever written. Landowska(9) writes that "Frederick the Great, after the battle of Colin, wrote a Minuet in his tent. Socrates danced. Now the least manufacturer of sonatas and quartettes is too grave, too serious to write real dance music. He composes la grande musique"—and the grandeur is but sham.

When the Ballet Russe danced the last movement of Brahms' *Fourth Symphony* as *Choreartium*, there was a tremendous argument over the advisability of "desecrating" such a sacred composition. Well, and why not? This particular movement is a Passacaglia, a scholarly, scientific development of an old dance form which was originally more scholarly and grave than the Chaconne. True, musicians diverted the Passacaglia from its original purpose, because writing intricate variations on a fixed ground bass afforded such a splendid opportunity for them to display their talents. But, as it happened, Brahms shaped his Passacaglia in eight-bar units, in strict conformity with the usage of the classic ballet. What crime, then, did the dancers commit? Edwin Evans states further that Brahms took his eight-measure theme from the Chaconne (also an old dance form) which concludes Bach's 150th Church Cantata, *Nach dir, Herr, Verlanget Nich.* Brahms' development consists of thirty amazingly diverse variations (all but the last in eight bars) and a coda.

Others who have used the Passacaglia as a single movement are Ravel and Ernst Bacon. Ravel's *Trio in A Minor* has this dance form as a third movement, though it is not in the traditional form, since it lacks the ground bass. The second movement of Bacon's *D Minor Symphony* is an Aria and Passacaglia: a theme and a series of variations carried by the orchestra to a steadily recurring theme in the bass. It is individual, and is characterized by stark simplicity, distinctly American, with interesting dissonant suspensions in the bass.

Brahms once ironically called his *E Minor Symphony* a mere "chucked-together set of Waltzes and Polkas," according to Robert Haven Schauffler(10).

Mendelssohn wrote, while he was in Rome and Naples, an *Italian Symphony.* The better to express Italian life, he made the fourth and final movement a vivacious Saltarello. "This," he wrote to his sister, "will be the gayest thing I have ever done." Perhaps it was inspired by the Roman Carnival, of which Mendelssohn was an enchanted spectator. At any rate, he scored his Saltarello movement so that flutes lead off into the merry dance after a short introduction. The other instruments are impelled to join in "as if they, too, had caught the mad contagion(11)." Though the violins go into a more serious strain, the wind instruments do not allow the dance to

be forgotten, even though their reminders are fragmentary.
A Tarantella enters after a short reprise of the Saltarello, and
the two rhythms, alternating and combining, make a glorious
Finale.

Other folk dances have been included in large symphonic
works. Lalo had a Tango rhythm in his *Symphonie Espagnole*
for violin and orchestra. Dvorak had a Furiant (a Czech
dance form) as the Scherzo to his *Third Symphony in D Major*.
Its strange accents and unusual rhythms are characteristic of
most Slavonic dance music. Dvorak also used the Polka as a
movement in trios and quartettes, as well as another purely
Czech dance, the Skočna, in the finale to his *E Flat Quartet*
op. 51 where he treated it in Sonata form, with two leading
themes. Smetana had a Polka in a string quartet, *Aus Meinem
Leben*. Karl Goldmark's *Country Wedding Symphony* has a
picturesque country dance as its fifth movement. Joseph Holbrooke wrote a first Symphony called *Les Hommages* op. 40,
with a Russian Dance (movement IV) as Homage to Tschaikowsky.

Many a dancer has sighed over the lovely, flowing Waltz
melody in Tschaikowsky's *V Symphony*, for the form is so
compact, and it is so closely knit that it is impossible to cut it
to the length needed for dancing, something which must glad-
den the hearts of the purists as it is brought to their attention.
Tschaikowsky also used a Tempo di Polacca (movement employing the Polonaise rhythm) in his *Third Symphony in D
Major*, op. 29. In most movements employing this rhythm, the
meter is three: a group of an eighth and two sixteenth notes,
followed by four eighth notes.

Beginning on March 18, 1878, there was an exchange of
letters between the Russian composer, Taneiev, and Tschai-
kowsky(12). These have a decided bearing on our subject, so
it will be interesting to quote excerpts from them here. Taneiev
threw a bombshell when he told Tschaikowsky that he couldn't
bear the trio of his (Tschaikowsky's) *Fourth Symphony*, since
it seemed like a ballet movement. In his opinion, this was an
irreconcilable defect in the Symphony: "In every movement

there are phrases which sound like ballet music: the middle
section of the Andante, the trio of the Scherzo, and a kind of
march in the Finale. Hearing the symphony, my inner eye
sees involuntarily our prima ballerina which puts me out of
humor and spoils my pleasure in the many beauties of the
work."

In reply, on March 27, 1878, Tschaikowsky wrote: "I
have no idea what you consider ballet music or why you should
object to it. Do you regard every melody in a lively dance
rhythm as 'ballet-music'? In that case, how can you reconcile
yourself to the majority of Beethoven's symphonies, in which
you will find smaller melodies on every page? Or do you
mean to say that the trio of my Scherzo is in the style of Minkus,
Gerber or Pugni? It does not, to my mind, deserve such
criticism. I never can understand why 'ballet-music' should be
used as a contemptuous epithet. The music of a ballet is not
invariably bad—there are good works of this class. And
when the music is good, what difference does it make whether
our prima ballerina dances to it or not? I can only say that
certain portions of my Symphony do not please you *because
they recall the ballet*, not because they are intrinsically bad.
You may be right, but I do not see why dance tunes should
not be employed episodically in a symphony, even with the
avowed intention of giving a touch of coarse, everyday humor.
Again I appeal to Beethoven, who frequently had recourse to
similar effects. I must add that I have racked my brains in
vain to find in what part of the Allegro you can possibly have
discovered 'ballet music.' It remains an enigma."

In our own day, there is the case of Harl McDonald who,
to re-create in music the hectic, dynamic pulse of the present
and to express the fact that despite great contemporary scientific accomplishments our appetite for gaiety and entertainment
is insatiable, wrote a Rhumba (a Cuban dance-form) into his
latest Symphony, as the third movement. *Reflections in an Era
of Turmoil*, he called it. McDonald(13) had previously
learned a great deal from the writing of a ballet suite in 1920.
He now applied his knowledge to a larger form. He was well

aware of the fact that a dance movement in a Symphony is not an innovation. "I feel that I am making use of a twentieth century dance-form much as earlier composers have used the dances popular in their day. I have only emphasized slightly one facet of large scale composition which has been present in a good proportion of standard literature." Of course, the Symphony excited much comment. It was thereafter known as the *Rhumba Symphony*, and writers rejoiced. Here was a subject for comment! Almost all of them termed it "sincere" music, but the phraseology of at least one of them might be questioned. "No dance symphony must be imagined in these pages," wrote he. "He is an intensely serious creator." One cannot help but wonder whether its being—or not being—a dance Symphony would have affected the *seriousness* of McDonald's creation. When the dance is used as sacred ritual, is the accompanying music less sacred than the dance itself? Can one not create dance music as seriously as one creates abstract music?

There were critics who lightly dismissed the *Rhumba Symphony*, terming it "dance-music." They, too, might be questioned, for though it is a larger composition in dance form, it would be difficult to dance to it. This was not the case with the classic symphonic dance movements. It is, rather, a psychological study of masses of people. It is confused, incoherent. It rises to a tremendous, inarticulate climax. Even the heavy orchestration tends to substantiate this feeling, with the melody subordinate to the accompaniment and the nervous maraccas (rattling gourds) sounding at intervals. McDonald also employed in this tympani; triangle; castanets; small Indian tom-tom; cymbals; snare, military, bass and big Indian drum. There is no interplay of thematic material in the Rhumba movement as there is in the first and last movements of this Symphony. These are noticeably in Sonata form.

Another reason, and a very simple one, for McDonald's use of the insistent Rhumba rhythm is that *he likes it*. Mozart and Haydn probably had the same reason for writing Menuets, but in their time pedantic people had not begun to make it necessary for them to justify their tastes with written words.

Outside of the dance movements in formal Symphonies, there are literally hundreds of symphonic dance movements which exist for themselves alone. Those mentioned here are possibly not the most significant of all: they are stray examples selected at random from the music of both modernists and classicists. For example, Haydn wrote twelve German dances for orchestra as no. 4 of *Das Musik-Kränzlein*, composed for the Masked Ball of the Pensionfund Society of the Vienna Masters of Plastic Arts in 1792 in the Imperial Redoutensäle. These vanished in 1829 and for more than a hundred years were lost. They were finally published in 1931.

There are many dance movements for unusual combinations of instruments. Mozart wrote five Country Dances for Chamber Orchestra, the first (on a theme from *Figaro*) composed in 1786, the rest probably in 1791. Cyril Scott once wrote three dances for Nathaniel Shilkret's unusual combination of string quartet and four humming voices.

Another English impressionist, Delius, wrote a symphonic poem, *The Dance Goes On*, prior to 1899. Later he revised it and titled it *The Dance of Life*. In 1908 he wrote *A Dance Rhapsody* for orchestra. Toward the last years of his life, he completed a short orchestral piece called *Fantastic Dance*.

Several composers have attained recognition with symphonic dance movements. Roger-Ducasse had a bitter struggle until 1910, when his orchestral *Sarabande* was performed. Pierre Octave Ferroud also won his first acclaim with an orchestral *Sarabande*. The ballet-symphony *Callirhoë* first brought Chaminade before the public. The creative fame of the American Ernest Schelling seems to rest largely on his orchestral *Victory Ball*, music of a graphic nature in which the dancers' frantic unheeding gaiety has an undercurrent of the bitterness and horrors of war. Its lovely Viennese Waltz is confused and slightly off-pitch, as is the rest of the dance music in this composition.

Though Aaron Copland's *Dance Symphony*, the win-ner of a Victor Company prize, is said to be uncertain in style, it is also considered a source-bed of all his later music. This composer's *Music for the Theatre* includes a Dance, with effective instrumental devices. A jazz piano is prominent. It is decidedly theatrical, decidedly satirical, decidedly rhythmic and choreographic. Paul Laval has composed a *Symphonic Rhumba*.

Perhaps the large number of symphonic dance movements is due to the greater ease with which large ensemble effects can be mirrored in the orchestra. A lone instrument may give us the effect of a mere dance accompaniment. An orchestra may picture the dance itself, its attendant audience excitement, and even characterize those who dance!

CHAPTER 10

NOTES

(1) Rockstro, *General History of Music,* p. 267
(2) MacDowell, *Critical and Historical Essays,* p. 251
(3) Parry, *Studies of Great Composers,* p. 95
(4) Mozart, *Letters,* p. 2
(5) Pound, *Antheil,* p. 120
(6) *The Étude,* September, 1924, p. 593
(7) Upton, *The Standard Symphonies,* pp. 68-69
(8) *The Étude,* October, 1916, p. 748
(9) Landowska, *Music of the Past,* p. 33
(10) Schauffler, *The Unknown Brahms,* p. 179
(11) Upton, *The Standard Symphonies,* p. 185
(12) *Life and Letters of Peter Ilyich Tschaikowsky,* p. 292
(13) In a letter to the author from Philadelphia, Pa., dated February
        13, 1936

*

CHAPTER 11

*

BALLETS IN LATER OPERAS

The leitmotif was not Wagner's only contribution to modern opera. Some of the theories he advanced and put into practice have had a direct bearing on the use of dance music in large theatrical productions. Of course, some of these theories were not entirely new with Wagner; but never before had they been stated so forcefully as to have influenced the works of other composers in the same field. Wagner believed that opera should abandon all those forms that do not spring freely from the dramatic nature of the subject. In other words, if the subject demands a ballet, the composer should include a ballet. If a ballet must be thrown in indiscriminately, it will have no value, except as entertainment for undiscerning people. In 1849, Wagner wrote to Theodor Uhlig(1): "So on January 16, 1850, I go to Paris. . . . First of all, I attack the five-act opera form, then the statute according to which in every great opera there must be a special ballet." Later, when he arrived in Paris and was in bad circumstances, he was advised to see the ballet master at the opera house, as he might want music for a certain dance. "I contemptuously refused this proposal," Wagner wrote. But—that he realized the value of dance music, *in its proper place*, is evidenced by his creative work.

Because Wagner thought a ballet belonged in his *Rienzi*, he wrote one. *Rienzi* had a tragic pantomime in the second act, and a Warriors' Dance. The latter was in F Major, ¾, to be performed by men in old Roman costume, according to the composer's letter to Wilhelm Fischer: "The last great ballet, as a festival ensemble-dance, illustrates the union of ancient and modern Rome. It should be a sort of chain-dance; the première danseuse would, however, have an opportunity of showing herself. I should assign to her the passage in ⅝ time G Major, and that in ¾ time C Major to the two solo dancers." Later in his instructions, Wagner gave explicit directions for cuts in almost any contingency of performance, with his reasons for each suggestion. In one place, for instance, he ventured to suggest the omission of twenty-four bars which, he said, would not amount to much, and only robs the close of its force. Wagner wanted *Rienzi's* tragic pantomime to produce an inspiring effect, and to this end he asked to have engaged for it "members of the comedy-troupe who are accustomed to play similar parts in spoken drama," these members to form a cast of chief characters in the pantomime.

In the words of Searchinger(2): Beethoven had created a type of music that in effect is nothing but one closely connected melody. Now Wagner strove for a parallel achievement in opera. Needless to say, in order to do this, he had to break altogether with what he calls the dance forms: to create the poetic counterpart to the symphonic form which at the same time conforms to the laws of dramatic form.

When *Tannhäuser* was about to be produced in Paris, the manager of the Opéra was anxious to convince Wagner of the necessity of rearranging the second act, so that a grand ballet could be inserted at this point. Wagner found his insistence annoying, but he determined to accede, in a measure, and make extensive choreographic additions to the Venusberg scene in the first movement. "I thought," he wrote, "that this would give the staff of the ballet a choreographic task of so magnificent a character that there would no longer be any occasion to grumble at me for my obstinacy in this matter. The

musical composition of the two scenes occupied most of my
time during the month of September." Wagner thought
wrongly, however. Custom was not to be flouted so easily.
In the first act, declared the management, a ballet counted for
nothing. Appropriate or not, it had to be in the second act,
since the rich patrons of the Opéra dined late and always
arrived correspondingly late at performances. Wagner remained adamant. The ballet belonged in the first act, and
there it must stay. Confidently, he tried to enlist the aid of
Petipa. He asked this ballet master for combinations never
before used in ballets, and astounded him by suggesting that
his pupils dance as might Maenads and Bacchantes. Petipa
politely explained that Wagner had himself renounced the
ordinary step-dancers of the Opéra by his obstinacy in placing
the ballet in the first act, and that the best he could do was to
offer him three Hungarian dancers to enact the Three Graces.
After much argument, Wagner discovered that the management was not disposed to spend a thing on his ballet, which
was regarded as so much wasted energy. Finally, a veritable
fight arose at the performance (presumably instigated by the
nobility whose dinner hours had been desecrated) over the lack
of a second act ballet!

Wagner's *Parsifal* had a reversion to the communal
elements of music: choral polyphony and the dance. There
was a Dance of the Flower Maidens in Klingsor's Castle. In
the Dance of the Apprentices in *Die Meistersinger* Wagner
cut out the eighth measure of the Waltz each time it came
around. Norwegian sailors in the *Flying Dutchman* danced
and made merry on the deck of their vessel at the opening
of Act III, while the Dutchman's ship, near by, remained silent
as the grave. For this, Wagner wrote a spirited ²⁄₄ chorus,
strongly accented and peasanty in feeling. Of course, this cannot be termed a ballet in the strict sense of the word. But it
serves to present operatic dance music in a *reasonable* way.

Edwin Evans(3) has made a very flat statement which
one may accept with reservations: "After Wagner, ballet in
opera disappeared and the independent ballet was left to second-

rate composers, often to hacks. The independent ballet has now succeeded in rising from that abyss and even Wagner's successor, Richard Strauss, has composed two works for it." He might have added that even Wagner's son, Siegfried, had a ballet in his own fifth opera, *Sternengebot*.

However, Richard Strauss (always very fond of dance music, according to Paderewski) has composed ballets in several of his operas also. Even his thoughts on the subject are now available, since the publication of his correspondence with his librettist, Hugo von Hofmannsthal. Strauss' *Arabella*, based on von Hofmannsthal's novelette, *Lucidor*, contains several Waltz themes built on "broad melodic lines of sensuous brilliancy" according to a critic. Martens tells us (4) that the success of Strauss' opera, *Salome*, with its Dance of the Seven Veils, made dancing Salomes an almost obligatory feature of the dramatic and musical stage for several years. It is Haskell's opinion that there is only one way to perform *Salome*. That is to do it in doubles: a singer and a dancer for each rôle (5).

In 1909, von Hofmannsthal (6) wrote to Strauss that he had spent three peaceful afternoons in writing the complete scenario for an absolutely new and original libretto in which the situations were broadly humorous, the action almost as obvious as a pantomime, and with opportunities even for a short ballet. This turned out to be none other than *Der Rosenkavalier*. Later he asked Strauss: "For the last act please think of some old-fashioned Viennese Waltz measure, half-sweet, half-piquant. It must pervade the whole act." Still later he wrote that he was trying to get a bustling, grotesque ending in the ballet manner for Act II "in which you can introduce your charming Waltz motif."

Later, they wrote *Le Bourgeois Gentilhomme* (after Molière) with a divertissement at the end of Act II: *Ariadne auf Naxos*. This is really an opera within an opera, a rehearsal scene at which the composer and the music and dancing masters are present. Strauss was advised by his librettist that the dances in this must be quite short. He replied that there was an opportunity for some charming "conversation-music" during the ballets of the dancing masters, cooks and tailors. Hofmannsthal then omitted a serious dance and substituted for it a jolly dance of the young tailors, so that there would be no imitation of an old world dance-form. Later, both composer and librettist became concerned about a producer, since they needed one who would follow their own careful calculations as to gestures and steps, the whole resembling a combined concert and ballet. If Reinhardt were to do it, they reasoned, the whole thing would become a singing blossom, the incarnation of the dance.

For *Die Frau ohne Schatten*, Hofmannsthal asked whether it would fit in with Strauss' rhythms to include a sort of Witches' Dance, since that was the way he visualized the passage.

In 1917, regarding *Jourdain*, Strauss wrote (7), "Are we keeping the little dance at the end, while they are fetching the notary? If so, we might make up a quartet to sing a lovely wedding-madrigal in the old Italian manner, while the dancers in the previous ballet (tailors and scullions) can be doing a dance in honor of the bridal pair. This combination of song and dance would make a charming finish." Hofmannsthal disagreed. Since there was a mixture of operetta and ballet in this Turkish ceremony, and since there was opportunity for the solo dance for the sylph in the short melodrama at the beginning of Act III, another ballet at the end of the same act would be too much. Wrote he (8), "The more experience one gets, the more importance one attaches to the weighing of the several parts, and the balance and correspondence of the different elements. That is what the French understand so splendidly. We must try to learn it from them." Then Strauss countered by saying that since the other two acts had brilliantly successful climaxes: the Tailors' Dance, Minuet and Dinner Scene, there should be a vocal ensemble with a ballet at the end of Act III. Evidently Hofmannsthal complied, for Strauss later wrote that the new Finale to Act III seemed very good, though he couldn't understand from the manuscript whether they dance while the madrigal is being sung, or later, or both.

ROBERT SCHUMANN

in his twenty-second year when he wrote his op. 2,
Papillons, from a portrait taken at that time

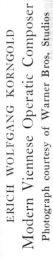

ERICH WOLFGANG KORNGOLD
Modern Viennese Operatic Composer
Photograph courtesy of Warner Bros. Studios

IGOR STRAVINSKY

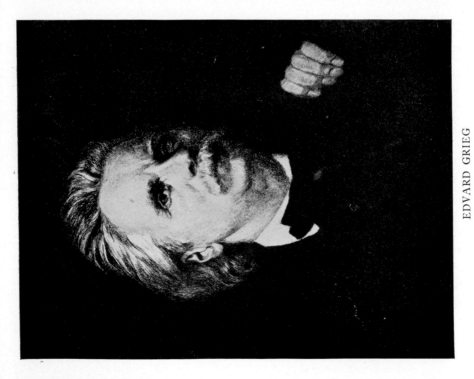

EDVARD GRIEG

Etched from life in Christiania in 1903 by
William Peters

"In any case," he concluded, "The final melodrama and Lully's Minuet will make a very good ending."

Strauss' symphonic poem, *Tyl Eulenspiegel*, was not the only musical work built on the same subject. Hans Stieber, a German who was born in 1886, wrote *Der Eulenspiegel*, a series of scenes with musical accompaniment, song and dance. In it, the composer sought to convey a deep philosophic meaning to his hearers. He had a puppet introduction, representing the metaphysical birth of Tyl.

Ernest Krenek has written an ultra modern, contrapuntal opera, with jazz Fox Trots in a masked ball scene and with a mystic making clever human puppets dance. It is named *The Leap over the Shadow*.

Although Arnold Schönberg has never written an independent ballet, his opera *Moses and Aaron* has a scene of about half an hour's duration which he says (9) probably could only be performed by dancers and mimes, and which nevertheless asks them to fulfill tasks which are very unusual. In his one-act opera, *Die Glückliche Hand*, the action is mimed by three dancers about a central figure, a singer, so it is really almost a complete ballet.

Korngold has ballets in all of his operas except his new one, *Die Kathrin*, about a modern girl. There is, for example, a Carnival Scene in *Violanta*, while *Die Tote Stadt* (The Dead City) presents a solo dancer in many moods. Korngold also wrote a Hornpipe called *Mummery* in his incidental music to *Much Ado about Nothing*.

Ernst Toch's *Princess and the Pea* contains a scene where the servants build up the bed. It is in effect a ballet, for the rhythmic music was intended by the composer to be danced. His opera, *The Fan*, has a scene in a dance hall. It is thus connected with dance, though not written directly for it.

Not to be forgotten are the charming dances in Humperdinck's *Hansel und Gretel*: the Knusper Waltzer and the Polka.

We are told that Verdi was very rarely happy in his ballet music: He did not think naturally in terms of the dance, which suggested to him no musical ideas. It was not primarily a question of temperament. Nevertheless, though he (like many another operatic composer) was fond of the ordinary ¾ rhythm and was uninventive as to meters for his opera ballets, he made judicious use of the corps de ballet with which he knew every operahouse would be equipped. The dance figures prominently in most of his works.

La Traviata, for instance, has a ball scene with a background of Spanish Dance and Waltz music. Indeed, Act I contains a vocal Waltz. *Aïda* has a short Dance of Priestesses in Act I and a Dance of Slaves in Act II. Both of these are in common time. The music is not unusual. There is also dancing in the Triumphal Scene. *Forza del Destino* has its first act opening with a danced chorus. There is a vocal Tarantella, with purely instrumental interludes, in Act III. The famous Minuet in *Rigoletto* is danced almost at the outset of Act I at the back of the stage, while characters sing in the foreground. This music has an almost classic purity, and is followed by a short instrumental ⅝, the Perigordino, danced on the stage after the singers exit. *Macbetto*, as Verdi pictured it, had the Witches' Scene in the form of a ballet. *Othello* contains ballet music. *Un Ballo in Maschera*, said to be so named because of difficulties with the police, has a Mazurka-Minuet, a death-dance melody, and a Masked Ball Scene in Act III. In this the dance music comes from within, while a complete dramatic scene, called " 'Mid Whispered Love and Dancing" occurs outside. One writer has termed Verdi's *Masked Ball* a splendid farce, since it is an Italian opera presenting a brilliant court ball in a palace in Puritan New England, by aristocrats instead of pilgrims.

And what of Puccini, that writer of splendid melodies and of exotic harmonies? His *La Rondine* has, at the end of Act I, a long scene where nothing is sung, but the orchestra plays a wistful Waltz while Magda, dressed as a servant, pirouettes her way through the moonlight to attend the students' ball. The last strains of the Waltz are heard as the curtain falls. *Le Villi* is a veristic opera in which the villis, or witches, sweep the faithless lover away in a death-dance, La Tregheda. There is a Minuet of Manon's friends in *Manon Lescaut*, and there is the famous Waltz song of Musetta in *La Bohéme*. That these dance scenes were not thrown into Puccini's operas at random and that they represented an entirely new feeling for the dance in opera is evidenced by the composer's letter to the publisher of *Mme. Butterfly*. In this he said(10) that "the flower scene is danced almost throughout." Certainly no composer before the time of Puccini had had the breadth of vision to be able to conceive an operatic scene as a ballet: to write the music to fit the atmospheric, dramatic and rhythmic needs of the moment; then to discard the element of dance and to allow the motivating rhythm to be sensed by the audience!

We hear dainty ballet music—almost puppet music—by Leoncavallo in *Pagliacci's* play within a play. This composer wrote *I Medici* in 1893, with charming dance music in Act II, an improvised song and dance festival in the streets. His opera *Maia* contains folk dances. And, while *Cavalleria Rusticana* is notoriously lacking in dance music, Mascagni atoned for the deficiency in his opera, *Iris*. Umberto Giordano has a ballroom scene in *Andrea Chenier*.

Ildebrando Pizzetti, one of Italy's moderns, has composed music to d'Annunzio's drama, *La Pisanella*, including a Dance of Poverty and Perfect Love, and a Dance of Love and the Scented Death. The latter climaxes the opera. Italo Montemezzi has a brilliant orchestral Dance of Seduction as the Prologue to his opera, *Il Nave*. In Act II, there is a passionate Dance of the Seven Candelabra. Sardinian folk dances (a Danze Montanare with accordion accompaniment) appear in this composer's opera, *Giovanni Gallurese*.

Catalani is the operatic composer to whom (his countrymen believe) understanding will come twenty years hence. In his opera, *Loreley*, he has a Nuptial March, a Danza della Ondine, as well as a charming Valzer dei Fiori, with short vocal phrases alternating with short instrumental phrases. Dancing elves appear in Respighi's *La Campana Sommersa*. First one after another enter to the ⅜ music, sung in moderate tempo di danza. The singing and dancing is simultaneous. The music is charming, lilting; the harmonies warm, piquant, distinctly elfin. The melody takes unexpected turns, the rhythm is sprightly. Tito Schipa has employed much the same device in his opera, *Princess Liana*. The vocal (tenor) Tango in Act II is an accompaniment to the dancers' steps.

Often during the past few paragraphs, vocal or instrumental Waltzes have been mentioned. Let us offer a probable explanation for the frequency of this phenomenon. A ballet in an opera is done by trained dancers. But when the leading character must dance, the accompaniment becomes a problem, since most singers are ignorant of the art of Terpsichore. However, almost anyone can waltz creditably, so to save his own opera, the composer will write a brilliant Waltz song (the Waltz rhythm easily admits of many vocal pyrotechnics) or he may simply allow the orchestra to play a Waltz. There are, of course, many arias in Waltz rhythm that are not intended to be danced. There are also instrumental Waltzes in operas which merely create or intensify moods. It cannot be denied that some composers literally pushed Waltzes into their operas because of the extreme popularity of that dance after its inception. Sometimes, unfortunately, this was done when the libretto of the opera placed it in a period before the origin of the Waltz. This inconsistency necessarily hampers the choreographer, who must somehow manage to fit an authentic early dance to the Waltz music.

There is a famous Waltz in Act II, scene 1 of Tschaikowsky's *Eugene Onegin*. The act opens upon a ballroom scene honoring Tatiana's birthday and containing a typically rhythmic Mazurka to which the guests dance, when the Cotillon begins. It is not long before voices break in, and the action begins while the dance continues. Thus it has a definite function in the drama. Act III has a longer Polonaise, written much as it would have been danced in a fashionable house of the period. Act I contains peasant songs and dances.

Most of Tschaikowsky's dances for his operas are national dances. There is a reason for this: most of the operas were based on subjects that were national in character. Tschaikowsky was not one to throw an Egyptian ballet into an opera concerned with a Russian legend. He was far too wise. In his opera, *Vakoula, the Smith* (later published as *Les Caprices d'Oxane*, the subject of which also served Rimsky-Korsakow for his opera, *Christmas Eve Revels* and inspired the Cossack dance in it) the devil and the witch dance a Gopak in the second act. In the third act the Zaparogue Cossacks dance a Gopak for the Tsar. The opera, *Maid of Orleans* opens with a village festival at Domremy. There are dances in Act I, scene 1 of *Mazeppa* in the garden, as well as a dance of the Drunken Cossack before the place of execution. Mamirov dances a Mummer's Dance in *The Enchantress*. *Pique Dame* has a fancy dress ball as well as a Dance of the Young Girls—before their governess puts an end to it. *Opritchniki* and *Tcherevichky*, both four-act operas, contain dances.

Tschaikowsky's first opera, *Voyevode*, most of which he destroyed during the seventies, contained a much-admired, orchestral Dance of the Serving Maids. This was written before 1865, many years before the completion of the opera itself. When Johann Strauss conducted it, its composer was filled with delight, since it was one of the first public performances of his music. Surely, it was more successful than Tschaikowsky's own attempts at conducting for, on one occasion, when he was asked to conduct the dances from *Voyevode* at a charity concert, he grasped the baton in his right hand while his left "firmly supported his fair beard" in the fear that, unless he managed somehow to restrain it, his head might fall off. He was distracted and timid. Someone has remarked that on this particular occasion the orchestra played well in spite of Tschaikowsky. The men had determined to pay no attention to his nervous beat!

Tschaikowsky was inspired to bring about the serious recognition of dance music by Glinka's splendid dances in the Italian style in *Russlan and Ludmila* (which also contains an oriental ballet in Act IV). Stravinsky writes(11): "It is true that Rimsky-Korsakow appreciated these dances—or rather, forgave Glinka for them—but he in his operas gave the preference to character or national dances." Glinka's *Life for the Tsar* contains Krakowiak and Mazurka, the latter in the Forest Scene, when the chorus of Poles sings an unchanging Mazurka (three) rhythm, while the orchestra must play four beats to a measure.

Rubinstein wrote many operas and included in them many ballets. Musically, they are as unimportant as some of his other attempts at composition. No one will deny that Rubinstein had inspired moments, but the music he created for the dance was doubtless written off-schedule. Nevertheless, Bessel wrote(12) of Rubinstein's first playing of his opera, *The Demon*: "Notwithstanding the marvelous playing, the new opera made no very favourable impression on the audience. The dances, the March . . . pleased them best." More, we find that Act I of *Feramors* has a graceful ballet piece called Dance of Light of the Brides of Kashmir, which has escaped oblivion.

A great, spectacular performance at the Marie Theater was planned by the dramatist, Gédéonov. He wished to have a blend of opera, ballet and fairy pantomime and selected an attractive, fantastic Slav legend of the tenth century (from the Balkans) called *Mlada*. For this, many Russian composers: Cui, Borodin, Moussorgsky, and Rimsky-Korsakow were each to write music for a single act. Minkus was to supply some of the dance tunes. The project was almost sure to meet disaster. It did, almost at the outset, due to lack of finances! Later, the economical composers used the material they had gathered for *Mlada* in other ways. Borodin's excellent last act, with its Indian and Lithuanian dances, was posthumously finished and orchestrated by Rimsky-Korsakow. Long before that, Liadov had suggested that Rimsky-Korsakow make his fragment into an opera-ballet, and the latter had accepted the suggestion. *Mlada* is featured by the worship of pagan gods. The central character, killed by a poisoned ring, returns to haunt her bereaved husband and his sweetheart, the murderess. Such a subject offers untold possibilities.

Rimsky-Korsakow's *Mlada* is in four acts and an apotheosis. In it, the composer employed folklore substance as the basis of a number of episodic songs and dances. In its second act is a circling dance, or Kolo, from which Russian peasants derive their Khorovodes. The composer had been fascinated at the Paris Exposition by the sudden blows struck by a Negro as the dancer approached in the Algerian Café. He promptly borrowed the effect for a scene in his own *Mlada*, the Dance before Cleopatra. (This music was employed many years later for the entrance and unveiling of the Queen in the Russian ballet *Cléopâtra*, the glorious musical hodge-podge.) In *Mlada* there are said to be harmonic traces of Wagner. Rimsky-Korsakow himself confessed that the leading motifs were worked out in a fashion not entirely his own.

That Rimsky-Korsakow was alive to all local and national color is proved by the sequences of dances in his operas. *A Night in May* has choral games and dances. Another opera is distinguished by a song and dance called "Hops," an old Autumn ceremonial. The *Snow Maiden*, *A Night in May*, *Kitej* and *Kastchei* all contain Trepaks and Gopaks. For *Kitej*, Rimsky-Korsakow took the theme of the Bear's Dance in the second act from his own collection of folksongs. Folk melodies being modal, he put the Dance of the Maenads in *Servilia* into the Phrygian Mode. His *Sadko* has a curious subject: lots are drawn to see who will appease the anger of the Sea-King. Sadko wins and is cast adrift on a raft. He then plays such delightful, irresistible music that the Sea-king and his court cannot refrain from dancing to it!

Snegourotchka, Rimsky-Korsakow's opera, has in it a Spring festival with laughing music to accompany the dances of the wood creatures. Russian folk melody is drawn on heavily in this opera, in fragments and in combinations. The Prologue consists of a Dance and Song of the Birds, and an animated Carnival Scene by a crowd of Berendeys on their way to the forest. Act III contains a vivacious, heavily-accented Dance of the Buffoons in ¾ meter, the melody reminiscent of the folk. High, mocking bells ring during the course of this dance.

Le Coq d'Or, Rimsky-Korsakow's last opera, was an attempt to reconcile ballet and opera, according to Haskell(13). Yet it was evidently not intended to be so, since, when it was first given, the singers declared it impossible for them to sing and dance at once. It was Fokine—not the composer himself —who hit on the idea of having singers sit at the side of the stage, as though they belonged to the inanimate setting, while the action was mimed by trained dancers. Over vehement protests from the composer's family, the scheme was carried out and has been in vogue ever since. Montagu-Nathan(14), in telling us that the comedy inherent in the story is effectively realized in the music and that the melo-declamatory method has been resorted to in the solos, has also called *Coq d'Or* a "satire on human foibles, a specimen of nationalistic art and a final chapter in the story of Rimsky-Korsakow's musico-dramatic development." Pushkin wrote the poem on which this work is based. It is preluded by an astrologer who assures the audience that there is a moral in what they are about to hear. Sombre chords introduce the fantastic tale, at the end of which the astrologer informs the audience that it was, after all, entirely unreal.

The ballet figured in the opera reforms of the Russian Five, as it had done in those of Gluck and Wagner. In order to make opera a dignified dramatic art, they had to exclude unnecessary ballets which interrupted the plot, which was then a mere excuse for virtuoso vocal and choreographic effects. They wanted a perfect fusion of music and drama.

Behold, then, the result! Because Dargomijsky's *Stone Guest* contained neither chorus nor ballet, it was dubbed by one critic a "recitative in three acts." Nevertheless, this composer's *Russalka* included dances. When Moussorgsky first submitted his opera, *Boris Goudonoff* to the Russian Imperial Theaters, it was rejected because (among other things) it contained no dances. One can imagine the composer's dejection. He must have been torn between two fears: that of losing his ideals and that of oblivion for his work. At last he capitulated and added the Polish Scene in order to overcome all objections.   In this, a gay Polonaise is danced in the castle gardens in Act III, scene 2.   This has a ring of festal splendor. Moussorgsky's original intention was to orchestrate it for strings only, in imitation of the "quatre-vingt violons du Roi," but he was forced to the conclusion that it was impossible to create a brilliant musical setting without the aid of woodwind and brass.   The archaic folk feeling is secured through the use of the Lydian Mode.   In 1872 Moussorgsky sent the score of this Polonaise to Balakireff and asked him (15) to present it in concert if he thought it worthy of the place, since it would be a great help to him to hear the Polonaise performed: "It is essential that I should hear my music played by orchestra alone, without the chorus, and I have not had a chance to do so until now."

Moussorgsky's first plan for the *Fair at Sorótchintzy* (left incomplete) called for a short Gopak at the end of Act I, a solo Dance at Dawn in Act III, and a danced duet some time before the Finale.   The Gopak he wrote for this is the familiar one that has become so popular, beginning with the sounds of the instruments tuning up.   The Persian Dances in Moussorgsky's *Kowantchina* occur in the first scene of Act IV, when Khovansky orders the Persian dancers to dispel his gloom.

Of Borodin's Polovetsian Dances in *Prince Igor* (when the princes' captors treated them as honored guests rather than prisoners, and regaled them with a banquet and the dancing of warriors and their women) Goossens says (16) : "No dance music ever written can match it for that intolerable throbbing rhythm that can set men madly leaping in the air, and leave their women swooning with desire."   In this opera, there is yet another dance scene of a sort, when the guards get drunk on fermented mare's milk (koumiss) and dance.   One by one these drunken dancers drop to the ground, exhausted.   The music is striking.

Among other Russians in the operatic field, Prokofieff has written dance music into his *Love of the Three Oranges*; Serge Youferoff into *Anthony and Cleopatra*; Cui into *Le Prisonnier du Caucase* (Danses Circassiennes) and into *Le Filibustier* (Breton folk dances); and Rachmaninoff into *Aleko* (Gypsy dances).

French operatic composers seem to have had no misgivings as to the advisability of adding ballets—rather, of adding dances—to their dramas. Almost all of them have enhanced their works in this way.

To accustom the public to Massenet's *Thaïs*, the Opera directors associated with it one of the standard ballets. When it was evident that *Thaïs* pleased the public, they worked to make it fill an entire evening and requested the addition of a tableau (The Oasis) and a ballet. The ballet in Act II, scene 5 begins with an Allegro Vivo (a low melody with high accompaniment); a Melopée Orientale (with a running melody); an Allegro Brillante, Allegretto con Spirito, Mouvement de Valse, La Charmeuse (with voices) and Finale. Massenet composed the ballet for *Le Cid*, based on exploits of the legendary hero of crusading Spain, in a Marseilles hotel room, with long latticed windows that looked out upon the old port. The prospect was fairylike. It was Spring, and his room was scented with fresh carnations. The motif he used at the beginning of the ballet he first heard in the very country of *Le Cid*, when he was living in a modest Spanish inn. To celebrate a wedding, the people danced all night in the room below him. Several guitars and two flutes repeated a dance theme until they wore it down. An ordinary traveler would have been angered at the continued sound. Massenet was a composer—and a thrifty one at that. He noted the tune, kept it with him, used it when he was ready for it. He had made use of local color, and turned to good account a sleepless night! The ballet of *Le Cid* was intended for Mlle. Rosita Mauri of the Opéra, to whom he "owed several interesting rhythms." The popularity of dancing and dancers at that time is attested by the fact that the star of *Le Cid's* incidental ballet was given equal billing along with the vocal artists!

Massenet also wrote a *Don Quijote*, to the libretto of the French poet, La Lorraine. This called for a festival in the house of Dulcinea in the fourth act. Accordingly, Massenet wrote into it a Spanish dance. Greek, Nubian and Assyrian slave girls danced in Massenet's opera, *Hérodiade*. His *Le Roi de Lahore*, on the other hand, contains voluptuous dances in Indra's paradise, to the flute accompaniment of the god Nareda. In *Bacchus*, the ballet occurs in the forests of India. *Le Mage*, based on the story of Zoroaster, has an important ballet, staged in a fairylike way. Massenet's *Cendrillon*, with its Louis XIII atmosphere, has a charming Gavotte. His *Le Jongleur de Nôtre Dame* is an opera in which the juggler sings and dances the profane steps of the market place for the Virgin, to her joy and his deliverance.

Mignon was supplied by its composer, Ambroise Thomas, with an actual ballet in the Finale of Act II, as well as with many moments literally sparkling with Waltz and Polka rhythms. The opera contains the oft-sung vocal Polonaise, in addition to a Gavotte. In Act I there is a Gypsy Dance in 2/4 meter, to a strumming accompaniment over which a sprightly song is heard later.

The libretto of *Timbre d'Argent*, opera in four acts, was accepted by Saint-Saëns after other composers had rejected it because of its difficulties. The principal rôle calls for a dancer, with the rôle of the vocalist subordinated to it. This caused much difficulty in casting, since the manager begged the composer to transform the dancer into a singer on his own wife's account. The setbacks in production were constant, the difficulties enormous. The opera was therefore much delayed. The basic idea was said to be profound and mysterious: an artist realizes a lofty ideal in his painting of a dancer (a musical phrase, taken by the horn, symbolizes his high aspirations both in major and minor modes), then the picture comes alive, and the purity is lost. A vast gulf between the ideal and the reality! This opera contains a Valse Vénitienne. Reynaldo Hahn declares Saint-Saëns to be essentially a "man of the theater." He also considers the dances in Saint-Saëns' *Ascanio* a supreme triumph of taste and intelligence: the entire Renaissance in a few pages. Saint-Saëns himself esteemed this incidental ballet more highly than his fragile *Javotte*. It contains an Ancient Dance, Gavotte, Bacchanals, Apparition of Phoebus and the Muses and other classic pictures, with a Grand Waltz as Finale.

The ballet in Saint-Saëns' *Samson et Dalila* has been called an episode perfectly connected with the dramatic action, of which it forms an integral part, and no mere divertissement. It has a Dance of the Priestesses of Dagon in Act I, an Allegretto ¾: not unusual music. The celebrated Bacchanale is in the second scene of Act III *Parysatis* has airs de ballet, while the third act of Étienne Marcal has a ballet and choral ensembles in the square of Nôtre Dame. Saint-Saëns' *King Henry VIII* has a ballet in the first scene of Act IV, in Anne Boleyn's chamber. Gounod describes this scene(17). The curtain rises on a graceful song and dance, during which Norfolk and Surrey carry on an aside conversation very ingeniously interwoven with the dance music. The whole divertissement in this opera consists of The Entrance of the Clans, Scottish Idyl, Dance of the Gypsy (employing tympani and cymbal), Gigue and Finale. The opera as a whole is said to make effective use of English folk dance melodies.

Another famed Waltz song occurs in Gounod's *Romeo et Juliette*, which also has a Ball Scene. This composer's *Mireille* has a joyous Valse-ariette known as Rondinella Leggiera. It was written for soprano and was not in the original version of the opera. Gounod added it later. In Act II, peasants dance the Farandole. A Moorish ballet is seen in Gounod's old-style grand opera, *Le Tribut de Zamora*. Still another Waltz occurs in Gounod's *La Nonne Sanglante in* Act III: *Un Jour plus pur*. When the *Faust* ballet is presented independently of Gounod's opera, it is called *Walpurgisnacht*. It is said not to be essential to the story of *Faust*, though in Gounod's time it was considered one of the finest parts of the opera, since it was melodious and well scored. It occurs during the fourth and fifth acts in the Vale of Tempe. In addition to Faust and Mefistofeles, there are present Helen of Troy and other figures relating to Greek mythology.

It is interesting to note that in 1869, Hervé wrote an opera in which Faust is condemned by Mefistofeles to dance for all eternity. Its name: *Le Petit Faust.*

When Bizet was in sad circumstances, he did many strange things to earn money. He wrote music for hire, taught, and even went so far as to compose music for dances! Though the latter occupation seems to be regarded by commentators as being one of the lowest possible, it may have had a great deal to do with the success of Bizet's later dance music.

On the occasion of *Carmen's* 1875 presentation in Vienna, the corps de ballet of the Opera appeared in the last act, where a divertissement from *La Jolie Fille de Perth* was interpolated. Halévy described this Viennese version as an opera-ballet. Bizet is said to have had a pupil whose mother was a South American, who frequently sang Spanish songs to Bizet. The celebrated Habanera was thus inspired. Finally, Bizet inscribed the song: "Imitated from a Spanish song, property of the editors of *Le Ménestrel.*" He had written and re-written this piece at the insistence of the singer, Galli-Marie, who wanted an effective entrance. The composition, as we know it, is the thirteenth version. Bizet either copied, or faithfully remembered, an old *Chanson Havanaise* which appears among the works of Sebastion Yradier, once very popular with singers. Nor was Yradier really the originator. The tune is actually of the Spanish folk, a dance rhythm. But both he and Bizet made good use of it. Tiersot(18) claims that Bizet did more than borrow folk themes. He assimilated the forms, rhythms and accents of the songs, after which he created new themes, wherein the folk impulse lived again, imbued with Bizet's own personality. Tiersot names the Habanera as an exception, but both he and Parker hesitate to believe that Bizet actually created the last entr'acte in *Carmen*, since it is so strongly impregnated with the character of Spanish dance. Tiersot says he cannot find this in any collection, but another writer (Gaudier) declares it to be a Polo, from a musical piece called *El Criado Fingido,* composed by Manuel García in 1804.

L'Arlésienne has been accounted Bizet's finest work after *Carmen.* Because the action of this takes place in Provence,

Bizet drew on Provençal songs and dances. For his Farandole, he is said to have made a version of the *Danso dei Chivau-Frus*. Parker (19) finds the chorus in F Sharp Minor to be somewhat in the character of a Bolero. He also believes (20) that the Danse Bohémienne in the *Fair Maid of Perth* is Bizet "nearly at his best." The *Pearlfishers* contains a savage dance chorus in Act III and Bizet's *Vasco da Gama* has a ballet in the last act. The opera *Djamileh* has an exotic dance of Egyptian Almees with monotonous bass and high, chromatic melody in the oriental style, which has occasioned another of those fascinating controversies: Reyer (21) calls it the true music of the East whereas Parker (22) feels that Bizet's East is the East of imaginative convention. A comparative study of oriental music and of Bizet's dance leads one to believe that Parker is correct: the latter is, after all, pseudo.

One Frenchman, Raoul Laparra, has based his operas on dance forms. He wrote *La Jota* and *La Habanera*, in which the Habanera theme is taken alternately by voice and orchestra. Both were meant to be beginnings of a cycle of Spanish operas, into which the dances would enter as the actual motifs of the operas. Laparra wished to complete the cycle with *Malagueña* and *Tango*, bearing in mind the fact that the original dance form of the latter was with the feet largely stationary.

Delibes' venture into the operatic field must not be forgotten. *Lakmé* contains the dance airs: Terana, Rektah, Persian Dance. Van Vechten (23) says they are the best part of the opera. After Delibes' death, Massenet completed his opera, *Kassya* with a ballet: Obertas, Ruthenian Dance, Sumka and Trepak, as well as a Mazurka for the Finale of Act I and a Polonaise later. There was a Ball Scene in Delibes' incidental music for *Le Roi s'Amuse*, with dance melodies in the ancient style.

Nor must Chabrier's *Le Roi Malgré Lui*, with its Danse Slave, Fête Polonaise and Waltz be overlooked. Charpentier once wrote a symphony-drama for solos, chorus and orchestra called *A Poet's Life*. Later this was transformed into the opera, *Julien*, where, in the last act when the Poet has sought a low dance hall in Montmartre, the opposing dance orchestras, vying with each other, supply a realistic background for his tragic downfall. Even César Franck, who devoted so much of his life to the composition of works imbued with a lofty religious feeling, composed a theatrical work, a four-act opera called *Hulda* (1882) after Björnstjerne-Björnson. In it is a colorful Ballet Allégorique, depicting the struggle of Winter and Spring. Rabaud's *Marouf, the Cobbler of Cairo* contains dances in the wedding festival scene.

Roussel made an interesting departure in the opera-ballet, *Padmâvotî* (Daughter of the Lotus). The scene is laid in India in the thirteenth century. It is an episode in the conquest of India by the Mongols. It includes Hindu secular dances, with the dances of the palace entertainers patterned after the Pshari frescoes in the Anjuta Temple; and a funeral dance in the Temple of the God of Death. The story concerns a wife's fidelity. When the Mongol king covets his enemy's wife, she stabs her king and dies with him on the funeral pyre. The singers play a more important rôle than the dancers, yet *Padmâvotî* was recognized as one of the most remarkable stage works of its time (1923) since there was inherent a real pretext for choreographic action, as well as the usual operatic vocal opportunities. The music is said to be of barbaric directness and to sacrifice convention to attain dramatic truth. It is vivid and exotic, perhaps due to its use of Hindu melodies. Two years later, Roussel wrote *La Naissance de la Lyre*, an opera with a lovely, classic ballet and a "Finale in Rameau's pure and lofty manner."

Ravel's *L'Enfant et les Sortilèges* is also a ballet-opera. Martens (24) says of this: Dance and song are associated throughout the score, rich in delicate, poetic, ingeniously rhythmed melodies. A lyric fantasy, symbolizing the griefs and joys of childhood. It contains Minuet, Gigue and American Waltz, all danced by the "inanimate" objects the child has destroyed in a fit of naughtiness, for in this work the child is the announcer.

Honegger portrayed musically, in his *King David*, the famous Dance before the Ark. Both he and Eugene Goossens wrote operas called *Judith*, with dances. The ballet in Goossens' opera is important, and occurs in the camp of Holofernes when he summons his dancing maidens for the entertainment of Judith. This music is well scored, colorful, bizarre. It is rhythmic, but not rigidly so. At times it is broadly lyric. It is, in fact, ballet music that is actually dramatic! A splendid, modern score. In his new opera, *Don Juan de Mañara*, Goossens employed an early form of Fandango to accompany the dancing of one of the principal women characters.

Perhaps because Leo Janaček's opera, *Jenufa* has national Moravian dances underlying the action's tragic moments, Newman made this apt remark: "Apparently . . . in these middle European countries . . . you shave yourself to a Krakowiak, cut a man's throat to a Mazurka and bury him to a Czardas." Be that as it may, many operas with dances have been written by composers in that very region, and many of them are highly esteemed.

Without directly using native themes from Poland's highland, Stanislas Moniuszko succeeded in transmitting their rhythmic and melodic characteristics in his opera, *Halka*, first performed in 1848. Since it is believed that no Polish dramatic composer has previously expressed by dance scenes the Polish national temperament so perfectly, *Halka* achieved its one thousandth performance in 1935! Its first act contains a "grave, noble and courteous" Polonaise, and culminates in a Mazurka, one of Moniuszko's finest achievements. Original dances and amusements of Polish mountaineers are depicted in the first part of Act III. This composer's opera, *La Comtesse*, with a Polonaise as an entr'acte, was first performed in Warsaw in 1860.

Schwanda, opera by Jaromir Weinberger, stemmed directly from the people. Its popular character brought bitter condemnation at first, but was later accepted more cheerfully, as the present renown of its Polka attests. *Schwanda* is a background for other Czech dances also, and for Waltzes. Smetana's *Bartered Bride* depicts the exuberance of the Bohemian folk in their songs and dances. He also wrote ballet music into his *Zwei Witwen* (Two Widows). Bohuslav Martinu wrote an opera called *Les Jeux de la Ste. Vierge*, a group of Miracles of the Middle Ages, in which chorus and ballet are outstanding. This is in five popular tales, the second being the Dutch Miracle Play, *Mariken of Nimeguen*, with singers and dancers alternating in the execution of the action. The music contains lively polyrhythmics. The fourth tale is of the French legend, *Sister Pasqualine*, with a fire dance around Pasqualine's funeral pyre.

Dvorak's opera, *The Devil and Kate* is based on a folk tale, beginning with a saint's festival in a country tavern. Of course, there is dancing. Kate boldly offers to dance with the devil if he should appear. He does; she keeps her promise —finally dancing away with him. In the infernal regions a ballet of demons appears and succeeds in dancing Kate off the scene, for she, with her little cross, has become a source of annoyance to her captor. Village dances in the folk festival of Act II occur in Dvorak's *The Peasant a Rogue*.

One American composer has built an opera around a dancer : John Alden Hugo who, in writing *The Temple Dancer*, with its Snake Dance, was said to show the effect of religious prostitution on the intellect.

A more important American opera is *Merry Mount* by Howard Hanson, in which the Maypole Dances in the second act form the ballet. These dances have to do with celebration of Mayday by the cavaliers who have settled at Merry Mount. A later scene, the Hellish Rendezvous, opens with dances by witches and goblins and continues with a processional which has been used as material for dancing. Robert Russell Bennett's opera, *Maria Malibran*, returns to the pre-classic dance forms, such as the Bourrée, since the scene is laid in 1826.

One can mention only the most famed of all light operas and operettas in connection with choreographic music, because dances are the very backbone of such productions, and because much of this music is light in character. A good deal of it is similar in style to every other composition for this type of opera. There are, for example, dances in the last act of Nicolai's *Merry Wives of Windsor*. The ballet is one of insects and elves. Some of the lively dances are accompanied by chorus, but it is notable that, whereas a chorus of elves preceding the ballet is utterly charming, spritely music, the following dance music drops immediately into the commonplace. Offenbach had dances in the *Tales of Hoffman* and so far forgot the conventions in his *Orpheus in the Underworld* as to place in Act II a Bacchanale in which the Olympians dance the Cancan. There are many Galops in his operas (as in most works of this type). These have an even ¾ meter, but the actual dance step is limping though lively. It is said to be descended from a German peasant dance called Hopser.

Modern incidental music is rich in dance compositions. Perhaps the best known of all is Grieg's music for Ibsen's *Peer Gynt*, from which the suites are taken. In the beginning, Ibsen wrote to Grieg that he needed incidental music for *Peer Gynt* and specified that "the scene at the house where the wedding is celebrated must be made, with the aid of the ballet, more effective than it is in the book. For this it will be necessary to compose a special dance-melody, which is heard softly to the end of the act(25)." Finck names Anitra's Dance as expressing the voluptuous mystery of the East. Then he terms the Hall of the Mountain King also a kind of dance, but of different character, when Peer Gynt is pursued by spiteful gnomes. In the second suite from this incidental music is a quaint Arabian Dance which appears (in Grieg's original score) as a chorus of maidens. In the original music, some of it unpublished, Grieg had a Halling in the Wedding Scene, then a Spring Dance played by a peasant fiddler on the stage. There was still another dance episode in the music to the Mountain King Scene. In later life, Grieg(26) wrote this of an orchestral concert where Anitra's Dance was played as a quick Waltz: "It could not please me, as it was rather too much to stand . . . the most remarkable thing about it is, however, that people can listen to this and digest it."

Robert Russell Bennett wrote incidental music to Philip Barry's *The Wild Harps Playing*—music that is strictly choreographic, though the subject is lugubrious. The play takes place at the death of a young girl. Bennett wrote his music in that style because he felt that within the girl and her doctor, at that precise moment, a sort of dance was occurring.

Coleridge-Taylor wrote much ballet music into his incidental music for various plays, as did Ernest Chausson, Giuseppe Mule, and others. Debussy had an Ecstatic Dance in his music to d'Annunzio's mystery play, *The Martyrdom of Saint Sebastion*.

In days of yore, a ballet was a necessity in opera. Today, composers add or omit ballets at their own discretion, and nothing ever is said of the lack or the inclusion more than ordinary comment, should their works be fortunate enough to be given a hearing. Sometimes modern composers make an effort to unearth an opera subject which will give them a logical opportunity for a ballet, or for a dance of some sort, not because they feel it is customary, but because they are aware of theatrical possibilities, and are acquainted with human endurance and appreciation from the standpoint of their hearers. When the ordinary audience hears music, it finds its listening made easier by a momentary diversion and may even, as a contrast, later appreciate pure sound all the more. After all, an opera may be both a work of art, capable of appealing to the deepest emotions, and an entertainment. A ballet, inserted judiciously, may entertain, and may heighten the emotional appeal as well.

Certain modern composers have become so fond of the opera form that they prefer it above all others. In the words of Korngold(27): "Why write a ballet when the opera is so much more attractive, when the opera (which is the combination of all elements) may include the ballet with far greater effect?"

CHAPTER 11

NOTES

(1) Wagner, *Letters*, p. 18

(2) Searchinger, *Art of Music*, vol. 9, p. 301

(3) *The Dancing Times*, June, 1933, p. 225

(4) Martens, *Thousand and One Nights of Opera*, p. 13

(5) "Diaghileff himself experimented in the reform of opera in his famous production of 'Le Coq d'Or', when he found the only possible solution, the leading dancers of the day to act and mime, the leading singers as voices, and the programme was divided logically into a choreographic section and a vocal section, with a double cast . . . this is the only manner in which Strauss' 'Salome' can be performed."
Haskell, *Balletomania*, p. 186

(6) Strauss and von Hoffmannsthal, *Correspondence*, p. 30

(7) Strauss and von Hoffmannsthal, *Correspondence*, p. 302

(8) Strauss and von Hoffmannsthal, *Correspondence*, p. 306

(9) In a letter to the author from Hollywood, dated April 16, 1936

(10) Puccini, *Letters of Giacomo Puccini*, p. 166

(11) Stravinsky, *An Autobiography*, p. 40

(12) Riesemann, *Moussorgsky*, p. 228

(13) *See footnote 5, supra*

(14) Montagu-Nathan, *A Short History of Russian Music*, pp. 230-231

(15) Riesemann, *Moussorgsky*, p. 234

(16) Propert, *The Russian Ballet in Western Europe*, p. 113

(17) Gounod, *Gounod*, p. 217

(18) Parker, *Bizet*, p. 222

(19) Parker, *Bizet*, p. 238

(20) Parker, *Bizet*, p. 90

(21) Parker, *Bizet*, pp. 199-200

(22) Parker, *Bizet*, pp. 199-200

(23) *Musical Quarterly*, October, 1922, p. 609

(24) Martens, *Thousand and One Nights at the Opera*, p. 343

(25) Finck, *Grieg and His Music*, pp. 130-131

(26) Finck, *Grieg and His Music*, p. 226

(27) In an interview with Korngold at Warner Brothers Studio in Burbank, California, on March 12, 1936

MUSIC INSPIRED BY DANCE

This is really—some might say—a chapter on reading meanings into music. But who will deny a conscientious author a bit of speculation, especially if it be founded on fact? However, the writer does not wish to emulate those critics who complacently label as "dance music" everything that is regularly and piquantly rhythmed, or who simplify their own work by prescribing everything listed as a "Dance" as being purely and definitely choreographic. Neither premise is entirely correct. The writer will merely advance certain thoughts and repeat certain facts. The reader is to draw, from them, his own conclusions.

Much of music is indebted to the dance for its existence, whether the composers realized it or not. If it was not definitely written *for* the dance, it was inspired by it, as was Schumann's *Carnaval*. Conversely, many composers have used dance forms in the broader sense to express musically phases of life and death. When Howard Hanson's *Pan and the Priest* was danced, it was used to portray the eternal conflict between conservatism and revolt, between the spiritual and sensual elements in life. This work, however, was not written with the dance in mind, according to the composer, yet it adapts itself particularly well to that purpose. Malipiero's *Symphonies of Silence and of Death*, composed in 1909, contain a Danza Tragica. *Liszt's Todtentanz*, a Danse Macabre for piano and orchestra, is a series of tone sketches illustrating the pictures in Hans Holbein's *Dance of Death* at Basle. Each of these pictures is skillfully characterized by a variation. Spohr once wrote a symphony called *The Consecration of Tone*, describing the relation of sound to the various phases of life. It began in the Silence of Nature, went on to the Cradle, the Dance, the Serenade, the Battlefield, the Grave—showing that music accompanies man from the beginning to the end of his career, in all his moods. Others, besides composers, have used the dance, as a theme, to express Life. Havelock Ellis, in the belief that all Life is rhythm, named his book *The Dance of Life*.

Because of the stigma attached to the writing of frivolous dance music, composers, attracted by the piquant rhythms and seeing in them great possibilities, often used them in disguise —sometimes giving the music an abstract title, sometimes incorporating dance themes and rhythms into programme music. Such occurrences are frequent, but because they are necessarily veiled in the obscurity of the composers' minds, few definite assertions can be made about them.

There is yet another side to the question: a strange side. Many compositions with titles suggestive of the dance were never meant to be glorified by any sort of choreographic interpretation! Nor would some of the composers of such music be happy today if they were to see this done. There is the case of Alexandre Tcherepnine, who always has difficulty in finding names for his compositions. To him, music is simply music. Thus he wrote several pieces, as pure sound, though (for want of better titles) he called them Dances. His surprise was great when these pieces actually were used as dance accompaniments, for he had never intended them to be danced, just as he'd never thought of his *Bagatelles* as being music for dance. Similarly, people often dance to his religious, ecstatic *String Quartet*, opus 36, built around the subject of a Saint before canonization took place. Another instance is that of

Ernst Toch's *Jongleur* so often danced. This was definitely not meant for dance. After the war, when young composers liked to have fun, and festivals of modern music were given often, Toch was pleased to imitate a juggler occasionally. He needed an accompaniment for this imitation, but found no one able to play as he wished. He therefore jotted down his own accompaniment, which later became the effervescent *Jongleur*. It was then played, published and danced.

Unlike most composers, Joseph Achron not only suggests a choreographic use for his compositions, such as his *Improvisations, Four Fantastic Pictures, Coquetterie, Serenade, Les Sylphides*, and his *Statuettes*, but would seem to welcome an interpretation more fulsome than that of the concert stage. Perhaps he did not intend these compositions to be absolute music; perhaps he really wrote them with dance movement in mind! Tansman so far approved of the practice of dancing to his music that he made for Kurt Jooss a new version of his *Sonatine Transatlantique*, which has resolved itself into good ballet music. The same thing happened with Tansman's *Sextuor*. The idea had come to Tansman solely as a musical composition. He wrote it, but Adolph Bolm saw a dance in it. Therefore, he and the composer worked out a dance called *The Tragedy of the 'Cello*, picturing the rivalry of the 'cello and violin who court the flute, when the violin kills the 'cello in a duel. When the dance was completed, it was said to realize more completely the idea in the back of Tansman's mind when he created the original music.

In some instances, Adolph Bolm (being a dancer) feels that music has been given color and has thus achieved a greater success through the dance, especially when the treatment is so logical that it is difficult to believe that it was not originally created for the dance. Rimsky-Korsakow's *Schéhérazade*, for example, was not composed with the dance in mind, but Bakst, Diaghileff and Fokine invented a story so logical and so accurate that it is difficult to believe (declares Bolm) that it did not belong to the dance at the outset. When Bolm choreographed his Mechanical Ballet to Mossolow's *Iron Factory*, he worked only from hearing a four-hand piano score and from looking at the conductor's score. At the first orchestral rehearsal, Bolm had a momentary tinge of nervousness. Neither he nor his dancers were familiar with the music in its orchestral version. Disaster or not? His fears proved groundless. The complicated score was minutely expressed in the dance. Every movement corresponded to something in the music. Success greeted the performance, and Bolm gradually came to believe that this was an isolated case where, had he presumed to give the composer the idea beforehand, it might not have turned out half so well.

Korngold, while declaring that none of his music was inspired by dance movement, seemed delighted with the fact that much of it, particularly the *Rübezahl*, has been danced. "It doesn't spoil it at all!" he cried. Cyril Scott is more complacent about the wide use of his music by dancers: "I can't say that many of my pieces have been inspired by dance movements as such. Dancers, however, often make use of my pieces. My *Ballad* for piano was once used in this way by a group of dancers who invented a scenario around it." Joseph Schillinger, on the other hand, actually admits that his orchestral *March of the Orient*, his pianistic *Excentriade* and his *Two Dance Vocalisés* for voice and piano were definitely inspired by dance.

Of Bach's *Peasant Cantata*, Ernest Newman says[1], "Not only are the songs delicious in themselves, but most of them are cast in well-known dance rhythms, and they seem to cry out for the accompaniment of the ballet." Bach's *Phoebus and Pan*, when presented as a sort of opera by Sir Thomas Beecham, utilizes the French Suites as a sort of incidental ballet. However, on the whole, *Phoebus and Pan* is more reminiscent of the dance than that. It is a secular, allegoric cantata, intended by Bach to be a satire. Phoebus represents serious music, while Pan typifies lighter composers, whose music "tickles the ear without stimulating the brain." As Rutland Boughton[2] puts it: "Bach's problem in *Phoebus and Pan* was to show whether the simple peasant dance rhythms and tunes or the elaborate development of polyphony were of the greater value. What he really stated was, that a great musician does not oppose but incorporates earlier and lowlier expressions of his art . . . his songs for Pan are as fine as the others. Even for the greatest of musicians, the music of simple people was a thing of great value."

From 1830 onwards, Rossini dashed off many elegant, graceful drawing-room compositions. There was a Bolero and a Tyrolienne—but the best known is *La Danza*, a Neopolitan Tarantella, first written for mezzo-soprano, later sung by tenors. When Respighi built the ballet *La Boutique Fantasque* out of Rossini's long-buried concert pieces, *La Danza* was included. Later in his life, Rossini wrote satirical pieces, one of which is a *Tarantelle Pur Sang*, a realistic picture of a Tarantella as danced in a little Italian town. This was later added to other pieces that formed the suite, *Rossiniana*. This also contains a *Petite Valse*.

Cyril Scott(3) tells us that "with Schumann, the title of a piece was an aid to its comprehension. And yet—significant fact—the piece was conceived first and the fitting title afterwards; which goes to show that Schumann, instead of circumscribing his musical inspiration by a literary idea, allowed the former to have full sway. The *Carnaval* and the *Papillons* are a series of small pieces placed under one comprehensive title. His inherent simplicity made him write so often in small forms." The dance titles in the *Carnaval* are Valse Noble, Lettres Dansantes, Valse Allemande, yet it is generally conceded to be almost wholly inspired by dance. Schumann wrote that "It was written mostly for different occasions, and excepting a few of the pieces is all founded on the notes A, S (A Flat), C, H (B Natural) which form the name of a little Bohemian town where I had a musical friend." When the *Carnaval* was later orchestrated by Rimsky-Korsakow, Liadov, Glazounow and Tcherepnine and finally danced, there was said to be a perfect fusion of music and action. In one ballet version, however, the astute Francis Kendig(4) found that the ballet did not interpret the glowing pantomime indicated by Schumann.

Said he, "They employed the notes which he left, but little else."

Schumann wrote well-defined Viennese Waltzes and German peasant dances into his *Papillons*. He also wrote a vocal duet called *Tanzlied*, with "whirling dancers, fluttering garlands, tantalizing maidens, love-sick youths, aching hearts . . . all in the dance." *Paradise and the Peri* was the title of a Cantata written by Schumann in 1843. It made up for a lack of oriental color by containing a Dance of the Houris.

Schumann (op. 20), Dvorak (op. 101, two books) Grieg and Tschaikowsky, were a few composers who wrote *Humoresques*, short, quaint pieces generally in some dance rhythm. All of these are not whimsical, since it has now become difficult to express humor in music by strange harmonies. Those that once seemed strange are now commonplace (witness the flatness of the Rubinstein *Étude on False Notes* in our day) and rhythms can be used only to depict whimsies.

When Berlioz was nineteen, he made his first attempt at programme music in his op. 14, *Symphonie Fantastique* or *Episodes in the Life of an Artist*. Movement II, Le Bal, introduces the hearers to a Ball and to sensual Waltz rhythms, a scene of festivity. Meanwhile, a single musical figure, the *idée fixe* recurs, to represent the face of the artist's beloved. Technically, this movement shows Berlioz's skill in the symphonic handling of a Waltz rhythm. The melody of the beloved continually interrupts the brilliant dance music as it is re-asserted. In the final movement, when love has proved false and the artist is about to be buried by demons, the melody recurs as a common, vulgar dance theme, fully expressing the demoniac satire involved.

The work of Berlioz has been unsung for many years. Would it not be possible, then, that he (wherever he is) would today be grateful for any sort of recognition, so long as it be intelligent? Yet when Massine decided to dance to this *Symphonie Fantastique* (based, at the outset, on a dance idea) English musicians held a spirited debate in print. Constant Lambert led the opposition, while Ernest Newman(5) led the defence in several such pertinent sentences that they are well worth recording here: "Berlioz has never been, among 'sensitive musicians' the Sacred Person, the sort of Grand Lama of Music, that Brahms has always been to certain communities. The *Fantastique*, indeed, so obviously calls for balletic treatment that many people must have wondered why it was not taken in hand by some choreographer or other long ago. . . . One feels, indeed, that had Berlioz had a choreographer like Massine to his hand it would have been in some such form as this that he would have planned to have his work presented. But in that case he would probably have modified the musical part of it at one or two points. Having to tell the whole story to a concert audience in music pure and simple, he naturally turned his incomparable gift for orchestral description on the business of suggesting the atmosphere of the scene to the eye through the ear; and now and then he has done his own part of the job so thoroughly that nothing that the choreographer can put before the eye can be anything but the faintest shadow of what Berlioz makes us visualize, so to speak, through the ear . . . for if ever there was a 'visuel' in music it was Berlioz. . . ."

Shall we say Brahms' *Capriccios* were *not* inspired by some feeling of dance movement? (Fuller-Maitland(6) describes the one in C Sharp Minor, op. 76, no. 3, as a "glorified Courant.") And what of Schubert's many *Moments Musicales* in dance rhythms, of Beethoven's *Bagatellen*, op. 33, no. 6, and of Grieg's whimsical *Puck*? Liszt(7) once called Chopin's *Seventh Prelude* the *Polish Danseuse* who lifted her little feet slightly from the floor and executed her dance with consummate grace and charming postures.

Scriabin's *Prometheus, Poem of Fire* had a programme, but was evidently not intended to be danced, though later it was. According to the composer's intention, it was to take the form of a mystic ceremony. The chorus was to be clothed in white vestments and the atmosphere to be that of a service rather than a concert. Also, the color keyboard was to be used.

Balakireff's symphonic poem, *Tamara*, was created as the

composer went along the Nevsky Prospect. He wrote to Tschaikowsky that he did not walk, but danced along, and composed part of *Tamara* meanwhile. It was based on a poem of Lermontoff which recites the legend of a Georgian princess who first attracted strangers to her castle, then invited them to join her in an animated, exhilarating dance, at the climax of which she stabbed them and threw the corpses into the river Terek. *Tamara* was regarded as one of Balakireff's finest works. He derived much of its gorgeous coloring from what he heard while on a tour of the Caucasus. It is oriental in melody and harmony. Martens(8) describes it in this fashion: Orgiastic dance themes ride rhythms of torrential sweep. This symphonic poem was later danced. And why not? Was it not inspired by a poem which was, in its turn, inspired by dance?

The fertile imagination of Vladimir Rebikov (1866-) widened the scope of musical composition when it produced his melo-mimicry, a blend of music and pantomime. His six melo-mimics or mimo-dramas, op. 11, were based on a legend. Often he disregarded tonality. His *Idyl*, op. 17, no. 2, is a dance of two little fauns to a flute, played by an old faun in the darkening woods.

In Moussorgsky's *Pictures at an Exhibition*, the Ballet of Unhatched Chickens is based on a costume design by Hartmann for a performance of the ballet of Trilby. Moussorgsky has given it to us as a scherzino, musically. This composer also wrote a song called *Gopak*. "Hoi, hop! dance the Gopak. I am young, my man is an old Cossack!" sings a young woman as she whirls in an amorous dance with an irresistible swing to it. Many other composers have written songs dealing with the dance. Moses Milner's *Tanz, Tanz, Meidele Tanz* is said to have a melodic swirl of enchanting agility and delicacy. Satie wrote a song called *Danseuse,* while in Coleridge-Taylor's *Bon-Bon Suite,* op 68 (written in 1909), the last song is *Say, What Shall We Dance?*

For his *Spanish Caprice*, op. 34, Rimsky-Korsakow used Spanish themes of dance character, and they gave him a rich basis for varied orchestral effects. Tschaikowsky(9) wrote to him: "Your Spanish Caprice is a *colossal masterpiece of instrumentation,* and you may regard yourself as the greatest master of the present day." Truly, it was epoch-making in the field of orchestration. Number four in the Caprice is a savage, passionate Gypsy dance song, with the one wild theme serving for the whole movement. The final movement is a Fandango Asturiano. When that other symphonic poem, *The Thousand and One Nights* by Rimsky-Korsakow, was danced as *Schéhérazade,* the composer's widow strongly objected to its use, claiming that it was not meant for such treatment. It was danced anyway, in 1910, with Fokine's choreography.

It is rather generally admitted that Chabrier's *España Rhapsody* was inspired by Spanish dance, for when this composer visited Spain, he wrote back to a friend(10): "The national music of Spain is of an incomparable richness. I am jotting down all that I can scize. . . ." as indeed he did. He jotted down guitar rhythms, heel rhythms, and even the rhythm of a man seated near the dancers, beating on the floor with his cane!

Many are the compositions inspired by balls, or festivals. Aaron Copland in 1935 wrote El Salón México (the name of a dance hall in Mexico City) based on popular Mexican themes. Respighi's *Feste Romane* is a musical picture of Rome's festivals. Massenet's *Fête Bohéme* in *Scènes Pittoresques* was doubtless inspired by a students' gay ball. Glazounow wrote a *Carnaval Overture,* Édouard Lalo wrote carnival music entitled *Arlequin,* and Smetana wrote *The Carnival of Prague,* containing subtitles relating to dance—all for orchestra. Gounod's *Souvenir d'un Bal* for two flutes and strings, is a posthumous work. Michael Ivanov's *The Insects' Ball* is an orchestral composition. In Tschaikowsky's first suite for orchestra, the fifth movement was an *Écho du Bal,* but was eventually named *Giant's Dance.* Bizet included *The Ball* in his *Jeux d'enfants.*

Although Joaquin Turina's orchestral *Danzas Fantásticas, Bailete, Danzas Gitanas* and *Danzas Andaluzas* all have titles suggestive of dance, the composer evidently did not intend them to be dance-pieces and declares instead(11) that they were not only inspired by the Andalusian dance, but were based on popular Andalusian dance rhythms.

Debussy's *La Mer* has a final episode in which the wind dances with the sea. Probably many more of his compositions are inspired by dance—certainly by a feeling of movement! The *Arabesques*, perhaps, or the *Iberia Suite*.

The early *Sarabandes*, *Gnossiennes* (based on Flaubert's *Salammbo*) and *Gymnopédies* of Satie have been danced so often, in spite of their extreme gravity, that it is difficult to believe that they were not intended for just that purpose. Later in his life, Satie's ironic humor began to assert itself. He wrote *childlike* music for children, too—not such music as Schumann wrote: as an adult speaking to children. Ravel wrote a series of duets, *Ma Mère l'Oye* for children. They were so descriptive, so atmospheric, so detailed and so charming in spite of their brevity (the *Pavane de la Belle au Bois Dormant* is not more than twenty measures in length) that they were later transformed into a ballet.

Vincent d'Indy openly admitted that his *Ishtar*, a set of seven symphonic variations, is a dance-poem. Each variation represents one of the steps of Ishtar's descent. They begin with rich and complex forms and grow simpler as they progress till, at the close, only the theme remains. With this unusual musical scheme, Ishtar is stripped of her veils and is supposed to be nude at the end.

Goossens is silent on the question of whether or not his *Eternal Rhythm* was inspired by dance, as is Infante on the subject of his *Ritmo*, although Turina admits that his symphonic *Ritmo* is based on Andalusian dance rhythms and was conceived in the form of a ballet.

Two Americans have written noteworthy compositions in characteristic vein: Douglas Moore with his *Barnum Suite* and Deems Taylor with his *Circus Days*. Of the former, John Tasker Howard(12) said, "Here is music that comes from the dance-halls: not of today, but of the era of the country fiddler and brass bands, when people were not afraid to be sentimental." For the latter, Taylor found inspiration in the peculiar rhythm of life behind the big top: waltzing elephants, equestrians and trapeze artists. All this forms itself into a sort of dance, the spirit of which Taylor caught admirably in his music.

One might continue indefinitely to cite cases where commentators have read a dance meaning or feeling into compositions which were intended to be abstract music. Very few works have escaped being so described at one time or another, no matter how lofty their aims, since the dance, too, (on occasion) also has lofty aims!

CHAPTER 12

NOTES

(1) Newman, *A Musical Motley*, p. 199
(2) Boughton, *The Reality of Music*, p. 177
(3) Scott, *The Influence of Music on History and Morals*, p. 65
(4) *Saturday Night*, July 18, 1936
(5) Controversy recorded in the Sunday issues of the *New York Times*, in John Martin's column, beginning on November 1, 1936
(6) Fuller-Maitland, *Bach's Keyboard Suites*, p. 8
(7) *Étude*, March, 1926, p. 179
(8) Martens, *Thousand and One Nights at the Opera*, p. 139
(9) *Life and Letters of Peter Ilyich Tschaikowsky*, p. 521
(10) *Musical Quarterly*, October, 1935, p. 458
(11) In a letter to the author from Madrid, dated March 7, 1936
(12) Howard, *Our American Music*, p. 526

IDEALIZED DANCE MUSIC

In many lands, modern musicians are trying desperately, in one way or the other, to preserve their native folklore, whether it be by recording, annotating, photographing, describing or transcribing. The effort is noteworthy from a historical standpoint. It also aids in giving a "national" character to the music of the individual. Since dance-songs form such a large part of folk music, they have been idealized by composers throughout the ages.

Moreover, the other dance forms that have been idealized by composers are legion. Consider the many who have written Minuets: Puccini, Respighi, Satie, Ravel, Debussy, Casella, Schönberg, Prokofieff. The latter has modernized and given new life to many old dance forms. His Gavottes are charming. They have a precision similar to Gossec's classic Gavotte (1734-1829) with a decidedly piquant harmonic coloring added. Dohnanyi and Respighi have also created music within the limits of classic dance forms. Respighi has transcribed liberally for piano the old dances and lute arias of early Italian composers, as well as including a dance of different character in his *Brazilian Suite* for orchestra.

Some writers have the audacity to claim that the idealized

JOHANN STRAUSS JR.

Leading his orchestra in 1853

From a lithograph published at that time

ADOLPH BOLM

PAUL WHITEMAN

dance forms of the masters were never meant to be danced! While this may have been true in some instances, it was not always so. One must be wary of generalizations in cases like this. Whatever the original intention, modern dancers have proved these writers to be unobservant by adapting almost every rhythmic composition—and some not so rhythmic—to their own needs, much to the disgust of conservatives. No one should condone flagrant misinterpretation of any music, but surely judgment as to whether a composition should or should not be used for dancing should be rendered on the basis of the excellence or inferiority of the individual use to which it is put. Then, if dancers *must* dance to the classics, is it not far better for them to utilize compositions that originally stemmed from the dance than abstract music which will surely have a different meaning for everyone who has previously known and loved it? Finally, the writer is not so sure that the majority of idealized dance pieces were not intended for dancing. It is the habit of admirers to become far more austere and zealous than those whom they admire, and it is just possible that the admirers of the classicists have built around them a wall of austerity that they never possessed nor wished to possess, as evidenced by many of their letters.

Those who play idealized dance music should be well acquainted with the particular dance and with its steps, even to the extent of learning and dancing those steps themselves, if they cannot visualize them, else their interpretations will fall far short of the mark. Idealized dances are far more charming when played easily and naturally than when "interpreted" with all the fury and artifice of the virtuoso. As an illustration, let us cite the case of Berlioz's *Roman Carnival Overture,* originally written as an introduction to the second act of his opera, *Benvenuto Cellini.* The Saltarello in the opera is also found in the Allegro section of the Overture. A conductor of Berlioz's time (Habeneck) once conducted this deliberately and slowly. The dancers, at their wits' ends, appealed to Berlioz, who agreed that the tempo should be quicker. In his irritation, Habeneck struck his desk with the violin bow, which broke.

Berlioz exclaimed, "Good Heavens! If you were to break fifty
bows that would not prevent your time being too slow by half.
It is a Saltarello you are conducting." Habeneck ended the
rehearsal angrily. Years later, Berlioz presented the same
Overture in concert and it was encored in spite of the fact that
the woodwind players had had no rehearsal and the Allegro
Vivace was played in the whirlwind tempo of the Transteverine
dancers. Habeneck was present, and Berlioz thought he
actually seemed disappointed at the success. Yet, if Habeneck
had unbent long enough on the former occasion to understand
the Saltarello step and movements, the trouble would never
have occurred.

There are three ways in which composers may use folk
dance tunes. One is to harmonize the entire song and present
it, as it were, *au naturel*. Another is to build a large composition on a particular dance theme, embroidering it until it seems
much larger than it really is. Still another way is to adopt
the spirit and style of the folk tune without employing any
recognizable theme in the process. The latter involves the
most genuinely creative impulse of the three. Saminsky(1)
believes that all national music must be constantly re-vitalized
by new harmonies in order to live, just as absolute music must
be periodically re-vitalized by the folk stream in order to
endure. The tremendous amount of folk music idealizations
now existing shows that many composers agree with him.

The modernizing of dance forms, MacDowell(2) tells
us, has been undertaken by almost every writer from Scarlatti,
who died in 1757, to our day. Scarlatti joined sections together with isolated measures, repeated sections and phrases
before completing the period, and added short codas to periods
indiscriminately. Since then, everyone has added to or cur-
tailed the accepted forms by putting two forms together: hence
the Fantasie-Mazurka, and so forth. (Schumann(3), in speaking of Taubert's *Alla Polacca*, where Waltz and Polonaise
rhythms cross each other, declares that it is an "old, but always
agreeable idea.") Wagner represented the culminating point
of the modern tendency to disregard forms which had their

origin in dances.   Indeed, the dance played an important rôle in the shaping of the art of music; for to it music owes periodicity, form, the shaping of phrases into measures, even its rests. And in this music is not the only debtor, for poetry owes its very "feet" to the dance.

So true is this, that the statement has recently been made that the average musician's acquaintance with the dance music of different peoples is largely through the music of various national composers.

Russia is said to be the richest country in the world as regards folk dance-songs, because of her great size and the different types of people she mothers.   It is on these many folk songs and dances that the neo-Russians sought to base their music.   Stravinsky (4) has decried, to a certain extent, the cult of idealizing folklore, mentioning that "naïve but dangerous tendency which prompts them to re-make an art that has already been created instinctively by the genius of the people.   It is a sterile tendency, and an evil from which many talented artists suffer."   Doubtless Stravinsky explains his own excursions into the folk realm with the knowledge that there is a difference between cosmopolitanism and nationalism.   The same music may have an entirely different significance in the hands of different composers.

When one speaks of idealized Russian folk music, his thoughts immediately jump to Glinka who was, in a sense, father of that cult.   It is noteworthy that Glinka's most famous, most praised idealizations were those of folk dances!   Not only did he write a Russian *Kamarinskaia* but he explored the dance music of other lands with a view to his own musical composition.   (Here, lest we forget to give credit where it is due, let us mention Carlo Canobio (1741-1822) who, fifty years before Glinka, wrote the Overture and Interlude to the Russian opera, *Oleg*.   In the prelude to Act III he used the traditional Kamarinskaia tune, changed into the rhythm of a court Minuet and worked out in variations.   That his venture did not win the acclaim of Glinka's may be the result of many causes—perhaps because Russian music was not then ready for this innovation, perhaps because it had not the force of Glinka's later idealization.)   Wrote Tschaikowsky(5) : "How astonishingly original is Glinka's *Kamarinskaia*, from which all the Russian composers who followed him (including myself) continue to this day to borrow contrapuntal and harmonic combinations directly they have to develop a Russian dance tune! This is done unconsciously; but the fact is, Glinka managed to concentrate in one short work what a dozen second-rate talents would only have invented with the whole expenditure of their powers.   And it was this same Glinka who, at the height of his maturity, composed such a weak trivial thing as the *Polonaise* for the Coronation or the *Children's Polka*, of which he speaks in his Memoirs at such length, and with such self-satisfaction, as though it had been a masterpiece."   And later(6) : "In symphonic music (such as *Kamarinskaia* and the two *Spanish Overtures*) Glinka simply played about like an amateur, and yet we are astounded at the force and originality of his gifts.   What would he not have accomplished had he worked as did the great masters of Western Europe?"   Indeed, the *Kamarinskaia* was an inelegant peasant wedding dance, heard by the composer in his native village, though it was fresh and fine melodically.   Glinka's genius glorified it.

Liszt wrote(7) in a letter of Glinka's *Jota Aragonesa*: ". . . the lively and piquant originality of this charming piece, so delicately cut and proportioned, finished with such taste and art! How the happiest surprises spring constantly out of the logical developments . . . without a single moment of heaviness or fatigue!"   Coming from Liszt, this was high praise indeed, for he also made use of the Jota Aragonesa.   Tschaikowsky, too(8), mentioned the simplicity of Glinka's *Jota Aragonesa* theme and the splendid structure created upon it. Glinka's Spanish material was gathered during his two years in Spain.

Dargomijsky (1813-1869: not one of the Russian Five, although mentioned in a previous chapter in connection with their reforms) composed a *Cosatschoque*, an orchestral fantasy on a little Russian Cossack Dance.   Moussorgsky's *Trepak* and *The Commander* are each a Song and Dance of Death. The former depicts a suffering peasant who has lost his way in the snowstorm. Death sympathizes with him and promises him comforts he has been denied in this life, to the tune of a Trepak. The entrancing dance tune becomes mocking and satirical just before the close of the song. These Songs and Dances of Death are said to rank among Moussorgsky's finest compositions. Liadov wrote a Russian Dance for orchestra as well as an orchestral Mazurka (a rustic scene near the village tavern), an orchestral Polonaise in memory of Pushkin and another dedicated to Anton Rubinstein. In 1915 Spendiarov wrote a symphonic *Dance-Song of the Crimean Tartars*. National Russian dances were composed by Rubinstein, Nápravník, Tschaikowsky, Rimsky-Korsakow and many others. Many were the Russian masters who idealized the dance music of other lands, such as Borodin in his two Mazurkas in the *Petite Suite*, and Glinka, Glazounow, Scriabin, Taneiev and Glière in their Mazurkas.

Poland, to which land the Mazurka belongs, claims to find traces of national folk dance melodies even in its ancient Christmas carols. Outside of the country, Polish dances made their entrance into art music toward the end of the sixteenth century. By the seventeenth century, they were widely popular. The dances of this epoch seem to fall into a particular form composed of two parts, the first part slow, in duple time; the second part faster, in triple time, but based on the same theme as the first.

Chopin is doubtless the most famous of all those who have idealized Polish dance tunes, though his music is often not recognized as dance music when it is so misinterpreted as to lose its inherent rhythmic vitality. Chopin, in turn, was himself idealized, when in 1901 Giacomo Orefice wrote the opera, *Chopin*, utilizing themes from Chopin's dance pieces and other compositions to tell his love story. Chopin remained almost entirely within the already-set dance forms, but within their limits did novel things. For example, the Polonaise is a dance that originated in 1573, when Henry of France became King

of Poland. At one of the grand ceremonials for his coronation, a stately procession of his court nobles passed before
him. The music accompanying this formal march was the first
Polonaise. It was adopted as a special feature of German
state balls in the earlier part of the nineteenth century, with
the guests touring the room in couples with a peculiar, halting
step. Prince Oginski's Polonaises were said to have enchanted
the Polish people in 1800. The Polonaise was also used as a
part of some instrumental suites. Bach, Handel, Weber and
Schubert wrote splendid ones.

When Chopin decided to write in this form, did he write
music for a stately procession with a peculiar halting step?
Not at all. An example of his power to inject drama into
conventional forms is the warlike Polonaise in A Major, often
termed the *Military Polonaise*, the rhythm of which gradually
gathers force, and which ends defiantly. It is said that Chopin,
while composing it, was terrified by the vision of a procession
of knights and warriors advancing upon him. Another Polonaise of note is the *Grosse Brilliante Polonaise* in E Flat Major
for piano and orchestra, with its preceding Andante Spianato.

Yet Chopin owed much to Poland: its people, the country,
its folk songs and its dances. He was steeped in Polish folklore, and (particularly in his Mazurkas) he utilized the folk
modes, even when no folk theme was apparent. Felipe Ped-
rell(9) declared that "Hadow says the great artists have no
nationality, but his sentence is refuted superbly by Haydn,
Glinka, Dvorak, Chopin. . . . All the essentials of Chopin's
works speak of the assimilation of the Slav element: sometimes
it is visible, and seems copied from the natural, as in some
Polonaises and Mazurkas; at other times that element is invisible, assimilated by the rare and suggestive divination of the
creator." That Chopin was aware of this characteristic is
evident from a letter written by George Sand to the American
Henry Harris (about 1867) that "the splendid lusty peasant
of Berri is a thing gone by now, and that pretty old dance the
Bourrée is replaced by stupid country dances; our folk songs

of the district once so admirable, which roused the enthusiasm of Chopin . . . are taking a back seat."

Cyril Scott has recognized Chopin's source of inspiration as being the folk, as has Mme. Lobaczewska(10), who said: Chopin discovered in folklore the passions and magic of the Past. And he took from it the emblem of a pure musical form. Here Chopin ceased to be a romantic to become the most daring of innovators. The patriot transformed the Polonaise and the Mazurka into highly developed modern dance forms. Schumann's(11) comment on the subject was: Chopin has elevated the Mazurka to a small art-form.

Chopin, like Mozart, was a composer who knew the dance-forms for which he wrote so well that he could dance them himself on occasion. On November 14, 1829, he wrote in a letter (12) that "She insisted on my dancing, so I had to dance the Mazur. . . ." Later, from Vienna, he wrote(13): "Yesterday at the Bayer's we danced the Mazurka."

In various ways, the Mazurka is mentioned often in Chopin's letters. From Dresden on August 26, 1829, he wrote(14): "We had to write our names in Hauke's book, which is devoted to those who visit the Prague Museum. . . . So each of us had to think of something to say. . . . What was a musician to do here? Luckily, Maciejowski hit on the idea of writing a four-verse Mazurka [Translator's note: These old national dances have words] so I added the music and inscribed myself together with my part, as originally as possible. Hauke was pleased; it was a Mazur for him, celebrating his services to the Slavonic world." On another occasion (April 10, 1830), he wrote, "Here is some comic news: Orlowski has made my themes into Mazurkas and Galops; however, I have asked him not to print them." Later, in regard to his own compositions, he wrote, "I don't send the Mazurkas because they are not copied yet; they are not for dancing." In 1848 he spoke of Mme. Viardot *singing* his Mazurkas and having to repeat them at a Covent Garden concert.

Many of Chopin's Mazurkas are strongly contrapuntal,

ranging from simple canons to more complicated structures. Few among the many he has written resemble each other, declared Robert Schumann(15) of these Mazurkas. He mentioned among the four Mazurkas comprising Op. 30, one with a sudden close in fifths "which will make German cantors throw up horrified hands above scandalized heads. And yet, different epochs seem to have different ears!" Schumann, as musician and critic, was undeniably an admirer of Chopin. In reviewing a Mazurka by Bergson, Schumann(16) said, "The above-mentioned Mazurka evidently has Chopin on its mind. . . . Even Chopin himself has lately altered in many ways. Imitators usually appear a few years after their original, and now we must listen to wonderful Chopinian embroideries from others as something new, though their inventor already considers them out of fashion." Again, Schumann commented aptly on salon dance music: "If we wish to find a reflection of Chopin's visionary, somewhat Mazurka-like Waltz music, or Liszt's stormy Hungarianisms, in elegant Viennese union, we need only take up the Waltzes of Thalberg. They might be reviewed without being looked at. Nothing more is to be expected but glittering, fluttering pianoforte dance music. Chopin and Liszt have also written for the dancing room. We may perceive the difference between them and Thalberg."

Chopin wrote in other dance forms besides the Mazurka and the Polonaise: Waltzes, a Bolero, Ecossaises, Krakowiaks and a Tarantella. If one compares the Ecossaises (Scotch Dances) of Beethoven and Chopin, one finds them equally charming, but totally different in conception and treatment. Also, they are both different from Weber's six *Ecossaises* for piano, written in 1802 and dedicated to the beautiful sex of Hamburg. Chopin's two idealizations of the Krakowiak were early works and are said to be uninteresting. (Other Polish and Russian composers who have written Krakowiaks are Paderewski, Blumenfeld, Zarembski, Noskowski.) One of Chopin's Krakowiaks is for piano and orchestra: the *Grand Concert-Rondo* in F Major, op. 14, written in 1827.

Chopin's *Tarantella*, op. 43, today seems charming, but

tame. Yet, when it was composed, Schumann commented (17):
"In Chopin's most daring manner, we see the madly-whirling
dancers before us, until our own senses seem to reel. We will-
ingly forgive the master for the wildness of his imagination."
In 1841 Chopin himself (18) wrote to Juljan Fontana, "I send
you the Tarantella. Be kind and copy it; but first go to look
at the *Recueil* of Rossini's songs, or rather songs edited by
him, in which there is a Tarantella in la; I don't know whether
it is written in ⁶⁄₈ or in ¹²⁄₈. People write both ways; but I
should like it to be the way Rossini has it."

Modern Polish composers are not content with a mere
harmonization of old themes, or even with writing in the old
dance forms. They try to write free stylizations of the folk
melody, adding to it folk harmony, rhythm and spirit. In
short, they retain the essence of what Chopin accomplished, but
they have far departed from any suggestion of a salon style.
They wish to draw closer to the source. Szymanowski first
indicated this style, in such works as his *Mazurkas*. Roman
Palester's orchestral *Dance of Osmoloda*, the dance suites of
Wiechowicz and Maklakiewicz, the *Symphonie Montagnarde*
of Kondracki, and Tansman's *Four Polish Dances* and *Mazurkas* for nine instruments, are also examples of this style. The
latter composer, according to Schwerké, often transformed the
rhythms of Polish dances into a Scherzo or Trio, as in his
Symphony in A Minor, *Symphonietta*, *Third String Quartette*
and *Suite Divertissement*. Extremely popular at the present
time in Poland is the orchestral *Houblon* by Stanislas Wiechowicz, professor in the Poznan Conservatory. *Houblon* is a
Polish wedding dance.

Though Paderewski wrote a brilliant and commanding
Polonaise in addition to his larger works, such as the opera
Manru with its spirited Gypsy dances, none of these works is
as well known and as beloved as his *Minuet in G*. This is the
case with many composers whose big compositions pass unnoticed while their tidbits are played unceasingly. This Minuet
was originally written by Paderewski in the style of Mozart,
without ornaments, to hoodwink two old gentlemen who be-

lieved that Mozart had written the world's most beautiful music and that there could never be anyone quite like him. Their discovery of Paderewski's hoax was a bit of a shock to them, but later they became very fond of the new Minuet. When Paderewski first showed this to Leschetizky, the latter accurately foretold its popularity and launched it on the road to fame by having his wife, Mme. Essipoff, play it at one of her concerts.

Although one of Smetana's early desires was to idealize the Polka as Chopin had idealized the Mazurka, he later was accustomed to fly into fits of indignation over the mere thought that he owed anything to folk music(19)! Therefore, his debt must have been unconscious. Yet, he wrote many Bohemian Polkas, and other dance forms. His *River Moldau*, a tone poem, employs the Polka. He wrote scarcely any music without the imprint of the folk.

The Moravian Vojtěch Řihovský, born in 1871, wrote *Bohemian Dances* for orchestra, op. 18. J. Móry, Moravian, who was born in 1892, wrote for orchestra (op. 18) some *Slovac Pastoral Dances*, as well as a *Slovac Dance Suite* (op. 19) called *At the Foot of Krivan Mountain*. Many years before this, the Jugoslav Vatroslav Lisinski (1819-1854) had proved himself a worthy successor to Haydn in recognizing the charm of Croatian folk tunes and had written orchestral Polonaises and other dances. Wolfgang Fortner has lately written a piano *Rondo on Schwabian Folk Dances*, using typical rhythms from the traditional peasant merrymaking and containing popular Plattschuh Dances. The Rumanian Filip Lazăr has several dances in his *Wallachian Suite* for orchestra.

Dvorak's *Slavonic Dances*, in two series, took the world by storm. They were fortunate enough to appear at a psychological moment. Old forms in music were being discarded; musicians were groping for something new. Dvorak supplied the answer to their questions by returning to the folk for his material, just as Diaghileff once, after having exhausted the ballet novelties at his command, created a sensation by returning to pure classicism. The *Slavonic Dances* were first written for piano, though they are now frequently heard in orchestral versions. The first series is Czech in character. In the second series, some of the dances are Yugoslav, and one is a little Russian Dumka. Both series contain stormy, high-spirited Furiants. The Minuets are slow, reminiscent of those danced in classic days. These dances have been called barbaric. Certainly they are full of fire and temperament. Hoffmeister(20) describes them as bearing also the stamp of classical purity, clarity and fastidiousness of workmanship. Their structure is delicate, the counterpoint characteristic, the figuration original and the orchestral colors masterly. In every respect the dances are symphonic in technic.

Dvorak broadened his own style to include characteristics of all the Slav peoples, not merely those of his own land. He wrote two albums of Waltzes for piano, one album of Mazurkas, a Furiant, and a *Goblin's Dance*. His *Polonaise* for 'cello and piano was a posthumous work. Dvorak's father came of a family of village musicians, and the composer himself spent his youth in rural surroundings. Is it then surprising that long-forgotten dance themes and rhythms should recur to him in later years, and should repeatedly be evident in his works? "Probably he drew upon them, as from some secret source, for the rhythmic power which lives with such intensity in his music. This, and other . . . characteristics, influence the content and form of his compositions," declares Hoffmeister(21). It is interesting to note that despite his own family's interest in music, Dvorak's father objected to it as a career for his son. When Dvorak wished to gain paternal consent to such a career, he proudly brought the orchestral score of a Polka to be played by the village band and he was struck dumb when, instead of harmony, hideous discords assailed his ears. He did not know that trumpets are transposing instruments, and he had written for them in the key he expected to hear. This fiasco did little to change his father's mind, and he was later forced to pay for his own musical tuition by playing viola in a popular dance band.

"Probably," venture Bauer and Peyser(22), "No other

music is so dependent on language as is the Hungarian. The syllables and their accent are the bases of the rhythm which is fundamentally dance music." We may then assume that what we know as Hungarian music is really folk dance music, or based on folk dance music.

The controversy over the various idealizations of this music will surely never be settled satisfactorily. For that there is much controversy there is no doubt. On the one hand, Brahms' arrangements have been called masterly. On the other hand, Cecil Sharp says(23) that "Modal folk airs have suffered grievously at the hands of modern musicians. Curiously enough, Brahms, who had the deepest affection for folk music, is one of the worst offenders. Of his modal airs, no one is harmonized in its own mode . . . and the spirit of modulation is usually foreign to folk airs, though it is the modern habit to modulate with great frequency."

When a Gypsy band was criticized for not playing one of Liszt's fifteen *Hungarian Rhapsodies*, with its dance tunes, as Liszt wrote it, the leader of the band said vehemently, "Is it my fault that Liszt was unable to put down on paper the music as he heard it played by my father?"(24) Then, along came Béla Bartók who, with Zoltán Kodály, has transcribed many of the national dances of Hungary—with the claim that Liszt utilized no authentic Magyar music, but passed off period street airs as the typical folk tunes of his native land. To that statement, Leonard Liebling added that, in any case, Liszt's choice of Hungarian music was decidedly more attractive than Bartók's collection of stark, dry melodies! Liszt admitted, of course, that his Rhapsodies were inspired by Gypsy dance music. (In this connection, Sarasate's brilliant *Zigeunerweisen* —Gypsy dances—for violin, must be noted. Sarasate was also the composer of Spanish Dances for violin.)

On the one hand, Brahms is said to have obtained the melodies of his *Hungarian Dances* from a poor Hungarian musician who played the tunes while Brahms and Remenyi notated them. On the other hand, Dohnanyi declares that Remenyi himself gave the tunes to Brahms, and that they were not arrangements of tunes by unknown folk composers. They were written by known composers shortly before the time of Brahms. These composers—or composer—sued Brahms' publisher over the melodies.

Perhaps Hungarian folk music is tempting to composers because, as Bartók declares(25) : In the Hungarian melodies with a fixed dance rhythm the most curious, most inspiring and novel rhythmic combinations are to be found. He and Kodály acted as historians when they took phonograph records of Hungarian peasant music and stowed them away in the National Museum at Budapest. The creative work of both of these men has been influenced by their excursions into the realm of the folk. Their music is alternately joyous and melancholy, passionate and languorous, barbaric and lyric. Often it is strongly accented. Bartók wrote many Rumanian Dances, also orchestral Transylvanian Dances, in addition to the Hungarian (among these are the orchestral *Hungarian Sketches*, including a humorous Bear Dance and a jolly Swineherd's Dance), while Kodály has composed the symphonic *Dances of Galanta*, with the themes taken from an 1800 edition of music "after several Gypsies from Galantha," a small market town near Budapest where the composer lived during his childhood. These have been called probably the best Hungarian Rhapsody since Liszt and have been said to be colorful, lusty, folklike and full of rude energy, with an almost blatant orchestration.

Alois Haba, whose rhythmic *Tango* is widely danced, made many experiments with quarter tones, inspired by his observations of Slovakian folk dance music, made when he traveled among the peasants making music at inns after dark, and when he later returned with a recording apparatus to check up on the accuracy of his observations.

That the precepts of Felipe Pedrell started the cult of folklore in Spain is now a generally accepted fact. He it was who preached the study of all Spain's precious folk records, lest young musicians become German or Italian in feeling, and fail to be Catalonian. "If one is to fulfill completely the ends of Folklore," he asserted(26), "He must have first of all an intelligent and exact transcription of the song as it is presented by the folk. He must, second, apply to the recognized document whatever harmony corresponds to the mode of the melody, then enrich it with modern polyphony." Massenet(27) was of the opinion that Granados' beautiful *Danzas Españolas* made him the "Grieg" of Spain: The music of Granados is written with an interesting musical purity; the harmonies are new, and its picturesque character reveals a new personality. Grieg himself(28) wrote of these dances: There is in them a freshness and a national perfume that pleases and interests me.

Albeniz wrote a great deal of salon dance music: Mazurkas, Cotillions, and Waltzes—for commercial reasons. He never took such efforts seriously. He did take seriously his dances in the Spanish vein: Malagueñas, Tango, Zortzico, Seguidillas —and rightly so, for they are more characteristic, and more worthy of his talent.

Falla, whose music is redolent of the folk, does not believe that Spanish composers should stay in one locale to write national music. His way is that of travel, to absorb different atmospheres. The third movement of his *Noches en los Jardines de España* is reminiscent of a Zambra, old Moorish nocturnal revelry (including music and dance).

Joaquín Turina, in his pianistic *Rincones Sevillanos* has written a delightful *Rondes d'Enfants*, as well as a grave *Danse de Seises dans la Cathédrale*. He also composed and dedicated to Segovia a guitar *Fandanguillo*. Moreno Torroba's *Fandango*, for guitar, is also dedicated to Segovia. Joaquín Nin composed an *Iberian Dance*, while Ernesto Lecuona, Cuban, has paid homage to his Spanish blood in *Andalucía*, a complete suite of Spanish dances, of which many of the themes must come from folk sources since, as in the case of his famous *Malagueña* (included in this Suite) several other composers (one of them Francisco Avellan) have idealized the same theme. The oft-sung *La Paloma* (in Habanera rhythm) is generally supposed to have come from folk sources, though Yradier's name appears as composer. Tomás Bretón, who was born in Spain (1850-1923) in 1894 wrote an orchestral Spanish dance suite dedicated to the Infanta Paz de Bourbon, Princess of Bavaria. He named this suite *Escenas Andaluzas* and had in it a Bolero, a Polo Gitano (Gypsy Dance), a March-Saeta and a Zapateado.

Like Pedrell, Alfredo Casella enjoys itemizing the names of composers who were indebted to the folk(29) : The popular contribution has been the basis of all great art. To cite only Haydn, Mozart, Beethoven, Verdi, Moussorgsky—how much did they not owe to the people? I ardently hope that our young Italian composers will listen to the voice of their land! Casella himself has written much music reminiscent of lusty peasant songs and dances. His *Pieces Enfantines* contain a ribald Giga.

The work of Ottorino Respighi in preserving the dance music created by old Italian masters has been noted before. Marco Enrico Bossi wrote a great deal in the old dance forms. His *Intermezzi Goldoniani* are really suites of old dances. His son, Renzo, has emulated him by devoting much time to the restoration of ancient popular Italian ceremonies and celebrations in music. Leone Sinigaglia (born 1868) worked in inspired fashion to immortalize the dance of his native Piedmont, while Sonzogno's *Tango* for orchestra, described as being thoroughly Italian, sensual, dramatic, picturesque, impassioned, tragic and sumptuously orchestrated, is not unlike Ravel's *Bolero* in its dynamic gradation and climax.

In 1925, Mario Castelnuovo-Tedesco wrote *Le Danze del Re David* for piano, a Hebraic Rhapsody on traditional themes, in which the entire history of the Jewish Race is told in dance music at once graphic and simple. The text is from the Psalms 37:25: "I have been young, and now am old; yet have I not seen the righteous forsaken. . . ." For the most part, each dance is separated by a fragmentary melodic theme (appearing each time in a different form) with a shofar-like accompaniment. In this rhythmic, powerful, passionate, wailing music, the piano is made to sound like an orchestra. At the end, a warlike march leads into a supplication, thence into a rhythmic war dance which grows stronger with each phrase.

The rhapsody concludes with a regal fanfare.   Joseph Achron is another composer whose greatest success has come in Jewish music. His *Stempenyu Suite* for violin, based on folk dance themes, is said to be "supremely inspired."   He has also composed a *Chassidic Tanz*.   Jacob Weinberg composed the orchestral *Ora*, a Palestinian folk dance.   Ernest Bloch has written an exotic Jewish Dance as one of his orchestral *Three Poems*.

But Castelnuovo-Tedesco has not only idealized the Jewish dance in music. His *Alt Wien*, in the style of Viennese Waltzes, is often played. His *Tarantella Scura* in the Neopolitan Rhapsody of 1924, is graphic in its depiction of folk merrymaking. It is safe to say that no other folk dance has been idealized so much and in so many ways by natives and foreigners as the Tarantella.   A few of the composers who have written Tarantellas are: Heinrich Schultz (Tarantella in A Minor for piano and small orchestra); Szymanowski (Tarantella for violin); Cui (final movement in the *Suite Concertante* for violin and orchestra, op. 25, also an orchestral Tarantella, op. 12); Saint-Saëns (Tarantella for flute, clarinet and orchestra, op. 6, first performed secretly at the Rossini home in Paris); David Popper (Tarantelle for 'cello and piano); Nápravník (Tarantella in the suite for violin and orchestra, op. 60); Henri Vieuxtemps (Tarantelle for violin and orchestra, op. 22, no. 5); Weniawski (Scherzo-Tarantelle, op 16, for violin and orchestra); Ernest Schelling (Tarantella for orchestra); Erwin Schulhoff (in his *Five Burlesque Pieces for String Quartette*); Alfonso Castaldi (Tarantella for Strings); Michele Esposito (in his *Neapolitan Suite for Strings*); Rebikov (in the *First Suite Miniature* for small orchestra); Liszt (no. 3 of Venezia e Napoli from *Années de Pélerinage*); Coleridge-Taylor (in his *Petite Suite de Concert*); Halévy; Thalberg; Raff (in the piano duet: *Fisherwomen of Procida*); Rossini (in *La Danza*); Auber (in *Masaniello*); Chopin; Moskowski; Heller; Gounod and Debussy (*Tarantella Styrienne* for piano, 1890, orchestrated in 1922 by Ravel and played under the title of *Danse*.)   And these are by no means all of the Tarantellas written.   It would be impossible to enumerate them here, even if one were able to discover every existing one.

The work of French composers has leaned more strongly toward the idealizations of dance forms, rather than of folk themes. For the most part, they prefer to borrow the spirit of the folk, while leaving actual folk creations in the hands of mere recorders. There are cases, of course, like that of Adolphe Piriou, the French composer who based a ballet-opera on the folklore and dances of Bretagne, with a village fête, betrothal scene, etc. It was in two acts, and was entitled *Le Rouet d'Amor*. But this work has never won wide renown. Better known are the compositions of Rhené-Baton, which were also inspired by the rhythmic and melodic form of the Breton folk song. Their colorful harmonies provide a true portrait of Brittany. Rhené-Baton, conductor for Diaghileff, was noted as the first conductor of many famed ballets. In this composer's orchestral medley, op. 5, appears a piece of dance music with this curious title: *Menuet for Monsieur, Brother of the King*.

The *Sarabandes* of Satie, composed when he was twenty-one, have made musical history since they were so simple, yet so daring. Their melodies were attractive, their harmonies contained the revolutionary ninths. Thus they were said definitely to foreshadow the style of Debussy's maturity. In fact it began to be rumored that Satie had accused Debussy of stealing his *Sarabandes*, whereupon Satie determined to stop the gossip by tearing up his own compositions. Fortunately, Calvocoressi was on hand to prevent the destruction.

Vaughan-Williams states that Debussy's *Sarabande* is an example of pure modal (or folk) harmony, as are the cadences in the Minuet from Ravel's *Sonatine*. The Menuet and Passepied in Debussy's *Bergamasque Suite* are among the first examples of his fondness for the eighteenth century manner, though colored with his own individuality. In 1890, however, he had written a *Valse Romantique*, *Mazurka* and *Dance*.

When Roussel, on the contrary, in 1909 wrote his *Suite* for piano, op. 14, he gave his own interpretation of the dance

forms. There was no reversion in thought or feeling to an
olden style.

Of Ravel, Hammond says (30) : "If he writes a Pavane, he
does so with the full consciousness of the twentieth century
mind and calls upon all the technic at the disposal of modern
composers." Indeed, his *Pavane pour une Infante Défunte*
is deeply emotional (in contrast to Faure's orchestral and
choral *Pavane* in characteristic Watteau atmosphere) and his
Minuet-Antique in more or less archaic style contains "scholastic
artifices in opposition to charming boldnesses." His *Pièce en
forme de Habanera* is satirical. The by-now famous *Bolero*
is said to have been inspired by a painting by Goya. It is
nothing more nor less than a technical tour-de-force, depending, by its very nature, on a full orchestra for a successful
performance. It has been so often mis-danced!

Milhaud wrote his *Saudades do Brazil* (two series of Brazilian dances) while he recalled the native dances he had seen
and heard during his two years as an attaché of the French
Legation in Rio de Janeiro. To express adequately the dances
that had so charmed him, he wrote his *Saudades do Brazil*
in polytonal fashion. It is not so much ultra-modernity as it is
an accurate recording of the way native music is often heard.
One sometimes wonders why sophisticated audiences are unable
to accept such translations as Milhaud's as being authentic.
Why should they expect native arts to be diluted for their
benefit? Milhaud's music has the acrid tang of savage folk
dance songs. His rhythmic figurations are also fascinating and
colorful.

One idealization of the *Habanera* (by Louis Aubert, born
1877) was at one time recommended to other composers as a
model. The orchestral style was declared to be at once supple
and solid, tasteful, clear, colorful, skillful, and exotic.

Grieg is renowned as the foremost Norwegian musical
folklorist. Doubtless, he is the *foremost*, but the credit for
being the *first* in that field goes to Grieg's friend, Halfdan
Kjerulf (born in 1815) who was greatly appreciated in Nor-
way, since all of his one hundred songs and forty piano pieces

are tinged with Norse color. In 1875, Kjerulf published in Stockholm a volume of *Selected Norse Folk Dances* for piano. In its preface, he stated that only he had had the foresight to publish a keyboard version of the Norse dances for people abroad, though he was himself indebted for melodies to Lindemann and Berggreen, and that it was a third person who had influenced his treatment of the tunes. He expected all those who had had the desire to see folklore preserved to appreciate his efforts; he cautioned against overuse of the pedal before the dances were thoroughly learned; he declared that the pronunciation of certain vowels had influenced his treatment of the tunes. The variety in the thematic and rhythmic material of Kjerulf's dances is surprising. In addition, though his settings were engagingly simple and folky, he imbued them with many attractive qualities.

Most of Grieg's *Dances*, op. 35, are in ¾ meter, fast sections contrasting with slow sections. They are harmonized in typical Grieg fashion, in what we have come to recognize as the Norwegian folk fashion. Of his peasant dance arrangements, Grieg said(31), "My object was to attempt to raise these folk tunes to an artistic level by harmonizing them in a style suitable to their nature. It is obvious that many of the little embellishments characteristic of the peasant's fiddle and his peculiar manner of bowing cannot be reproduced on the piano, and had therefore to be left out. By way of compensation, the piano has the advantage of enabling us to avoid excessive monotony by virtue of its dynamic and rhythmic capacities and by varying the harmony in case of repetitions. I have endeavored to trace the melodic lines clearly, and to make the outlines of forms definite and coherent." In spite of the fact that someone said that "Grieg, struck with the freshness of the native dances, transplanted them boldly into his academic flower pots," Finck(32) declares that Grieg's national music was not borrowed tunes; he composed his own melodies. What we accept as being Norwegian was really Grieg's own harmonic scheme. Grieg wrote much music in other dance forms beside the folk.

Grieg made the statement that "Percy Grainger plays my
Norwegian peasant dances as none of my own countrymen can
play them." But Grainger went further than that. He was
impressed enough by Grieg's ideals to become his pupil and
later, to follow his master's lead in transcribing many folk
dances and in adapting his style to the creation of tunes that,
when not native, contain at least the spirit of the folk. His
most-played composition, *Country Gardens*, based on an old
English dance tune, is reverently dedicated to the memory of
Edvard Grieg. Grainger's music is difficult to play, but not
in the accepted sense of the word. It contains no nonsense, no
fol-de-rols. His transcriptions of folk melodies, despite the
infusion of his own personality, remain robust, peasantry
melodies, in the words of Joseph Arnold(33). Grainger has
also idealized American folk dance tunes, such as *Turkey in
the Straw*. His Irish Reel, *Molly on the Shore*, is based on
two Cork Reel tunes: *Temple Hill* and *Molly on the Shore*. It
is scored for string orchestra. His *Mock-Morris* is No. 1 of
Room-Music Tid-bits for strings.

Cecil Sharp's restoration of early English folk tunes was
a service to English musicians, who thus gained a foundation
for a national school of composition. Perhaps they all felt
as did the writer who said that "The Highland Fling meant
something when it was danced upon the hills in the striking
costume of the glens. Transplanted to the modern ballroom,
it would be like a thistle in a conservatory: beautiful, but out
of place. It is therefore quite clear that much of our picturesque music of the future will be historical resurrections and
glorifications of forms and ceremonials of the misty past, as
indeed are the *Passacaglias* (nos. 1 and 2 for orchestra, published in 1922) of Cyril Scott (who also wrote English
Dances) and the *Rigaudon* of Grieg."

Vaughan-Williams, who has even used the Morris dancers'
instrumental combinations in writing for the modern dance, has
spoken of how the younger English composers were dazzled
by the extraordinary wealth of beautiful English folksongs
which Sharp brought to their attention; how they wanted to

preach a new gospel (as the Elizabethan Virginal composers did in introducing English folk dance songs into their compositions), and how they wanted to rhapsodize on the tunes, so that some clever journalist invented the phrase, "synthetic folk song." In justification, Vaughan-Williams (34) has remarked, "Personally, I think it is just as good for the student to write synthetic folk songs as synthetic Strauss, Debussy, or Elgar. . . ." The work of Vaughan-Williams in the folk fields has an unusual depth, a richness of orchestral color and great sincerity. Nonetheless, Herbert Hughes in 1932 wrote in the *London Daily Telegraph* to the effect that "In England the cult of folk music has gone too far. It was from the beginning too self-conscious." Many years before, Cecil Sharp prophesied just that. Rather, he believed that the English musician will not necessarily write English music simply by going to English folk music for his themes. The English school of music will be founded after the younger generations have been familiarized with folksong.

English folk dances, then, have been widely idealized. Gustav Holst's opera, *At the Boar's Head* contains no less than thirty-five Elizabethan folk tunes and dances. Edmund Horace Fellows wrote for small string orchestra some short Elizabethan dance tunes by anonymous composers, gathered from the British Museum: *James His Gaillard*, *A Toy*, *My Robbin*, *Hollie Berrie*, *Daphne*, *The Wychie*, *Tickle my Toe*, *Strawberry Leaves*. The third of Fred Adlington's *English Folk Tunes* for string orchestra is a sixteenth century clown's dance from Ilmington, Warwickshire. Rutland Boughton also wrote *Three English Dances*, op. 23, for string orchestra.

Sir Edward Elgar was more inclined toward other dance forms than the folk, though he did compose for orchestra *Three Bavarian Dances*, op. 27. These are taken from the choral suite, *From the Bavarian Highlands*. He also wrote an orchestral Mazurka and a Menuet for strings alone. Then he made an interesting musical venture entitled *Contrasts: The Gavotte A.D. 1700 and 1900*. This was his op. 10, no. 3.

That English dances traveled far is evidenced by Vaughan-

Williams' (35) statement that *Sellenger's Round* (36), English dance tune, lost its lilt in crossing the channel and reappeared in Germany as a stately chorale: *Valet will Ich dir Geben* which we know so well in Bach's great setting from the *Passion According to St. John.* Prince Henry of Prussia became intrigued with the English Dances composed by the American Emerson Whithorne for Lady Randolph Churchill's famous Shakespeare Ball, before 1914. Prince Henry asked for the original manuscript, then had the pieces played by military bands throughout Germany. Whithorne also demonstrated his fondness for old English dance melodies by writing for violin a Bourrée, a Rigaudon and an Air. Godowsky wrote some piano duets on old English country dance themes. Granville Bantock has a *Hornpipe and Sailor's Dance* in his *English Scenes*, an orchestral suite. He also wrote an *Old English Suite* from pieces in the Parthenia and Fitzwilliam Virginal Book, as well as a String Suite called *Scenes from the Scottish Highlands* containing Strathspey, Quickstep and Reel.

No one dares to doubt that German dances have been idealized by some of the world's most distinguished composers. One has but to name these composers and the titles of their idealized dance pieces (some inspired by the dance forms of other lands) to prove this point. One of Bach's idealizations has not yet been mentioned: the *Chaconne*, which is so gigantic that it surely belongs in the category of dance pieces that were never meant to be danced. Beethoven's first *German Dance* in C Major is an idealization of the heavy York Dance in ¾ meter, its characteristic being a strong accent on the second beat of the measure. Beethoven wrote twelve orchestral German dances for the masked ball given by the Pension-fund Society of the Plastic Arts of Vienna on November 22, 1795. At the same time, his twelve orchestral *Menuetten* were performed. His twelve *Contretänze* were composed in 1802. An orchestral *Allegretto-Minuet of Congratulations* was first performed in November of 1822, although its manuscript is dated November 1823. Beethoven wrote six *Menuetten* for piano solo, published in 1796. In 1805 was published a Menuet in E Flat

Major, said to have been completed at the age of thirteen, according to an unknown hand on the printed copy. Beethoven was the composer of a *Polonaise in C* as well as thirteen Ländlers and twelve variations on a Menuet.

Mozart wrote six German dances. Schubert wrote many Menuets, as well as an original piano duet, a *Polonaise*, op. 61, no. 1, and *Five German Dances with Coda and Seven Trios* for string orchestra, in 1813. Weber wrote a rhythmic, gay, arresting *Polacca Brilliante.*

The present German government has endeavored to uncover real, native musical talent. To that end, it has sponsored such competitions as the one for hausmusik masterpieces. Recently, Paul Hoffman's *Four Chamber Pieces in the Style of German Folk Dances*: Kermesse-Dance, Schwabenliesel, Romance and Schüttel de Büx were discovered in this way. These compositions are said to be fresh, full of rhythm and of folkloristic melody.

A form of dancing very popular in the old days was Torchdancing, music for which has been written by many composers. In 1854, von Bülow wrote that he had received an invitation to hear the band of eighty men play the military music composed by Count Redern for the Torch-dancing in his entrance hall. This dance is termed a Marche aux Flambeau, or Fackeltanz, when idealized. The dance form most closely resembles that of the Polonaise. Those written by Spontini and Flotow are now forgotten, though they were tremendously popular in their day. Rubinstein and Guilmant wrote them also. Those of Meyerbeer have become best known. They were composed for royal weddings. In all, they numbered four, of which the first honored the nuptials of the Crown Prince of Bavaria and Princess Mary of Prussia.

Idealizations often extend farther than the idealizer. In the present day, several noted composers have idealized the dance music of those who first idealized dance forms. The five *Wiener-Tänze* for piano go under the name of Friedman-Gaertner. Friedman himself, though he has written a Passacaglia and several lyric Polonaises of his own, has transcribed for piano some of the dance music of Rameau, Grazioli, Gluck, Beethoven, Scarlatti. Seiss has arranged some of Beethoven's *German Dances*. Godowsky's *Renaissance* is built on works of the old masters (mostly their dance pieces) such as Rameau, Schubert, Corelli, Lully, Dandrieu, Loeillet. He treated their music in a more polyphonic fashion. The forms and harmonies are not ultra-modernized or distorted in any way, but are just modern enough to retain more of the flavor of the atmosphere of the age in which the music was first composed. So appropriate are his harmonic enrichments and added rhythmic figures that it seems the composers themselves would have written them just so had modern harmonies and instrumental resources been available. Godowsky's aim was to transform archaic, neglected pieces into modern, logically developed compositions. An interesting departure is his *Walzermasken*, two dozen fantasies in Waltz time for four hands. These mask the personalities of such people as Schubert, Brahms, Chopin, Liszt and Johann Strauss in their moods, fancies and characteristics.

The Swedish folklorist of note was John August Soderman, born in 1832, who had a distinctly national spirit and an original feeling for harmony. During the last part of his life he treated originally the Swedish folk song and Polka. They are now monuments to his work and his music. P.O. Ferroud once orchestrated a tuneful ballet on Swedish folk tunes, *Le Porcher*, based on a fairy tale by Hans Christian Anderson. Max Bruch wrote some orchestral Swedish Dances.

Kaddara immortalizes Greenland's tribal dances. Hakon Borresen, a pupil of Svendsen, wrote this opera in 1921. Its musical climax is the Dance of the Whale's Capture. All of its music is said to be based on genuine folk themes.

The spirit of the Negroid dance and its music has spread over the world. Many composers have idealized this dance in orchestral works. Rivier wrote a Negroid *Danse*, inspired by accounts of André Gide's travels in Africa. Henry F. Gilbert's *Dance in Place Congo* is said to contain the rhythms of the Bamboula, Counjaille, Calinda and Chacta. This music is termed a pantomime-ballet. Gilbert once made his living (while studying with MacDowell) by playing the violin in theaters and for dances. Later he wrote much music in attempts to idealize Negro and Indian themes. Many are the Negro Dances he has written for two and four hands on the piano. He took the Bamboula theme as Gottschalk did, from the Negroes in New Orleans.

Coleridge-Taylor also wrote a *Bamboula* for piano, (simpler, therefore better, than Gottschalk's) a composition which merely formed the groundwork of a grealy enlarged orchestral rhapsody that he composed in 1910. It is apparently different from the piano piece, though both are brilliant, but the composer himself wrote that the four bars of the actual theme are identical. In 1896, Coleridge-Taylor wrote a Danse Nègre which later became the fourth episode in his *African Suite*. It was inspired by a characteristic quotation from Paul Lawrence Dunbar:

> "Civilised?"
> "Waal. . . !"
> "Sing?"
> "Waal. . . !"
> "Dance?"
> "I'll be *cursed* if they can't!"

It was late in Coleridge-Taylor's life before he became an enthusiastic apostle of color in music. "What Brahms has done for Hungarian music, Dvorak for Bohemian and Grieg for Norwegian, I have tried to do for these Negro melodies," he said(37).

Harl McDonald has made extensive use of dance rhythms in his *G Minor String Trio*, in his *Second Trio* and in his *Negro Quartet*. This was because of his keen interest in the spontaneous character of most types of folk music and not with any thought of providing tonal background for the dance.

In Brazil, where African culture has penetrated, we find the composer Villa-Lobos writing *African Dances* for orchestra.

Cuban composers consider Ignacio Cervantes (1847-1905) as their pioneer in the composition of idealized Cuban folk dance music. His *Danzas* conformed to the style of his own epoch—that is, the age of Salon music—yet were brief, individual and showed such penetration and advance into the spirit of modern modulation that they inspired and paved the way for Cuban modernists.

Amadeo Roldan in his *Motivos de Son* (Cuban dance-song themes, written in 1930) displays a richness of harmony, despite frequent dissonances, and a rhythmic sense so fascinating and yet so complex that one unaccustomed to Afro-Cuban music can scarcely comprehend or play them on sight. Alejandro García Caturla has written much music on Cuban dance themes and in those forms. In addition, his song to words of Alejo Carpentier, *Juego Santo*, speaks of the dances and of the native instruments that accompany them. The melody is much in the style of the primitive song one hears as one attends native fiestas on the outskirts of civilization; it rises above an interesting rhythmic accompaniment. The many dances written by Ernesto Lecuona are more in the popular vein, though all contain distinctly Cuban rhythms and themes. Eduardo Sanchez Fuentes, Cuban critic, has written several famed songs (*Tú* and *Cuba*) idealizing the Habanera rhythm.

Justin Elie, Occide Jeanty, Jules Heraux and Ludovic (all Haitians) have done much to preserve their native dance tunes, chief among which is the Meringuë, said to have originated in the army. Peasants today keep alive this dance that was formerly performed with guns and bayonets.

Ancient Peruvian dance melodies have been preserved in Carlos Valderrama's *Inca Steps*, said to be a published composition.

Memories of the dance music heard in his childhood in the state of Jalisco, Mexico, inspired José Rolon to write his *Tres Danzas Indígenas Mexicanas* for piano. They are slightly off-pitch, and their rhythms are piquant and unconventional: an attempt to reproduce on the piano the complicated Mariachi music. Manuel Ponce has also written a section called *Mariachi* into his symphonic cycle, *Chapultepec*, which idealizes the folk. Ponce has written, too, a *Danza y Canto de Antiguo México* for orchestra. José Pomar wrote a symphonic *Huapango* based on folk themes and Sones. In the score, the composer ordered the violins to bow short, so as to make the music more characteristic. In this work, Pomar did not idealize any known Huapango music, although he used the character, the outward form and the sensual abandon of the dance itself. Chavez has idealized certain folk dance themes in his Mexican ballets.

Frederick Jacobi, contemporary American, spent much of his time with the Pueblo Indians in New Mexico and Arizona, where he studied their music and was impressed by its spiritual beauties. The result was several abstractions on Indian themes, the most successful being the *Indian Dances* for orchestra. In a sense, Jacobi feels that Indian music has permanently influenced his own musical speech, though perhaps unconsciously. One of Bernard Rogers' *Two American Indian Frescoes* for orchestra is an Ojibway War Dance, with more rhythmic than melodic interest, following the character of most Indian dance-songs.

Many years after the majority of North Americans had forgotten the old-time fiddle tunes, Henry Ford started a return of recognition by his patronage of "Mellie" Dunham, an old-time fiddler for barn dances. Composers, however, had not forgotten. In 1917, Leo Sowerby wrote *Money Musk* for piano, an old country dance tune set. Later this was orchestrated. David W. Guion transcribed the *Arkansas Traveler*, an old fiddler's breakdown, for piano. He first heard it in West Texas at cowboys' dances and reunions. The second melody in his arrangement is *Whoa, Mule!* an original tune by an old slave who fiddled and sang while Guion listened and danced.

There are more splendid idealizations of folk dances and other dance forms in existence than it would be possible to describe or even to list in full. However, since the dance music of each country has been given attention by fine composers, those dancers who wish to avoid monotony in their musical repertoire and who wish to idealize the dances as the composers idealized the melodies, might do well to investigate the vast musical literature on the subject.

CHAPTER 13

NOTES

(1) Saminsky, *Music of the Ghetto and the Bible,* p. 57

(2) MacDowell, *Critical and Historical Essays,* p. 184

(3) Schumann, *Music and Musicians, second series,* p. 470

(4) Stravinsky, *An Autobiography,* p. 152

(5) *Life and Letters of Peter Ilyich Tschaikowsky,* pp. 377-378

(6) *Life and Letters of Peter Ilyich Tschaikowsky,* p. 607

(7) Liszt, *Letters,* Vol. I, p. 353

(8) *Life and Letters of Peter Ilyich Tschaikowsky,* p. 311

(9) Pedrell, *Lírica Nacionalizada,* pp. 114, 172

(10) Bauer, *Twentieth Century Music,* p. 44

(11) Schumann, *Music and Musicians, second series,* p. 484

(12) Chopin, *Letters,* p. 74

(13) Chopin, *Letters,* p. 129

(14) Chopin, *Letters,* p. 60

(15) Schumann, *Music and Musicians, second series,* p. 484

(16) Schumann, *Music and Musicians, second series,* p. 485

(17) Schumann, *Music and Musicians, second series,* p. 540

(18) Chopin, *Letters,* p. 227

(19) Vaughan-Williams, *National Music,* p. 100

(20) Hoffmeister, *Antonin Dvorak,* p. 59

(21) Hoffmeister, *Antonin Dvorak,* p. 110

(22) Bauer and Peyser, *Music through the Ages,* p. 103

(23) Sharp, *English Folksong: Some Conclusions,* pp. 49, 51

(24) *The Étude,* October, 1930, p. 694

(25) *Pro Musica Quarterly,* October, 1928, p. 34

(26) Pedrell, *Lírica Nacionalizada,* p. 8

(27) Pedrell, *Lírica Nacionalizada,* p. 31

(28) Pedrell, *Lírica Nacionalizada,* p. 32

(29) *The Étude,* November, 1927, p. 167

(30) *Modern Music,* January-February, 1928, p. 23

(31) Finck, *Grieg and His Music,* pp. 99-100

(32) Finck, *Grieg and His Music,* Chapter VIII
(33) *American Dancer Magazine,* June, 1934, p. 13
(34) Vaughan-Williams, *National Music,* pp. 82-83
(35) Vaughan-Williams, *National Music,* p. 138
(36) Chapter IV disproves the statement that *Sellenger's Round* is native to England
(37) Preface to *Twenty-Four Negro Melodies*

THE WALTZ AND ITS CREATORS

The Waltz has ruled the sophisticated dance floor the longest of any form of social dance! Stories of its origin are many. Yet all authorities agree that it began sometime during the Middle Ages. On the one hand, we are told that the Volte was the ancestor of the modern Waltz and that Arbeau described this dance as being "a species of Gaillarde familiar to the Provençals" danced in triple time: two steps and a leap.

On the other hand, we find that the German Dance and Ländler, a south German folk dance, were the earliest forms of Waltz, and were taken to France as the *Allemande*, entirely different from the old Allemande of 1600, or from Bach's stylized Allemandes. At first it was often danced in duple time, but toward the end of the eighteenth century, the triple rhythm was definitely established. Castil-Blaze adds vehemently that "The Waltz, which we took again from the Germans in 1795, had been a French dance for four hundred years." Still another authority ventures the opinion that the Waltz came from the Minuet, and that from the Passepied!

It was MacDowell's belief(1) that *all* triple time arose from the dance. "When a man walks, he walks fast or slow. But when he takes one long step and one short one, he no longer

222

walks, he dances. Thus we may say with reasonable certainty that triple time arose directly from the dance. A half note followed by a quarter note correspond to a 'trochee' in our poetry. The figure of dotted quarter and eighth notes, followed by a quarter, was probably developed to alternate the feet and lessen physical fatigue, corresponding to the dactyl in poetry."

An old Austrian Waltz, called "Dreher," was said to be in quintuple time. Vincent Lachner has a movement of this type in his orchestral *Ball Suite.*

No matter when or how it originated, the Waltz has had a lurid history. It shocked English society because of the proximity of the dancers. It was a great sensation but, needless to say, the English people still dance the Waltz. Byron scathingly satirized it in *The Waltz, an Apostrophic Hymn, 1812* under the pseudonym of Horace Hornem, Esq. This poet called on Terpsichore to own her none-too-lawfully begotten Waltz! Yet from the pen of the very same poet also came these lines:

> "Endearing waltz!—to thy more melting tune
> Bow Irish jig and ancient rigadoon . . ."

Richard Brinsley Sheridan spoke of the modesty of our first parents

> "When hand in hand through Eden's bowers they roved,
> Ere yet the devil with practice foul and false
> Turned their poor heads and taught them how to waltz."

The Waltz spread all over the world. The Colombian Pasillo is actually a shortened Waltz rhythm. In Venezuela the same movement is called a Joropo. It appears to be of Spanish origin, but now cannot be found in Spain!

There are, then, many kinds of Waltzes. But the three principal ones are the slow German Waltz, or Ländler; the livelier Viennese, or three-step Waltz; and the quick Waltz in double time. Modern popular songs in syncopated vein have given us a languid Waltz in addition to the three major varieties.

"Doubtless man could have invented a more enjoyable little musical form than the Waltz," writes Ernest Newman(2), "But doubtless man never did, and unless I am greatly mistaken, it will see a few of the more solemn forms out. They may turn up a contemptuous nose at other dances, but most great composers would be as ashamed to admit that they had never composed a Waltz as to have it said of them that they had never kissed a girl; indeed, a psychologist might infer that the composers who have been guilty of the one neglect have also been guilty of the other. Their music generally shows it. . . . Mozart, Beethoven, Schubert, Weber, Schumann, Brahms, Chopin, Wagner, Richard Strauss, Tschaikowsky, Berlioz, Debussy, Ravel, have written Waltzes. It may be that the Waltzes of some of these men will be remembered when their most ambitious works are forgotten. Brahms was the most serious of them all, and his Waltzes derive a special charm from their mere contrast with his work as a whole—the charm of an occasional smile on a usually grim face."

The only reference to the Waltz in the life of Handel seems to be with regard to his musical cook whose name actually *was* Waltz. This man later went on the stage and won fame as a singer. The composer often referred to him with pride.

Beethoven's youthful Waltzes were said by Saint-Saëns(3) to be utterly devoid of charm: merely pieces written in three-four time. But when it became the fashion to admire Beethoven (declared Saint-Saëns) everyone admired, played and sentimentalized his worthless music too. Perhaps just such a person was he who wrote that "Beethoven has composed thirty-three admirable variations on a Waltz tune of Diabelli. What, exactly, can a dancer dance in such a work? For Diabelli's theme is nothing. . . ." In 1822, Beethoven offered some variations on a Waltz for pianoforte to a publisher for thirty ducats in gold. Then, in the early part of 1823, he was asked to compose the variations on Diabelli's theme. He first refused the commission, later relented. Soon ten and twenty, then twenty-five variations were finished and still it was not the end. Beethoven was in a veritable creative fever and he wanted to show all he could do with a fairly commonplace theme. He dedicated these thirty-three variations (op. 120) to the wife of Ferdinand Ries, but couldn't write in the dedication as he did not know her name. Accordingly, he begged Ries to do it for him and surprise her with it. Later, when Beethoven became acquainted with one of Ries' own compositions, he exploded in anger—and thereafter refused steadfastly to dedicate anything to Ries or to his wife and forbade Ries to call himself a pupil of Beethoven. The matter was explained by outsiders who claimed that Ries stole too much from Beethoven, in spite of all he had previously done to spread the fame of Beethoven and his music, as evidenced by existing letters.

Nijinsky's "Spectre de la Rose" was danced to an adaptation of Weber's *Invitation to the Waltz*, once fashionable in European ballrooms. Litolff's charming *Invitation à la Polka* might have become better known than it did, were it not for the inevitable comparisons with Weber's renowned music, because of the similarity in titles. In the *Invitation to the Waltz*, according to Marion Bauer (4), Weber forestalled Liszt and Berlioz in writing program music. How true this is can be judged only by reading Sterndale Bennett's account of Schumann's verbal accompaniment to his playing of this music— to realize what visions it brought to another composer: "There!" he said as he began, "There, he bows, and so does she. He speaks, she speaks, and oh! What a voice—how liquid! Listen—hear the rustle of her gown! He speaks a little deeper, you notice. You cannot hear the words, only their voices blending in with the music. Now they speak together. They are lovers, surely. See, they understand—oh! The Waltz! See them take those first steps! They are swaying into time—away!—there, there they go—look!—you cannot hear their voices now—only see them!"

A fact for the "Strange as it Seems" column is that the composition known as *Weber's Last Waltz* was not written by Weber at all, but by Reissiger, a German musician born in Wittenberg. This composer's dance music (in his opera, *Adèle de Foix*) was praised highly by Schumann (5): "The ballet music deserves special mention; here Reissiger's pleasing talent shows for what it is." Yet Schumann, in his rôle of critic, declared that *Weber's Last Waltz* balances itself on the hair-breadth line that divides affectation from nature. It was published in 1824, and Reissiger himself protested against the name the publishers had given it. He termed it an injustice —which, indeed, it was.

It has been said that some masters, writing in the popular forms, cut, polish and elaborate on them. But Schubert, in his Viennese Waltzes (of which Brahms was fond) was pure Viennese. These might have been written by a Lanner or a Strauss. The earlier Waltzes were short, and were intended for actual use. The later ones were longer, and had trios. In none of them was there much attempt to elaborate the usual "one, two, three" Waltz accompaniment. It has been said that Schubert was obsessed by the popular origin of the dance. Really, he presented his Waltzes simply, without ornaments or pretension. Liszt put some of Schubert's Waltzes into his *Soirées de Vienne* as well as writing a *Valse Oubliée* of his own.

Virtually a contemporary of Schubert was Josef Lanner, from whom the Strausses inherited their Waltz-form. Where, from Mozart to Schubert, this form had been scarcely more than a three-part song-form with trio, Lanner enriched it to the point where it consisted of an introduction containing a hint of the principal theme, then a series of different Waltzes—in which one principal Waltz recurs, then a coda amounting to a summation of themes. Indeed, Lanner began the era of Viennese light music to which the Strausses provided the grand climax.

John Field, inventor of the Nocturne which was made famous by Chopin, wrote numerous Waltzes. Ironically, few people know of these, while Chopin's Waltzes constantly grow in popularity! If Chopin was national in his Polonaises and Mazurkas, he was distinctly suave, sophisticated and Parisian in his Waltzes. It is the polished, gallant man of the world who speaks through the Waltzes, not the soul laid bare through tragedy. Thomas Edison(6) merely described them as being "not conventional Waltzes." That Chopin(7) himself regarded them lightly is evidenced by his letter of May 15, 1830: "I meant to send you a new Waltz to amuse you, but you shall have it next week." A noteworthy fact about these Waltzes is that, despite their brilliance as a whole, there is at least one part in each of them that can be danced—that is, waltzed in the regular way, not merely "interpreted" by a concert dancer.

The Waltzes of Chopin have been known to have had curious and wonderful effects. At least, in one case, they opened the eyes of a young boy to the vast possibilities of romanticism in music, as contrasted to the formal classics with which he had previously been familiar. That boy was Frederick Delius. "My first musical experience," he wrote(8), "Was in hearing a valse of Chopin when I was ten years old. It made a most extraordinary impression upon me, and it was as if an entirely new world had opened up to me." Cyril Scott's very first composition was written down at the age of seven: a little Valse in Chopinesque style.

From Vienna, Chopin wrote in 1830(9): "Among the numerous pleasures of Vienna the hotel evenings are famous. During supper Strauss or Lanner play Waltzes. After every Waltz they get huge applause; and if they play a quolibet, or jumble of opera, song and dance, the hearers are so overjoyed that they don't know what to do with themselves. It shows the corrupt taste of the Viennese public." Again, in 1831, he wrote: "Here, Waltzes are called works! And Strauss and Lanner, who play them for dancing, are called Kapellmeistern. This does not mean that everyone thinks like that; indeed, nearly everyone laughs about it; but only Waltzes get printed."

The Strauss family (preceded in the Viennese Waltz field by Johann Heinrich Schmeltzer and his son Andreas Anton, who were mentioned in a previous chapter, and by Johann Joseph Hoffer) became a phenomenon to be noted at length in history books, biographies and commentaries. Many were the contemporary composers who, visiting Vienna, wrote home about the Strausses. Since letters of famous people have a way of being published sooner or later, we have now a fairly accurate record of the composers' feelings on the Strauss subject. Nearly all were enthusiastic!

It was perhaps natural for Wagner to display excitement over these glorious Waltzes, for, in his early youth, he considered the *Ypsilanti Waltz* the most wonderful of compositions—a feeling which was cured only by his hearing of one of Weber's compositions. In 1832, he wrote(10): "I shall never forget the extraordinary playing of Johann Strauss, who put equal enthusiasm into everything he played, and very often made the audiences almost frantic with delight. At the beginning of a new Waltz, this demon of the Viennese musical spirit shook like a Pythian priestess on the tripod, and veritable groans of ecstasy raised the worship of the magic violinist to almost bewildering heights of frenzy."

Count Sandor Apponyi(11) in his *Memoirs* tells of a visit by his cousin to Wagner's room, where the music of Johann Strauss' *Blue Danube Waltz* was open on the piano: "The conversation must have turned to this, for Wagner sat down at the piano and played a few bars of the immortal Waltz, enthusiastically praising its beauty. I envied my cousin this experience; it is not everyone who can hear Richard Wagner playing Strauss. This admiration for Strauss was characteristic of Wagner's attitude to other musicians. His highest admiration was reserved for those who stood completely outside his own sphere and whom he could criticize objectively."

Once, Hans von Bülow(12) said that the Waltzes of Johann Strauss the second (greatest of the Strausses) were appropriate material for the most serious concert programs, because they were not only great dance music but great music as well.

Berlioz described the balls of Viennese youth, in which ballroom dancing became an art, as far above the usual routine of balls as the Strauss Waltzes were superior to the Polkas in the dancing-salons of Paris(13). "I have passed whole nights watching thousands of incomparable waltzers whirling about," he wrote, "and admiring the choreographical order of the country dances, composed of two hundred persons in two

ranks, and the piquant look of the characteristic steps, which
for originality and precision I have never seen surpassed, except
in Hungary. And then there is Strauss, conducting his fine
orchestra. . . . There is no jealousy between dancing and
music, each shares with the other. This is only fair, for Strauss
is an artist. The influence he has already exercised over musical
feeling throughout Europe in introducing cross rhythms into
Waltzes is not sufficiently appreciated. So piquant is the effect
that the dancers themselves have sought to imitate it by creating
the deux-tempo Waltz though the music itself has kept the
triple rhythm. If . . . the public can understand the singular
charm frequently resulting from contrary rhythms, it will be
entirely owing to Strauss. Beethoven is too far above them;
Strauss has addressed himself to the masses. . . . Strauss's
Waltzes, with their fervid airs resembling love voices, have
the gift of putting me into a profound melancholy. . . ."

In MacDowell's opinion (14), Strauss remedied the defect
of unbroken regularity of rhythm in the Waltz by a marvellous
use of counter-rhythm, thus infusing into the dance a simulation
of intellectuality. On the other hand, it has been said that
Strauss, sensitive enough to read the tendencies of the time,
translated the sensuous and restless moods of the age into
artistically perfect musical pictures, inspiring the excitement
of pleasure.

"When Johann Strauss commenced to write for the stage,"
declared Victor Herbert (15), "He was helped by Genée, and
I played in the orchestra at Vienna when some of the Strauss
pieces were at the height of their success. The title of dance
king or Waltz king which fell on different generations was justly
won." (It will be remembered that Strauss also wrote a
comic opera called *Indigo* on the Ali Baba story in 1871; an
incomplete ballet named *Aschenbrödel* (later finished by
Bayer); *Die Fledermaus*, an operetta with a choral Waltz
and a sparkling ballet in 1874; as well as *The Gypsy Baron*
and other works. In all, there were fourteen light operas.)
There were many Strausses, however, several claiming to
write Waltzes, conduct dance orchestras, accentuate the weak

beat in three-four time, and so on. There was said to be one such in Paris who stayed away from Vienna out of consideration for Johann Strauss who, in turn, did not stay away from Paris for a similar considerate reason!

Lanner, predecessor of the elder Johann Strauss, had made a tour to Paris and London—a tour whose triumphs were eclipsed only by those of the elder Strauss, who had added to his accomplishments the introduction of the Quadrille. Even as the elder Strauss displaced Lanner, so did his son, Johann II, displace him. This son disobeyed his father's injunction to have nothing to do with music (even as Dvorak and Adolphe Adam) and soon his Waltzes rivalled those of his father in popularity and charm, when both were conductors of café orchestras. In the year of the triumph of Johann II, Lanner was dying of poverty in a corner of the Vienna that had once idolized him! Five Viennese cafés featured the music of Johann II, then he popularized it personally through Europe and in America. He even persuaded his brothers Eduard and Josef to become composers and conductors and to substitute for him on occasion. But, by reason of a pact between them, the music of Josef was destroyed by Eduard after the former's tragic death.

Johann Strauss II (October 25, 1825 to June 3, 1899) was an "electric" conductor. One who saw him in her childhood exclaimed, "I remember how he bobbed up and down the stage, and oh! How fascinating he was!" Years have dimmed the memories of the surviving members of Johann's various orchestras, but one such musician(16), when questioned about the Waltz king in recent years was able to reply only, "Ah! But he was a *charrr-ming* man!" to every question. In all, Johann II wrote nearly five hundred compositions of which his Waltzes (nearly four hundred of them) are best known. Edison(17) was interested enough to examine the themes of twenty-seven hundred "conventional" Waltzes, only to discover that, in the final analysis, they consisted of about forty-three themes, worked over in various ways. Of all the

Waltz composers, Johann Strauss proved to be the most inventive!

Strauss' three-quarter time was supple, elastic. His orchestral effects were distinctive. Some said that his operettas succeeded in bringing the spirit of the café to the opera house. Theodore Thomas(18) was once asked how he managed to impart such vitality and lightness to the Strauss Waltzes when conducting. "Have you ever noticed," he replied, "That I always beat the first strokes of the rhythm up instead of down? You cannot put the life and continuous motion of the dance into a piece of music if you knock the poor tune down at the beginning of every measure."

Interesting facts are related of a few of the more famous Waltzes. Strauss' wife said that the melody of the *Simplicimus Waltz* was conceived in a dream. The themes for the *Blue Danube Waltzes* were written upon cuffs when paper was lacking. Strauss' wife rescued them from the laundry. They were inspired by a forgotten poem by Carl Beck. Since the Vienna Male Singing Society had been promised a new work for its concert on February 13, 1867, the *Blue Danube Waltzes* were first written and performed for and by a choral ensemble. Strauss attached no importance to these Waltzes; did not even bother to play them on his public programs until they created a furore in a private orchestral concert. Thus Strauss' popularity was definitely assured over his predecessors and over his contemporary, the Alsatian Emile Waldteufel, who composed over eight hundred pieces of music and who made his home in Paris, the very city conquered by Strauss! Other nineteenth century Waltz writers who were surpassed by Strauss were Labitsky, Gung'l, Lumbye, Czibulka, Siefert and the composers of pianoforte Waltzes: Thalberg, Raff, Schütt, Godard, Chaminade and Moskowski.

Today, Strauss is honored by a film, *Waltz Time in Vienna*, depicting the famed Strauss-Lanner feud; by *Vienna*, an orchestral rhapsody by M. Konstantinoff, though Schwerké(19) accuses this of "engaging an entire orchestra in the expensive pastime of saying nothing"; by *The Great Waltz,* an operetta; by grand balls and torchlight processions in Vienna to celebrate each birthday of the *Blue Danube Waltzes*; and by many other devices, all of them utilizing the themes of his Waltzes. *Le Beau Danube* was first danced by the Russian Ballet in 1923 to Massine's scenario and choreography, the scene laid in a public garden in 1860. It was composed as a relaxation after the strenuous production of *Le Sacre du Printemps,* and although it appeared at a time when jazz reigned supreme, it played a part in launching a new vogue of the Vienna Waltz.

To most people, the Waltz is a symbol of great joy. Stier(20) relates how, when the rumor spread that the very unpopular Gustav Mahler had fallen victim to cholera, his orchestra spontaneously struck up a lively Strauss Waltz as a paean of thanksgiving! Surely, the Waltz has been a relaxation for serious musicians for many years, and—significant fact—when they wish to enjoy themselves so, most often it is the Strauss Waltzes that are selected for this diversion! (In spite of the pastime of Borodin, Cui, and Rimsky-Korsakow, according to Rachmaninoff's account, of paraphrasing the *Dog Waltz* in piano duets.) When, in 1913, a birthday party was given Paderewski in Switzerland by some fellow-artists, all of them: Paderewski, Schelling, Samaroff, Josef Hoffman, Rudolf Ganz and Stokowski performed at the same piano a ragtime version of the *Blue Danube Waltz.* It was the climax of the day. Henry L. Mencken(21) belongs to a group of musically-minded people who gather together of a Saturday evening to play. They end every evening with a Waltz and have, in their time, gone through every known Waltz of any consequence. "The Strauss Waltzes, with their enchanting, exhilarating rhythms, are some of the loveliest things in all music. What could be more beautiful than Mein Schatz from *Der Zigeunerbaron* [My Sweetheart from *The Gypsy Baron*]? But those English titles for a Viennese Waltz are like Pilsener beer with milk in it. . . . There was never any clash of debate over Strauss. It was unanimously agreed that he was first-rate."

"Unfortunately, not by Johannes Brahms," inscribed

Brahms under the four bars of the *Blue Danube Waltz* with which he had autographed the fan belonging to Strauss' widow. Brahms showed his allegiance to and his admiration for the Viennese Waltz in his sixteen Waltzes for piano. Newman's (22) statement best sums up Brahms' contribution: "What Brahms did in the Waltz was to give perfect and final expression to German sentimentality. . . . The amazing thing is the variety of expression Brahms gives to so rigid a form as that of the Waltz. When the giants unbend, they do so with a peculiar graciousness and no less strength."

Kreisler has idealized the Viennese Waltz in his *Caprice Viennois* and *Schön Rosmarin*, as has Godowsky in such compositions as *Alt Wien* and Castelnuovo-Tedesco in his satirical *Alt Wien*. While the American Henry Hadley was in Vienna, he spent three days in the composition of a series of Waltzes in the Viennese style, *Student Life in Vienna*. This he did to win a bet and (ironically enough!) to convince the leader of the Hapsburg Café orchestra that there really is good American music. Hadley gave the conductor something he could comprehend. Doubtless, if he had presented a composition in an American idiom, the conductor would have thrown up his hands in horror.

The part played by dance music in Vienna has always been great. The earliest musical memories of Karl Goldmark, Viennese composer, are of the dance tunes produced by four workmen on wind instruments fearfully out of tune. His first lesson (without a knowledge of notes or of technicalities) was to accompany a choir singer on the violin, in a Waltz. His first modest compensation as a composer was three florins, in payment for making an orchestral arrangement of a Polka sung to him by the leading lady of the ballet at the Ödenburg Theater.

When Tschaikowsky first began to improvise on the piano, his impromptu compositions were Valses, Polkas and Rêveries de Salon. It was he who included a Waltz in a symphony later in his life, and who wrote a Valse-Caprice for piano (op. 4); a Valse-Scherzo for piano (op. 7); a Valse-Scherzo for violin and orchestra (op. 34) ; the *Waltz of the Flowers* in the *Nut-cracker Ballet*; the Waltz in *Eugene Onegin*; the Waltz in the *Variations in F* and the *Melancholic Waltz* in the third suite, in D Major (op. 55). Incidentally, Taneiev also wrote a *Valse Mélancolique* in his second quartet, later arranged for small orchestra.

Moussorgsky is said to have used a Waltz theme or rhythm, in the most stupid style of Italian opera, to express a biting musical satire in a vocal composition. The Arensky Valse from the Suite for two pianos has become so popular that when noted piano-duos announce at their concerts that "We have received a request for the Arensky Valse," their audiences break into spontaneous applause. Arensky also wrote a haunting vocal Waltz, *But Lately in Dance I Embraced Her*.

Sibelius is said to have received two hundred and fifty dollars for the *Valse Triste* (a part of his incidental music for Avid Järnefelt's drama *Kuolema*) from a German firm. It was composed in 1903 within a week's time, and was originally scored for strings alone. Later, with quaint pathos, he mentioned to Edwin Evans the fact that his best works were scarcely known, while the *Valse Triste* was flaunted in every pleasure resort from Egypt to Alaska. He also wrote *Valse Romontique*, *Valse Lyrique* and *Valse Chevalieresque*. While Sibelius was in Vienna, seeing the Johann Strauss of sixty-five conducting his orchestra with all the fire of a young man, he conceived a lasting love for the Strauss Waltzes. The influence of these Waltzes and of Vienna is evident in his orchestral *A Ballet Scene*, performed for the first time in Helsingfors.

Nearly all of the French composers used their Waltz music to express something more than a dance rhythm, as indicated by their titles. Vincent d'Indy wrote his *Helvetia Waltzes*, each one named after a Swiss town. Satie wrote a *Valse du Mystérieux Baiser dans l'Œil*, *Trois Valses du Précieux Déguoté* and the *Valse du Chocolat aux Aumandes*, in his children's pieces.

The *Danse Macabre* of Saint-Saëns was first played by Colonne over the protests of his orchestra, but when, on first hearing, it was encored, Colonne's judgment was discovered to be sound. The entire poem is a Waltz, cleverly and grotesquely instrumentated. It is based on an eerie poem by Henri Cazalis. Death is a fiddler who summons skeletons from their graves to dance until the cock crows. There are two themes: one in dance measure, punctuated with the clack of bones, and the other a serious, nocturnal strain. Variations on those two themes are heard throughout the composition. The significant cock-crow at dawn is taken by oboe. Olin Downes asserts that this *Danse Macabre* is wittier than it is terrible; Saint-Saëns watched the revels from a safe place and calmly recorded the events of the night.

Several French composers have written romantic Waltzes. Debussy has a *Valse Romantique* which, along with his *Mazurka* and his *Danse* cannot be considered in his usual style. These three compositions might even be termed commonplace. Grovlez wrote *Trois Valses Romantiques*. A Parisian wit once complained of the exquisite bad taste of Chabrier's *Valses Romantiques*, for Chabrier did not scorn musical vulgarity when it suited his purpose. Before 1881, this composer had written a *Scherzo-Valse* into his *Dix Pièces Pittoresques* for piano, as well as a *Danse Villageoise* and *Menuet Pompeux*.

Debussy's *La Plus que Lente*, originally written for piano, was duly orchestrated by another musician and presented to the composer for his approval. His objections to this particular score may give us a clearer view of Debussy's own ideals, and of his conception of this lovely composition in particular. He wrote to his publisher (August 25, 1910): "Examining the brassy score of *La Plus que Lente*, it appears to me to be uselessly ornamented with trombones, kettle drums, triangles, etc., and thus it addresses itself to a sort of de luxe saloon that I am accustomed to ignore!—there are certain clumsinesses that one can easily avoid! So I permitted myself to try another kind of arrangement which seems more practical. And it is impossible to begin in the same way in a saloon as in a salon. There absolutely must be a few preparatory measures. But let's not limit ourselves to beer parlors. Let's think of the numberless five-o'clock teas where assemble the beautiful audiences I've dreamed of." Subtly, Debussy indicated that *La Plus que Lente* belongs to all that is elegant and charming in life, and that it should be treated orchestrally and interpreted according to its innate character.

The first performance of Ravel's *Valses Nobles et Sentimentales* was given by the Société Musicale Indépendante in Paris on a program of almost all new works, without the names of their composers being revealed. Many of Ravel's admirers were indifferent, some even disapproving. Some people ascribed the authorship to Kodály and others to Satie. Of course (declares Calvocoressi(23)) they liked them when it became known that Ravel had done them. They are characteristic of Ravel, and of his ironic humor and depth of sentiment, but were at the same time such an advance over his earlier works that they went unrecognized. It shows the utter impossibility of judging music on first hearing, and of judging its worth solely by a publicly-conceived idea of a composer's worth. These Waltzes are unified by an epilogue that summarizes them all. They were given a motto by Henri de Régnier(24): "The delicious and ever-new pleasure of a useless occupation." Says E. B. Hill(25). "In these dances the somewhat impoverished Waltz receives a new lease on life." They were later transformed into a ballet called *Adélaïde ou le Langage des Fleurs*.

If these Waltzes deserve the comment of E. B. Hill, what can one say of Ravel's *La Valse*, conceived as a potential ballet, and often referred to as the "Apotheosis of the Waltz?" This is amazing in its technical construction, and more amazing when one realizes that both it and Ravel's *Bolero* would have been utterly banal in the hands of a less gifted musician. Ravel invented for it themes of the Viennese Waltz type, but his harmonies are more sophisticated. Incidentally, Florent Schmitt's *Rhapsodie Viennoise,* originally for two pianos and later orchestrated, never won such fame as did Ravel's *La Valse*, in spite of the fact that Schmitt had the same ideal: transporting the brilliant Viennese Waltz into sophisticated surroundings. *La Valse* is also said to have been conceived for two pianos. Casella divides it into three parts: The Birth of the Waltz, the Waltz, the Apotheosis of the Waltz; thus making Ravel's poem a tryptich. "Whirling clouds give glimpses, through rifts, of couples waltzing. This is made clearer as they gradually scatter, revealing a large hall filled with a whirling crowd. The scene is illuminated. At the fortissimo, the light of the chandelier bursts forth. An Imperial Court about 1850."

La Valse may be the culmination of centuries of development. Perhaps, after Ravel, the Waltz form is destined to progress no further. But it is safe to say that composers will continue to write Waltzes as long as music is written in our idiom, so fascinating is the form. However, although the form itself is popular, the popularity of individual Waltzes is as unpredictable as that of any other piece of music. It is true that, during the course of three years in Europe, the *Merry Widow Waltz* sold at the rate of a million copies a year. On the other hand, the year 1922 found Karl Michael Ziehrer, Viennese composer of the *Old Vienna Waltzes*, penniless and starving. Lanner died in poverty while the world fêted Strauss.

Lady Waltz is indeed a capricious mistress!

CHAPTER 14

NOTES

(1) MacDowell, *Critical and Historical Essays*, p. 25
(2) Newman, *A Musical Motley*, pp. 216, 217, 218
(3) Saint-Saëns, *Outspoken Essays on Music*, pp. 82-83
(4) Bauer, *Twentieth Century Music*, p. 39
(5) Schumann, *Music and Musicians, second series*, p. 19
(6) Cooke, *Great Men and Famous Musicians on the Art of Music*, p. 30
(7) Chopin, *Letters*, p. 90
(8) Heseltine, *Frederick Delius*, p. 5
(9) Chopin, *Letters*, p. 129
(10) Wagner, *Life*, p. 77

(11) *Étude,* February, 1936, p. 76

(12) *Musical Quarterly,* October, 1935, p. 469

(13) *Memoirs of Hector Berlioz 1803-1865,* pp. 376-377

(14) MacDowell, *Critical and Historical Essays,* p. 27

(15) Cooke, *Great Men and Famous Musicians on the Art of Music,*
        p. 243

(16) Ernest Huber, now resident in Los Angeles

(17) Cooke, *Great Men and Famous Musicians on the Art of Music,*
        p. 30

(18) *The Étude,* January, 1928, p. 15

(19) *Musical Courier,* December 14, 1935, p. 38

(20) Stier, *With Pavlowa Round the World,* p. 231

(21) *The Étude,* May, 1936, pp. 277-278

(22) Newman, *A Musical Motley,* p. 220

(23) Calvocoressi, *Music and Ballet,* pp. 71-73

(24) E. B. Hill, *Modern French Music,* pp. 254-255

(25) E. B. Hill, *Modern French Music,* pp. 254-255

*

CHAPTER 15

*

IGOR STRAVINSKY

We have seen the gradual departure of music from the close fusion with the dance it enjoyed in primitive and ancient times. We have noted the fact that many people looked upon dance music with scorn. It has remained for the moderns to take up the composition of music for the dance in earnest, and to set the history of choreographic music well on the way toward the completion of an artistic cycle.

The coöperation of great musicians like Tschaikowsky helped to make this possible. But, without a doubt, the greatest single factor in the recognition of modern ballet music as music is Igor Stravinsky. This composer's greatest services to ballet music were the tearing down of existing rhythmic and harmonic forms; an insistence upon the right of ballet music to have an individuality of its own; and his vigorous demand for the respect due a composer. And thus, his music, especially *Le Sacre du Printemps*, has vitally influenced modern dance movement itself. Louis Horst(1) is of the opinion that the sensational renaissance of the dance has strongly influenced modern music. How, we wonder, can Mr. Horst account for the fact that *Sacre*, with its pulsing, primitive sound, demanding a certain elemental movement, antedated what we know as the modern dance? Even Anga Enters(2) (more closely allied to the dance than music) in 1930 asked "where was the 'modern dance' before the experimentation in new music forms was begun? Is there not a peculiar significance in the fact that until five years ago there was no 'modern dance' in America, though modern music was in a state of gestation at least twenty-five years and that the present American exponents of 'modern dance' had been, not less than five years previous to their sudden conversion, content with hackneyed forms?" Surely, a change in both dance and music was bound to come. Perhaps the element of "which came first?" matters not at all. It is nevertheless true that, thanks to Stravinsky, ballet music opened the door to all modern, abstract music.

Some consider Stravinsky a reaction against all conceptions belonging to the Schönberg order. Really, Schönberg and Stravinsky were both reactionaries, of a different sort. Richard Buhlig made the statement that the former is the only creative genius in the world today, but Schönberg considers himself more of an innovator than a creator. His pupils, who learn in six months the atonal principles on which he labored for twenty-five years, are apt to progress into marvelous, untold creative fields, according to his own admission. Why then, is Stravinsky not an innovator, a creator of the first order? At least, his music provoked anger. It was at first entirely strange to ears accustomed even to modern music, and it started an unmistakable vogue.

Many composers for the modern dance are spending their waking hours diligently turning out dozens of miniature "Sacres." The number of composers who borrow right and left from Stravinsky and who are rewarded with being thought original and daring is great. However, if the writer believed, with Erich Wolfgang Korngold that "after Stravinsky there was no development, only imitation(3)" this book would be about Stravinsky, not about choreographic music as a whole. Fortunately, that statement is a little too inclusive to be credible.

We do not deny that he occasionally used other themes. When this has happened, Stravinsky has usually been frank in acknowledging them. But, Edwin Evans(4) mentions discovering that the Russian tune of Ronde des Princesses in Stravinsky's *Firebird* occurs also in the second movement of Rimsky-Korsakow's *Sinfonietta*. He invited Diaghileff to play the arrangement of the latter with him, and when they arrived at the particular theme, Diaghileff jumped up, crying, "No! It isn't true!"

The statement that Stravinsky has been an astounding and at the same time, a dangerous influence on present-day composers was made by Bauer and Peyser(5). Yet here is the reaction of one of these modern composers (William Grant Still) : "*Petrouchka* was a revelation to me. I never knew anyone could score so elaborately and yet in such a telling fashion. I tried to imitate Stravinsky in an earlier composition, but the result was so bad that it forced me to branch out for myself. I was glad, for in a performance of my composition, I heard all the faults that a bad imitation of a good work can produce. Now my days of conscious imitation are over as a result of my early experience and of my admiration." Stravinsky was, in that case, far from being a "dangerous" influence. He did, on the contrary, much good. But, in all cases, one fact remains: the composer who has something to say *will say it*, regardless of the age in which he lives, his style or the influences that beset him.

No, Stravinsky simply heralded a group of composers whose ballets are among their best musical works. Why should these not be composed seriously and thoughtfully, instead of filling the place of a mere diversion, a passing interlude in a composer's life on earth? True, Stravinsky *was* an innovator, a reformer. More than that, he imparted the courage of their convictions to many young composers. No longer do they function as "Yes-men," subservient to the whims of a ballet-master. No longer are they timid if a choreographic interpretation displeases them. (Did not Stravinsky ban an English performance of a little ballet to his *Ragtime* in the fear that his music would be mis-danced?) No longer do they suffer in silence when a dancer is ignorant of the laws of music, and wait until the posthumous publication of their memoirs to vent their spleen upon an unsuspecting world. They are far more apt to confront the dancer and attempt to teach the rudiments of music upon the spot!

Stravinsky is at his best in his ballets. He uses dissonances and many rhythmic changes in quick succession. He once declared that "Romantic music was a product of sentiment and imagination; my music is a product of motion and rhythm. Nobody has found as yet a suitable name for this tendency in musical development(6)." He is wrong. There is a name for it, and that name is "Choreographic Music." The ancients had it, centuries ago.

In his remark, one can read the reason for the amazing success of Stravinsky's ballet music. He does not write mere connected sounds, expecting someone to drift along and fit movements to his sounds. His music grows out of movement, out of the rhythm of his thoughts, of his daily life, of his original idea. Small wonder that no imitations are successful! At best, an imitation is superficial. Stravinsky's creations come from the depths of his creative consciousness. They are then necessarily sincere.

This composer himself says(7) : "I want neither to suggest situations or emotions, but simply to express them. I think there is in what are called 'impressionist' methods a certain amount of hypocrisy, or at least a tendency toward vagueness or ambiguity. That I shun. Thus my methods differ as much from those of the impressionists as they do from academic, conventional methods. The one essential is to feel and to convey one's feelings."

Cowell(8) believes the Stravinsky music to be too interesting and detailed for dancing. If one watches the dance, one loses interesting musical values. If one listens to the music, the dance is not fully appreciated. No one seems to agree with Cowell on this score. White(9) asserts that "Ultimately Stravinsky's music was written to be heard as an accompaniment to a spectacle. Where the spectacle is satisfactory, the result is excellent. Where it is not, the music suffers." George

Antheil(10) considers that dancing is a social affair unless it draws attention to the music forcibly, while Ezra Pound(11) informs us that a fair test of the real art of the ballet is whether one does hear the music. Rutland Boughton(12), vehement anti-Stravinskyist, has this to say: "The pleasure many of us got from the *Firebird* and *Petrouchka* was only in a slight degree due to the music. Some sort of rhythmic noise had to accompany the otherwise silent show. And so the man rode to notoriety on the backs of the Russian ballet!"

Indeed, he did. Stravinsky's music alone accompanied the entire twenty-year span of life of the Ballet Russe. Other composers came and were forgotten, then were revived. Stravinsky went on continuously. His name became synonymous with that of the Ballet Russe. Had he remained in his homeland, his music might never have won a wide hearing. If it had, its reputation would probably not have spread so far abroad. None of his works were produced under Russia's old regime. The new government displayed a certain interest which waned quickly. Stravinsky and his music have both become expatriates!

The whole field of Russian music for the dance might today be obscure were it not for Diaghileff, the amazing man to whom even many foreign composers owe their first recognition. Above all things, Diaghileff preferred melody in music (Stravinsky once teased him about his enormous admiration for Tschaikowsky) though he never allowed his personal taste to govern his choice of music. Auric declared that if one placed twenty scores before him he would unhesitatingly select the best, and be able to give the reasons for his choice.

It was this Diaghileff who "found" Stravinsky, born in 1882, one of the most extraordinary of all musical talents. Cautiously, after having heard some of his music, Diaghileff merely asked the composer to orchestrate two Chopin pieces for *Les Sylphides*. Then he commissioned *L'Oiseau de Feu*.

While he was writing this first commissioned ballet, Stravinsky was intoxicated with the dancing in *Prince Igor* and *Carnaval*. This ballet, based on a Russian fairy tale, was written in complete collaboration with the choreographer, Fokine. The latter had seen, in the music of Stravinsky's early symphonic *Feu d'Artifice* (years later produced as a ballet by Diaghileff) darting flames. Nonetheless, despite the splendid impression Stravinsky's first efforts had made on both Fokine and Diaghileff, Liadov had seemed to them at the outset to be the logical one to write a ballet on this old folk tale. They broached the subject to him. Months passed. The Liadov music was long overdue. "Well," said Diaghileff to the composer at a chance meeting, "Is my ballet ready?" Responded Liadov, "It won't be long now, it is well on the way. I have just bought the ruled paper." Thus, Haskell informs us (13), did Stravinsky happen to write *L'Oiseau de Feu* and to score his first triumph. It was not the only time in his career that Stravinsky was destined to be "second-choice" and to emerge victorious. Many times he has had to jump in on the spur of the moment, figuratively saving many producers' lives and incidentally piling up renown for himself.

Perhaps because *L'Oiseau de Feu* was one of his first ballets, it shows traces of other influences. Goossens believes it to be the only one of Stravinsky's works in which one can clearly trace his artistic pedigree and recognize the different influences that have molded his own very personal idiom: Borodin, Dukas, Rimsky-Korsakow. Another observer believes that it stamped its composer as a worthy successor to the Kouchka: "His mentality is strongly oriental in type. Borodin . . . has left distinct traces on the mind of the younger man in the riotous splendor of the Danse Infernale and final tableau of *L'Oiseau de Feu.*"

Such was Florent Schmitt's (14) admiration for Stravinsky that he changed the name of his Villa to "Villa Oiseau de Feu" and muttered, after hearing one of Stravinsky's compositions: "This is to discourage all the others from writing music!" In 1910, another noted French composer (Debussy) wrote (15) to his publisher: "You haven't mentioned Stravinsky's *L'Oiseau de Feu*. It isn't perfect, but in a certain sense it is very good, since its music is not a docile servant of the dance. At times, one hears in it entirely unusual agreements of rhythms.   French danseuses would never agree to dance to such music!   But then, Diaghileff is a great man and Nijinsky is his prophet—at least, when Calvocoressi is not at hand!"   (It should be remembered that Calvocoressi did much to popularize Diaghileff's ventures outside of Russia.)

L'Oiseau de Feu was more than an expression of movement in music.   It was the beginning of Stravinsky's power to depict the workings of the human mind in tone.   So steadily did he work with Fokine in the composition of this ballet, phrase by phrase, that Kirstein(16) reports this admonition of Fokine, when Stravinsky brought him a beautiful cantilena on the entrance of the Tsarevitch into the garden of girls with beautiful apples: "No, you bring him in like a tenor.   Break the phrase, where he merely shows his head, on his first intrusion.   Then make the curious swish of the magic horse's return and then, when he shows his head again, bring in the full swing of the melody."   Who knows?   Perhaps the thoughtful admonitions of people as wise in stage lore as were Fokine and Diaghileff profoundly influenced Stravinsky's whole future as a creator for the stage!

Richard Strauss(17) wanted Stravinsky to surprise his audience with a loud crash in *L'Oiseau de Feu* (instead of a pianissimo at the opening) so that the public would listen and follow the trend of his musical thought.   But Stravinsky had as little difficulty in persuading the people to listen to him despite his quiet beginning as he has had in inspiring people to write about him, since his music, years after its inception, still remains a controversial subject.

L'Oiseau de Feu is a danced tale in two scenes.   Soon after its introduction, the Enchanted Garden of Kastchei is pictured, with its magical harmonies.   The sudden apparition of the Firebird is suggested by loud, almost converging polyharmonies. A Hollywood musician might call this "mood" music.   Seldom does a snatch of melody appear.   In the Dance of the Firebird, the music is suggestive of flames and has been said to depict the light given by a single feather of the Firebird.   The dance is in ⁶⁄₈ meter, but the tempo is Allegro Rapace and the accents so unusual that it seems anything but that. The dancer who could dance this music successfully without being a superb musician would have to be supremely intuitive. (Diaghileff once engaged Marie Rambert to teach all of his dancers the principles of Dalcroze Eurhythmics, since without them they were unable to understand the complicated rhythms of the Stravinsky works. Sokolova learned the first act of *Sacre* in a few rehearsals because her musical training made the difficult rhythms easy. Haskell used to see other dancers standing about with sheets of paper on which the principal rhythms were sketched out: the most difficult of methods.)

The Dance of the Enchanted Princesses in *L'Oiseau de Feu* is modal, and is in the form of a Khorovode, a grave and stately traditional Russian round dance. Fantastic, poly-rhythmical music depicts the subjects of Kastchei, while the famed Infernal Dance of Kastchei's subjects is a marvelous crescendo of diabolic energy, with a syncopated melody over a low accompaniment. The Andante signifies the Berceuse of the Firebird. This is followed by somber, rising chords marking the death of Kastchei. The second scene of the ballet is the one in which, to music that virtually shimmers, the palace of Kastchei disappears and the petrified figures come to life. The music ends majestically, jubilantly and brightly, the theme being taken ever higher and higher aloft as Ivan and the Tsarevna are united in love.

One cannot agree with the critic who said that Stravinsky's music is nothing without the assistance of an orchestra, for the greatest orchestral genius in the world cannot make a bad composition good by effective scoring. Nevertheless, there is something very definitely lacking in his piano scores. He needs the orchestra, as well as the complete production, for full expression of his creations. There has also been a change in Stravinsky's conceptions since the composition of these earlier works. When he was heard conducting his own music after years had passed since their creation, it was discovered that there was a great variation in his interpretation and in Stokowski's. And the latter had been extraordinarily careful to observe all of the composer's indications. Stokowski himself, a member of the audience on the later occasion, commented on the difference.

The theme of *Petrouchka* literally forced itself on Stravinsky while he was busy with *Sacre*, and from a piano composition grew into this poignant drama. Stravinsky calls his protagonist "the eternal and unhappy hero of all times, of all fairgrounds" and it is in this ballet that he is said to appear first as an innovator. Diaghileff assisted him in developing the theme. To its original conception may be attributed much of the pianistic treatment of the score. Goossens(18) gives still another explanation: "In *Petrouchka*, Stravinsky would pick up some common tune and let it blare out naked and unashamed, and then wrap it up in elaborate disguise through which we could catch the echo of its mocking laughter. One remembers how the orchestra fell silent when the puppets first broke through the crowd, and only the piano was left to represent their mechanical ecstasy."

Petrouchka is a burlesque in four scenes, the action taking place in the St. Petersburg of 1830. It is ironic, not humorous. Nijinsky is said to have thought of this ballet in a symbolic sense. The Charlatan represented Czarism, Petrouchka depicted the soul of the Russian people. Aptly enough, Petrouchka's final appearance is as a ghost, deriding the Charlatan and the people he has deceived. The ballet has been described as presenting the psychology of the inanimate.

The first Tableau is a *Fête Populaire de la Semaine Grasse*: excited, shimmering music, utilizing popular melodies derived from those Russian peasants who have begun to assimilate Western culture. These tunes are so artfully disguised and so perfectly blended that they seem to lose their identity, though not their character. Said Casella, of an excerpt from *Petrouchka*: "Curious example of a mixture of simplicity and extreme contemporary complexity." The first definite dance rhythm occurs almost at the outset, but does not remain long. In many cases, Stravinsky is merely polyrhythmic, not polyharmonic. But he has been so clever about it that the same effect is given to the unsophisticated ear. The Charlatan is heralded by a sinister, hypocritical theme taken by bassoon. Between tableaus, a military drum and tambourine cover the pauses. The second tableau is in Petrouchka's home, with erratic, inarticulate music portraying the wild joy and frustrated emotions of the puppet. He struggles to express himself : the music *makes* him articulate ! It is at once aimless and purposeful and it reminded Adrian Stokes of the snuffles and yells of animals. The Blackamoor dances to heavy music in the third scene : perhaps not intended for any deep psychological import. The Blackamoor's graceful and grotesque scene with the Dancer is in burlesque ballet style, an adagio in a regular three-four meter. The fourth tableau contains the excited and vari-colored Fête music, changing for each different character, but unified in feeling and in the repetition of certain musical figures. In this scene, as in *Pagliacci*, the gayest things occur while the audience knows full well that tragedy lurks just around the corner. Here occurs the famous Russian Dance, with its tone clusters. Petrouchka's dying music is taken by poignant strings, with tiny flute ornaments as he shudders, so faithfully does the music underlie the action. When Petrouchka's ghost has appeared, the muted string choir plays four notes in unison, after the final blackout.

When *Petrouchka* was first rehearsed in Vienna the orchestra men audibly called it "dirty music." Over their open hostility, it was produced and received well. Thus Stravinsky had a taste of what was one day to occur with his *Sacre*.

Now, Latin music-lovers are accustomed to show their likes and dislikes openly. When Mossolow's *Iron Factory* received its first performance in an Italian city, half the audience hissed; half applauded. The conductor announced that at the end of the concert the composition would be repeated and that everyone who did not wish to hear it could go. No one walked out ! Such demonstrations, then, are common. But *Sacre* did more than occasion a disturbance. It shook the musical world, and supplied critics and journalists with material of which they are still making use, more than a score of years after the first presentation in 1913!

Sacre was a headlong leap into dissonance, barbarism, emotionalism. Perhaps the world was unprepared for it. Let us consider first a few of the objections. We may gather from Mr. Boughton's rather vehement remarks that he does not like *Sacre*, a fact which will make very little difference to those who do, but at least he had the courage of his convictions: "*Sacre* has many features in common with a primitive voodoo sacrifice. It expresses country life and work in a way which no composer had previously thought to record in music. In the first pages of *Sacre* we find vagueness and monotony as in primitive music. With the full resources of the modern orchestra, Stravinsky managed to effect what the savage got from drums only . . . the prevailing conception that music is the art of disorder. *Sacre* is the will to force a composer's personality upon his art, a sign of 'mystical restlessness' which finds no truth in religion and no peace in art."

"*Le Sacre* is indeed full of one phase of Borodin's spirit," Gerald H. Abraham has said (19). "There is this difference, however, with Stravinsky, that he lacks the orderliness of Borodin's scientific mind, whereas the latter (even in the *Prince Igor* dances in the same mood) never becomes incoherent even in the expression of the most primitive and elemental human passions, the most naked savagery and ferocious exuberance. Stravinsky is very frequently unable to control his self-expression. . . . Nobody would be foolish enough now seriously to consider Stravinsky a lunatic, but there is no doubt that this failure to control an overheated imagination and to prune and train its products is a serious defect in an artistic mentality."

Lunatic? After reading the following quip by Antheil (20), one might rightly wonder whether it is Stravinsky or the academicians who deserve to be thought balmy: "One must never be suddenly jarred in either a restaurant or a concert hall. One eats food in the first and digests it in the second. Imagine the effect of the *Sacre* on 'the old gentleman who must be careful' !"

Which is precisely what did occur. Calvocoressi says the audience of 1913 was really roused, not bewildered, scandalized or personally hostile. The music was too much! Puccini(21) wrote of the première to Tito Ricordi: "I went to hear the *Sacre du Printemps*. The choreography is ridiculous, the music sheer cacophony. There is some originality, however, and a certain amount of talent. But taken altogether, it might be the creation of a madman The public hissed, laughed, and . . . applauded." (Nijinsky's choreography was said to be a sort of counterpoint in opposition to the music.) Muriel Draper(22) wrote of the London production: "The intensity of the score, which builds itself around and in you with each succeeding note and rhythm, leaving you no escape from its passionate logic, drove the audience to a pitch of frenzy. . . . It is common talk now among amateurs and critics of music that *Sacre* is not, after the third or fourth or tenth hearing so impressive." Van Vechten described the Paris première, and Copland says bitterly that "the shock produced by the rhythmic brutality of *Le Sacre du Printemps* has no counterpart in recent times. Our younger composers startle no one."

Even *Sacre* has become a classic of its kind. But for Diaghileff it was the first baptism of public bad feeling. There were other frenzied protests to which this amazing producer quickly accustomed himself. As for Stravinsky himself, he quietly withdrew from the auditorium when the first protests were made, so he is unable now to give his impression of the matter.

What, after all, is this ballet? It is simply tableaux of pagan Russia in two parts. It begins with a single melody. In fact, the method employed throughout is to continue one melody while others are added. Some of the themes are original with Stravinsky, though he created them after folk models. Others are definitely borrowed from the peasant folklore of north Russia, where ancient musical traditions have been preserved. Some of the melodies are modal. There is a great deal of ostinato accompaniment. The rhythms are complex. Some chords are strongly accented, off the beat. Many of the dances are in continually changing meters: $\frac{3}{16}$ $\frac{5}{16}$ $\frac{4}{16}$ in the course of a few bars, with ⅜ and ⅝ following soon after. At least, these meters are all allied in spirit. The first part of the ballet is called Adoration of the Earth, and includes an Introduction, Harbingers of Spring, Dances of the Adolescents, Mock Abduction, Spring Rounds, Games of the Rival Tribes, Procession of the Sage, and Dance of the Earth. The second part is the Sacrifice. It also has an Introduction which leads into the Mystical Circles of the Adolescents, Glorification of the Chosen One, Evocation of the Ancestors, Ritual of the Ancestors, and the Sacrificial Dance of the Chosen One.

Upon seeing this score, one realizes what caused the riot, as well as the recurrent dislike of some people. It is *purely choreographic music*, enhanced by fine scoring. It makes no claim to a musical or thematic development. People were so unused to the idea that they couldn't believe their ears. They had come to view a gay spectacle. Instead, their emotions and their minds were aroused. More, as one looks at the score for the first time, it is as if one were seeing a finer edition of the music of some of the younger composers for the modern dance. What sort of dance music, Mr. Horst and Mr. Engel, would you be composing today had there been no *Sacre* and no Stravinsky?

From time to time, critics have analyzed and decried many of Stravinsky's characteristics. They object, it seems, to his changing style for every composition, to what they term "this phenomenon of perpetual search," to his tendency to create an objective work each time. They believe this theory to be too objective, too literary, since they hold that his talents are best expressed in the purely musical domain. He has, however, often left the field of ballet and the theater to compose abstract music. This is still imbued with the feeling of movement (one might call it inspired by dance!) but it has never won the popular acclaim of his theater pieces, despite the ponderous praises of critics.

"This phenomenon of perpetual search" again proves his kinship with the ancients. MacDowell (23) declared that "the choric dances of Stesichorus and Pindar approached our modern

forms, because the form fitted the poem. Today, too often, we
make our ideas fit the forms." What is so strange about a
musician letting his methods be dictated by his subject? Must
Stravinsky limit himself to being always Stravinsky, to please
those who wish to fit the great into their own personal patterns
of greatness? The composer himself is rather headstrong.
He refuses to be compelled to do thus and so. "I live neither
in the past nor in the future," he cries to his critics, "I live in
the present(24) !"

Adolph Bolm is of the opinion that the real significance of
the Russian ballet began when Stravinsky used Russian folklore
—which is to say that the significance of the Russian ballet, in
so far as music was concerned, began with Stravinsky. Strangely
enough, this reform was not effected in Russia, but outside. Of
all the works in which Stravinsky has paid homage to the Russian folk, *Les Noces*, a scenic ceremony inspired by freely-
adapted old Russian customs, is most thoroughly impregnated
with that spirit. The work is dedicated to Diaghileff who said
of it(25) : "If you wish to know an essentially Russian work,
to my mind nothing reveals Russia as completely as *Les Noces*.
In fact, it uses peasant dance themes, some not exceeding a
fourth or a fifth in compass. Others of the themes are merely
founded on Russian scales. It is a choral ballet in four tableaux
without interruption, depicting a Russian peasant wedding festival in the nineteenth century. The ritual of peasant life is
enacted in the ceremony of plaiting the bride's hair; the blessing
of the bridegroom; the bride's departure and blessing of the
bride; and the wedding feast, or the Red Table. Two versions
of the orchestration preceded the final one, and a great deal of
time was wasted in an attempt to synchronize mechanical pianos.
The 1923 version is for chorus and four soloists, four pianos,
xylophone and battery of percussion. Some agree that *Les
Noces* is a product of a transitional period in Stravinsky's
career. John Martin wishes(26), after hearing it, that some
kind Providence would supply another Stravinsky or two to
turn out equally "poor" music for the dance hereabout. "In
its function as part of a choreographic collaboration it is ex-

traordinarily successful. It tends toward that kind of inspired sequence of sound effects that ultimately will solve the difficult problem of music for the dance."

"When Stravinsky writes for the chorus his mind must surely turn homeward to his native Russia with its choral songs and dances and the great liturgies of its church," presumes Vaughan-Williams(27), "And so I believe that it is in *Les Noces* and the *Sinfonie des Psaumes* that we find the real and great Stravinsky which will remain fresh and alive when all the clevernesses of his instrumental works have become stale from familiarity." Whereas some (as mentioned previously) regard *Les Noces* as a product of a transitional period, others group it with *Le Sacre* as a product of the composer's so-called "primitivist" period.

Renard, a burlesque of history, has often been called a "comic little brother of *Les Noces*." It is Stravinsky's own transmutation of the Russian folk song idiom. It is to be played by clowns, dancers or acrobats on trestles in front of a small orchestra in a small room. If a theater is used, Stravinsky wishes it played before a curtain. The orchestra includes four human voices: two tenors and two basses, singing often in falsetto, sliding and howling as would a fox. *Renard* begins and ends with a little march.

At the beginning of his career, Stravinsky had begun an opera called *Le Rossignol*. Later on, he completed it and presented it in its operatic form. Still later, he made a symphonic poem from the second and third acts and gave it to Diaghileff to use as a ballet. He then adapted a scenario from Anderson's fairy tales for that purpose. Goossens has written that the absence of voices in the ballet version of *Le Rossignol* robs the work of much of its former brilliancy and sonority, in spite of the richness obtainable by an economy of orchestral resources. "The first opera version was a lovely thing," he declares, "From the brooding Prelude to the last triumphant Song of the Victorious Nightingale."

L'Histoire du Soldat re-introduces the Speaker, or Narrator, to the stage. It was originally planned as a sort of ballet to be read, played and danced. There were fifteen pieces in the original score, which calls for only six instruments and a battery of percussion. Stravinsky decided to have his orchestra well in view, on remembering how he disliked listening to music with his eyes closed, not seeing the movements that produce it. The work as a whole is said to owe much to the army experiences of one Larionoff, an artist with Diaghileff, who was impressed with the contrast between the brutal soldiers and the elegant officers. It is bitterly satirical, reveals the "gaiety and spiritual poverty of post-war Europe," and uses Tango, jazz Waltz and Blues rhythms in novel instrumental effects. It contains a Royal March (in Pasodoble style); a Devil's Curse and a Chorale. Tone contrasts take the place of expression. In the musical pauses the soldier whispers secrets of his past to his bride.

One critic found the stage production amusing; the music secondary. Divorced from its stage action, he found the music interesting only in its rhythmic pattern. An English writer said the music matched the "simple-mindedness of the story." Still another wrote, "It says much for the genius of Stravinsky that, though severely handicapped by this formless method of composition (i.e., ballet music that follows closely the movements, step by step) he has yet succeeded in giving his works a certain unity of feeling, harmony and material. Even the dances that follow so quickly upon each other in the fourth tableau are carefully dovetailed together."

White (28) notices a change in Stravinsky's outlook on music, occurring almost at the end of the war. Certainly it was about this time that the composer's thoughts began to hark backward, that he began to think musically in what one might almost term "classic" fashion. Yet this is not so unusual. Almost all composers who startle the world with a new sort of ultra-modernism in music revert to a purer form of expression sooner or later. It is as if the former were a purging of the soul in preparation for the latter. We find this true of Schönberg, and even of the noisy Antheil. The latter admits publicly his change of feeling and advertises the fact that he believes the time has come to write melodies again. However, in Stravinsky's case, the change may be another evidence of "this phenomenon of perpetual search": the presentation of every idea in the form best suited to it.

Many are those who deplore Stravinsky's re-writing of the music of older composers. Yet none of these people flayed Godowsky for his rejuvenation of old dance pieces. Stravinsky's *Pulcinella*, based on Pergolesi's music, was the target for many a barbed dart of criticism.

Two who praised Stravinsky's venture were M. de Sales and Goossens. The former said that "Stravinsky skillfully threw into relief the beauties of the old master by underlining them." Goossens (29) was astounded at the failure of the general public to appreciate the resourceful reverence of Stravinsky's re-dressing of the beautiful Pergolesi music. "To some, any rearrangement of a classic constitutes an unpardonable sacrilege. Old music, like old china, calls for the utmost care in its handling. Some in the hostile camp, who thought it in bad taste because of the alleged disregard of traditional harmony, were blind to the wonderful homogeneity of technique and the comprehension of old forms and procedure displayed in every page of this masterly score. It is often difficult to detect where Pergolesi ends and Stravinsky begins."

One critic called *Pulcinella* officious, inappropriate to the eighteenth century composer's style, labored and deliberately vulgar. Another said of the same performance that it was gay, lucid, charming, witty, entertaining; that the duet for trombone and double bass may not be Stravinsky at his ablest, but that it is good, clean fun; that only the canny Igor knows how much of the music is his own and how much Pergolesi's; and that it is a product of his skill and wit and taste. Still another person remarked that it had never occurred to her to take the score seriously; that Stravinsky never meant it to be serious nor had any illusions concerning the value of a great piece of musical fooling; that he never intended to be appropriate in style to Pergolesi's period; that he was deliberately and amusingly artificial and purposely false in harmony and orchestration to the genre of Pergolesi. Olin Downes summed up these conflicting views by saying that they were not due to established rules of criticism; but to temperamental differences and personal taste, and prophesied that only a future perspective on all of Stravinsky's music would enable us to judge it more accurately.

Stravinsky says that the success of *The Good Humored Ladies* tempted him to work on *Pulcinella*. Perhaps he was surprised then when Trend later wrote that his work was a mere arrangement of arias and sonata movements from Pergolesi, which neither as orchestration nor music can be compared for a moment with the exquisite Scarlatti pieces, arranged by Tommasini for *The Good Humored Ladies* ballet.

As a matter of fact, it was Vincenzo Tommasini who was first asked to write *Pulcinella* (30), and for that purpose he was called to London by Diaghileff in 1918. But he disagreed with the producer on the method of treating the old Italian music, so he said: "If you want Italian music to sound Russian, why are you asking *me* to do that? Ask a Russian musician, and no one will do it better than Stravinsky." So, Stravinsky wrote *Pulcinella*. He later caused its choreography to be altered and adapted to his music. What would Petipa have said to such presumption on the part of a mere composer? Diaghileff and Massine accepted the dictum because "there was no other solution." Of this collaboration, it was said later that Stravinsky has embellished the admirable melodic line of Pergolesi with harmonic sarcasm, trombone persiflages, asthmatic bassoon hiccups. And Massine correspondingly exploited the elements of classic dance virtuosity in the sense of Irony.

Pulcinella is a ballet in one scene, the subject taken from a Neapolitan manuscript of 1700, containing many comedies utilizing the traditional personages of the popular Neapolitan Theater. The episode chosen to serve as a vehicle for this ballet was entitled *Quatre Polichinelles Semblables*. True, Stravinsky has planted one harmony on top of another in a manner that would surely have astounded Pergolesi, but which now seems quite natural—even, in a sense, classic. And the uses to which the themes are put are ingenious and refreshing, to say the least.

As Stravinsky jumped into the breach in the cases of *Firebird* and *Pulcinella*, so he was destined to do in still another case: that of *Apollon Musagète*. When Bolm was about to present a dance Festival program, he asked Bartok for a ballet, stipulating its duration and mentioning the number of people he would use. Bartok presumably began work. Came the eleventh hour—Bartok was not ready! Stravinsky was then approached and he, never at a loss, despite the fact that it had been four years since he had written a ballet, came forth with *Apollon Musagète*. For this, he had a vision of a white ballet. He admired the beauty of line in classic dancing and thus it appeared to him that a diatonic composition was most appropriate, and that the austerity of the style would determine the instrumentation. He deliberately turned to the creation of melody from a purely musical standpoint. He did as Diaghileff did: when he had exhausted the possibilities in ballet novelties, he reverted—at the psychological moment—to the severely classic, and won a tremendous success. So it was with Stravinsky. *Apollon Musagète* is simple music, polyphonic, growing into a smooth crescendo of rich beauty. But its very simplicity lends subtlety.

It is for strings only because, as a Parisian wit averred, it could scarcely have been otherwise. Did not Apollo flay Marsyas for daring to match his pipes against the stringed lyre?

Apollon is in the classic ballet manner. It is in two scenes, and is a piece without a detailed plot. Apollo is born in the Prologue. Apollo and the Muses are seen in a series of pas d'actions, then Calliope, Polyhymnia and Apollo have variations after which Apollo and Terpsichore danced a pas de deux. In the Apotheosis, when the music increases in power and expressiveness, they all ascend to Parnassus in a phaeton drawn by four horses.

Again, Stravinsky wrote a ballet after another composer in *Baiser de la Fée*, a serious imitation of Tschaikowsky. The comment was made that he created an ideal Tschaikowsky ballet without the formal defects of the original, but it is Tschaikowsky without nuance. "Thin and charming music" is another description of it. It is the longest of all Stravinsky's ballets, and is dedicated to the composer whose melodies appear in the score. It was commissioned by Mme. Ida Rubinstein, and is an allegory in four dancing scenes. The story is built around the mysterious kisses given by a fairy at the birth and at the death of a youth.

Stravinsky's *Mavra* is classed in one instance as a one-act opera bouffe, in another as a ballet. Stravinsky himself terms it an opera. It was his intention to have the movements of the *singers themselves* disciplined by the accepted standards of the ballet stage, and to that end, Mme. Bronislava Nijinska was called into action. The work itself is dedicated to the memory of Pushkin, Glinka and Tschaikowsky and is more harmonic, less contrapuntal than other Stravinsky works.

Persephone, a mimed drama in three scenes, is one of Stravinsky's latest compositions, the music on a French poem by André Gide. For the first performance of this work in 1934, Kurt Jooss was the choreographer.

At the present time, Stravinsky has completed a commission from the American Ballet. His new ballet is entitled *Jeu de Cartes en Trois Donnes*. Each deal of this card party is upset by the Joker, to whom ordinary rules do not apply; each deal begins musically with a short processional, a March, Polonaise or Valse. In numbered paragraphs paralleling the musical score, composer and librettist carefully indicated the choreography. When Balanchine had half finished making the dances, he showed them to the composer, who criticized them intelligently and who was meticulous as to correct tempi and other musical details. John Martin later admitted that he thought the ballet music quoted from every musician from Rossini to Ravel and that it was arbitrary, involved and calculating: "Indeed, it must be seriously questioned just how great an asset to the production the distinguished composer actually proved

CHOREOGRAPHIC MUSIC

to be." Another writer said the music was as superficial as its subject-matter.

NOTES

(1) *The Dance Observer*, February, 1936
(2) *The Drama Magazine*, December, 1930
(3) In an interview with Korngold on March 12, 1936
(4) White, *Stravinsky's Sacrifice to Apollo*, pp. 26-27
(5) Bauer and Peyser, *Music through the Ages*, p. 496
(6) *The Étude*, May, 1930, p. 322
(7) Propert, *The Russian Ballet in Western Europe*, pp. 102-103
(8) *The Dance Observer*, Vol. I, no. 5, June-July, 1934
(9) White, *Stravinsky's Sacrifice to Apollo*, p. 68
(10) Pound, *Antheil*, p. 109
(11) Pound, *Antheil*, p. 109
(12) Boughton, *The Reality of Music*, p. 171
(13) Haskell, *Balletomania*, p. 133
(14) Calvocoressi, *Music and Ballet*, p. 56
(15) *Letters of Claude Debussy to his Editor*, p. 85
(16) Haskell, *Balletomania*, p. 121
(17) Stravinsky, *An Autobiography*, p. 67
(18) Propert, *The Russian Ballet in Western Europe*, p. 105
(19) Abraham, *Borodin, the Composer and His Music*, pp. 203-204
(20) Pound, *Antheil*, p. 106
(21) Puccini, *Letters of Giacomo Puccini*, p. 243
(22) Draper, *Music at Midnight*, pp. 149-150
(23) MacDowell, *Critical and Historical Essays*, p. 27
(24) Stravinsky, *An Autobiography*, pp. 277-278
(25) *The American Dancer Magazine*, June, 1936, p. 17
(26) *New York Times*, Sunday, May 3, 1936
(27) Vaughan-Williams, *National Music*, p. 103
(28) White, *Stravinsky's Sacrifice to Apollo*, Chapter II
(29) Propert, *The Russian Ballet in Western Europe*, pp. 99, 98, 100
(30) In a letter to the author from Rome, Italy, dated February 28, 1936

OTHER RUSSIAN BALLETS

Actually, there are two Russian ballets. One of them lives now in the memories of those who witnessed and who participated in it, and in a modern attempt at re-creation. That was the ballet Diaghileff took from Russia. The other ballet is that which was left behind: still clinging to its old-fashioned traditions, to inartistic dance forms and to rather obvious accompanying music, for the most part. It is today not in the least an advance over what was done many years ago, without the refinement that must have existed then. The Russian ballet that came to Western Europe was not the real thing. It was Diaghileff's super-dream of the real thing!

This leads us to doubt Cyril Scott's statement (1) that "Folk dance music had already done much to imbue the Russians with boldness and patriotism, but it was the Ballet with all its enthusiasm-creating rhythms and tone colour which finally put a torch to the long-smouldering fire and endowed the leaders of the revolution with the essentials to set it in motion." Obviously, the Russian ballet Scott saw (unless he had been in Russia)— the ballet that he presumed started the Russian revolution —never existed in Russia at all!

Chaliapin's autobiography is by no means the only book that speaks of the tremendous service of Diaghileff for Russian music as a whole. The world now recognizes him as a ballet impresario, but he was not content to have the world think that the Russian ballet was the only fine thing in Russia. Therefore, he organized huge European festivals of Russian theatrical performances: operas and art exhibitions as well as ballets, and thus became the first to spread the gospel of the modern Russian music that took the world by storm.

Diaghileff actually began his artistic career as an inspiring composer, but was discouraged by Rimsky-Korsakow. Then this creative sense manifested itself in a different way, when he acquired a veritable passion for cutting, correcting and re-assembling ballets. The music for *Le Festin* and *Cléopâtra* was thrown together in this way. Later in his career, it was his pleasure to employ fine composers and to employ his own creative feeling in making subtle suggestions to them.

It was Diaghileff who first made possible the glorious fusion of music, painting and choreography and brought the finest artists (Picasso, Benois, Bakst); the most superb choreographers (Fokine, Massine, Balanchine); and the most talented composers (Stravinsky, Liadov, Debussy, Tcherepnine, Auric, Bax, Berners, Falla, Dukelsky, Glazounow, Hahn, Lambert, Milhaud, Poulenc, Prokofieff, Ravel, Respighi, Rimsky-Korsakow, Rieti, Satie, Sauguet, Steinberg, Schmitt, Strauss, Tommasini) into his productions. Not all of them were Russian composers. Some of the music was commissioned, some of it pre-composed and adapted to the dance. The result of Diaghileff's efforts was far greater than the mere propagandizing of Russian music and the glorification of his own name. To-day, there is scarcely one fine composer who has not thought of composing for ballet and for pantomime as a means of creative expression!

With Diaghileff, everything was a complete picture in which every element was carefully balanced, and the dancers were clearly just one of the elements. In all the discussions Arnold Haskell had with him, he never once claimed as his own ideas that Haskell *knew* had come from him. "His autocracy and leadership were understood things. It pleased him to be generous, it was the prerogative of being a Tsar(2)." A period of brilliant decadence and supercilious cleverness in music has been associated with the last decade of the Diaghileff ballet. This was, perhaps, to be expected. It is a great strain always to be producing something that is more of a novelty than the last effort. Diaghileff's Russian ballet was itself so much of a novelty that when it came to England, attention was concentrated on the brilliance of setting and dancing rather than the music(3). When its newness disappeared, there had to be novelty in its presentations, and so on. One of Diaghileff's clever moves in combating this situation has already been mentioned.

Glazounow is of our era, and his music was used by Diaghileff. But his ballet music belongs to a bygone day in Russia. He wrote three ballets, all in the regular rhythms associated with the old school, with scarcely a section that is musically outstanding. His *The Seasons*, op. 67, is in two parts. The first part consists of Winter: Frost, Ice, Hail, and Snow; while the second part is Autumn: Bacchanale, Petit Adagio and The Satyr (a variation). Glazounow's *Raymonda* is an attempt to picture Medieval times. The Saracen Abdourahman plans to abduct scornful Raymonda, but is thwarted by the return of her betrothed, Crusader Jean de Brienne, who kills him in a duel and marries Raymonda. This ballet, dedicated to the artists of the Imperial Ballet at St. Petersburg, is merely pleasant, tuneful music depicting moods and scenes. The pantomimic episodes have most of their melodies ornamented with arpeggios and short, rushing scale passages. There is a Valse Fantastique which, judged by modern harmonic standards, doesn't seem fantastic at all. Incredibly enough, there is also in the ballet an excuse for Arabian, Spanish, Hungarian and other characteristic dances, though to declare openly that the music for each of these dances is entirely characteristic would be to take too much for granted. Glazounow's *Ruses d'Amour*, op. 61, is a ballet in one act, a Watteau pastorale, originally choreographed by Petipa. The simple introduction is suggestive of an old French Chanson, and there follow many dances characteristic of that period in France. A departure from the usual is the fact that the divertissements in *Ruses d'Amour* come at the outset, rather than in the Finale. The music, unlike that of *Raymonda*, has about it a freshness and spontaneity that would indicate that the composer was more at home in the musical contemplation of Watteau than of Medieval times.

Prokofieff, like Stravinsky, was a reformer. He once composed a ballet on a mythological subject (the prehistoric Scythians who used to wander over the Russian steppes) which he submitted to Diaghileff, who was impressed with the music in spite of the fact that he did not condone the subject matter. He therefore commissioned another ballet from Prokofieff, at which the composer assembled the mythological ballet music into an orchestral *Scythian Suite*, or *Ada et Lolly*, op. 20. In it, the second episode is the Dance of the Dark Spirits. The *Scythian Suite* is said to be the only existing rival to *Le Sacre du Printemps* in the realm of barbaric emotional appeal.

For Diaghileff's commission, Prokofieff wrote *Chout*, a development of a folk tale of the Arkhangelsk region: a satirical tale of a buffoon in disguise. It has been described as being amusing, wicked, venomous, subtle and mocking. The music is at times broadly melodic, decidedly polyharmonic, brusque. It is left to the melodies and dissonant harmonies to supply the sardonic effect, since the meters are not at all unusual. Prokofieff made use of an ingenious device for unity: entr'actes extended from the same initial melody, treated differently in each case, only to end with the same peremptory, heavy two measures, identical in rhythm to those of the short prelude, heralding the coming scene. In some of these entr'actes, themes from the preceding scenes are reiterated. The story of the ballet is sardonic in itself. It ranges from a merchant's love scene to a young woman being transformed into a she-goat and buried. The ballet is said to be impregnated with the folk, though not in the sense that other composers have used folk dance tunes. It could be defined, says one writer, as an anti-fairy ballet. At all times it suggests the realistic, skeptical people who refuse to believe in miracles. It amuses us as an exaggerated farce.

Le Pas d'Acier, Prokofieff's "Bolshevik" ballet, based on life in Soviet factories, was also written at the instigation of Diaghileff who, at the première in London when Goossens conducted, insisted on sitting near him in the orchestra pit in order to be ready to leap onto the stage and calm any signs of protest from a very hostile audience. Nothing happened to warrant it, however. The ballet is a choreographic view of the most horrible year under the Soviet regime (1920) when people died, starved, froze and were tortured. It presents the rhythm of the time, the poetry of mechanics, and is a remarkable tour-de-force. Characters in it are peasants, commissaries, an orator, a sailor who becomes a worker. There are factories, hammers, and so forth. The music, then, is discordant, abrupt, complicated, angular, uncompromising, dissonant and reminiscent of pounding and frenzy. It gives the sensation of whirring, clanging machinery and of unceasing toil, of perfect mechanical organization and strength. All of this alternates with a frequent, consonant, peasanty melody. The dissonant chords amount almost to tone clusters, at once characteristic of the composer and of the subject he chose to portray. Even the changing scenery is accompanied by a long piece of music, starting in octaves with a running accompaniment figure, and gradually adding more notes and gathering intensity until the end.

About this time Prokofieff is said to have turned his back on modernity and returned to clear, simple musical design. Whether this was a lasting condition is problematical. At any rate, he now composed for Diaghileff *The Parable of the Prodigal Son*, which was a lyric work, redolent of the classic spirit, in keeping with its character. It was not merely picturesque, and its music has "grandeur" for the most part, with the exception of a few rare animated episodes. Prokofieff's *Sur le Borsythène* also returns to the old. It renews classic dance forms such as the Gavotte. It was produced at the Paris Opéra.

Lately, at the request of the Bolshoi Theater in Moscow (the national opera house) Prokofieff wrote a ballet based on Shakespeare's *Romeo and Juliet*, but a preview of it merely served to emphasize the incongruity of libretto and music: the former adhering to the worst of the old traditions, with a happy ending; the latter in a realistic idiom, successfully characterizing Shakespeare's lovers. Before the formal first presentation to the public, a change was expected to be made in the libretto.

A Russian composer who now seems to be part of the American scene by virtue of his adoption of the name of Vernon Dukes in order to write popular tunes for Ziegfield and others, is Vladimir Dukelsky, composer of symphonic music and of ballets for Diaghileff. (Dukelsky's adoption of the American name is ironic, in view of the affectation of foreign names by many American musicians who wish to make good in their own country.) At the age of twenty-one, while he was in Monte Carlo, Dukelsky wrote the ballet *Flore et Zéphyre* on a libretto by Boris Kochno. Because the music was reminiscent as well as melodious and ably scored, a critic of that day opined that later Dukelsky would "develope such qualities as inspiration, content, and the ability to discard the inessential." Part of the scenario and music of *Le Jardin Public*, portraying a poet's day in a public park, is said to be by Dukelsky. It is based on a fragment from André Gide's *The Counterfeiters*, and it is opened and closed (presumably at dawn and at night) by a sharp drum tattoo. Dukelsky's third ballet is entitled *Field Day*.

Before speaking of Soviet composers, it may be as well to mention the ballets of Alexandre Tcherepnine, the final creation of Alexandre Scriabin and the ballets of Liadov and Arensky. The latter's ballet, *A Night in Egypt*, op. 50, contained Dances of Slaves, Jews, Ghazis and Snake Charmers as well as a Waltz and the Solemn Entrance of Antony. Liadov wrote the ballets *Kikimora* and the placid *Enchanted Lake*. Scriabin's last unfinished work, *Mystery*, was conceived as a synthesis of three arts: poetry, music and dance. These were not to complement each other nor to be dependent on each other. They were to be three independent factors holding together in contrapuntal relationship, resulting in an insoluble, artistic whole. Scriabin's later ideals went far ahead of our mortal conceptions. He was a mystic and a philosopher.

Somehow, deeply rooted in the mind of Alexandre Tcherepnine(4), is the thought that choreographer, stage director, scenarist and composer must be in complete agreement in order to produce a perfect product. For that reason, he works toward just such a collaboration when he composes his ballets. It happened that Pavlowa returned from India at the precise moment that he became interested in the religion of the East, so it was but natural that he should compose a ballet for her on a similar subject. The result was *The Frescoes of Ajanta*, op. 32, a large series of divertissements on ideas of the ballet master. Pavlowa had been investigating the subject in India, and had thought to bring with her cloth for costumes as well as native records. Native themes had been gathered by her musical director, Theodore Stier, in a native theater. These appealed to Tcherepnine, so he made use of two or three of them. The characters in the ballet are Prince Guatama (Buddha), his wife, and their attendants. The theme is the Great Renunciation of twenty-five hundred years ago. The scene is the entrance to the Temple of Ajanta. The music is thematically unified. Its composer was happy in its creation, for he enjoys writing music with a purpose. He also wrote the ballet, *Training*, op. 37 no. 3, long before its first performance in Vienna. The story concerns two boxers and its form demanded a fugue, therefore Tcherepnine made it fugal. Then the music and dance forms corresponded: an entire ballet (though short) without stops. In 1936, the young Tcherepnine was hard at work on a new ballet for the Berlin Opera: *Fahrend Schuler mit dem Teufelcannon*, working from a large page of detailed notes as to duration and character. These notes were taken during a conference of the composer, choreographer and artists before Tcherepnine left Europe. He believes that music for the dance should be a different music than that which is abstract. But he also believes that music can play a strong part in assisting other arts, such as the dance, to revitalize themselves. In 1937 Tcherepnine wrote the ballet *Trepak* for Mordkin.

Delius was of the opinion that Russian composers are trying to give a strange, half-barbaric mixture of Orient and Occident; or Wagner and the *Danse du Ventre*. Casella also commented on the Russian output, though his remark referred only to the new Soviet composers: "Two things are especially noticeable: the disappearance of the folk and national elements, and a dangerous rhythmic laxity."

The frequent use of ostinato basses and strong rhythms in Russian music is said to be due to the Tartar influence. Harmonic exoticism comes from the Russian-Greek church. The atmosphere of the East is achieved by chromatic melodies and metrical irregularities such as ⅝ and ⅞, and by placing three, five or seven bars in a structural unit.

Best known of contemporary Russians in the new school of composers is Dmitri Shostakovitch. Since he is a product of Soviet Russia, he is more concerned with music in its social implications than in its artistic aspects. He is still very young, yet his recent ballet, *Limpid Stream*, was the cause of worldwide musical comment after it was banned in his own country. His first ballets were not so unfortunate. Both of them make use of the Polka. Galops and Waltzes also abound. *The Bolt* parodies these dances with bombastic humor. It is said to present the ironic conflict between two opposing viewpoints. The music reveals the composer's "amazing craftsmanship and splendid scoring." *The Golden Age* was criticized by Herbert Elwell, himself a composer, as having a "callow striving for originality, nose-thumbing antics, and juggling of banal tunes." Excerpts from these ballets have been played a good deal in concert outside of Russia.

When Shostakovitch came forth in 1936 with *Limpid Stream* (or *Sparkling Brook*, as some translate it) he met an entirely different reception from Russian authorities, who also looked askance on his opera, *Lady Macbeth of Mtsensk*. As far as they were concerned, a composer of Shostakovitch's renown is inevitably linked with his native land in the minds of audiences all over the world, and by his efforts all contemporary Russian music is judged. So, with the thoroughness that has characterized all of their moves, they banned the ballet on the ground that the composer had shown in his work formalism, eccentricity, skepticism, straining for effect. They wished (so they declared in print) (5) to put an end to the unwholesome, non-Soviet tendencies in his work, irrespective of the greatness of his talent and of his understanding of technique. They deplored his petty bourgeois methods. They deplored the fact that his new ballet music strums but does not express anything. They deplored the composer's susceptibility to Western influences, his loss of contact with his native soil and its people. They exhorted him to look to the limitless field of folk music and the heights of truly classical musical literature for his inspiration.

This field was explored by another modern Soviet composer, Boris Ber, in a ballet called *The New Russian Village.* For it, he transcribed modern Russian tunes as well as older songs. Music and dance showed thus a union of two psychologies, for in the dances, the feet did traditional steps, while certain hand movements and straight backs indicated a city culture. Goleizowsky was responsible for the choreography.

Glière, born in 1874, is known both as a product of the neo-Russian school, and of Soviet Russia. He and Serge Vasilenko were the first composers to appear after the World War, in the era known as "military communism." Because their music reflects the school of Rimsky-Korsakow, it cannot be termed "revolutionary." One of Glière's ballets, *The Red Poppy* (*Krasni Mak*) has always been extremely popular in Soviet theaters since its creation in 1927. In this ballet, the composer was prudent. He did not attempt a sudden break with tradition. Rather, he refreshed the old ideas somewhat. However, he did put forth a great effort to write music expressive of the new proletarian nation, and the result was strong dance music of a muscular, masculine, individual quality. It was said to have been written at a period of his development rather than maturity. The choreographic motive of *The Red Poppy* is the unloading of a steamer by Chinese coolies. The Dance of the Russian Sailors from this ballet has been played independently in many orchestral concerts. Glière's ballet *The Comedians* was said to have been lukewarmly received because of its uninteresting music. Other ballets attributed to this composer are the romantic *Red Moon*, *The Saporojzi Cossack* op. 64, and *Crisis*.

Vasilenko (born 1872) wrote the ballets *Joseph Le Beau* in 1924, and *Lola* in 1925.

Another neo-Russian who adopted Soviet thoughts in music is Kordenko, composer (in 1925) of *The Golden Calf*, a ballet-pantomime produced in Leningrad. It was symbolic of the struggle between proletariat and capitalist, with the former emerging victorious.

The subject of the ballet, *Flames of Paris*, by Boris Asafiew, born in St. Petersburg in 1884, is drawn from the French Revolution, based particularly on the march of the Marseilles battalion and the taking of the Tuileries on August 10, 1792. The music is a re-working of songs, hymns and dances of that period, with vivacious rhythms and sharp melodic outlines. A French critic said this of it: The trumpets of the funeral marches, to the sound of which the French revolution buried its heroes, as well as the ardent songs and dances of the revolutionists, have found a prodigious interpretation and expression in Asafiew's strong, forceful creation. Asafiew is known throughout Europe by his nom de plume, Igor Glebov. He also wrote the ballets, *The Hunchback Pony* (*Koniok Gorbounok*) and (in 1934) *The Fountains of Bachtissarai*, after Pushkin. The latter is highly romantic; its music is lilting and rhythmic. Asafiew's most recent ballets are *Partisan Days* and *Prisoner in the Caucasus*, also after Pushkin. The latter music was said to be undistinguished and typical of old-fashioned ballet music, though its dancing harked back to the folk, yet with a certain elaboration and refinement.

Since Nicholas Nabokoff's *Union Pacific*, to a scenario by Archibald MacLeish, is in the repertoire of the Ballet Russe now, it has become very well known outside of Europe. Nabokoff was born in Poland, of Russian and German parentage. His studies began in Russia. *Union Pacific* is built around the first American transcontinental railroad, completed in 1869. Therefore the music concentrates on folk songs of that period, some of which imitated the rhythms of chugging trains and galloping horses. Nabokoff took them from phonograph records. To retain the essential bareness of the original accompaniment, Nabokoff devised ostinato accompaniments for some of the tunes. The not-too-pretentious music was then orchestrated in collaboration with Edward Powell. Some sort of a record was set when this one-act ballet, in four scenes, was completed (scenario, music and choreography) in three weeks!

Union Pacific was not Nabokoff's first attempt at ballet writing. In 1928, Diaghileff presented his choral ballet, *Ode or Meditation at Night on the Majesty of God as Revealed by the Aurora Borealis*, a forceful, simple composition in oratorio form for large orchestra, chorus and soloists. The text was by the poet Lomonosoff, who lived in the time of Russia's Empress Elizabeth. There was no attempt at mere cleverness in the orchestration, and the motifs were strongly Russian in flavor. Over this ballet there was a critical controversy, one observer terming it childish, an English writer declaring that "Nabokoff will have to produce something more convincing than this before we begin to wave flags and hang out buntings," and a Parisian writer placing Nabokoff in the first rank of musicians, by reason of *Ode's* penetrating charm and the composer's rational use of dissonance, instead of a deliberate breaking of rules to force audience attention. Nabokoff also wrote the ballets *Aphrodite* and *Comédie*.

The Russian Maximilian Steinberg wrote for Diaghileff the ballet *Metamorphosis*, after Ovid, in which the dances and characters are Greek. He also wrote, in 1914, the ballet *Midas*, depicting the musical contest between Apollo, God of the Lyre, and Pan, God of the Shepherd's Pipes. Steinberg has the orchestra braying to denote King Midas' ass's ears, when His Royal Highness objects to Apollo's being awarded the prize.

The biting musical satire of the Russians is evident in the music of Lyof Knipper, born in 1898. His ballet, *Santanella*, displays intellectuality and romanticism. Ultra-modern Nicholas Slonimsky who now makes his home in the United States, has written a ballet called *The Prince Goes A-Hunting*, while all of the music of the modern Russian composer, Paul Juon (born 1872) is said to be impregnated with frenzied dance rhythms.

Julien Kreyn, born in 1913, wrote for Ida Rubinstein a ballet called *Galatée,* somewhat influenced by the modern French school. He is the nephew of the Russian, Alexander Kreyn, whose greatest success as a composer has been in the Jewish musical idiom. Arends, a modern Russian, wrote a successful ballet after Flaubert, *Salammbo.* It was produced in Moscow.

Now there must be mentioned another custom of Soviet theaters: that of re-writing established stage works to fit their own ideas or their own circumstances. Many works have been produced in Soviet theaters with a soupçon of propaganda added. Others have been created anew, simply because the subject-matter is desirable.

For example, the Russian Alexander Shenschin wrote the ballet *Carmen*, a choreographic expression of the source material of Bizet's opera, using fundamental Spanish rhythms and folksongs. Falla's ballet, *The Three-Cornered Hat*, was treated by Vasilenko in such a way as to pad the plot with extra scenes and dances. Spanish folksongs and melodies from other works by Falla were added to the original score.

Even Russian critics condemned the latter production (which was but one of many similar ventures) on the ground that it discloses the theater following the line of least resistance.

CHAPTER 16

NOTES

(1) Scott, *The Influence of Music on History and Morals,* p. 145
(2) Haskell, *Balletomania,* p. 109
(3) Ellen Terry wrote a book on the Russian Ballet, published in 1913 by Sidgwick and Jackson. In it she said, "The Russian ballerinas accomplish the feat of being fluent on their toes. They do not hammer out the steps. It is a false notion of rhythm that there is a hammer-stroke on every strong beat. But they take a collection of steps, as a singer takes a collection of notes, and calmly and gracefully phrase them." (From a review of the book in the *Dancing Times,* January, 1918, p. 234)
(4) In an interview with Tcherepnine in Los Angeles on March 28, 1936
(5) *Moscow News,* February 19, 1936

THE INFLUENCE OF THE ELEMENTS OF JAZZ ON THE WORLD'S DANCE MUSIC

It has been said that jazz is the folk music of America; that all great national schools of music have been built on the songs and dances of the common people, and that Mozart, Haydn and Chopin, were they alive today, would write Fox Trots as naturally and as inevitably as they once composed Gavottes, Minuets and Mazurkas.

The word "jazz" has occasioned scores of *authentic* anec-dotes (all entirely different) as to its origin. They need not be recounted here.

In spite of the fact that Diaghileff thought jazz in the United States was due to the "Jewish sardonic vein," one thing is indisputable: jazz is Negroid. Other influences may have come later, but the first impulse came from Africa. Some travelers who have observed closely African primitive music claim they can see in it no resemblance to jazz. Doubtless such people are not themselves musicians, and are so blinded by the clever instrumentation of modern jazz that they cannot recognize the basic characteristics. Hence they see no similarity.

One might remind these people of the note addressed by· George Antheil to Ezra Pound, in which he wrote(1), "I am beginning to get annoyed with Americans who tell me that jazz will be the music of the future.   My God, the African Negroes have the American Negroes stopped a mile for every kind of rhythmic and musical effect.   American whites must have a bad effect upon their Negroes, don't you think?"

As a matter of fact, syncopation itself was known to and used by the classicists.   Thus wrote Jean Philippe Rameau (pre-classicist) on syncopation in his treatise of music: "As soon as a Note begins on the unaccented part of the bar and one half of its value is heard on the first part of division of the next bar, that causes a shock to the ear and in that case, that note is said to be syncoped, and is called a Driving-Note."   Chopin once wrote, "I wish our letters would fly, like syncopations."

Jazz, then, is not just syncopation, as some people believe. It is a very special "something" that the Negroes added to what we have known as music that enables it to be called jazz. Many definitions of this have been advanced.   Paul Rosenfeld calls jazz an entertainment that temporarily removes people from contact with the realities.   Robert Edmond Jones believes that this rhythm is the outermost and thinnest layer of our consciousness.   Mary Austin wrote: "As we use the term jazz, it implies a particular kind of musical rhythm which requires the body to correspond to it by particular and unusual movements. Actually, jazz is a group of movements which have become exteriorized in musical intervals and accents."   Cyril Scott(2) has attributed to jazz much of the unrest of the present day. Said he, "The orgiastic element about jazz's syncopated rhythm, entirely divorced from any more exalted musical content, produced a hyper-excitement of the nerves and loosened the powers of self-control."

A curious fact is that the more one reflects upon the excellence of these definitions, and the more one considers the subject itself, the more one wonders whether anyone on earth will ever be able to describe in words exactly what jazz is, why it has taken such a hold upon people all over the world, and why it has influenced so many serious musical works, especially those in the ballet idiom.

The writer has but one explanation to offer: there is something *fundamental* about jazz, as well as something as fascinating and as exciting as the Viennese Waltz rhythm.

There is jazz in every country to which the Negro was taken, but in each case, it is a different jazz from that which came from North America, due to the different alien cultures that fused with the Negroid.

What the Jew in America did to jazz, according to Saminsky and Goldberg(3), was to add his racial poetry, a sort of homeliness in words, set to a singable tune. That is Irving Berlin. Almost all of America's popular music is for dancing, whether social or specialty. It became popular through its simple melodies, small in range (as are folk tunes), and through constant repetition of these melodies within range of receptive ears.

It is interesting to note that the dance movements that accompany jazz music have had the same effect on dance movement as a whole that jazz itself has had on music. Whereas in classic dancing, knees and toes were turned scrupulously out, jazz dancers now develop knock-knees to add to what is termed "sex appeal." Whereas classicism developed a beauty of line by extending the foot until one danced only on the point of the toe, jazz dancing uses flat feet and heels to emphasize its intricate taps. Whereas classic arm postures surmounted a rigid body, today the hips, shoulders and head do the major part of the dancing while the hands dangle loosely. Of course, this is a word portrait of contemporary jazz dancing: but any detailed study of the work of modern concert dancers will reveal that they have assimilated those actions, and made good use of them in quite a detached manner—in such a detached manner, perhaps, that they would even resent the suggestion of such an origin.

Many songs of identical epochs in the development of American popular music sound similar. This is no doubt due to the fact that a truly popular song was much copied, with the result that there are innumerable one-steps, two-steps and Waltzes that are practically identical, just as there were later ragtime pieces built on similar patterns and, still later, Blues and Fox Trots.

First (along with barn dances and such) came the era of the popular ballad and coon song, as well as soft shoe dancing. The Juba Dance was a dance of slavery days, and "the New York itch," as W. C. Handy terms it, is simply a more eccentric evolution of this old dance. When Handy(4) was a boy, the Jenny Cooler Dance was almost as foolish as Truckin'. In the 90's, there was a dance called the African Pas, consisting of raising hand to forehead in a salute and making four shuffles backward and to the left. Songs accompanied these dances. To do the Pas, the song went: "First you do this, then you do that . . . Stand up rightly, do it lightly, that's the Pas-a-ma-la." When Chris Smith wrote *Ballin' the Jack,* the song had words descriptive of the actions of the dance. Nobody thought of such a thing but the Negro. White people held to the folk dances of the mother country and of London music halls, until jazz engulfed them and forced them to change their dance movements to conform to its sound.

There.was a great vogue for Cakewalk music, and by white writers, some of whom picked up their tunes in Negro communities as played by local mandolin and guitar bands. Some of the best known Cakewalks were *Creole Bells, Georgia Camp Meeting, Eli Green's Cake Walk.* There were many publishers for this music in the country outside of New York: Iowa, Cincinnati, and so on. It mattered not whether the Cakewalk music was marked ¾, ¼ or Alla Breve—the Cakewalk tempo came out just the same, and the musical pattern remained as before, despite the constant improvisation of the dance steps and the fluctuation of the choreographic pattern. The beauty of the dance was in the self-expression and individuality of each couple. It is true that the Negroes often danced their Cakewalks to old English folk dance songs borrowed from Southern planters and elaborated upon in characteristic fashion. But it was the other—the genuinely Negroid Cakewalk music that paved the way for ragtime and the Blues. Scott Joplin's *Maple Leaf Rag* and W. C. Handy's *St. Louis*

Blues were the first of these types to be published. The kinship of the latter to spontaneous folk music is attested by its continued popularity. About the same time, the Airplane Waltz, Maxixe and Tango were popular, and music was written to fit their movements. The Hesitation Waltz also found great favor.

The Shimmy, which occasioned many a Shimmy song, was a purely Negroid dance—even, one might say, an ancient dance, for the colored people had done those steps and figures for many years before the dance became universal. There is a Shim-Sham-Shimmy in Harlem, danced usually to the *Call of the Freaks,* written by a colored band leader named Luis Russell. This, says E. Simms Campbell(5), is a "hot" number with a rolling bass and a fast, high treble introduction. Its rhythm (as well as that of the dancers' taps) is decidedly Negroid. Its pulsations are as old as time. Both music and taps blend in recurring crescendos and diminuendos. Two fast choruses usually suffice. Throughout the dance, they sing in low tones: "Oh, shim-sham-shimshamshimmy!" As W. C. Handy remarks, "They just can't dance like white people and enjoy it!"

The Charleston rhythm has been found by Handy to be similar to the Tango rhythm which came originally from Africa. There the Moors borrowed it from the Negroes and named it Tangana. They took it into Spain where the Spaniards called it Tango. The Habanera rhythm (also of African origin) is identical with that of the Tango, though the dances differ. The Fox Trot became a popular dance, with much music written to accompany it. Truckin', the Black Bottom and the Lindy Hop are evolutions of Negro folk movements. The only difference in the way these dances are done now is that sophisticated performers add to them something similar to what sophisticated composers have added to jazz.

Readers may be confused by several of the foregoing paragraphs, since many will recall that certain white performers have claimed to be the originators of several of the dances which were mentioned as being of Negroid origin. The truth of the matter is that these performers were better businessmen and women than the colored artists; they saw the possibilities in Negroid dance and music, listened intently and watched—sometimes even took lessons from—performers in Harlem, and then went out and sold the "new" dances and their accompanying music as their own creations. Had colored people tried to sell their own product in those days, it would doubtless have been refused, or would not have attained such wide popularity as it did through the intervention of others. "I can recall," declared a noted Negro musician, "When fellows sold a song for the price of a meal. It became famous under someone else's name, and they were forgotten."

Paul Whiteman's place in the history of jazz is unique. He is not a musician: he is a showman. He does not claim to be the originator of jazz, nor to be a song-writer or even an arranger. Yet, without him, jazz would not now be a household word. Shrewd and daring, Whiteman was the first to recognize jazz's possibilities and to orchestrate it. Under his regime, music for social dancing actually became symphonic. He recognized the fact that there is a substantial reason for the popularity of the old masters; therefore he did not frown when he had to admit that Mr. Bach, Mr. Handel, Mr. Chopin and Mr. Puccini had supplied themes for the biggest jazz hits in history. Whiteman was first to give a jazz program in a fine concert hall. To do this, he concentrated on novel instrumental effects. He tried to get his jazz band to produce extreme sounds: the deepest, the most piercing and the most seductively soft tones. Thus, when one was far enough away from his orchestra, only the rhythm was heard, while harmony and melody formed a subordinate accompaniment. Then, in spite of bright lights, immaculately tailored men and spangled women, the sophisticated atmosphere uncannily faded to primitive surroundings. The music was of the jungle, and the rhythm had the power to call one back!

Though Whiteman publicized jazz, there are still people who insist that he spoiled it: that he, by over-sophisticating it, had really denatured it. As a consequence, when everyone presumably turned from jazz as we know it to "swing" music, they were really turning back to jazz as it actually is, since swing is nothing more than rhythmic jazz.

Whiteman took jazz to Europe, where critics wrote that it showed not a greater skill, but skill of another kind: in diversity of rhythms and instrumentation. Whiteman did not apologize for the different new music he had brought out of America. Rather, he was as proud of it as Europe is of her own music. Consequently, Europe accepted American jazz for what it was. Paradoxically then (to quote William Grant Still) while American composers are derided for writing music in European molds, all the European composers who attempted to write in the jazz idiom (and there were many) were lauded to the skies. Their mental processes were analyzed and their achievements dressed up with a great many fancy adjectives.

These composers have had ample opportunity to appreciate jazz. After Whiteman's advent, scores of jazz bands, both white and colored, sprang up. The radio, the films, and all the sophisticated revues featured it. Today, wherever one travels, one finds American dance music. After being rowed through long lanes of beauty: the romantic flower-bordered canals of Xochimilco in Mexico, one arrives at the grand climax, a huge advertisement for a popular brand of beer and —an orchestra playing American jazz! In wealthier South American homes are books of music, copied painstakingly by hand—mainly composed of the latest jazz hits! Europe dances to it. At one time it bade fair to gain such a foothold in Germany that it and all "jazz in disguise" were banned from the radio, since an effort was being made to promote pure German dance music(6). This was rather a large order, since the Viennese Waltz is the only European dance form which can compare with jazz in point of rhythmic charm and piquancy. Other folk dances are charming, but the popular European dance music, written by second-rate composers, is as insipid as a certain cheap variety of American popular tune. Even Japan has found a use for jazz. A certain Japanese authority believes that it can save the silkworm industry from great damage by driving a parasitical worm into the body of the silkworm where it will die of asphyxiation. (This is from a Tokio news dispatch of December 5, 1936.)

Claude Debussy was the musician who antedated Whiteman in discerning the possibilities of jazz. Into his *General Lavine—Eccentric* he wrote a musical caricature in the form of a Cakewalk, as early as 1910! His *Minstrels* and *Golliwog's Cakewalk* are also in the ragtime idiom, but—such was his foresight—in them he actually anticipated some of the later developments of jazz itself! In other words, Debussy was—in jazz as in many other things—a prophet. Satie was another Frenchman who wrote ragtime, but he, in his *Ragtime du Paquebot* from the ballet *Parade* satirized it by utilizing all of its cheapest elements.

By his own admission(7), when Stravinsky composed his *Ragtime* for eleven instruments (including the Hungarian cémbalo which so fascinated him) he did it with the idea of creating a composite portrait of the new dance music, giving it the importance of a concert piece, as former composers had done for other dance forms. In his *Piano Rag Music* he stressed the piano's percussive qualities. The different rhythmic episodes were dictated by the fingers themselves.

Ravel came to the United States only to be impressed by jazz. He gloried in the music of Harlem night clubs and in the taps of the dancers at Roxy's, even as other visiting artists and critics had done. He accordingly made use of this new idiom. There emerged a Sonata for violin and piano in the Blues idiom, as well as *L'Enfant et les Sortilèges,* when the teapot and teacup sing a duet and dance a Fox Trot, in which jazz and Chinese music combine. Ravel later discarded jazz as a musical tool.

Marion Bauer quotes Milhaud(8): "Jazz was like a beneficent thunderclap which cleared the art-sky"; and declares that his tribute to jazz was the ballet *Creation of the World* in which he tried to release jazz from the narrow confines of the dance. He even dreamed of writing a jazz symphony, but wrote the ballet instead. This ballet had a Negro Adam and Eve, and was scored for a slightly enlarged jazz orchestra, treated as a purveyor of purely symphonic music. Milhaud also wrote a *Rag Caprice* and included a fugue on a Blues theme in his *Études*. His jazz is polytonal. Though his *Le Bœuf sur le Toit* is a cinema-symphony on South American airs, its syncopation gives the music the appearance of jazz. But that, again, is merely another case of the penetration of African dance music into widely separated lands.

La Revue de Cuisine for five wind instruments and piano, with a lively Charleston section, was Bohuslav Martinu's little musical joke. Jean Rivier wrote an overture for a Don Quijote of any age which is by turns noisy and sentimental, and which utilizes saxophone and jazz. Constant Lambert's *Elegiac Blues* is dedicated to the memory of Florence Mills, while his *Rio Grande* is cast in an idealized jazz form. The Tango, Boston, Shimmy, Blues and March rhythms have all been tumbled into Kurt Weill's *Three-Groschen Opera*. This composer has written an opera called *Mahogany* in jazz idiom. In 1919, Auric wrote a Fox Trot for two pianos called *Adieu, New York*. The rhythmic figures are authentic, but are clothed with such mournful, modernistic harmonies that the spirit of jazz is scarcely recognizable.

There is a good deal of tap dancing and a ballet doing the Charleston in Krenek's jazz opera, *Jonny Spielt Auf*. Critics said it sounded jazzy, but lacked rhythm. They also thought the composer had conceived some amusing ideas about our music and our customs. Since the writing of that opera, Krenek has utilized the jazz idiom in other operas, even introducing it into *Orestes,* a Greek drama, in the belief that he had discovered a new musical idiom and was employing the dance as a means of psychological expression.

These compositions by foreigners are most interesting in themselves. Further, they show the extent to which the elements of jazz—modern dance music—have influenced the world's abstract music, even as dance music has done through the ages. But, Mr. Haskell to the contrary, they are not jazz. No one but an American can write jazz successfully. Even Vaughan-Williams (9), an Englishman, agrees with that concept: "At all events jazz, whether you like it or not, is a purely indigenous art. No one but an American can write it or play it. Also, attempts by Americans to dress jazz in the European symphonic style are failures." In this respect, it is of value to note the observation by Charles Seeger(10): "Let it be said by one who *does* appreciate good jazz that there has not come to his notice one single treatment of jazz in the so-called 'art-music' that did not lower the value of the work as art and fail utterly to be one-tenth as good music as the improvisation of any good Negro dance-hall band."

Paul Whiteman(11) once remarked that "Jazz is a free form. It has no rules and I hope it never gets any." Yet there are almost unconscious rules in jazz. In its very freedom it is set, except for the fact that it is advancing year by year and that the popular songs of today are totally different and infinitely more pleasing than those of the preceding decade.

Popular songs in America are not long-lived because they are made to sell. Publisher and composer alike are eager for the huge royalties that the short-lived song will bring, not the money that would come in over a period of years from finer efforts. Martin Broones admonished a young composer: "If you would be popular, use only tonic and dominant chords. No diminished sevenths!" Ralph Rainger carefully wrote the lyrics for one of his new songs in words of one syllable. Domenico Savino heartlessly arranges everything for popular consumption by ruthless harmonic and rhythmic changes and implacably defends himself upon the grounds that he is making things commercial.

Things like this have caused many people to raise the objection that modern dance composers are untutored. This is not entirely true. Many have studied composition seriously. They are not so different from men like Rimsky-Korsakow and Verdi who, after having written some of their greatest successes, acknowledged that they needed technical training and set about to acquire it; except that the jazz composers are compelled to continue writing commercial music in order to make a living.

This commercial music was given a decided compliment by Percy Grainger (12) when he said, "I have in mind the extremely clever jazz manipulations of popular themes with marked rhythm that has taken place in the last few years. These orchestral arrangements are often made by musicians with unusual experience. To my mind, this form of jazz is the finest popular music known to me in any country of today or even of the past."

Irving Berlin was quoted thus by a studio publicity writer: " 'Never try to rush a composition. It's apt to take a day, or a week, or even a month to complete, so don't be hasty.' In one case," ran the item, "A particular song was written by him in a single night without changing a note or a lyric— but, of course, he's Berlin!"

One wonders what masters like Beethoven, Mendelssohn, Falla, Brahms and Debussy would say to a remark like that? It will be remembered that Beethoven painstakingly readjusted many times his simplest works. Mendelssohn criticized himself so severely that he removed eleven sections from *Elijah* after the first performance. Brahms withheld compositions for two years from publishers who had requested them, in order to perfect them. Falla wrote and re-wrote every bit of his music before publication. Debussy's *Pelléas et Mélisande* occupied him for more than eight years.

Robert Schumann (13) once wrote of "an alliance against a certain class of mechanical musicians who compose by the yard, today for the church, tomorrow for the ballroom." This is perhaps like some of our contemporary jazzists who, however, bring the ballroom to the concert hall and gain thereby critical acclaim as pioneers rather than critical sneers as upstarts.

Thus, jazz has its pioneers, too. Those who wish to criticize those pioneers should remember that the pioneers of many schools of music have been untutored. Were it not for them, the scholars could not have added the finishing touches.

That the elements of jazz will make a typical American symphonic music eventually, when handled tastefully by the finest composers, is a fact that cannot be denied. When Stokowski played Morton Gould's *Chorale and Fugue in Jazz*, he spoke of the widespread influence of jazz. Gould was but twenty-two years old when he wrote this interesting, sometimes frankly funny composition.

Jazz is used as an American musical idiom in Frederick S. Converse's opera, *The Immigrants;* in Werner Janssen's orchestral *Christmas Eve in New York* and in many of Copland's works. Of the latter, Saminsky says, "Stylization of the jazz-pattern, the condensing of the jazz-spirit into a cultured form, and even the peculiar neurotic exhilaration of jazz, is not native to Copland; the unsavoury, shrieking cartwheels in *Music for the Theater* is the artificial, casual Copland."

Louis Gruenberg had an entire period during which he believed that jazz had a definite place in the scheme of musical composition. He then wrote a *Jazz Suite*; *Jazzberries*, op. 24 for piano; *Jazzettes* for violin; three sets of piano pieces: *Jazz Masks, Jazz Dances* and *Jazz Epigrams*, op. 30; and *Daniel Jazz* for voice and eight instruments to a poem by Vachel Lindsay. Today, Gruenberg mentions this period as one from which he has emerged very definitely.

Emerson Whithorne's *New York Days and Nights* is a serious work containing jazz effects. This composer lives in New York where, when he has composed for many weary hours at a stretch, he turns on some jazz records, smokes a cigarette and accumulates enough energy to return to work.

This, then, is the way the elements of jazz will enter into the true American music: the finest American composers will absorb it and, having allowed it to become a part of themselves (as it is of the daily life of the American people), will write splendid music with no thought of idealizing jazz. But—it will be there, in one or the other form, lending a harmonic and rhythmic glamor and an exotic instrumental color to the whole.

Moreover, just as dancers and composers have accepted the Viennese Waltz and other national dance forms as a permanent part of their repertoires or their creative consciousnesses, so they have accepted and will continue to accept jazz. In crude and sophisticated dance music the world over it is a well-defined and undeniably strong influence.

CHAPTER 17

NOTES

(1) Pound, *Antheil,* pp. 87-88

(2) Scott, *The Influence of Music on History and Morals,* p. 152

(3) Saminsky, *Music of the Ghetto and the Bible,* p. 108

(4) In a letter to William Grant Still from New York, dated March 4, 1936

(5) *Esquire,* February, 1936

(6) *Musical Courier,* October 26, 1935, p. 16

(7) Stravinsky, *An Autobiography,* pp. 122-123

(8) Bauer, *Twentieth Century Music,* p. 270

(9) Vaughan-Williams, *National Music,* p. 127

(10) Cowell, *American Composers on American Music,* p. 341

(11) In an interview in Los Angeles on September 28, 1926

(12) *The Étude,* September, 1924, p. 593

(13) Schumann, *Music and Musicians, second series,* p. 27

*

CHAPTER 18

*

THE BALLETS OF JOHN ALDEN CARPENTER
AND
WILLIAM GRANT STILL

"The ballet, with its kaleidoscopic freedom and rhythmic interest, easily appears to be the ideal solution for the creation of large-scaled musical works indigenous to America."(1) While that bit of intelligent thought was being formulated in Walter Anderson's brain, two native American composers of widely different temperaments and musical styles were busily proving that he was correct. One was a businessman by the name of John Alden Carpenter, the other an Afro-American of steadily growing talent named William Grant Still.

Still and Carpenter are among those few composers to stride definitely away from the regular-rhythmed dance music to which the public is accustomed. Their music is at once valuable as music, racially fascinating, not imitative, and choreographic. Both of them first wrote ballets with foreign backgrounds; both of them later came to write ballets expressing the American scene in good-humored, satirical music. The later ballets are thus doubly significant.

Carpenter's ballets are interesting for another reason. The first two, *Birthday of the Infanta* and *Krazy Kat,* were created simultaneously with the choreography, when Carpenter him-

286

self was in the closest collaboration with Adolph Bolm. *Birthday of the Infanta* was based on the Oscar Wilde story (also set in different ballets by the English Imogen Holst, the Hungarian Nicholas Radnai and the German Bernhard Sekles; in an opera by Alexander von Zemlinsky and as an orchestral piece by the Austrian, Shreker) though the actual working scenario was planned by Carpenter.

Between Carpenter and Bolm there exists a great personal sympathy, perhaps represented by the fact that the former is godfather to Bolm's son. At any rate, this sympathy doubtless greatly facilitated their artistic collaboration and left them, throughout the years, with the deepest admiration for each other. Bolm declares(2), however, that during the creation of the ballet, he left Carpenter entirely alone, until the composer began to send him completed parts of the score from time to time. In one instance, Bolm asked that his own solo dance be shortened. He had recognized instantly that no human being could hold an audience's interest, or have enough breath for that length of time. Carpenter carefully considered the matter and shortened it by at least one half.

On the other hand, Carpenter(3) avers that the *Infanta* was written in the beginning with definite choreographic groupings and movements (as suggested by Bolm) in mind. It was a successful fitting of music to action, but was nevertheless a score which, for its complete effectiveness, depended on the dance. In other words, says the composer, such a score is apt to be quite ineffective for concert purposes without violent eliminations and rearrangement.

Since the subject was of the old Velasquez period, Carpenter had to write in a Spanish idiom. The ballet contains a festival for the young princess, gifts brought to her, Spanish dances, a mimic bull fight and the caperings of the dwarf Pedro who fell in love with the charming Infanta when she threw her handkerchief to him, but died of shock and surprise when he repeated the dance he had dedicated to her in the palace antechamber and saw his own image in the mirror.

Krazy Kat was conceived in a definite desire to write some-

thing typically American. It was to last about twelve minutes
—because, after all is said and done, one American trait is
brevity: the art of saying much in few words. Why should
it not be so in music? George Herriman, creator of the
Krazy Kat comics, devised the actual scenario, so that the
music is an attempt to re-create the whimsicality of that strip.

Carpenter's Krazy Kat is the world's greatest optimist:
Don Juan and Parsifal rolled into one, and it is Ignatz Mouse's
function to burst the bubbles as fast as Krazy blows them.
Krazy is discovered asleep under a tree at the outset of
the ballet, to which Herriman adds "which isn't a bad way
to discover any Kat!"

Barrère conducted the 1922 performance of *Krazy Kat*
in Town Hall, and in this Bolm was eminently successful as
Krazy Kat himself, more so than anyone has ever been since.
If such a character is difficult to express musically, it is more
difficult to dance effectively. One must be prepared to cope
with the preconceived ideas of a public who nightly devour
Herriman's cartoons. John Tasker Howard has written at
length about this ballet. It is a charming tonal picture of
Krazy, Ignatz Mouse and the rest of them, including Officer
Pup. Among American works it is recognized as being
thoroughly American. Its humor is exaggerated, its caricature
slapstick and its effects jazzy. Howard says it was an interesting experiment in transferring the jazz idiom to respectable
company. Krazy's happy psychology runs through the score,
and the whines and laughter assist the buffoonery. In fact,
it is termed a "jazz pantomime." Carpenter is intensely subtle
in *Krazy Kat,* though Howard says it would have been quite
possible to make the music as superficial as the cartoon appears
on the surface. Krazy is really a human creature with the
weaknesses and vanities common to us all, and the brutal
derision of Ignatz Mouse is Life, bringing us to earth from
our dreams. Carpenter, he finishes, has sharpened the elemental nature of these passions and given us appropriate music
even in the quasi-Broadway tunes.

There is in *Krazy Kat* a little—but only a little—of the

JOHN ALDEN CARPENTER
American composer

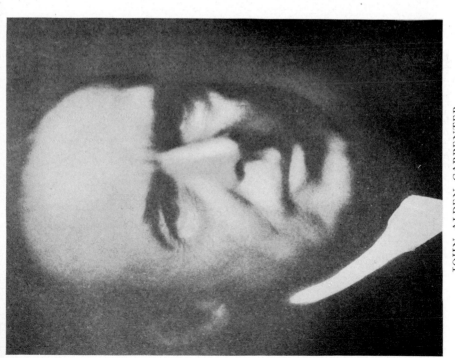

WILLIAM GRANT STILL
Afro-American composer

ÉCOLE DE DANSE

The costumes have changed, but the music and the dance steps remain the same as in the old ballet

After a painting by Degas (1834-1917)

Carpenter we find in the later *Skyscrapers*. It is frankly slap-stick. If anyone but the tasteful, musicianly Carpenter had written it, we might easily term it "cheap" music, and in that case writers like Mr. Howard would not have devoted so much space to it. Dare we believe that Carpenter in *Krazy Kat* leaned backward in his eagerness to picture the dance in music, that he was overly-influenced by too-simple patterns? Carpenter himself admits that as between the two methods of composing a ballet, the one he used in *Skyscrapers* (writing the music first, to follow the basic idea inherent in the subject; leaving the choreographic details to be imposed on the finished score) is to him far more congenial and logical. There is no comparison between the two methods, he declares!

Diaghileff commissioned *Skyscrapers* in 1924, after seeing the score of *Krazy Kat* and photographs of the action. He asked for a ballet dedicated to the modern city. It appears that the lack of story in *Skyscrapers* (later the cause of many hectic incidents) was occasioned by the great impresario him-self, for Diaghileff suggested writing the music in general terms of contemporary American life without regard to story or action, the details of which, he assured the composer, would be supplied later by himself and his associates. Indeed, Diaghileff *did* make some suggestions after the score was completed: suggestions which Carpenter adopted. Though Diaghileff's production of the ballet never took place, it was once produced in Germany under the title of *Wolkenkratzer*.

As a starting point, Carpenter worked out the broad out-lines of a dance sequence to be played in about thirty minutes, based on the alternating ideas of contemporary American work and play as reflected in the superficial life of 1926, when the ballet was written—a comparatively simple problem, according to the composer. The title was to be *Song of the Skyscrapers*, and it was to be based on the premise that American play-noises are jazz. Carpenter completed his score, based on that rough scaffolding of ideas. Then, and only then, were the detailed actions and dances imposed on the music, having been worked out in a collaboration of Carpenter, Robert Edmond Jones and Sammy Lee. Working according to this method, Carpenter believes that any composer has greater freedom and a better chance of achieving a general unity of form with a resulting work which should be available for concert purposes without rearranging.

Whether he realized it or not, it was evident in the music of *Skyscrapers* that Carpenter had thoroughly absorbed the feeling for dance movement that Bolm had imparted to him during work on the first two ballets, for in *Skyscrapers* he spontaneously and without limitations wrote excellent choreographic music! Moreover, much more mature music than in the two previous ballets, but that may have been due to his growth as a composer, or to his fancied freedom from limitations.

When he planned his ballet, he remarked informally to Bolm, "I am composing a ballet which I want to be free, and to have scope and breadth." They both glanced briefly, in passing, at a huge building that was being erected near Bolm's hotel. Bolm replied, "Then I hope you will put into it plenty of this modern sound!" Carpenter smiled whimsically and answered, "That's what I've already planned!" Of course, he was right. There is plenty of "this modern sound" in *Skyscrapers*.

Nevertheless, Bolm and Carpenter disagreed on some points. The latter had been impressed by jazz, and by such things as a police strike in Boston, while Bolm visualized a scene looking through a New York alley, and all that would happen there. He made no bones about saying that he considered Carpenter's subject weak: Lacking a logical sequence of events, or even an organized plot. And this in spite of the fact that the scenario of *Krazy Kat,* which Bolm sanctioned, is extremely simple—in fact, almost elementary! His premise is that a ballet is essentially of the theater and, being so, should have all the attributes of the successful theatrical drama, plus fine music and superlative dancing, in which case it would exceed in entertainment value any other form of theater art.

Carpenter's fragmentary, incomplete thread of story led to the application of strange remedies in a later (1933) Hollywood Bowl production of the ballet. No one approves of dancers ruthlessly changing scores to suit their own ideas, nor dancing a totally different ballet and calling it *Skyscrapers*. But perhaps there is a little to be said for them, in view of the circumstances. It appears that one of the reasons for changes was that some imaginary authorities had obligingly opined that life had greatly changed since the ballet was composed. Whereas in 1926 people ate hot dogs for diversion, in 1933 a hot dog constituted a full meal. For that, and similar reasons, the ballet was changed. Robots worked on the Skyscraper and waited on table in the cabaret, while a bloated plutocrat known as The Boss had a dream in which angels sang, a seductive lady charmed him and demons pursued him. Into the mêlée was thrown a prizefight. The new scenarists openly admitted that their "reasons" permitted them to retain the title of the ballet and eliminate the subtitles. Lo, the poor composer! Has he no jurisdiction over his brainchildren?

Skyscrapers introduced saxophones, banjo and tom-tom into the orchestra of the conservative Metropolitan Opera House. It is also scored for full orchestra, two pianos and two solo voices. The music accomplished several things. It placed Carpenter in the front rank of American composers, for many believed that his greatest strength lay in composing serious jazz (of this sort) with a view toward dynamic and forceful characterization. It brought him to the attention of musicians as an orchestrator, a producer of rich effects and varied tone colors. And it definitely pleased people like Henry O. Osgood(4), who could recognize in it clever distortions of such old tunes as "When ye ain't got no money, well, ye needn't come around." In addition, it portrayed the rush and confusion in contemporary America and was frankly based on the cacophony and rhythmic movement in our city streets.

In the printed score, Carpenter gives yet another reason for the lack of plot: it proceeds on the simple fact that American life reduces itself essentially to violent alternations of work and play, each with its own peculiar and distinctive rhythmic character. The action of the ballet is merely a series of moving decorations reflecting some of the obvious external features of life, as follows:

Scene   I : Symbols of restlessness
Scene   II : An abstraction of the skyscraper, the work that produces it and the interminably passing crowd
Scene III : Transition from work to play
Scene IV : Any Coney Island and a reflection of a few of its activities, interrupted presently by a "throw-back" in the film sense, to the idea of work, and reverting with equal suddenness to play
Scene   V : Return from play to work
Scene VI : Skyscrapers

The ballet opens with a stirring, unquiet ⁵⁄₄ rhythm (Allegro molto) strongly accented, the small repeated notes giving the effect of restlessness. Thereafter, changing rhythms and accents lead quickly into Scene II, in the same tempo, but with fragmentary melodies (perhaps depicting faces in the crowd) over the same accented, changing basic rhythm. The Strutter's Solo Dance is one of the smoothest, nevertheless most obvious, melodies in the entire ballet. The Negro scene is based on a slow, ecstatic tune with intervals and cadences suggestive of Spirituals, though at the Hollywood Bowl it became an angelic scene. This progresses to a lively ⁴⁄₄ with accents on the last halfbeats, reminiscent of those ragtime fiddlers who continually stamp on the floor when the regular beat has passed. The return from play to work is emphasized by a reiteration of the main theme of the ballet, again in fragmentary fashion, after which comes the seemingly unending "Skyscrapers" rhythm. The ballet ends in a burst of glory, a final animated section.

In this music is heard the tapping of hammers, the screaming of rivets. Somehow the effect of altitude is given, of a rising ever higher, and of people returning from ambitious work in the clouds to small pleasures closer to the beloved earth: to human company and loves and hates, to contemplation even of the prosaic sandwich man. *Skyscrapers* teaches that pleasures are close to God's creations; work nearest man's ideals. Howard(5) finds, deep in the music, an underlying irony and pity for the seeming futility of it all. He finds the themes to be more fully developed than episodic and declares that Carpenter was finely restrained, had climactic *moments* only and allowed himself the effectiveness of contrasts, when it would have been so easy for him to be common! Evidently Carpenter, like Pavlowa, never chooses "the easiest way."

Robert Edmond Jones(6) describes the method by which he and Carpenter drew action out of the completed music: "Carpenter would play the music, giving me an idea of the changing orchestration. He played each passage over and over again for hours. This gave me certain ideas of movement for which I drew tentative designs to be discussed with him. Countless patterns were made during six months of grueling, unremitting labor. From those we selected the final succession of designs, one growing from the other, parallel with the music." The foregoing description was read avidly by a critic(7) who had just heard a concert performance of the music. He wrote sarcastically, "The average listener cannot spend six months listening while the composer plays over the same passage hour after hour," and further intimated that the music, stimulating when accompanied by dancing, seemed far less significant when deprived of it, because the action in the operahouse so thoroughly engaged the eye that the ear failed to notice monotonies. Though *Skyscrapers* uses American tunes to depict American scenes, he found it Russian in its rhythmic pulse and dissonance. Because of the uneven meters, one wonders? Surely the Russians have no monopoly on that. Too, one might inquire, what exactly is the difference between a Russian and an American dissonance?

Be that as it may, Carpenter is also the composer of the famous *Tango Americaine, Polonaise Americaine* and *Little Dancer and Little Indian:* idealized dance forms. He is vividly contemporaneous and his works are considered by folk like Olin Downes to be the most brilliant that are being produced today in American music, because he is constantly drawing closer to life and constantly growing more mature.

A totally different phase of the American ballet is expressed by the younger William Grant Still, himself representative of all the presumably necessary attributes of an American composer. He is known as an Afro-American, yet the blood of the American Indian also runs in his veins. He was born of intellectual parents. He studied earnestly with Chadwick and with Varese, opposite poles of musical thought. At one time or another, he has played most of the instruments in the orchestra, whence comes the intimate knowledge that leads to his striking orchestrations. He was once associated with jazz, that typically American expression. To his youth may be attributed his spontaneity. With such a background, his music cannot fail to be individual, racial and national. Moreover, it contains the elements of greatness and of permanence, for it makes a direct appeal to people's hearts. Still prefers to let his Negroid characteristics display themselves in the structure of his works, rather than on the surface. He stands head and shoulders above the rank and file of Negro musicians, for he is not a copyist—not even of motives established by others of his Race.

The most American of all Still's ballets to date is his *Lenox Avenue*. For many years, he had been gathering themes and putting them into a little notebook, almost all of them exact, as he later used them. Suddenly, Columbia Broadcasting System invited him (along with five other prominent American composers) to create a musical work designed especially for radio. Soon then, *Lenox Avenue* (a series of eleven orchestral episodes with intermittent spoken lines for the announcer) sprang into being. It was seemingly the inspiration of the moment, really the accumulation of years of thought. After the composition was complete in its orchestral form, Still realized that it would also make an effective ballet: a series of choreographic street scenes typical of modern Negroid life, and he immediately set to work to give *Lenox Avenue* a new form. It has thus a dual identity. He avows a similarity in the theme of this orchestral piece, or ballet, to that of his opera, *Blue Steel* and insists that it happened purposely, to ally the voodoo theme of the opera with the raucous rhythms of contemporary life as expressed in the shorter work.

If Still's *Lenox Avenue* is jazz (and many will insist that it is, though it was not intended to be) then the source of jazz is truly established once and for all. For these motives are characteristic, though entirely original with the composer. They were suggested to him by infrequent excursions into night club life and frequent visits to revival meetings in search of little-known Spirituals, for which he has a genuine fondness. In this way he succeeded in re-creating the actual atmosphere while not adhering to themes invented by strangers. If Still's ballet music is primitive, it is because he is himself sincere and can therefore create only what comes to him naturally—*as do primitives!* Except that Still has added to his creations the sophistication, the polish and the knowledge he has gained and that is, in effect, his heritage, strange as it may seem.

Still's approach to the composition of dance music is unique. He had seen Pavlowa dance, and though her artistry impressed him deeply, he was even then searching for newer, broader forms of choreographic expression in music. Thus his music is rhythmic in such a distinctive way that it can only be adequately choreographed with modern, free movements: the realization of his mental vision. His music is also conducive to sustained movements, not erraticisms. Instead of mentally picturing actual dance steps, he visualized the general trend and feeling of each dance. While he composed his dance music, he would sometimes rise and dance about the room, not only to ascertain the tempo, but also to determine the characteristics and feeling of the music in relation to the movement. Often he would conceive a dance in its elemental form and make the music, in pitch and in rhythmic values, correspond to that form: the pitch determining the dancer's movement in space; the rhythm determining the foot or floor patterns.

Still's realization that the ballet was a form that even he might adopt for musical expression came about through none other than Adolph Bolm who, while on a trip to South America, became fascinated by Lafcadio Hearn's tales of Martinique and wished to visit that island. He was prevented only by an iron-clad steamer schedule. On his arrival in New York, he sought out Still as being the one American composer who would be most likely to feel such an atmosphere accurately. He loaned Still the book by Hearn, suggested the theme of *La Guiablesse* for a ballet, as well as one dealing with the Mardi Gras which he had also suggested to Griffes before then. Then, from Chicago, Bolm actually commissioned Still's Ballet, *La Guiablesse*. Ruth Page produced a scenario after Hearn's story, and Bolm promised her that she might dance in it when it was completed.

Bolm made many excellent suggestions on receipt of Still's first score. Therefore the composer took the ballet back, for extensive revisions. One of Bolm's precepts about ballet-writing appealed to Still as being applicable to anything one might create, in any form: to say what one has to say as briefly as possible (8).

Still's earliest compositions were all scrapped and whatever was good in them incorporated into a larger work. Thus the *Dance of Love* became a part of the *Sorcerer* ballet, and the *Dance of the Carnal Flowers* was, with very few changes, written into *La Guiablesse*. The former ballet is rather more pantomimic than active and was never produced, though it was composed at the suggestion of Dr. Howard Hanson. It had not as much vitality as his other ballets. Still planned to transform it into a one-act opera and did use its themes elsewhere. The latter ballet (*La Guiablesse*) is a tri-cornered story against a colorful background of intrigue and vitality: an excellent setting for dance movements. It was written in first draft before Still's *Sahdji*. Its revision followed the creation of *Sahdji*.

The music has an individual appeal, more a blend into dance movement than subservience to it. Critics wrote that it was far above the average ballet music. La Guiablesse herself is a devilish creature who appears in the guise of a beautiful woman to lure the susceptible youth to his death. The score of the ballet is vigorous and sophisticated, and the rhythmic patterns are (as always in Still's music) bizarre. It is, on the whole, choreographic music, which is actually true of very little music written for the dance. That is to say, it needs a choreographic interpretation corresponding to the lack of superficiality in the music. Before writing *La Guiablesse,* the composer studied West Indian and Creole musical material, but was not impressed by it. He determined to create his own themes as being truer to scene and mood.

The scene of *La Guiablesse* is laid on the Island of Martinique. The opening theme is that of the temptress. This appears also throughout the text and finally in the concluding funeral march, giving a strong unity to the ballet. However, the "she-devil" herself is introduced by a distant contralto solo: a haunting, wordless melody.

"*La Guiablesse* is a work of talent. *Sahdji* is a work of genius!" once remarked an observer of Still's music(9). Indeed, it is only after a careful study of these two ballet scores that one realizes the truth of that remark.

Sahdji is Still's ballet for orchestra, chorus (singing a text relating incidents in the action), and for bass chanter (reciting ominous African proverbs). The scene is laid in old Africa: a hunting feast of the Azande tribe, when Sahdji, a woman who loves life intensely, must die with her dead husband, the chieftain Konumbju, while her sweetheart, Mrabo, assumes the leadership of the tribe. The scenario is by Richard Bruce and Alain Locke.

Even as Still had investigated West Indian and Creole material for *La Guiablesse,* so he spent approximately eighteen months studying African lore in preparation for the writing of *Sahdji.* This time, the effect of his study was more satisfactory because his thoughts at the outset were more sane. His first desire was simply to absorb the atmosphere so that he would be able to write in an African idiom without using folk material. The Invitation Dance (named so by Dr. Hanson), where Sahdji tempts Mrabo, came to him first. Around it the ballet was built.

Still had no idea that he was reverting to ancient ideals when he wrote this ballet, yet it would be difficult to find any other modern work which contains so many elements of the old Greek drama without being constructed on a Greek subject: the chorus moving rhythmically as it sings, morals pointed by a portentous, lonely figure (the Chanter, a bass soloist) as well as the masterly orchestral accompaniment, skilfully mirroring the moods of each moment.

The dramatic quality of the music is apparent even in the short introduction to the ballet and in the melodic prologue sung by the Chanter before the ballet begins. This is a late addition to the ballet, the most important change made during Still's recent revision of *Sahdji*.) In *Sahdji*, the dances were so completely visualized that the composer was able to write a description of them into the score. During the chants, Still indicated stage actions, such as the women's rhythmic clapping during the men's chant, or the men's stamping while the women are dancing.

Nathan Emanuel (10), who danced the leading rôle of Mrabo in the initial presentation of *Sahdji*, considers it the easiest to perform of all the American ballets presented at Rochester, since the music is so dramatic and so suggestive of every emotion, and since the composer had spared no energy to give the performers detailed notes as to the way he wished his creation presented. Carpenter's *Skyscrapers*, being more abstract and containing fewer indications for the performers, was more difficult to interpret, though equally enjoyable. There was one difficulty in the production of *Sahdji*. One of the more lyric dances (in the orchestral version) had sounded intensely dramatic in the piano reduction to which the dancers had made their dances. They had, of course, suited their actions to the sound. When they heard the orchestral version they had to re-cast the entire dance.

The music of *Sahdji*, praised by the Rochester critics who twice witnessed the ballet, and by Olin Downes (11), who was struck by the intensity of the score, is a classic of its kind. Adelaide Hooker termed it "good theater," but it is more than that. It is elemental drama because it is a stylization of the folk impulse, of folk ceremonials, and of the emotional tempests underlying primitive life. In addition, there is shown in Still's ballet music detailed attention to the dramatic meaning of each dance, or episode, in relation to the complete ballet. Everything is part of a harmonious whole. Nothing is wasted, nothing superfluous. Once, in speaking of the creation of ballets, he remarked, "I love to write these things. I create little worlds of my own and live in them for a while." This, perhaps, best explains the utter reality of each composition in the choreographic idiom. It *is* real to its creator.

For Thelma Biracree, who danced the name rôles in *Sahdji* and *La Guiablesse* in Rochester, William Grant Still has lately written a ballet called *Miss Sally's Party,* in an attempt to preserve by re-creation certain peculiarities of American folk music and dance. The time of this ballet is "Not Long Forgotten" and the scene is The Old South.

There is a short ballet in Still's opera, *Blue Steel,* but this, far from being thrown into the proceedings with a total disregard for its necessity as opera ballets used to be, arises from a need in the story and serves as a symbol of the opera's theme: a keynote of mysterious tribal rites in the swamp. This composer's second opera, *Troubled Island,* also contains a stirring ballet. A coy dance of French pattern, in the Haitian banquet hall, suddenly becomes a savage voodoo rite, and the voodoo drums continue their bizarre pattern long after the dance has ended, to spell the doom of Haiti's Emperor Dessalines, central figure in the drama. Still is of the opinion that his own style is best suited to works for the stage. "I am naturally an economical person," he has declared, "and it is hard to be economical in large works for orchestra."

From the Black Belt, Still's short suite for chamber orchestra, contains a dance movement. His *The Black Man Dances* for piano and orchestra, consists of four Negro dances depicting as many phases in the life of the Race, from Africa to North America. Still used an original Blues theme in this, as he did in *Lenox Avenue.* He also based his entire *Afro-*

American Symphony on just such a theme, developed and inverted. He did not write jazz, as such, but succeeded in making it portray his subject. He believes the Blues to be more characteristically Negroid than many Spirituals, since they exhibit no trace of Caucasian influence. Many dancers have created original dances to Still's shorter piano compositions.

Other young Americans are following the lead of Carpenter and Still. The output of good ballets is increasing yearly in the United States. Both musicians and public are becoming dance-minded. This writer believes it to be a necessary development in the evolution of American music, and an unbounded field for inspired creation.

CHAPTER 18

NOTES

(1) *The Greater New York Weekly,* May 5, 1934
(2) In an interview in Hollywood on December 14, 1935
(3) In a letter to the author, dated December 3, 1935, from Chicago, Ill.
(4) Osgood, *So This Is Jazz,* p. 31
(5) *Modern Music,* November-December, 1931, p. 15
(6) L. A. Sloper in the *Christian Science Monitor,* December 10, 1927
(7) L. A. Sloper in the *Christian Science Monitor,* December 10, 1927
(8) In an interview in Los Angeles, California, on March 10, 1936
(9) Harold Bruce Forsythe
(10) In an interview in Los Angeles, California, on March 10, 1936
(11) *New York Times,* May 22, 1931

*

OTHER AMERICAN BALLETS

"If Charles Griffes had only lived. . . ." people are wont
to say, in the belief that if that had happened, Griffes would
have produced *the* great American music. This composer
was greatly attracted by ballet music. He asked Adolph Bolm
to give him a suitable scenario, but at that time, Bolm thought
that Griffes would best serve himself by concentrating on
purely symphonic music for the American public, and he was
then instrumental in getting a hearing for Griffes' *Pleasure
Dome of Kubla Khan,* the first notable attention Griffes had
received. Some time before, Griffes had completed the *White
Peacock,* for piano solo. Bolm took it, invented a story around
it and persuaded the composer to orchestrate it so that he could
dance to it in a theater prologue to a film. Later, Michio Ito
created a dance of his own to this music.

However, during the last years of the world war, Bolm
planned a concert in which Ito was to dance in a little sketch.
Ito had an idea. He wished to dance *The Spirit of the Wine.*
Everything was available but the music. For this, Ito had some
authentic Japanese melodies tucked away in his agile brain.
Griffes heard them, and on these themes, he wrote and orchestrated a little Japanese ballet, *Sho-jo* for that appearance.

Meanwhile, he continued to beg Bolm for a ballet subject. Bolm's suggestion had to do with the Mardi Gras, but they both hesitated about going ahead with it because it involved the question of race prejudice, a precarious one in the United States. From that day to the day of his death, says Bolm (who saw him but two days before the end) he was awaiting word from the choreographer to continue work on the Mardi Gras ballet.

Griffes may have sneaked off without Bolm's knowledge, however, to satisfy his amazing craving to write ballet music, since there is credited to him a dance-drama called *The Kairn of Koridwen,* scored for celesta, harp, five wind instruments, and piano.

Another American composer formerly associated with Bolm is Henry Eichheim, who in 1924 wrote *The Rivals,* a Chinese ballet lasting about twenty-five minutes. One writer says that the thematic material in this ballet is Mongolian city and country folk tunes, heard by the composer in China. Bolm, on the other hand, declares that he and Eichheim first discussed the music, then went from one Chinese theater to another in San Francisco to feel the atmosphere. This was partly so that Bolm himself could get acquainted with the movements and duration of Chinese theatricals. He and Eichheim made up a sort of detailed dummy of the ballet, describing exactly what would happen in each space of time. After that the music was created easily and quickly, much to the composer's surprise. Eichheim in 1926 wrote *A Burmese Pwe* for the Neighborhood Playhouse in New York, lasting about twenty minutes; as well as another Chinese ballet lasting but ten minutes, *The Moon, My Shadow and I.*

The American George Antheil created almost as much discussion with his ballets as did Stravinsky. There was a striking difference: no one was bold enough to insinuate that Stravinsky wrote noise instead of music, whereas such accusations constantly greeted Antheil. The exceptions were people like Ezra Pound and Gertrude Stein. Now that Antheil, from his safe seat in the film colony of Hollywood, has renounced ultra-modern noises and has declared that composers should return to writing melodies, one cannot help but wonder what the decisive Pound thinks of his wayward friend. Long ago, Pound wrote(1): "As for the machine shop, Antheil has opened the way with his *Ballet Mécanique;* for the first time we have a music, or the germ and start of a music that can be applied to sound regardless of its loudness. The aesthete goes to a factory and hears noise and goes away horrified; the musician, the composer hears noise, but he tries to hear what kind of noise it is."

This mechanical trend started when Antheil concluded, upon hearing a player piano, that any unmechanical music had reached its doom. He was naturally averse to having his own music stillborn, so from that moment on, the music he wrote was mechanical: ballets characterized by motion and a steel-like rigidity. The *Ballet Mécanique,* written in 1923-25, is scored for an orchestra of Antheil's wild dreams: anvils, airplane propellers, electric bells, automobile horns and sixteen player pianos. Half an hour of this caused ecstatic literary people to dub it "music of the future" and musical people to call it "naïve, infantile, passionless, forceless." Once that was out of his system, Antheil began to grope for his true métier, away from violent sounds. His fondness for jazz rhythms and tricks once made him take a trip to collect, in the heart of Africa, native forerunners of jazz. In 1929 he wrote a ballet after W. B. Yeats called *Fighting the Waves.* He also, in 1922 (before the *Ballet Mécanique*) wrote two ballets which have never yet been performed. His *Flight* is a chamber opera, or ballet for marionettes, written in 1927-30. His *Les Songes* is noted as the first score to be composed directly for the American Ballet Company. In his opinion, two long dances that he wrote for Martha Graham amount to ballets. One is called *Course,* an ensemble dance, the other is *Dance in Four Parts* arranged from his *One Hundred Preludes to the Woman with One Hundred Heads* after Max Ernst. Perhaps Antheil's interest in this form of composition arises from the fact that he is fond of dancing in its theatrical aspects and because he believes that America loves it too and will become a great dance country (2). Hence his desire to follow the trend of the times.

Aaron Copland's unproduced ballet, *Grohg*, has for its subject a fantastic necromancer who loves the dead and has the magic power of making them dance. The music, written during the years 1922-25, partly in Paris and partly in the United States, was orchestrated at the MacDowell Colony. The castle-like abode of Grohg is suggested in the opening measures; then there is a dance of an adolescent, later a dance of a young girl who moves as in a dream. The finale of the ballet is one in which all Grohg's servants and victims mock him. These dances were said by Paul Rosenfeld to suffer from rhythmic rigidity. Nevertheless, when in 1929 Copland could not complete a composition in the allotted time for the RCA Victor competition, he seized upon this ballet music, extracted a suite of three dances from it, called it *A Dance Symphony*, sent it to the judges and won $5000. It was later given a hearing by Leopold Stokowski and the Philadelphia Orchestra.

In his later ballet, *Hear Ye! Hear Ye!* Copland realized his dramatic powers to the fullest extent and composed music entirely representative of the American scene. This is a travesty on a murder trial, with three witnesses' conflicting views of the tragedy propounded. The jury compromises by believing every one guilty. Though the music has many lyrical passages, it is a running commentary on the action. It includes a motive of accusation, appearing each time a new person is accused. The three scenes are separated by music, and the score is flanked at beginning and end by a parody of the *Star Spangled Banner*, representing a distortion of American justice: the theme of the ballet. The debating attorneys are represented by polytonal episodes. The first scene introduces delightfully bromidic night-club music. For a chorus routine, Copland wrote piquant jazz. The rhythms are percussive throughout the ballet, but logically developed. The wittiest and most subdued music in this whole affair is said to be a parody on Mendelssohn's *Wed-*

ding March. For the Ballet Caravan, Copland wrote *Billy the Kid* which was received enthusiastically by audiences, and in which a typical saga of the West is related with stylized and sophisticated dance movements.

Robert Russell Bennett once composed a little ballet that was never produced, on a Pierrot and Columbine theme treated in the modern manner. So long ago did this happen that he has now even forgotten the name (3), but he thinks it was called *The Stolen Rose.* Though it was a very young work, it had vitality, and it served as a sort of prelude to his opera-ballet, *Endymion.* This was written in 1927, when Bennett was studying with Mme. Nadia Boulanger. In response to her advise to write something forceful, the American composer searched through old books and finally discovered this poem in old French, in five acts—obviously a libretto for someone like Rameau. As far as Bennett knew, it had never before been set to music, so he decided to do it. He went even further back than the time of Rameau for his musical material. Its ideal form was a combination of orchestra with dancers, chorus and soloists (the latter in the orchestra) but when it was presented at Rochester in 1935, the voice and dance were combined. The leading characters were Diana, Pan, and Endymion. The composer now considers this work stilted and artificial.

Now, for five years, Bennett has been planning to write two ballets on scenarios he has in his possession, one of them based on cartoon characters. The fact that he has hesitated so long before writing them leads him to believe that the ideas weren't sufficiently gripping. The modern method of getting some casual musician to write effective but worthless dance music after a dance has been completed interests him immensely, though he fervently hopes he will never be drafted into that sort of work. When he writes for the dance he thinks only of the mood and the ultimate effect rather than of the means by which it is produced. That is, the dancer's actual movements are extremely vague in his mind. Usually, his music for dance is part of a large work, in which the various situations engender different rhythms, and sometimes a momentary or continued combination of rhythms.

A curious coincidence is the fact that Werner Josten, born in Germany in 1888 but now living in America, in 1933 also wrote a pastoral, diatonic ballet called *Endymion*, with some dramatic moments. Before that, he composed (1928) a short ballet called *Jungle* and (1931) the ballet *Batouala*, lasting an hour. His most recent ballet is *Joseph and His Brethren* in six scenes, between which a narrator reads the Scriptural story. Each scene is developed as an independent musical form, indicated by the leading titles. The music is lyric and modern, yet archaic in feeling. There is much writing in the old forms, including whole fugue-like sections. The ballet depicts the principal incidents in Joseph's life: Preludio, Jacob's House; Pastorale, The Beloved Son; Joseph Sold into Egypt; Canzona, Joseph and Potiphar's Wife; Ceremonia, Joseph Interprets Pharaoh's Dream (and is oblivious to the charms of a court dancer); Sinfonia, Joseph Makes Himself Known to His Brethren.

The only one of Howard Hanson's works conceived directly for ballet was his short contribution to the general pageant of the California Forest Play in 1920. In 1926, this *Prelude and Ballet from a Forest Play* was produced at the Eastman School in Rochester, along with John Beach's twelve-minute ballet-pantomime, *The Phantom Satyr*. (Beach also wrote a half-hour ballet in 1925, *Mardi Gras*.) The work of the Eastman School and its choreographer, Thelma Biracree, in presenting American ballets is noteworthy, especially when one considers that, due to the fact that this school is largely devoted to music, there is a lack of many well trained dancers. Therefore the choreography in these initial presentations must be simple and direct, excepting that for the few splendid and expertly trained dancers who act as soloists. Many American ballets were first performed under Dr. Hanson's direction at the Eastman School; some were repeated elsewhere, and some were performed there after their introductory presentations by other organizations. The ballets of both Still and Carpenter were danced in Rochester, as were *The Marriage of Aude*, a lyric drama in three scenes, and *Three Japanese Dances* by Bernard Rogers. Burrill Phillipps' *Princess and Puppet* was presented in 1933. Phillipps, incidentally, wrote also *Courthouse Square*, with the flavor of rural America, and *Play Ball!* on an idea by Miss Biracree. Deems Taylor's *Circus Day* was presented in 1935. The following year saw the production of Schelling's *Victory Ball*.

In 1883 Anthony Comstock penned these lines: "Our youth arc in danger. Let no man be henceforth indifferent. Read, reflect, act!" And on that theme Martha Alter composed her ballet, *Anthony Comstock*, or *A Puritan's Progress*, in five continuous scenes, presented at Rochester in 1934. Her first step was to write a Comstock hymn in the Comstock style. This hymn is later used in large, strident form to signify Comstock's wrath. The ballet represents Comstock the fanatic, and the sorely tempted. Scene I is a panorama of the seventies, including a pseudo square dance. (Near the end of the ballet appears a more syncopated, more dissonant square dance tune.) Scene II depicts the Satyr, while Scene III is at the Art Students' Ball in New York City. Scene IV is Comstock's Vision and Scene V is conflict.

The Happy Hypocrite, on a story by Max Beerbohm, treating of the transformation of a young English waster into a serious man through his efforts to win a young girl, when his saintly mask finally becomes his own face, was composed in 1925 by Herbert Elwell, and produced at Rochester seven years later. The music neatly reflects the story, though, from the choreographer's standpoint it was too abstract to be easily worked out in dance form.

Emerson Whithorne's *Sooner and Later* is a dance satire on the progress of civilization. The music is modern, brilliant, clever, full of interest and contrast. It was written in 1925, is in six scenes, lasts two hours and is scored for chamber orchestra and chorus. The first part is a tribal ritual, working up to a sophisticated frenzy. Part II is the machine age in a city, with puppets burlesquing metropolitan scenes and the music satirizing popular songs. Part III is Life, a geometric pattern in the Crystal Age of the imagined future, with detached and dehumanized crystalline music.

In Lazare Saminsky's one-act Biblical ballet, *Lament of Rachel*, the traditional Synagogue chant *Lamnatzeach* was used to depict the aggrieved Leah, rejected elder daughter of Laban. (Jacob Weinberg wrote a ballet on a different aspect of the Hebraic scene: *Carnival in Palestine*.) Saminsky's ballet was composed some time between 1914 and 1920. He also wrote an opera-ballet in one act in 1915 called *The Vision of Ariel*; a merry symphonic dance-song of Estherka, medieval Jewish Queen of Poland in his *Song of Three Queens*; the one-act opera-ballet, *The Daughter of Jephtha* in 1928, a vivid ritual dance for piano, and *Gagliarda of a Merry Plague*, a chamber opera on Poe's *Red Death* (the Gagliarda is the dance to which the Red Death enters the castle). Shreker also planned to set Poe's *Red Death* to music. At one time André Caplet wrote a Fantasy for harp and bow instruments inspired by the same subject, but never developed it into a ballet as Calvocoressi suggested to him (4). Calvocoressi then submitted the idea to Ianco Binenbaum, a Turkish citizen resident of France. Binenbaum turned out a piece of grim, forceful, impressive, extraordinarily dynamic music on the subject, but all of his work came to naught, since by that time Diaghileff had announced a *Masque of the Red Death* by another composer.

Ruth St. Denis once wrote a tale called *The Spirit of the Sea*, a simple story of a fisher boy and a sea sprite who loved for a moment. This was made into a ballet by R. S. Stoughton, who sometimes made use of harmonies associated with French impressionism and of those associated with jazz, but in a most refined way. It is an attractive ballet, though not at all outstanding.

An utterly charming ballet on a delightful scenario by Winthrop Ames is Deems Taylor's *Kiss in Xanadu*, op. 16. This pantomime in three scenes was performed in the play *Beggar on Horseback* by George S. Kaufman and Marc Connelly. It is no marvelous psychological specimen, nor yet an extraordinary, compelling ballet, but it is certainly one of the inspired compositions for that type of theater that for so many years took the place of standard ballet in America. The duties of the attendants, the wistfulness of the Princess of Xanadu and the exit of the attendants are all mirrored in the music, even to her surreptitious reading of the yellow-backed novel after they have gone. Both Prince and Princess disguise themselves in fantastic fashion and slip away to a public park where they flirt and kiss, then return to their separate bedchambers. Here they awaken in the morning. The Princess, at breakfast, presents an apathetic cheek, which the Prince dutifully kisses. How different, says the slow, memorably romantic music, was last night's stolen kiss! They resume their seats with a sigh as the ballet ends. Taylor also wrote rhythmic ballet music for Gilbert Miller's production of the play, *Casanova* by Lorenzo de Azertis at the Empire Theatre in New York.

Joseph Achron has been the first to write an independent ballet for the screen, an impressionistic score which may be played by orchestra or piano. It was written in 1935 and is called *Spring Night*.

Two ballets on Negro themes were Lamar Springfield's symphonic *Legend of John Henry* and David Guion's primitive *Shingandi* for orchestra and two pianos. The latter lasts twenty minutes and was intended for the colored dancer, Hemsley Winfield, who died a few years after 1930, when the ballet was created. Guion wrote a *Mother Goose* ballet in the same year. In 1927, March Blitzstein wrote an orchestral ballet-suite called *Jig-Saw*, and in 1930, the ballet *Cain*. Long before Henry Cowell became interested in tone clusters, he wrote a ballet called *The Building of Banba* (1922, scored for fourteen-piece orchestra, chorus and vocal soloists) and one called *Atlantis* (1926, for theater orchestra and three voices). Now he writes percussion accompaniments for modern dancers.

Wayne Barlow was, in youth, obsessed by the idea of doing

a ballet on a social theme of conflict, so he wrote the as yet
unproduced *False Faces* on the theory that everyone presents
a false face to the world about him.   The score contains a
dynamic Workers' Dance.   Walter Piston's ballet, *The Incredible Flutist* was danced by Hans Wiener.   Eugene Loring
choreographed Paul Bowle's ballet, *Yankee Clipper*, said to be
clever musically, and to provide a sustained musical background for dancers.   Like conventional ballets, it is straight-
forward and episodic.   It contains tuneful sailor dances.   For
dancing, Robert McBride wrote *Show Piece*.   Elliott Carter
has written two ballets, *Pocahontas* (commissioned by Lincoln
Kirstein for the Ballet Caravan, Inc.) and *Bombs in the Ice
Box*.   For the Littlefield Ballet, Murray Cutter wrote *Snow
Queen,* and Herbert Kingsley wrote *Terminal* and *Ladies'
Better Dresses.*

The Ballet Russe has produced *Ghost Town* (scenario by
Marc Platoff after a story by Mark Twain) to a score by
Richard Rodgers, of the musical comedy team of Rodgers
and Hart.   It deals with an American town after the gold-rush
era.   The American Ballet Caravan has produced *Filling Sta-
tion* by Virgil Thomson, a pointed satire on the way Americans
think about the different classes of their society.   Rather than
underlining the dance action, move by move, Thomson's score
forms a running background aiming to enhance situations and
characters.   For the Ballet Caravan, Henry Brant composed
City Portrait, with his subject the struggle for existence by
an overcrowded metropolitan population.

Thelma Biracree has found that American ballets, on the
whole, demand a much more elastic technic on the part of
dancers than any other type of ballet.   Every form of dancing
must be used to express the American scene (i.e., ballet, modern
movements, pantomimic action, tap dancing and acrobatic
dancing) just as music expressing the American scene must
partake of many different idioms, most of them entirely
divorced from accepted European standards.

Declares Isabel Morse Jones, "The sense of creative joy
in a fundamental art movement is taking hold of American

audiences, who feel a closer participation in the dance than they do in merely listening to music." (5) But, though America has an increasing appetite for the dance, her appreciation of it is as yet in the earlier stages. She cannot appreciate a dancer from a purely artistic standpoint, as they did in Russia when the finesse of every movement was discussed and analyzed and when, it must be admitted, the artists of the Imperial Theaters played always to the same titled audiences, while the audiences in America are transient and the performances open to all who can afford them. America cannot yet appreciate a fine dancer in the abstract as she appreciates a fine musician. No, her enjoyment of dancers is tempered by the new, unusual creations they present. The fact that every dancer must of necessity be a creator today limits the dancers' rôles in the artistic world, but broadens those of composers, for each dancer is eager for new ideas and new music that will be interesting and have depth enough to be lasting. It is not to the costumer or scenic designer that the American dancer looks when inspiration fails—it is to the American composer!

CHAPTER 19

NOTES

(1) Pound, *Antheil,* p. 138
(2) In a letter to the author dated April 17, 1936, from New York City
(3) In an interview in Hollywood, California on April 13, 1936
(4) Calvocoressi, *Music and Ballet,* pp. 100-102
(5) *Los Angeles Times,* September 27, 1935

MODERN FRENCH BALLETS

No group of composers has written so many excellent ballets as the modern French. Their works are generally equally fine as theatrical spectacles and as music. In nearly every case, the music can stand alone, independent of the dance it should accompany. Perhaps the desire of Frenchmen to write lasting music for the theater was prompted by some thought similar to Saint-Saëns': We have had enough of opera without singing and ballet without dancing. He might have added "intellectuality without basic thought," for such was the state in which music once found itself, lacking in all human qualities.

French composers, too, have been the most influenced by jazz. They seem to have been fascinated by the rhythmic combinations, though their harmonies remain peculiarly their own. This preoccupation with a foreign musical idiom is shown chiefly in ballet music. This is logical, since jazz has always been identified with physical movement.

Paul Dukas' *La Péri*, in one scene, was said to be the first lyric poem danced on the stage, and to "introduce a new principle in the ballet: a free-form musical work, intimately united with mimic action, in which the mere picturesque had no part." An oriental motif permeates the score and gives rise to varied and ingenious harmonic and contrapuntal combinations. The music is delicate, impressionistic. The piano score looks much like a reduction of a symphonic poem, unplayable in the sense that it is not nearly as effective without its instrumentation, and Dukas has scored it excellently. It has a complexity of rhythms that must have delighted the souls of the listeners and dismayed those who danced it. There are occasional stretches of broad melody, but few outstanding musical themes, thus keeping the structural web more coherent. The ballet itself has but two characters. The scenario was Dukas' own. The music reinforces the action, and yet can produce an atmospheric illusion for the imaginative listener when played in the concert hall. It is interesting to recall that Burgmüller also wrote a ballet-pantomime called *La Péri* in Paris in 1843.

Dukas' success with *La Péri* perhaps might not have been so pronounced had not another composer a few years before (1882) braved the wrath of the Parisian public by writing symphonic music for dancing. This composer was Lalo (1823-1892), and his ballet was *Namouna*, in two acts. With only three months to complete this ballet before its scheduled performance at the Opéra, Lalo worked so far beyond his strength that he had a paralytic stroke. He recovered and, with Gounod's aid in orchestrating the last act, managed to finish the music. He was unhappy over it also, because he had had to make compromises with the ballet master and to write what he termed "music for legs." Actually, much of the score was melodic, with a picturesque, oriental flavor. It included Moroccan and Cymbal Dances, a Mazurka, and a Valse de la Cigarette. It was, apparently, exactly the sort of thing the French public would like. But, as so often happens, predictions went awry. True, musicians liked it. The public condemned it in advance as being the work of a symphonic composer. It was denounced as being too heavy and too dissonant. It was the first time ballet music had caused such a scandal. Someone suggested to Lalo that he should write some "danceable" music, to which he replied, "Do you want me to do *Giselle* over again?" They insulted his ballet music by calling it symphonic,

according to Julien Tiersot(1), and ever since it has lived as
art music, for it has been most successful in the concert hall.
Before 1905, Debussy wrote: "Among too many stupid ballets,
Lalo's *Namouna* is something of a masterpiece. Who knows
what dumb hatred has buried it so deeply that we never hear
of it now? What a loss to music!" Lalo wrote also an unsuccessful opera, *Fiesque*, the ballet music of which (under the
title of *Divertissement*) was successful in concert.

Since Erik Satie (1866-1925) never disdained dance
rhythms or melodies, his writing was said to reach the negation
of music itself! His first actual ballet was *Parade,* in one scene,
to a scenario by Jean Cocteau, whose enthusiasm for dancing,
syncopated music and the music hall atmosphere had inspired
the composer. This realistic ballet was the incentive for many
other similar sketches by other composers. (In fact, Satie
was said to have copied *Parade* himself, in the last ballet he
wrote. This was entitled *Jack* and the composer firmly believed that the manuscript had been lost in a taxi. His chagrin
vanished when he discovered it in the pocket of an old over-
coat.) There was no general dancing in *Parade*, rather, a
series of separate tunes. It was a jest, a caricature, a discon-
certing little affair. Its noise and its discord were dictated by
a clever brain, a brain whose guileless simplicity was an effective
screen for its depth. The music is diverting, and in perfect
accord with the scenario. *Parade* represents a traveling theater,
the advance ballyhoo of which the public mistakes for a performance. When it is finished, the audience departs and the
exhausted managers collapse. There is a fugal prelude, a Ragtime du Pacquebot, and a short, ironic, fugal epilogue to depict
the final surrender of the managers.

Satie's satirical humor again showed itself in the ballet,
Les Aventures de Mercure, a series of plastic poses burlesquing
the gods of ancient history. A suite from this ballet contains
the Dance of Tenderness, Dance of Mercury, Dance of the
Graces, Letter Polka and New Dance. *Relâche*, a ballet in
two acts by Satie, has more or less uneventful music which
French critics thought witty and amazingly ingenuous, while

heartily deriding the ballet itself. They wished to see the music attached to a more worthy spectacle! An American writer (Martens) (2) agrees as to the negligibility of the music. It employs popular tunes for the sake of the mood. The ballet as a whole expresses "aimless movement and the thoughtless joy of the moment." The authors described it as "Life without a morrow, nothing for yesterday, nothing for tomorrow, all for today," and as a "snapshot ballet in two acts, with a film interlude and the tail of Francis Picabia's dog." There is no plot. The music includes a big drum solo imitative of a railroad accident. It was evidently a satire on the opera-ballet, for its backdrop bore these words: "Do you *still* like the opera-ballet? Poor wretch!" Small wonder that on the eve of the première of *Relâche*, all of Paris turned out. The Avenue Montaigne was full of luxurious automobiles, the occupants wondering whether or not the farce would take place and dubbing it a "grave illness" rather than a joke.

Because Satie's ballet *Uspude* contained but one character, the manager of the Opéra ignored it when it was sent to him, refusing even to send a receipt for the manuscript. Then Satie angrily challenged him to a duel. The challenge was withdrawn only when a formal notice was sent to the effect that the ballet had been received, examined and found wanting. One presumes that Satie's final quip in ballet form was never written, since the composer was wont to announce publicly that he was carrying material for these ballets in his head and would soon prepare them. "They" were to be a series of three ballets: one in two acts; one in three acts during which no one appears on the stage; and one in four acts in which there were people on the stage and a miraculous apparition in Act III.

Debussy was more occupied with the music of his ballets than in trying to accomplish supreme irony. At least two of his three ballets contain some of the finest music he ever composed. In all of his works, his harmonies are pagan, his rhythms expressive of a feeling for movement. His ingenuity in imitating styles of composition has already been noted. Consequently, he fitted well into the creation of music for ballet.

Khamma, said to be a posthumous ballet in three scenes by Debussy, was actually composed in 1912, to a scenario by Maude Allan and W. L. Courtney. It is the least interesting of all this composer's ballets, because of his departure from his own idiom. The scene is laid in the interior of the temple of the Egyptian god Amun-Ra, but the opening music depicts a distant tumult. The prayer is a broad melody in octaves, while in Khamma's dance, open fourths are used, in the accepted oriental manner. Much of this ballet might be termed "mood music." However, critics have praised it. One says that the composer achieved a miracle of suggestion with the simplest means, another that it reflects musically all Debussy's powers of atmospheric evocation. Debussy himself described it as a "curious ballet, with its ringing of trumpets which makes one feel riotous, alternately hot and cold!" He was in feverish haste to complete *Khamma* to oblige Maude Allan, who was coming to Paris from South Africa with but one desire: to work on it with him. He did this because he wrote (in a letter of April 10, 1912) that a woman who could accomplish such perilous voyages without fear must know no obstacle to her will!

In the same year, Debussy was approached by Diaghileff for a ballet but since the composer had no subject handy, Diaghileff suggested placing the ballet in eighteenth century Italy. Naturally, Debussy thought this a bit contradictory for Russian dancers. The result was that Nijinsky supplied an inconsequential scenario, *Jeux*, on which Debussy went to work. His music for this was subtle, inventive, elaborate, poetic, intensely beautiful at moments, sensitive and a bit ironic. It belonged more to the realm of symphonic poem than to the ballet. At Nijinsky's instigation, however, Debussy maintained throughout a clear rhythm and well-marked themes, perfectly evident through the tonal embroidery that surrounded them. Diaghileff asked for one change in the music: the lengthening of the end, with which the composer was happy to oblige him. "It is true in the matter of the ballet," wrote Debussy(3) of *Jeux*, "That immortality passes through the legs of the dancer and finishes in a pirouette." (December 12, 1912). It is well known now that Debussy was not in the least pleased with Nijinsky's choreography for *Jeux*. "This man watches music pass by with a wicked eye: it is villainous; it is even Dalcrozian," he wrote to a friend.

After the slow, impressionistic musical prelude of *Jeux*, a tennis ball arrives on the stage to a charming descent of notes. This heralds the ballet itself, a slight tale of stolen kisses, jealousy and play. The theme is bandied about, and volleyed back and forth. The music is as nimble as the dancers. If, as Debussy once told Cyril Scott(4), his own style was limited, it still retains a definite fascination for its admirers and it is elastic enough to admit of sarcastic tone clusters, polyrhythms, polyharmonies, and so on. The ballet *Jeux* ends as it began, with the tennis ball falling on the stage. As the curtain falls, the motif of the prelude is heard again.

On July 25, 1913, Debussy wrote(5), "Now I am extracting confidences from the old dolls of Chouchou, and I'm learning to play the tambourine in anticipation of the *Boite à Joujoux*." The latter was Debussy's final, most ingratiating ballet, written with clarity and with humor, in a conscious attempt to avoid acrobatics. "The gods," wrote the composer, "aided me for the rest." He felt that it was written in "the true French spirit." This ballet is *for* children, rather than *of* them, from an adult standpoint. It is pervaded by a "mockheroic, naïve, humorous spirit, befitting the subject: a box of toys whose adventures are echoed in music where parody and poetical feeling combine in the most singular manner." The scenario was by André Hellé. Debussy urged a quick presentation of this little ballet and pointed out the dangers of hesitation. But it was destined that he should pass on before the orchestration was completed. This work was finished by André Caplet.

Outside of the utterly charming music in this ballet (a description of this would be useless; it must be heard to be appreciated) there are one or two interesting departures. The elephant dances to heavy music, to which is added an old Hindu melody in 5/4 meter, constructed on a Hindu theme for five o'clock in the morning which "serves even today to tame elephants." The high-pitched, syncopated piccolo melody over a low drumlike bass to which the English soldiers dance, is reminiscent of ragtime. The Waltz of the Doll is accompanied largely by a reiterated F in the bass and, to prove that Debussy thought definitely of movement while composing, a section of short staccato notes in the Waltz is marked "pointes." When the little troops march, the Soldiers' Chorus from *Faust* sings sweetly in the bass. When the soldiers use little peas for their bullets, these are indicated musically by staccato notes appearing in the silences between the times of conflict. In the third, pastoral tableau, Debussy has captioned a lively piece of 2/4 music thus: "The enthusiastic children dance a Polka with an evident disrespect for the author's thought." Little by little, the music becomes more reminiscent of the first. The bugle sounds when the curtain falls finally. The head of the little soldier appears and he gives the military salute.

Another Frenchman who wrote music for Maude Allan was Marcel Remy, whose *The Vision of Salome* pictures Salome as being but fourteen years of age. The music matches the character in innocent guilelessness.

Florent Schmitt wrote an epochal *Tragédie de Salomé*, a danced poem in two acts and seven scenes. Martens has described its music: "It evokes fragments of drunken song, strangled by a rain of bitumen and cinders, snatches of dance tunes, clapping of hands, stifled passion-sighs, maniac laughter." This ballet, in the impressionistic idiom with an oriental flavor, is dramatic but not melodramatic. The music is direct, complex, powerful. This score was important in the history of French music. It was actually a pioneer work in the ballet as we know it today. The music was sufficient without the stage spectacle; with it, it became extraordinary. It was first mimed by Loie Fuller in 1907, according to reports, although the printed score gives the first performance in 1913. It was not based on Wilde's drama, but on a poem by Robert d'Humières.

In the second part of the ballet, Schmitt employed a folk song of Aica, found by Salvator Peitavi on the shore of the Dead Sea. It is distinctly oriental. A single female voice backstage begins to sing wordlessly, then the melody is taken up by other female voices. It grows in intensity as it is amplified by the orchestra. Salome's Dance of Seduction is done to the lowest, slowest, most sensual, luring melody that can be imagined. The frenzied accelerando leading to the end and the final destruction of Herod's Palace form a huge climax, a veritable musical tour-de-force. Since the music expresses so much, there is little left for a realistic stage action to accomplish. *La Tragédie de Salomé* is said to be second only to Ravel's *Daphnis et Chloé* as a product of individual invention.

Schmitt's latest ballet is *Oriane-La-Sans-Égale*. It utilizes a chorus and tenor soloist. The scene is laid in Avignon in the fourteenth century; the story built around a lovely girl who scorns her admirers and, because of her cruel past, loses the Prince of Love. She finally dances with Death, and with a horde of madmen. Critics enthused over this brilliant score, for it was said that the composer seems to achieve his noblest aims when he has images to evoke and actions to paint, rather than when he is preoccupied with cerebral intricacies of pure music. In addition to his *Three Dances*, op. 86 for piano, Schmitt has written two other dance compositions: *Pupazzi*, a ballet of eighteenth century Italy (1907) and *Little Elf Shut-Eye*, a ballet on Hans Anderson's fairy tales combined into the dream of a little boy whose toy box came to life. It was originally a suite of seven rollicking piano pieces. The scene is laid in 1850. It contains a vocal berceuse and a Chinese fairy tale. The music aptly describes widely varying moods and is skilfully orchestrated. In 1909, Schmitt was engaged in the writing of the ballet *Urvasi*, to Calvocoressi's libretto, then gave up the idea. It was not the only French ballet never written, for once Maurice Delage began to write a sort of ballet inspired by Kipling's *Bridge Builders*. He made a fine start, with forceful and original ideas, then couldn't get permission to use the tale. The ballet was discontinued and the already-formulated ideas used in a later choreographic tone poem on Indian themes.

A ballet, *Le Carillon*, by Massenet, was once produced in Vienna. Massenet has to his credit two other ballets: *Cigale* (The Grasshopper) and *Espada*, the story of a Spanish dancer who must hide her emotions and go on with the show as her lover is killed in the bullfight arena. *Cigale* was composed in Monte Carlo at the instigation of Henry Cain. In 1904 it was presented at the Opéra Comique. So pretty and picturesque was it that Massenet(6) wrote that he himself was "by far the most entertained of those who attended the rehearsals of *Cigale*." (Was this remark, one wonders, double-edged?) At the end of the ballet is a touching, poetic scene where an angel appears in the distance and sings. The story is told that Massenet, when young, was taken to visit Théophile Gautier by a kind friend, who told the poet that Massenet was a deserving musician and that a ballet with Gautier's name attached would open to him the doors of the Opéra. On the spot, Gautier developed two ballet subjects, one of which (*The Rat-Catcher*) Massenet liked. However, nothing came of it. The Opéra refused his ballet, since the name of Gautier was so dazzling that that of young Massenet was completely lost in its brilliance. Nevertheless, a fine future was prophesied for him.

The most successful of all French ballets in the last twenty-five years is said to be Ravel's *Daphnis et Chloé,* on an old Greek romance re-written by Mereszowsky. Here, it is obvious that the excellence of the music was the ballet's chief claim to merit, for the subject matter lacked interest for many people. It has been called Ravel's masterpiece, since it was written in a burst of inspiration. Subtly and colorfully it depicts the moods of the old romance and, in the words of E. B. Hill(7): The music achieves a graphic delineation of character and has a plastic quality which incites mimetic response. Goossens(8) terms Ravel's ballet a "subtle web of instrumental complexity. The spell of its music holds us enthralled, so enchanting are

ÉMILE JAQUES-DALCROZE

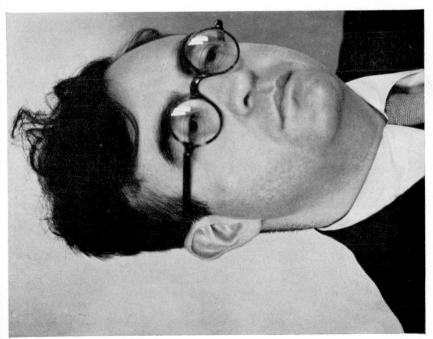

CARLOS CHAVEZ
Mexican composer

MODERN DANCERS
and their percussion instruments
Photograph courtesy of Lester Horton

its melodic and harmonic cadences. It contains choral singing." This singing chorus, over a moving orchestral fabric, provides a woodsy, faunlike atmosphere and it may be replaced (if necessary) by variants engraved in the orchestra score for this purpose. Goossens speaks also of "the perfect balance of the orchestration, the clarity and skill of the scoring."

Calvocoressi(9) tells us that Ravel, truly French, read all of the classics in French translations. Thus he grew to love the character that Greek art had acquired at the hands of its French imitators, hence his settings of Greek folk songs and *Daphnis et Chloé's* Greek subject-matter. Actually, Ravel was as fond of the old French as he was of this story. In 1909, Diaghileff submitted to Ravel many conventional libretti. From them, *Daphnis et Chloé* was chosen, Fokine finally casting the libretto into shape to Ravel's satisfaction. The first bars of the music were inspired by Ravel's memory of a wonderful leap sideways that Nijinsky used to do in a solo in *Le Pavillon d'Armide*. He wished to provide musical opportunities for more such leaps. The pattern was a run and a long pause, running through Daphnis' dance. In the score are also many impressionistic nature-imitations.

The ballet is in three tableaux. The first is an introduction and religious dance with rich, reverent harmonies, almost pagan in their emotional quality. When the young girls surround Daphnis with their dances, Ravel employs closely intermingled ⅞, ¾ and ¼ meters. The grotesque quality of Dorcon's dance is emphasized by strange accents rather than by irregularity of meter. Ravel has indicated individual motifs for each of the principal dancers, and the expression of the varied emotions or actions (terror, gaiety, flight) is achieved perfectly without for a moment abandoning the general harmonic scheme. Ravel has achieved consistency without monotony. There seems to be no pause in the music at all, even for a change of scenery. The latter apparently disappears conveniently during the course of the music, and is replaced. The ballet ends on a final fortissimo chord after a tremendous crescendo. Here, indeed, is music! Stravinsky attacked the problems of the stage, the dance, the mood and so forth, and surmounted them. Ravel makes it appear that they were already surmounted in his mind before he began to compose. Therefore he was able to devote himself entirely to the writing of fine music.

The French "Six" were said to be united by their radicalism and by their devotion to the ballet. The Six are: Milhaud, Durey, Honneger, Poulenc, Tailleferre, and Auric. All have written for the modern dance. It was a sort of cult with them. Often, the flavor of lusty music-hall tunes has crept into their ballet music, but it has served only to define more clearly the moods of the moment. Muriel Draper says that "the greatest distinctions of Les Six, that half-dozen of intelligent musical investigators and compilers of rhythm and sound, have been in the works written for Diaghileff's production."

Milhaud has been the most prolific of them all as regards ballet. One of his earlier works was *Les Songes*, a fantastic toy ballet. *La Bien Aimée* he composed after Liszt and Schubert. In 1921 appeared his *L'Homme et son Désir*, a symbolic pantomime to ultra-modern music wherein a nude man does the Dance of the Soul. The libretto was by Paul Claudel. That for Milhaud's ballet, *Le Retour de l'Enfant Prodigue* was by André Gide, while Jean Cocteau supplied the scenario for *Le Bœuf sur le Toit* (translated "The Bull on the Roof" but nicknamed "The Nothing-Doing Bar"). The latter, a cinema-symphony, refers to American prohibition, now a historic episode. The scene is a barroom, the characters all the possessors of huge papier-maché heads, the action deliberate. South American syncopated melodies (a version of jazz, but without its rhythmic complications) supplied the animation and the vitality for this ballet. They are sometimes treated polytonally, in the Milhaud manner, and at other times in a cheap cantina style. At the outset occurs a theme with a decided Rhumba feeling. This recurs constantly during the ballet, and serves to unify it, as does the unmistakable Latin-Negroid character of the rest of the thematic material for, in a sense, none of the themes is very different from the others, due to their constant rhythmic similarity. The Negroes, the Women and the Men

10 B⁺ de Clichy
Paris

Chère Mrs Verna Arvey

Puis que vous désirez des renseignements sur mes œuvres chorégraphiques . je vous en adresse ci dessous la liste exacte

Le Bœuf sur le Toit (scénario de Jean Cocteau)
Saudades do Brazil
L'Homme et son Désir ("   " Paul Claudel)
La Création du Monde ("   " Blaise Cendrars)
Salade ("   " Albert Flament)
Le Train Bleu ("   " Jean Cocteau)
La Bien Aimée (d'après Schubert et Liszt)(" " Alexandre Benois)
Les Songes (" " André Derain)

Veuillez agréer je vous prie . l'assurance de mes meilleurs sentiments

Darius Milhaud

Darius Milhaud's Contribution to Choreographic Music

all have their own themes (of considerable length) on their entrances. There is, decidedly, no trace of French impressionism in this ballet! One critic called it a "novel, fiendishly-complicated, slapstick satire."

"It was a logical step from the rhythms of South America to jazz—and Milhaud was an easy convert," declares Marion Bauer (10). "The *Creation of the World* is a curious combination of Bach and jazz, a form of pleasantry in which Stravinsky also indulged." The latter is an original, picturesque, cacophonic ballet. What else could one say of a dance-pantomime on such a subject, set in a Polynesian scene, with a dusky Adam and Eve? In *Salade,* Milhaud's sense of satire came to the fore, with violent rhythms, strident sonorities, and with an orchestra composed of both singers and reciters to accompany the dancing.

In spite of the fact that Milhaud's *Le Train Bleu* parodies musical comedy songs and ragtime, the music is said to be thoroughly congenial to the subject. The scenario is also by Jean Cocteau, and it is termed a danced operetta, rather than a ballet. The action takes place in the very year in which it was produced: 1924. Again, the combination of Milhaud and Cocteau could be nothing but bitingly satirical. Throughout, the music is banal, with the exception of a few melodies that are at once peasanty and classic in feeling. The ballet as a whole, however, reminds one of cheap music hall music, without the saving quality of inspiration with which, for example, Lord Berners endowed his *Luna Park.*

Arthur Honegger reached the "emancipation of his talent" and the "realization of his own power" in his ballet *Horace Victorieux* in 1921. It was the first of his important works, and was once described as being an athletic symphony. The libretto was by Fauconnet. Honegger also wrote the ballets, *Le Dit des Jeux du Monde* (libretto by the Belgian poet, Meral), *Semiramis, Amphion, Roses en Metal* (a ballet of the machine age), *Verité et Mensonge* (libretto by André Hellé), and *Skating Rink* (scenario by Canudo, 1922). In the latter ballet, a bored throng joylessly revolves in a rink. Honegger's 1938 ballet *Le Cantique des Cantiques* was written to dance rhythms already created by Serge Lifar who believes, incidentally, that no art should try to illustrate another art and therefore that it is not possible to dance *music*. What one does is to dance to the accompaniment of music. Accordingly, one critic called Honegger's ballet a monotonous composition of no great musical value, a series of clashes and accents orchestrated with violence and not conducive to interesting musical discourse. Another critic found it more appealing, and described it as having an intensely "archaic and evocative beauty."

Auric wrote the ballets *Pastorale*, *La Concurrence*, *Les Fâcheux*, and *Les Matelots*. The latter was on a scenario by Boris Kochno and was in two acts and five scenes. It was produced by Diaghileff in 1925. There are lyric passages in it, but it is mainly musical satire and burlesque. It has been described as a series of Hornpipes based on noisy, jocular, rhythmic folk songs. Even the tender passages are scored for brasses. In *Les Matelots* Auric was thought to have attempted to graft the Stravinsky style onto the French tradition. French critics admired its humor and the theatrical qualities in its music. They asked whether it was less classic than Lully's ballets, since both had the virtues of a clean articulation of themes, rhythmic pulsations, preponderance of binary themes, strong accents. The fact that the coarse joke has supplanted the Minuet, they wrote, doesn't in the least alter the mechanism and the plan!

Mme. Germaine Tailleferre has an impressionistic ballet to her credit: *Marchand d'Oiseaux* (The Bird Merchant).

Poulenc, besides his choreographic concerto for piano and eighteen instruments (*Aubade*), wrote several ballets. *Cocardes* was composed in 1920 to depict the Parisian bals publics on July 14th, Bastille Day. *Diana* followed a mythological subject, while *Football* included an autograph collector and football star and used two grand pianos instead of an orchestra. It lasts about five minutes. Then, Poulenc wrote a decadent ballet, *Les Biches*, on a satirical literary subject. It is in one act. Both music and text are based on popular French songs.

Most of the melodies, then, are reminiscent of the folk. "Say, what is love?" the singers ask (for there are, of course, singers in this novel ballet) articulating in exaggerated fashion. In a melodic section they all seem to agree that love is a cat with a velvet paw that will catch you soon. A Rag-Mazurka alternates with a musical mood reminiscent of Scarlatti. There is a contrapuntal Fox Trot. Of such unexpected, delightful contrasts is *Les Biches* composed!

Each of the French Six wrote part of a ballet to a scenario by Cocteau. It was called *The Couples at the Eiffel Tower* and cannot fail to call to mind a similar coöperative venture on the part of several Russian composers in a bygone year.

A description of the contemporary Opéra ballet in Paris was written by an Englishman in 1927(11) : "The class lesson lasted for one and one half hours and seldom in so short a space of time have I heard so much Chopin. After a few years of training, ballet dancers must heartily hate the Polish composer. . . . In the Rotonde de la Danse, Signor Nicola Guerra was conducting a rehearsal of M. Inghelbrecht's ballet, *Le Diable dans le Beffroi*. The pianist was being advised by the composer, sitting by his side, as to tempi. 'Would you recommence that movement, M. Guerra?' asks the composer, 'it should go a little quicker.' 'Kindly begin again, Mesdames, Messieurs,' says Guerra, 'and take it a little quicker,' indicating the new tempo with his stick." How different from the old School of the Dance even up to the time of Degas, with the inevitable violinist sawing out dance tunes for budding ballerinas!

D. E. Inghelbrecht also wrote the ballet *El Greco* or *Évocations Symphoniques*, first presented in 1920. It consisted of Orage, L'Impie, Cortege Funebre, La Jeune Fille Chrétienne, Assomption. It was built on a tale of a Toledan blasphemer. The scene was constructed around an El Greco masterpiece reproduced with living figures.

Yes, writes Reynaldo Hahn in a characteristic letter(12), he knew Nijinsky, Pavlowa and other dancers well. And he still has ideas about and memories of the dance, but to communicate them would require time, care and work far surpassing the limits of an ordinary letter. Therefore he remains silent. From other sources, one may learn of his choreographic music. His *Le Dieu Bleu* was created by Nijinsky. It was on a scenario by Cocteau and Madrazo, and was in one act. This was a legend of fabulous India, with sensuous music, a Dance of Memories, Dance of Ecstasy and Solemn Dance of Exorcism. Hahn's *La Fête chez Thérèse*, written in 1908, is placed in a fashionable modiste shop in the Paris of 1840. To this shop comes Carlotta Grisi, famous danseuse, with her friends, to select gowns for the Duchess' fête. The score contains Dance of the Grisettes, Mimi Pinson's Waltz, Violent Dance, Courteous Dance, Trying-on-Scene, Mournful Dance, Mimical Duet, Pompous Minuet. Hahn wrote a ballet called *Le Bal de Béatrice d'Este*, the scene of the sixteenth century in Milan. Though Hahn was born in Venezuela in 1875, he may be regarded as a Frenchman, musically speaking, since his training and environment were French.

Albert Roussel has written a ballet, *The Spider's Feast*, which has been termed a masterpiece of contemporary French music. The score contains the Entrance of the Ant, Dance and Death of the Butterfly, Birth and Dance of the Day Fly, Death and Burial of the Day Fly. The scenario is by Gilbert de Voisins and it is, strangely enough, like the play *The Captive*, in which the principal character is absent from the stage throughout, for the feast never takes place. The spider is stabbed as he is about to begin his repast. The work is sensitive, imaginative and humorous. It is fitting that a miniature orchestra should accompany the insects and worms in their microscopic, tense drama. It is said to be alternately dramatic and dissonant, ingenious and subtle, since the insects actually delineate human passions. In 1925, Roussel's *La Naissance de la Lyre* was given its première at the Paris Opéra. It, like this composer's *Padmâvoti*, is an opera-ballet, wherein the chorus sings and dances. This return to the Greek model (appropriate, since the ballet was founded on the Greek legend of Hermes and Apollo) was amazingly successful, despite the technical problems involved. It also contained declamation unaccompanied and with orchestral support.

Gabriel Grovlez wrote two ballets, *La Princesse au Jardin* and *Maïmouna*, inspired by the Orient. It so happened that Andreas Pavley and Serge Oukrainsky heard the latter ballet at the Paris Opéra in 1921. Later, when Mary Garden (then director of the Chicago Opera) commissioned a ballet from them, they evolved a scenario around strange events happening at the Robinson Café in Paris and, since Pavley was more fond of fitting dances to music than music to dance, they resolved to find a French composer. Remembering *Maïmouna*, they approached Grovlez on the subject of the music and, after consulting with him as to duration of scenes, points of emphasis and other technical details, left the matter entirely in his hands. In two months, it was completed. The time of the ballet was 1850, when costumes were so charming, and when Robinson was the gathering place for Bohemian young people. Grovlez (13) conceived his music in the spirit of the ballet of that period, with its Polkas, Mazurkas, Galops and Schottisches: all the choreographic forms of the time of Elssler and Taglioni, though the composer's musical setting is a bit more modern, more scintillating than that. The *New York Times* thought it the most elaborate ballet since *Petrouchka* and *Coppélia*. Grovlez's piano compositions are much inspired by dance rhythms, and when he composes for ballet he carefully interprets in his music real movement, not mere pantomime, fixed attitudes, gestures and the psychology of the characters as do other French modernists. In fact, he seems to disapprove a little of the exaggerations of most French modernists in their use of jazz and Negroid rhythms. He even seems to regret—wistfully—the passing of the old ballet form in which Delibes so excelled; and he finds that modern French ballets are written for the concert hall, not for the dancing stage.

Jacques Ibert (born 1890) has written *The Gold Standard*, a ballet wherein a young girl marries for money, but is at last reunited with her true lover. The spectacle ends with a gay Can-can. Its saucy and ironic music is permeated with a real music hall wit. The policeman's whistle, heard at the end, has been termed "Ibert's favorite instrument" by one reviewer. Others of his ballets are *Les Recontres, Diane de Poitiers* and *Angélique*.

Also given to fantasies and to burlesque is Yvonne Desportes, whose ballet *Trufaldin* is a Prix de Rome work, written according to the real spirit of Italian comedy.

One must not forget Henri Constant Pierné, composer of the delightful ballet *Cydalise et le Chèvrepied*, in which a dancer is taught the art of love by a faun. Pierné also wrote the ballets, *Bouton d'Or* and *Images*. Nor must one forget *Dolly*, a fanciful ballet about a spoiled little girl, written by Fauré in 1913. In this same year Alfred Bruneau composed "*L'Amoureuse Leçon*" in which the beaus and belles of Watteau's paintings dance their old time dances. Bruneau's ballet, *Les Bacchantes*, was composed after Euripides. Before 1900, Paul Vidal wrote a romantic ballet called *La Maladetta*. He is the composer also of the ballet *Guernica*, with its Habanera. Rhené-Baton is said to have a ballet to his credit.

La Chatte, the ballet composed by Henri Sauguet for Diaghileff, was undertaken with a little advance counsel from Rieti and Milhaud, and emerged "sonorous, varied, expert" according to Virgil Thomson. Sauguet wrote *David* for Ida Rubinstein and *Night* for Balanchine.

More recent French ballets are Gaubert's *Alexander the Great* (1935); Deodat de Severac's *Adonis*; Samuel Rousseau's *Promenades in Rome*; Borchard's *Bagatelles*; Marcel Bertrand's *Ileana* and Guy Ropartz's *L'Indiscret*. It was the latter composer who wrote *Un Prélude Dominical et six Pièces à Danser pour chaque Jour de la Semaine*, first danced in 1931 in France, though written in 1928-29. The character of each day's music is indicated by the tempo mark. Sunday has chimes and counterpoint, reminiscent of church; Monday bustles with a piquant leading rhythmic figure; Tuesday is decisive, with a persistent accompanying note; Wednesday is nervous; Thursday is grave, sustained; Friday is alternately tender and whimsical; Saturday is jolly, rising to climaxes and retiring, then ending in a burst of happiness. This set of pieces is in the impressionistic style that we have learned to regard as being typically French.

George Migot has written the ballet *Confessions and Promises*, also a choreographic symphony called *Hagoromo*, after a Japanese print, on a libretto by Louis Laloy. In the latter ballet, where song is part of the accompaniment, there is a sort of counterpoint of painting, music and dance. According to Schwerké, the singers' voices and the gestures and poses of the dancers are all treated as elements in an expressive ensemble. Lifar starred in a ballet by Jean Françaix at the Paris Opéra: *Le Roi Nu*. This portrays a stylized, ravishing seventeenth century. The music is said to be full of quick, nervous life, to sparkle with a deft orchestration, and to be reminiscent of the froth on champagne. It was composed after Lifar had completed the choreography, so that Continental critics termed it restoring music to the music-less ballet. Jean Françaix also has to his credit the ballet music entitled *Jeu Sentimentale*, of which a critic wrote: Once again this young musician delights us by his fresh charm and natural grace. Free as he is from all traces of heaviness, it is still difficult to predict the future of such a talent, so attractive in its early stages. Françaix composed, too, the imaginative ballet, *Lutherie enchantée*.

On the whole, one must admit that modern Frenchmen have ably carried on the ballet traditions set for them by such as Lully and Rameau. And, it must be granted that even as Lully and Rameau knew the audiences for which they wrote, so do the modernists know their public. Some of them keep pace with that public, offering satire that is more and more biting in order to maintain interest in the ballet as a musical form. Some have even succeeded in writing superlative music besides!

Chapter 20

NOTES

(1) *Musical Quarterly*, January, 1925, p. 20
(2) Martens, *Thousand and One Nights at the Opera*, p. 438

(3) *Letters of Claude Debussy to His Editor*, p. 111
(4) *The Étude*, February, 1924, p. 79
(5) *Letters of Claude Debussy to His Editor*, p. 284
(6) Massenet, *My Recollections*, p. 244
(7) E. B. Hill, *Modern French Music*, p. 271
(8) Propert, *Russian Ballet in Western Europe*, p. 117
(9) Calvocoressi, *Music and Ballet*, pp. 77-78-79
(10) Bauer, *Twentieth Century Music*, p. 236
(11) *The Dancing Times*, June, 1927, p. 274
(12) In a letter to the author from Paris, France, dated March 12, 1936
(13) In a letter to the author from Paris, France, dated April 23, 1936

*

CHAPTER 21

*

SPANISH, ITALIAN, LATIN-AMERICAN
BALLETS

A modern Italian (Vincenzo Tommasini) (1) has written
his view of the ballet: "Isn't the modern ballet a musical reaction against the invasion of verismo and the learning of the
music drama—a kind of unbridled race toward the plastic and
primordial power of rhythm, to diminish the clutch of realism
and of loquacity? Isn't it to re-assure itself that theatrical
music has renounced song, has kept its actors mute and preferred to let them speak with their feet?"

It is for just such a reason that many modern Spanish and
Italian composers have turned to the ballet as a freer means
of musical expression. Some, who felt more strongly on the
subject, devoted part of their time to writing music for marionettes, for how else could their musical creations be accompanied by a perfect production that did not in the least detract
from any interest the audience might feel in the music? The
marionette music of Respighi and Falla deserves a place as
ballet music since it is, after all, movement-music. Respighi
felt that the grotesque nature of the puppet is accentuated in
dancing and that the dance is a passive art, entirely dependent
on the music which it makes visible. But, since marionette
music is amply covered in articles devoted solely to it, merely

332

the titles of the compositions for this theater will be mentioned here.

Undoubtedly, sophisticated contemporary Spanish dance music owes more to Felipe Pedrell and his folklore cult than the world believes possible, for composers like Falla studied with and were inspired by him. Falla's ballet music, especially, shows that he thoroughly assimilated Pedrell's assertion, that music should be born from the same national consciousness that produces folk song. Though Falla did not usually "quote," he invented material that is at once popular, authentic, characteristic and true to the pulse of the folk. Thus he gives a truer picture than if he had restricted himself to folk melodies. None of his music was written for effect. He is more sincere than that. People who are acquainted only with pseudo-Spanish music are oblivious to his subleties. He removed the coarse embellishments from Spanish music and gave it a mystic tinge. His ballet music is based on *real* Spanish dancing: capricious, insinuating, fantastic, langorous, rapid, and breathless in its sudden pauses. Falla's dance music has made him an international figure in the world of music.

Yet no one is more annoyed than he over the tawdry thing that sometimes passes for dancing, and more angered by its association with his creations. César de Mendoza, Spanish conductor, on visiting Falla in Granada, was thus addressed by the composer: "I congratulate you for having played the first act of the 'Vida Breve' without cuts. I am tired of these shreds one tears from my works and on which the most ordinary dancer stamps her feet. I feel they are cutting me into pieces and I have given strict instructions to my agent for all that to stop."

Spanish dance music also owes much to the dancer, La Argentina, for, during her lifetime, she was the inspiration for a new piece of ballet music from an outstanding composer every time she returned to Spain. For example, Ernesto Halffter, a young composer from Madrid, had La Argentina as the choreographic creator of his ballets, *Escriche* and *Sonatina*, with its Danza de la Pastora and Danza de la Gitana. Halffter also composed the orchestral *Divertimiento Coreográfico*. The superb La Argentina also danced *Le Contrabandier*, a one-act ballet by Oscar Aspla, and later interpreted in movement six songs by Joaquín Nin as they were played by their composer and sung. Her association with the music of Falla won for her some of her greatest plaudits.

Falla has borne on his capable shoulders the brunt of Spanish ballet writing. His masterpiece for the marionette theater is *El Retablo de Maese Pedro*. His short opera, *La Vida Breve*, with its interludes of Andalusian song and dance, has a final choral dance scene, at the end of which Salud falls dead at the feet of her faithless lover on the day of his marriage to another. The "background of thoughtless dance music has given way to tragedy."

Falla, like many another modern composer, has not "renounced song" in his ballets, as the remark by Tommasini would indicate. Mute actors are not enough for many modernists. They must use the human voice to clarify or to intensify the emotions in their ballets. Thus both of Falla's ballets include song. Their earlier versions were for something like a double quartet.

The scenario of *The Three-Cornered Hat* (once expanded into an opera by Zandonai, *La Farsa Amorosa*; and into *Der Corregidor* by Hugo Wolf) was adapted by Martinez Sierra from a story by Alarcon (1833-1891). The scene is laid in eighteenth century Spain. In Falla's version, the few quotations of folk music were deliberate, and were done with humorous intent. The music is sometimes polyrhythmic, sometimes polyharmonic. There are castanets in the orchestra, and from time to time single melodic phrases of intense beauty are heard. There are characteristic Andalusian vocal turns on notes preceding cadences in the song. The second part of the ballet opens with a melodic nocturne which recalls one of those "Spanish gardens where Falla spends his nights" as an enthusiastic English critic put it. An emphatic knock at the door is told in the theme, exact as to interval and key, of Beethoven's *Fifth Symphony*. Rachmaninoff once used this theme to open a song in his op. 21, *Fate*, to words of Apuchtin. One cannot refrain from noting that in this matter, both Falla and Rachmaninoff scorned to write something reminiscent, so that they could be accused of copying. They actually copied, so that they might then be accused of cleverness! The four notes of Beethoven's theme are now as familiar to the world at large in their particular implication as the theme song of any film, radio program or theatrical presentation.

El Amor Brujo is a *Gitanería* in one act and two scenes, with text by Martinez Sierra, based upon an Andalusian Gypsy tale, in which the ghost of the dead lover appears when the new lover tries to supplant him. The rhythms and the actual phrase-lengths were all conceived in terms of the dance. At the outset, Falla had the theater in his mind, and there it stayed. Thus, *El Amor Brujo* must be seen as well as heard. The music is compact and passionate, with an almost hypnotic monotony at times. The stirring, insistent rhythm of the Ritual Dance of Fire has few emotional rivals in music. The slow, rhythmic, voluptuous section of the Pantomime music is like the seething of a volcano before an eruption. Yet, parts of *El Amor Brujo* are tender and sweet, or tranquil and mysterious. It is inspired music. The piano and vocal score is but forty pages long. Compared to many ballets it is short, but brevity is the very soul of Falla's music. Every note means something. Nothing is misplaced or wasted, overdone or underdeveloped. He says simply what he must say, and the emotional effect is heightened thereby. Comparatively speaking, for such a short work, more of it has become widely popular than of any other such creation, for almost the whole of the ballet is now familiar to audiences, whereas many larger works languish in well-merited or unmerited obscurity. Almost all of the piano music by Falla that is played hails from his ballets, so that countries infested with resident or visiting pianists know him by his choreographic music alone.

Falla (2) believes that music is not to be understood before it can be enjoyed: it must be felt. ("La música no se hace para que se comprenda, sino para que se sienta.") Perhaps the best, terse summary of his music is given by Trend, when he says: With Falla we feel that the music has already been going on for some time elsewhere, when the performer by art or magic begins to let us hear it.

As was the case with Ravel's *Bolero*, the musically suggestive paintings of Goya inspired Granados to write two books of piano pieces, among them many Spanish dances. These were later transformed into the opera, *Goyescas*, with its famed Fandango. Albéniz is also noted as a composer of Spanish dances in the folk style: some popular, some subtle. Recently, some of his music was gathered together by Infante and made into a single ballet in one act called *L'Amour Trahi*, to a libretto by Louis Laloy.

The ballet *Good Humored Ladies*, danced by Diaghileff's company, was based on a story by Goldoni, great Venetian humorist. The music was culled from the best of Domenico Scarlatti's Sonatas and was arranged by Vincenzo Tommasini. Massine's choreography is said to have utilized wonderfully every note of the music, particularly in the fugue. Goossens (3) feels that Tommasini's ballet is remarkable for the manner in which the atmosphere of the eighteenth century and the archaic spirit of Scarlatti's music has been conveyed orchestrally with a minimum of resource and a maximum of effect. With this declaration, Guido M. Gatti (4) heartily agrees, his own version of the matter being a slightly different wording of the identical thought: "It is a veritable model of orchestration of the Sonate per clavicembalo, wherein the sonority and the very spirit of the epoch and the instrumentation are symphonically re-created in a way that leaves nothing to be desired." So well received was this ballet that Tommasini was promptly scheduled to do *Pulcinella* and Cimarosa's *Le Astuzie Femminile*. As things turned out, Stravinsky did the former ballet and Respighi the latter. Tommasini then interested Diaghileff in a ballet on Paganini's music, treated very freely, but had to abandon this project when he broke off relations with the impresario. His material was not wasted, since he wrote and published the last part of this ballet as a symphonic work, *Il Carnevali di Venezia.* Incidentally, Roland Manuel has lately scored another ballet from Scarlatti's Sonatas, called *Elvire.*

Respighi, composer of the marionette score, *The Sleeping Beauty*, also wrote a *Scherzo Veneziano*, in 1920, a ballet-picture of Goldoni's Venice, including a Forlana. His ballet, *The Birds*, was on a scenario by Claudio Guastalla, also librettist for Respighi's *Belkis, Regina di Saba*, a ballet in seven scenes with song. Perhaps Respighi's greatest fame in the field of ballet arose from his suggestion to Diaghileff that a ballet be made up of the small pieces that Rossini composed for the entertainment of his guests. This resulted in *La Boutique Fantasque* with its splendid contrasts in charm and vitality. So graphic is Respighi's music that years after one has seen the ballet, a phonograph recording can recall perfectly each of its details!

Pantea, a symphonic drama for one dancer, baritone soloist, invisible voices and orchestra, is undoubtedly one of Malipiero's most unusual and most powerful creations. Written in 1918, it is in five parts wherein Pantea desperately seeks liberty and finds death. Really, there are two persons on the stage: Pantea, and the Shade. During the Prologue, there is loud, impetuous music over a broad bass melody as the small room is illuminated with multi-colored, flaming lights. The insistent music becomes calm, when Pantea arises and dances to the Symphony of the Dawning Day. Invisible voices sing the morning songs in vocables. Pantea's movement is arrested by the sound of a nostalgic male voice that continues after the others have stopped. When that voice ceases, she vainly tries to open the door. The curtain falls. In the next agitated scene, Pantea struggles against her first hallucination and tries to sweep away the tempest that prevents her escape from the summit of a high mountain. She is heedless of the voices that summon her as she dances. Darkness envelopes her as she attains the heights. The second hallucination finds Pantea in a green field. Her dance begins gaily, but rises to frenzied vivacity as the voices intone an exultant hymn. In the third hallucination, Pantea runs frantically about among great trees, standing somberly close in the dark night. The harmonies here are very close, very dissonant. Pantea becomes exhausted. When the curtain again discloses the scene of the Prologue, she is contemplative. Again the nostalgic, sad voice is heard. This time Pantea succeeds in opening the door, only to admit the Shade. A funeral rhythm becomes more agitated and the music more contrapuntal as Pantea expires. Lugubrious, pianissimo music accompanies the fall of the curtain as the voices breathe "Ah!" in languishing fashion. All is harmonically rich and atmospheric, dramatically and psychologically speaking.

Malipiero is the composer of the humorous puppet ballet, *The Savages* as well as the one-act ballet called *The Masquerade of the Captive Princesses*, given its première in Brussels in 1924.

Both scenario and music for *Il Convento Veneziano* ("Le Couvent sur l'eau") were written by Alfredo Casella. This is a buoyant choreographic comedy with voice in two acts. It was created in 1925, and is also a picture of Goldoni's Venice, based on a theme of J. L. Vaudoyer, and containing a Festive March, Children's Round, Barcarolle, Sarabande, Walk of the Aged Ladies, Nocturne and Final Dance. As might be expected, Casella's *La Giara* is Sicilian and pastoral—since it is based on Pirandello's comedy of the same name. It has been said by Martens to be brilliantly Rossinian. Marion Bauer declares that the composer has shown in it unusual charm and ability in handling a folk type in which for a moment he left the path of dissonance he travels so easily. One may easily disagree with Miss Bauer on the latter point, because *La Giara* is decidedly dissonant and contrapuntal, but in a rustic manner. The style serves his peasanty subject well, for it makes the music sound as if it were created by folk who have no acquaintance with artistic prettinesses. It also accurately catches Pirandello's literary style.

La Giara has to do with the repairing of an old jar by a hunchbacked potter who is trapped inside it. There is a prelude during which all the leading characters pass before the curtain, when the music graphically describes each one. The first General Dance recalls the Tarantella, with contrasting rhythms and both consonant and dissonant themes. Don Lolló's music reminds one of an old harpsichord exercise and one suspects, indeed, that Don Lolló himself (the landlord) is intended to portray a certain decadent aristocracy. Later, a popular melody (taken from a volume of Sicilian Songs of the Land and Sea, by Alberto Favara) is sung backstage. To this melody, Casella added an accompaniment typical of his own musical individuality. The ballet contains a rough, strongly accented Waltz in the German style. It concludes with a general village dance: fast, loud and heavily accented. The ballet was a little over a month in the writing. Casella began it on July 12, 1924 and completed it on August 27, 1924.

Vittorio Rieti, composer of the ballets, *Le Bal* and *Madrigale*, really acquired prominence with his *Barabau*, produced by Diaghileff. This is a burlesque ballet on Rieti's own libretto, inspired by Italian country life in Tuscany, the actors being peasants and soldiers, but containing authentic folk music. It lasts about an hour and a half and is more or less in the form of a suite with marches and peasant dances. Wind instruments predominate in the score. It was first intended for production on a small German stage, when Diaghileff heard it on its completion in 1925. He liked it, and requested the addition of some pieces. It was then settled that he should produce it. Part of the music was written for *a cappella* chorus, but when it was first produced in London, because Diaghileff hated the idea of a chorus for a ballet (according to Rieti) (5) he took his revenge in placing the singers on the stage, dressed in absurd fashion. Says Rieti: "The effect was very comical, and proved to be one of the reasons for the ballet's success." in thus admitting Diaghileff's astuteness, Rieti agrees with at least one London critic (6) : "*Barabau* is provided with a chorus (screened to their necks) and this chorus with its spasmodic commentaries on the doings of the dancers, is almost half the fun. Rieti's music is so simple and unassuming as nearly to disarm criticism. No doubt, if he had wanted to show how clever or how audacious he was, the opportunity was there. But he evidently preferred to be just appropriately light-hearted, as befitted his theme. His scoring is light, his harmonies thin, sometimes to the point of bareness. There is, though, humor of a genuine brand in the phrases he has given to the chorus." On the other hand, another observer considered *Barabau* just another ballet-cantata for which Stravinsky had supplied the formula—a formula which bade fair to become a pattern soon. He remarked on the fact that the recent creations of Diaghileff resembled each other musically: youth parading its individualism and stooping to a communal discipline, when even in the turbulence the work of musicians appears conceited and homogenous. These observations were made after listening to the ballet scores that succeeded each other within a space of three years.

Le Bal, on a libretto by Boris Kochno, was Rieti's second ballet for Diaghileff, a tiny intrigue occurring during a nineteenth century ball. It was presented just a few weeks before the death of the impresario, association with whom Rieti believes to have been the high point of his artistic life for, he declares, we shall never again see such a wonderful man. Rieti also orchestrated part of Chabrier's music for a ballet, and re-orchestrated Chopin's music for *Les Sylphides*. His latest ballet is *David Triomphant,* produced in Paris by Serge Lifar. The effect of this ballet is arresting, as percussive instruments play an important part. It was composed with a view to perfect musical adaptation to body movement. Rieti is still much attracted to ballet music and wishes to write more of it.

Renzo Bossi, son of Marco Enrico Bossi, wrote *Rosa Rossa*, a lyric choreographic poem in one act after an Oscar Wilde novel; and *Burla Valdostana,* a mimed and danced scherzo in one act; as well as *Fantocci Animati,* six little pieces for small orchestra to be illustrated with dance and pantomime. Castelnuovo-Tedesco composed a vocal ballet *Bacco in Toscana,* which sparkles with Dionysian lightness. Franco Alfano's *Eliana* is a ballet on popular Italian motifs with an optional chorus. It is in four parts. Before the turn of the century, he wrote two other successful ballets: *Napoli* and *Lorenza*. Santolíquido's contribution to this sort of theater is *The Bayadère with the Yellow Mask* in one act. Alfredo d'Ambrosio (1871-1914) wrote a ballet on Alfred Mortier's libretto: *Hersilia*, with dances of Ondines, Naiads and Sirens. Carlo Gozzi's eighteenth century Neapolitan piece *The Love of Three Pomegranates* inspired a recent ballet of the same name by G. C. Sonzogno. The music, stretched over a fantastic succession of scenes, is colorful, joyous and full of rhythmic contrasts. Renato Simoni, in writing the scenario, enriched the tale with greater color and variety of situation, while yet retaining its original charm.

Riccardo Pick-Mangiagalli has been both librettist and composer for most of his ballets: *La Berceuse, Il Carillon Magico, Mahit* and *Salice d'Oro*. His *Sumitra* in one act is to a scenario by C. Clausetti. G. Adami was librettist for his ballet, *Casanova a Venezia*, in eight scenes.

Italy has had many propagandist ballets. *Balilla*, by Guarino, was one. *Fiordisole* was another. The latter, produced at La Scala, was by Franco Vittadini to a libretto by Gino Cornali. The theme was political, but the music was merely pleasant and rhythmic. Previously, Vittadini had written another ballet called *Vecchia Milano*, in eight scenes, to a scenario by G. Adami. His finest feature in this was said to be the resolution of the theme.

Amadeo Roldan (Cuban) has composed an Afro-Cuban ballet called *La Rebambaramba*, as well as *El Milagro de Anaquillé*, a one act choreographic mystery, also Afro-Cuban. *La Flor del Irupe*, Constantino Gaito's ballet, was presented at the Colón Theater in Buenos Aires. This composer's *El Cangeo* was said to have been danced by Bronislava Nijinska. *Amancay*, by H. Iglesias Villoud, was produced in Buenos Aires in 1938. In 1940 Juan José Castro, the Argentine composer, had his vivid ballet *Offenbachiana* based on themes culled from Offenbach, presented at the Colón Theater. However, it is Villa-Lobos, with so much of his music reminiscent of primitive Brazilian dance chants, who is best known in South America as a composer of choreographic music. His *Amazonas* is an Indian ballet, the movements of which (designed by Maria Oleneva, ballet mistress at the Municipal Theater in Rio de Janeiro) were said to have been perfectly synchronized with the music. The theme is of a captive warrior who is seen as he dances for the medicine man's daughter, and is killed by tribesmen. Villa-Lobos' Choros no. 10, *Razga o Coração* is said to have been originally composed as a ballet, an exotic tribal dance, with the melodic material made up of combined Portuguese folk song and an Incantation. Withal, it was purely a symphonic conception and was performed as such after its performances as a ballet in Paris and Rio de Janeiro. Villa-Lobos, as head of music in the public schools of Rio, recently organized an open-air chorus of children who accompanied their songs with appropriate rhythmic movements.

In Mexico, though Antonio Gomezanda has written eight ballets on Aztec themes, and José Pomar is the composer of the novel proletarian ballet called *Eight Hours of Work,* it is to Carlos Chavez that the honors for ballet composition really go. In his ballet *The New Fire,* Chavez used Indian themes literally. For the first time, he looked away from Europe and scanned the resources of his own country for inspiration. The music was of the soil: unsmiling. Paul Rosenfeld called it "astringent, robust, dry, impassive."

Chavez's second ballet, *The Four Suns,* for symphony orchestra and women's chorus, was written in 1926. It is based on an Aztec legend, is made up of simple, clear-cut rhythms, and has its roots so firmly in the ancient culture that it sometimes assumes the monotony of the actual Indian dances. The music is inherently choreographic and has a ritual quality, though it is also bare, brusque and unvoluptuous. Rosenfeld says this one has an almost distemper-like quality, as if it, too, were inscribed upon an ancient temple wall. Writes a New Yorker: "A movement from his *Four Suns,* played by Mr. Chavez on the piano with an accompaniment of groans, hoots,

whispers and stamping, to show how it would sound orchestrally, has the same quality of individuality rooted in racial
and national character."

The same writer says that Chavez's third choreographic
score, *H.P., Sinfonia de Baile,* has unmistakable vitality.
This, for large symphony orchestra, was composed in 1926-27.
The name means "Horse-Power." In it, Chavez was assisted
by the ironic Diego Rivera as scenic and costume designer.
The ballet is symbolic of the relationship between northerners
and tropic dwellers. The tropics produce raw materials; the
north has the machinery with which to manufacture the raw materials into the necessities of life. Each needs the other.
Part I of the ballet is the Dance of the Man, expressing the
unknown forces about him. Part II is a cargo ship at sea,
expressing the commerce between north and south, with gym-
nastic sailor dances, and seductive, nonchalant and sensual
mermaids. Part III is the loading of tropic cargo. Part IV
is the city of industry, with skyscrapers and ticker tape and men
insatiably collecting the raw materials of the earth. As themes,
Chavez used Anglo-Saxon sea chanteys, the Huapango (of
Mestizo origin, though Chavez's abstract interpretation makes
it lean more toward the Indian than the Spanish, with its
contrasting rhythms and exotic instrumental effects) and the
Sandunga. The rhythmic treatment of the latter theme, one
of the loveliest of all Mexican folk melodies, makes it among
the most charming music ever to come from Chavez's dry pen.
Not for nothing did Rivera say that the music of *H.P.* could
exist successfully without dance or scenery. In the final scene
of the ballet, all the themes are suggested.

"Once again," declared the *New York Times,* "A musician
has issued a formidable challenge to a choreographer."
Chavez himself said that *H.P.* is a symphony of the music that
is in the very air and atmosphere of our continent; music that is
heard on all sides, a sort of review of the epoch in which we
live."

Lately, Daniel Ayala of Mexico has completed a ballet
that is essentially Mayan. It is in two acts and is called *Uchben*

X' Coholte. It is a legend treated in a modern manner, but
it has all the strength and grandeur of the ancient Mayans.
The music is of two epochs. The prologue hints at what is to
come; but the first section is laid in the pre-Cortez era. When
the curtain rises, warriors battle so enthusiastically that they
all die, causing the spot to be haunted by evil spirits. In the
second section of the ballet (laid in modern times) a fiesta is
planned for that very spot. The orchestra starts to play a
Jarana (here this dance is a Mayan expression of the Spanish
Jota) when someone recalls the apparitions and everyone
leaves, panic-stricken. Incidentally, Ayala used the human
voice as an orchestral instrument in this ballet.

In San Salvador, Central America, María M. de Baratta
has also been writing choreographic music in an attempt to
express the cries of her race through the rhythms of its music.
She has published indigenous dances—one of these being a
ritual on the setting of the sun, who is father of the corn, whose
mother is the earth. To some of her dances she has set words,
in Spanish and in the native tongue, "Nahuatl," as well. One
of her finest works is *Nahualismo,* a long piano composition
inspired by the autochthonous spirit. This is, in effect, a ballet, with a scenario based on the strongest traditions of San
Salvador's Indians, and with well contrasted moods in the
vigorous music. Señora de Baratta is now preparing a book on
San Salvador's folk music.

CHAPTER 21

NOTES

(1) From an article "Del drama lirico" by Vincenzo Tommasini, in
the *Rivista Musicale Italiana,* vol. 39
(2) Trend, "Manuel de Falla and Spanish Music," p. 45
(3) Propert, "The Russian Ballet in Western Europe," p. 98
(4) *Musical Quarterly,* July, 1926, p. 469
(5) In a letter to the author from Paris, France, dated March 11, 1936
(6) *London Daily Telegraph,* December 12, 1926

CHAPTER 22

*

MODERN GERMAN BALLETS

The father of modern German ballet compositions was none other than Ludwig van Beethoven, known in the annals of music history as the link between the classic and romantic eras. About 1790, Beethoven wrote a ballet of knighthood. It was produced in Bonn, the city of its creation, during the following year. Orchestral excerpts from it are still played occasionally. Some of them are: March, German Song, Hunting Song, Romance, War Song, Drinking Song, German Dance, Coda.

When Beethoven was thirty, he composed no. 43 of his works: the ballet *Prométhée,* presented in Vienna (as renowned a ballet center in the old days as was Paris) in 1801 by Vigano. Beethoven had been enchanted by the beautiful figure of Vigano's Spanish wife, María Medina, and dedicated to her a Menuet, "à la Vigano." But when *Prométhée* was written, another dancer (Mlle. Cassentini) had supplanted her, and Beethoven became enthusiastic enough over her to write for her his *Twelve Variations on a Russian Dance.* Haydn and Beethoven had bitter words over *Prométhée.* Thayer, in the *Life of Ludwig van Beethoven,* has elaborated on the incident thus: "Hayden met Beethoven on the street and said, 'I heard your ballet yesterday and it pleased me very much.'

345

"Beethoven replied, 'Oh, dear Papa, you are very kind, but it is far from being a "Creation"!'

"Haydn was surprised and offended and said, 'That is true. It is not yet a "Creation" and I can scarcely believe that it will ever become one.' Both men, embarrassed, said their good-byes."

Though *Prométhée* was more in the form of a series of divertissements than a logically constructed ballet d'action, it has been termed a landmark in the history of the dance. Why this should be so is something impossible to fathom, except by unconditional admirers of Beethoven. Is it because some people like to think that every effort of this great German master tops every effort by anyone else? Is it because the mere *idea* of greatness takes precedence over the work itself? Was the actual music more charming than Mozart's ballet music, or more significant? Perhaps the answer may be found in its enormous success, for sixteen performances of it were given in its first year (1801) and thirteen in the following year.

Prométhée was on a mythological subject, with Prometheus himself appearing in the opening scene. It consisted of Overture, Introduction and sixteen numbers. Two themes from the Finale appear elsewhere in Beethoven's works, one in a symphony, one as one of the twelve *Contre Tänze,* and one as a theme for the *Variations and Fugue for Piano,* op. 35. The ballet music itself is still performed, though seldom.

Modern Germany presents a different aspect with regard to music for the dance. This is partly due to the development of what is known as the new German dance, which is consciously antimusical, in itself a denial of any subordination of movement to sound or to literary idea. Whereas, some of the finest French composers scored successes in the realm of pure music by means of their ballet scores, many of Germany's finest composers have put the dance farthest from their thoughts. Some have written ballets in their youths, only to discard the form later as being of no value to them. Modern German music has departed from the dance as far as the dance has departed from music!

Richard Strauss' best known ballet, of course, belongs to the Diaghileff period. Strauss himself once wrote a sketch for a three-act ballet to be called *Kythere,* on the subject of Watteau's picture in the Louvre. Hofmannsthal liked this pretty, picturesque conception, but the ballet was never written. Then in 1912, when Diaghileff (who was also something of a politician) wished to give something of its own to each country he visited, Strauss was commissioned to write *Josephslegende.* Kessler and Hofmannsthal wrote the scenario, with Nijinsky (the most extraordinary stage personality of the day) in mind for the boyish rôle. It was an ideal combination of scenarists, composer, painter and choreographer. Hofmannsthal first sent the scenario to Strauss with the injunction to read it with special regard to its picturesque and beautiful elements, in "the spirit which once moved you to devise a ballet in the Boucher-Fragonard-Watteau manner(1)." Hofmannsthal was enthusiastic over the idea, since it presented the problem of dressing a Biblical subject as Paolo Veronese would have done. And this is no more incongruous than the settings selected by many medieval painters for their Biblical scenes.

Strauss thought *Joseph* was splendid. He immediately wrote back to Hofmannsthal(2) that "It will go like hot cakes. I have already begun the first sketch." Later, he wrote that the ballet was not progressing so quickly as he thought it would, because the chaste Joseph was hardly in his line, and he found it difficult to write music for a character that bored him: "However, perhaps I may yet find lurking in some queer ancestral corner of my nature some pious melody that will do for our good Joseph(3)."

Hofmannsthal then suggested that Joseph's music be found not in any "queer ancestral corner(4)," but in the purest region of Strauss' brain, that of absolute intellectual freedom. He agreed that if Joseph were a figure of such chastity, he, too, would be bored and would be unable to create suitable music. He insisted that the Joseph he had had in mind at first was quite a different character, partaking rather of an ecstatic holy search. His argument must have won the day, for Strauss later completed the sketch of Joseph's Dance to his own satisfaction. When he apprised Hofmannsthal of this, the latter wrote exuberantly that the ballet was perhaps the only art-form that allows a really close collaboration between two people who happen to be gifted with "a certain imaginative way of seeing things(5)." Strauss then attended the London performance of the ballet, and returned to say that it had had a great success, although most of the critics abused it, and the lewder sort of Englishwomen even went so far as to find it indecent. He said that the main thing in the ballet, Joseph's Dance, was still not up to the mark, and therefore tedious(6).

The foregoing correspondence, containing Strauss' own misgivings, may shed a bit of light on the controversy that raged over the ballet. We might even presume that Strauss was loath to relinquish the commission, and wrote the ballet for that reason, not as an inspired work, for Bolm declares that he was one of the highest paid of all Diaghileff's composers. Some critics enthused that Strauss had created a new form of art, a music-drama without words. But there were more people to condemn than to praise. Almost everyone considered this music inferior to what others had written for the ballet. Goossens(7) thought it too dull to be even decadent; devoid of inspiration; ostentatious and empty. These qualities were all camouflaged with a consummate dexterity of orchestration which served only to accentuate its futility. Bolm says that the ballet was a failure because Strauss' heavy, Teutonic music did not fit the movement or color of the period: Strauss and Veronese had nothing in common. There may be a very simple reason for the accusation of dullness, divulged by a mere glance at the piano score. At the time when most ballets are finishing, it is still going blithely on. Strauss evidently wished to earn his fee. The reason for the great length is that Strauss, understanding the musical idiom better than the dance, developed all of his themes musically and extensively, with long modulatory passages and contrapuntal sections, some of which couldn't be other than tiresomely pantomimic on the stage, since a single dancer has a certain amount of breath, or endurance, and no more. *Josephslegende* is overly consonant, though ordinary melodies often take an unusual turn. What few dissonances there are emerged logically from a harmonic development.

This was not Strauss' only ballet. Of comparatively recent vintage is his *Schlagobers* or *Whipped Cream*, the action of which takes place in a Viennese pastry shop. In one scene, forty-eight dancers emerge from a bowl of whipped cream beaten by a mechanical cook. The music is light, gay and typically Viennese, with many Waltz themes. Marion Bauer thought it retained the outer shell of his orchestral skill, but with nothing to say: much technical ado about nothing. Another writer lamented Strauss' downfall from the heights to the "opulent aridity" of a *Josephslegende* and thence downward to the shamelessness of *Schlagobers—!*

Schönberg(8) declares very simply that he has written no ballet because he has no understanding for dancing. He has the attitude of a person dealing primarily in sound, not movement. Even when he is writing songs, says Gerald Strang, he thinks primarily of the music, not of the medium. This is perhaps the reason that he has not been sufficiently interested in the ballet as a form of expression. However, several of his works amount to ballets. He has made an interesting experiment in *Die Glückliche Hand*, op. 18, in which a silent man and woman enact the rôles in the pantomime. There is a vocal soloist and a singing choir in the orchestra. The composer terms it an experiment in operatic form. In comparison with contemporary ballets, it *is* a ballet, though it is perhaps not so active as most. Although Schönberg has written Minuets in his *Piano Suite*, op. 25, in his *Suite for String Orchestra* and in his *Serenade;* and a Waltz in his op. 23 for piano, none of these were written as dance music, nor have they any relation to the original except in form.

Paul Hindemith was once a professional musician. That

is to say, he was once a dance musician. Despite this lowly beginning, he has become a noted composer with a decided influence on the younger generation of German musicians. At the outset, he wrote dance music. His op. 20, composed in 1921, is called *Das Nush-Nushi,* and is a dance-like ultra-modern score designed for Burmese marionettes. Hindemith's op. 28 is *Der Damon,* a dance-pantomime in two parts. This was described by a supercilious observer as being "objectionable" because it portrayed two girls engaged in prostitution. Hindemith wrote this music for a single purpose: the stage. Therefore he accompanied the score with a note to that effect, adding that the music was not to be performed separately in concert. Lest some zealous writers persuade an over-credulous public that Hindemith has forever forsaken the field of dance music, let us hasten to correct that impression. It must be admitted, in all fairness, that he sometimes uses dance rhythms far more subtly than is usual. For example, his Concerto for viola and chamber orchestra is built on four folk songs of the fifteenth and sixteenth century, and is called *Der Schwanendreher* after one of them. This explanatory note prefaces the composition: "A minstrel entering a merry company displays what he has brought back from foreign lands: songs serious and gay, and finally a dance piece. Like a true musician, he expands and embellishes the melodies, preluding and improvising according to his fancy and ability. This medieval picture is the inspiration of the composition." Hindemith's Sonata for violin and piano contains a Tarantella in which ¾ and ⁶⁄₈ meters oppose each other. Lately, for the dancer Massine, Hindemith has written the music for *Nobilissima Visione,* the name changed to *St. Francis* for the American public.

Jaap Kool(9), of the Netherlands, first began to write dance music because he believed that rhythmic, winged (rather plastic, moving) music best suited his musical turn. Opera he discarded as being too heavy: concert music as being too static. Nevertheless, he composed a symphony that was performed several times, though it, also, was plastic, built to express the labor in the building of machines, and the feelings of the workers. Most of his other compositions have been inspired by dance, and often composed directly with the dancer, when he would try to comprehend the body movements and translate them into musical form. This is a difficult task, since the music cannot then be developed naturally, but must be molded into the dance form. The procedure is distinctly a development of the new German dance, with which this composer is affiliated. Kool's latest ballet, *Ständetänze,* is built from Dutch workmen's dances, inspired by the paintings of the painter, Pieter Breughel. Here the question was not only to conceive musically the characters and rhythms of the different craftsmen, but to catch the atmosphere of a great painter, a difficult task which served only as an inspiration for Kool. The dance *Zimmermannstanz* from this ballet (evidently also called *Der Hausbau*) is in a vigorous triple rhythm, with a single rhythmic figure often repeated in varied forms, much as a modern dancer would repeat and amplify a movement figure. Kool has also written Japanese dances and dance scenes for piano; *Elexiere des Teufels, Schiessbude* and *Leierkasten*—all ballets; *Titcki,* a Chinese ballet; and *Tänze im Alten Stil* for piano and orchestra. He has also written books on the dance and on the saxophone, and has compiled a study of various dance forms which is now in use in modern German dancing schools.

Because little is known of Kool, it may be wise to mention his musical beginnings. He started out as a chemist. Incidentally, he studied music, with no thought of making it a permanent occupation. It happened that he visited a museum of music history five minutes after Richard Strauss had left it. Strauss had been interested in a glass harmonica to use in his opera, *The Woman Without Shadow,* but it was impossible to repair the glass. Kool immediately set to work in the capacity of musico-chemist, and finally managed to build a glass harmonica. Curiosity made him compose for this instrument; the lure of music then took such a strong hold upon him that he began also to compose for other instruments.

At the ripe old age of eleven, Erich Wolfgang Korngold wrote his first composition, *Der Schneeman*. It was in the form of a ballet in two scenes, because that form is the easiest for a child of that age to comprehend. When it was performed, the conductor didn't change a note, despite the composer's youth. It is "incredibly rich music" and it left critics gasping at Korngold's ability and predicting a great future for him. That it was not entirely a stunt is shown by the fact that this little ballet is performed even today! The knowledge of pantomime gained by the young composer in writing it assisted him in his climb toward his great ambition: the writing of operas.

Anna-Anna was the London name for Kurt Weill's *Les Sept Péches Capitaux*, a mimed cantata. He also wrote a ballet of bell-hops and waiters into his opera, *Royal Palace*.

Egon Wellesz wrote a ballet, or dance symphony, called *Die Nächtlichen*, a fantasy which "translates the nocturnal experiences of the soul, from delicate psychic dreams to wildest outbursts of passion, in a physical dance-pantomime to ultramodern music." This was composed in 1924, following Wellesz's modern ballet, *Das Wunder der Diana* (1919) and preceding his ballet *Achille auf Skyros* (1925) with its sword dances.

Young Werner Egk, a German musician, recently wrote a ballet called *Der Weg*. He is also the composer of *Auf der Alm* (Bavarian dancing scenes) full of rough, boisterous humor. Folk tunes of the Bosnian Hill people are perpetuated in Joseph Bayer's ballet, *A Bosnian Wedding*, with its flowing melodies and piquant rhythms. Joseph Schlar had an interesting adventure when he wrote the modern ballet, *Sardanapal*, based on an original Paul Taglioni score. It is spectacular, and is climaxed by a mad Dance of Delirium. *Ein Tanzspiel*, by Franz Shreker, is a dance play to be performed out of doors, with a Sarabande, Minuet, Madrigale, Gavotte.

The Viennese Franz Salmhofer is one of the most often mentioned of modern ballet writers. His *A Woman Dreams* includes jazz and Waltz rhythms, and is doubtless inspired by the episode of a Carnival on the Riviera. His humorous *Good-for-Nothings of Vienna* was extremely popular when it was produced at the Vienna State Opera in 1930. The libretto is by Eichendorff. Another Salmhofer ballet, in which the motif of the music is identical with that of the ballet, is *The Luring Phantom,* depicting the succumbing to the lure of sweet wines and the chase for the phantom. The music itself is said to be youthful, sympathetic, unspoilt and full of rhythmic and melodic pleasure.

Strauss wrote a ballet called *La Vieja Vienna,* while Bachrich wrote *Sakuntala,* a ballet with graceful music in the Viennese style. Johann Strauss' Waltzes have been used in ballets by many later composers to express the life of gay Vienna. For example, *Der Lieber Augustin,* a ballet recently written by Alexander Steinbrecher to a scenario by Margarete Wallmann, ballet mistress of the Vienna State Opera, uses a Strauss Waltz in addition to *Prinz Eugenius* and *Ach du Lieber Augustin.* The music is lively, popular, well orchestrated.

If modern Germans have withdrawn from the ballet-form through lack of interest or understanding, modern Viennese composers (who are classed as German by those who take into account the similarity of language and customs) have more than made up for the lack, and thus they are true to old Viennese operatic tradition. It cannot be denied that their ballet music (on the whole) leans strongly toward the popular, whereas the existing German ballet music is heavier, more abstract, more apt to be classed as pure music. Yet, remembering the joy that the Waltzes of Johann Strauss have given to the world, who can say that one or the other is of greater value?

CHAPTER 22

NOTES

(1) Strauss-Hofmannsthal, *Correspondence,* p. 182
(2) Strauss-Hofmannsthal, *Correspondence,* p. 185
(3) Strauss-Hofmannsthal, *Correspondence,* p. 193
(4) Strauss-Hofmannsthal, *Correspondence,* p. 194

(5) Strauss-Hofmannsthal, *Correspondence,* p. 206

(6) Strauss-Hofmannsthal, *Correspondence,* p. 230

(7) Propert, "Russian Ballet in Western Europe," p. 115

(8) In a letter to the author from Hollywood, California, dated April 16, 1936

(9) In a letter to the author from Germany, dated April 9, 1936

*

ENGLISH BALLETS

In speaking of the English Ballet (which has been steadily improving for many years and which has ranked among the world's finest) one must of necessity quote that tireless, critical globe-trotter, George Bernard Shaw(1). For when, in 1893, Shaw wrote complacently of the French Ballet, he was really advertising the Ballet of his own land: "Of course, the ballet, like everything else in Paris, is a provincial survival, fifty years behind English time, but still it is generally complete, and well done by people who understand ballet." This statement may perhaps be taken with a grain of salt since Paderewski(2), in speaking of Shaw as a critic, tells us that "he wrote as an opponent of public opinion."

For, no sooner did Shaw praise the English ballet thus than (in 1892)(3) he decided to disparage the ballet in London: "Perhaps by the next time I visit a music-hall the ballet will have found its Wagner, or at least its Meyerbeer. For I have had enough of mere ballet: what I want now is dance-drama." In 1893(4), he spoke of the composer, Mr. J. M. Glover, and his ballet, *From London to Paris:* "Mr. Glover has entered thoroughly into the spirit of the piece: his score grows naturally out of the action, and is consequently free from the stereo which makes most ballet music so worrying. The allusions to popular comic songs come in with a musical humor and a daintiness which makes them quite witty and pretty; and some of the points—for instance, the sea-sickly harmonies to *Rule, Brittania* in the storm scene—are irresistibly funny. In short, Mr. Glover's music has all the liveliness and adroitness of the ordinary imported French ballet music, without its staleness and without its foreignness." The ballet went on vivaciously to a pure ballet divertissement, "relieved by a funereal clog dance and can-can at the end." This Glover of whom Shaw wrote was undoubtedly the James Mackey Glover (conductor, composer and writer) who was born in Dublin in 1859.

Five years after Glover's birth, Sir Arthur Sullivan's ballet, *L'Ile Enchantée*, was produced at Covent Garden. It was said to have been more or less the result of an accident, and to have hindered rather than helped his progress in spite of the few gems of melody it contained. "On one occasion," he said in his biography(5) "I was admiring the 'borders' that Beverly had painted for a woodland scene. 'Yes,' he replied, 'they are very delicate, and if you could support them by something suggestive in the orchestra, we could get a very pretty effect.' I at once put into the score some delicate arpeggio work for flutes and clarinets, and Beverly was quite happy. The next day probably some such scene as the following would occur. Sloman, stage machinist: 'That iron doesn't run in the slot as easily as I should like, Mr. Sullivan; we must have a little more music to carry her across. Give us something for the 'cellos if you can!' 'Certainly, Mr. Sloman; you have opened up a new path of beauty in orchestration,' I replied gravely, and I at once added sixteen bars for 'cello alone. No sooner was this done than a *variation* (solo) was required at the last moment for the second danseuse who had just arrived. I said to the stage manager, 'I haven't seen her dance yet. I know nothing of her style.' 'I'll see her,' he replied, and took the young lady aside. In five minutes he returned. 'I've arranged it all,' he said. 'This is exactly what she wants (quoting it to me rhythmically) tiddle-iddle-um, tiddle-iddle-um, rum-ti-rum-tirum sixteen bars of that; then rum-tum, rum-tum, heavy, you know, sixteen bars, and then finish up with the Overture to William Tell last movement.' In ten minutes I had composed it, and written out a répétiteur's part, and it was at once rehearsed."

In this way he was hampered by the stage limitations of a ballet. "It means to me," he declared(6), "That I've got to do a carpenter's job. When I do get into my stride I am reined in with brutal suddenness because what I have labored on, in order to give the best that is in me, is going to ruin the show. I am a musical carpenter, and I like the trade so well that I am going to get out of it." He did get out of it, but not for all time. Later in his career, he agreed to write a ballet called *Victoria and Merrie England,* to be produced in 1897, the Queen's Diamond Jubilee Year. His bad health caused the ballet to be postponed in 1896, but it was finally written. Since it was intended to reflect England's life, Sullivan made the music national: "His melodies seemed to wander through England's many centuries."

So, English ballet composers are not without their traditions. It is notable that modern composers of this school have developed some of the most interesting of all ballets— that is to say, interesting psychologically as well as musically.

Despite the fact that in 1922, Vaughan-Williams built a ballet on old English country dances, called it *Old King Cole* and had it presented at Cambridge, he was forced to confess his ignorance of many accepted ballet traditions when Adolph Bolm commissioned him to write a ballet in three scenes on Dickens' *Christmas Carol.* Bolm found it easy to help in details regarding durations, treatments and so on, and shortly, since Vaughan-Williams was inspired by the project, the ballet was completed (1927) and success greeted its presentation. It was really a Masque, combining carols, folk dance tunes and artistic folk songs by means of original material in the same spirit. Together, this music produced a well-knit fabric, making an effective background for the dreams and visions of Scrooge.

Vaughan-Williams has written another Masque for dancing, called *Job,* and founded on Blake's illustrations for the Book of Job. It is in ten scenes and an epilogue, for full symphony orchestra. The drama of conflict in the soul of man humbled by adversity is presented. This drama is ancient, so there are suggestions of something archaic in the music, though it uses contemporary devices for rhythm and color and is fresh, original, erudite, modern and gravely dignified. A Danish review called the music "expressive." Another said it was melodious, at times full of character, but more often banal. Still another declared that "toward the ending there is heard in the music's apotheosis an echo of the English Church's hymns of Handel, which together with the introductory and concluding Pastorale constitute the ballet's most beautiful musical parts." The scenes of this ballet are played partly on earth and partly on a staircase rising toward Heaven. It contains a Saraband, Pavane, Galliard, and a Minuet of the Sons of Job and Their Wives, a measure "formal, statuesque and slightly voluptuous." Satan has a Dance of Triumph. Constant Lambert has made a version of Job for small theater orchestra.

Lambert, born in 1905, though one of England's younger composers, is decidedly vital. Before he was twenty, he met Diaghileff. The latter was so impressed with Lambert's music, his sure technic and his new idiom, that he urged the composer to prepare a ballet for him. Lambert did. The ballet was *Romeo and Juliette* in two acts, and it got off to a flying start. It had Paris in such an uproar when it was first produced that one could scarcely hear the music above the free-for-all fights that accompanied it. Needless to say, it effectively brought Lambert's name to the attention of the musical world.

In 1927, Lambert wrote *Pomona,* a ballet in one act on a theme by Thomas McGreevy. Pomona is the goddess of fruits; the scene is laid in a Roman wood. The music is scored very simply. The writing of passages in one key simultaneously with other voices not very far from the leading melody gives rise to much dissonance and a very rustic quality. There is an Intrata, a heavily marked Coranto, a Pastorale, Menuetto, Passacaglia, Rigadoon, Siciliana, Marcia. There is some fugal writing, and a good many banks of consecutive thirds moving against each other. One bass theme serves to unify the music. In a sense, it is reminiscent of Casella and his adoption of the rustic treatment in music: his chords of major and minor seconds and his modernistic, contrapuntal, biting style. Yet, it is extremely individual. Lambert is Lambert; Casella is Casella. Lately, Lambert has completed the ballet *Horoscope.*

Lord Berners is the psychologist of modern English music. His ballet, *Freaks,* depicts the wax works. His *Luna Park* is a fantastic ballet in one act to a scenario by Boris Kochno. There are five in the cast, the showman and four freaks, each portrayed by characteristic music. At the ballet's conclusion when they, really humans, decide to leave the sideshow and go out into the world, their music re-asserts itself as the showman innocently opens their niches and their freakish mechanical appendages perform alone, uncannily. The return of the showman gives Berners the opportunity for a welcome musical recapitulation. The showman's horror when he sees what has happened and then hides himself is shown by a furious accelerando, crescendo, and a crashing chord. Then there are four significant final chords in unison. It is interesting to observe how both the scenarist and composer have realized the Russian Ballet's capacity for satire, fine acting, brilliant dancing and technical display. It is all music that one would be liable to hear in a place like *Luna Park,* but it is too much infused with Lord Berners' ingratiating individuality to be cheap.

The same is true of his *The Triumph of Neptune,* in twelve tableaux to a book by Sacheverell Sitwell. This is surely inspired music, with no lack of genuine melody. It is a mixture of reality and fantasy: the nervous shifting of scenes and the rapidity of the tempi corresponding to the rhythms of everyday life and the few older dance forms with their simple music giving a feeling of Queen Victoria's era. Nevertheless, some of these old dance forms (such as the Schottische and Polka) are very definitely satirical, proving that it was intended to be a joke on Victorian England, after all. Fanfares, some reminiscent of bagpipes, separate the sections. The Allegro Giocoso Prelude is strongly accented and, for the most part, contrapuntal. A section representing London Bridge gives way to the satirical Schottische. Later in the ballet are several jolly Hornpipes which are honest and infectuous. The Polka music alternates and combines with a slow vocal bass solo consisting of the first phrase of *The Last Rose of Summer*. The ballet ends with an apotheosis, a tremendous dynamic climax with huge chords piling on top of each other.

It has not been long since Lord Berners completed another ballet in satirical vein, this one called *The Wedding Banquet*, an impression of a middle-class wedding about thirty years ago, presumably in France. In the initial presentation, the opera chorus sang explanatory comments supplied by Gertrude Stein. The ballet is said to be amusing, to "love the people it mocks" and to be splendidly sound from a dancing point of view.

Gustav Holst wrote for Hubert Stowitts a ballet called *The Lure,* on a scenario by Alice Barney of Washington, D. C. Though the subject was the old one concerning the moth and the candle flame, the score is said to contain excellent modern music. This composer also wrote a choral English folk ballet entitled *The Morning of the Year* as well as a ballet suite. The latter was written in his first experimental period of composition (about 1900) when he was more occupied with music than with mystic significances.

Three ballets are Cyril Scott's contribution to the choreographic world. His *Karma* was produced by André Charlot in a Revue, as was his *Dance of the Red Death,* after Poe. These ballets are short, lasting about ten minutes. A longer ballet in two acts, lasting about forty minutes, was suggested to Scott on viewing one of Pieter Breughel's pictures in Vienna. The subject is humorous, the title: *The Shortsighted Apothecary*. It is more pantomimic than active, and the stage and characters are required to copy Breughel. This ballet had not been performed up to 1936. Scott's(7) musical themes for his ballets are suggested to him by the scenes, emotions or atmosphere that must be reproduced. Once created, the music then suggests the movements.

Joseph Holbrooke once collaborated with a young English dancer on the ballet, *Aucassin and Nicolette*. He also wrote *The Moth, The Red Mask* and *Pierrot and Pierrette* (op. 36) with dances by Harlequin, Columbine, Pantalon, Clown. Rutland Boughton wrote two ballets: *Snow White* and *May Day*. Granville Bantock's *Pan in Arcady* is an interesting choral ballet. One of his earliest works was the ballet suite, *Rameses II*. Arnold Bax's music is said to be Celtic in feeling. He is the composer of ballets for *Between Dusk and Dawn* and *The Frog-Skin*. Samuel Coleridge-Taylor, after much planning and procrastination, actually wrote a *Hiawatha* ballet which was later made into suites.

William Walton wrote a ballet called *Siesta* as well as a small ballet to be heard in C. B. Cochran's Revue, *Follow the Sun*. It was an "impudent trifle" with "piquant and individual scoring" and contained a "grand 1910 Waltz tune." Walton's *Façade*, later made into a ballet, was originally an instrumental suite to be accompanied by a voice reciting Edith Sitwell's poems through a megaphone. It is, as one would expect, cleverly humorous. That it originally contained the elements of a splendid ballet is evidenced by the dance-forms on which Walton constructed it: Polka, Valse, Swiss Yodeling Song, Tango Pasodoble, Tarantella, Sevillana. With the utmost of gravity, Walton made delightful parodies of each of these dances. It is as if he were a listener to each piece, presenting his sly reactions in musical form to a responsive public.

Adeline Genée, celebrated dancer, produced in London a ballet called *La Camargo* to music by Dora Bright (who also compiled the ancient and period music for Genée's *La Danse,* (reconstructing the Golden Age of the ballet) as well as *Spring,* a ballet especially composed by Sir Frederick Cowen. Walford Hyden's *Three Virgins and the Devil* was choreographed by Agnes de Mille. A recent ballet-pantomime or Masque produced in London was said to be neither more nor less than ballet music should be. It was composed by Maurice Jacobsen, was entitled *David* and was based on the Biblical story. The music was not oriental, but was said to return to such sources as the *Tonus Peregrinus* set to a Hebrew text and sung during David's Dance before Saul.

Ninette de Valois is the choreographer of an English ballet, *The Rake's Progress,* to music by Gavin Gordon, distinctly national in flavor. Miss de Valois also choreographed *Checkmate,* a new ballet by Arthur Bliss. The score is rich, effective and reflective of the atmosphere of medieval strife, jousting and jealousy suggested by the rivalry of chessmen. The tension and powerful energy of the music was said to add greatly to the general effect of the ballet as a whole: the battle of the Reds and the Blacks.

Incidentally, Ireland has had a word or two to say in the field of sophisticated choreographic music, for Arthur Duff, graduate of Trinity College, is an Irish composer whose first ballet was performed by the Abbey Theatre School of Ballet. Moreover, Joseph M. Crofts wrote the ballet *Doomed Cuchulain,* performed in Dublin in 1937. Both music and dance are clearly symbolic and in the old Gaelic vein. They express the true Irish spirit.

CHAPTER 23
NOTES

(1) Shaw, *Music in London,* vol. iii, p. 56
(2) *Saturday Evening Post,* February 20, 1937, p. 85
(3) Shaw, *Music in London,* vol. ii, p. 66
(4) Shaw, *Music in London,* vol. iii, p. 241
(5) Lawrence, *Sir Arthur Sullivan,* pp. 57-58
(6) Sullivan and Flower, *Sir Arthur Sullivan,* p. 67
(7) In a letter to the author from England dated February 24, 1936

*

*

MISCELLANEOUS BALLETS

It was really Dohnanyi's wife(1) who interested him in writing ballets though, strangely enough, it was through a pantomime-ballet he had written before he met her (*Der Schleier der Pierrette* to Arthur Schnitzler's book) that their friendship began. This ballet is characterized by a harmonically rich Viennese Waltz in the wedding scene. Later, when Pierrette is locked in the studio with the dead body of her lover, Pierrot, she goes mad to the tune of an insistent, frenzied Waltz. She frantically dances herself to death. Other dances in the ballet are a Jocose Funeral March and a Minuet. Since this ballet was popular throughout Europe, especially in Russia, Mrs. Dohnanyi saw it and visualized improvements in it long before she met the composer whose wife she was to become. Later, she wished to make a ballet on a Hungarian theme. It so happened that at this precise moment, Dohnanyi had in preparation a series of masterly symphonic pieces which were then only in piano score. They were based on folk dance themes and were called *Ruralia Hungarica*. When his wife wished to create such a ballet, these compositions assumed a new significance to Dohnanyi. He promptly added two pieces and it became *The Holy Torch,* in eleven scenes, an "iridescent, sensitive score."

Together with the dance, into which Mrs. Dohnanyi tried to get the folk feeling, *The Holy Torch* music forms a monumental work. As Dohnanyi worked with folk tunes, so did his wife develop folk dance patterns in the abstract. Since the tulip predominates in Hungary's art, she made dances whose formations and arm movements suggested tulips. She also succeeded in perfecting a system of dance notation, noting the steps and floor patterns in connection with each measure of music, which was interpreted correctly by ballet masters in distant cities. Only the main movements, of course, were indicated, the rest being left to the imagination of the artists and the ballet master. Her system, if adopted by other dancers, would help to make more permanent the art of the dance, by allying it minutely with the music it accompanies.

Bartok's pantomime, *The Wonderful Mandarin* was put into rehearsal but never performed, since the composer objected to certain stage actions that rendered the graphic symbolism of his orchestra meaningless by loosening and dissolving the clear relation to the scenic development. *The Prince Carved in Wood,* another Bartok ballet, met a different fate. In it, Bartok employed two leading themes. The lyric theme is intended to transport the audience to the past, while the grotesque theme portrays the stark realism of the present. At times, the rich music in *The Prince Carved in Wood* rises to great shrieking dramatic climaxes. It contains Dances of the Trees and of the Waves.

Kodály's ballet is entitled *Kurucmese.* Another Hungarian composer who is given (like Bartok and Kodály) to the exploration of many different types of folk music, is Ladislas Lajtha, born in 1892. He has written the ballet *Lysistrata.* Jenö Hubay, also Hungarian, is the composer of *The Selfish Giant,* a ballet based upon an Oscar Wilde tale.

Modern Polish composers have made outstanding contributions to musical literature for the ballet stage since the time of Adam Minchejmer (1831-1904) who, with Moniuszko, composed the ballet *The Devil's Tricks.* He was the ballet master at the Grand Theater in Warsaw and therefore must have

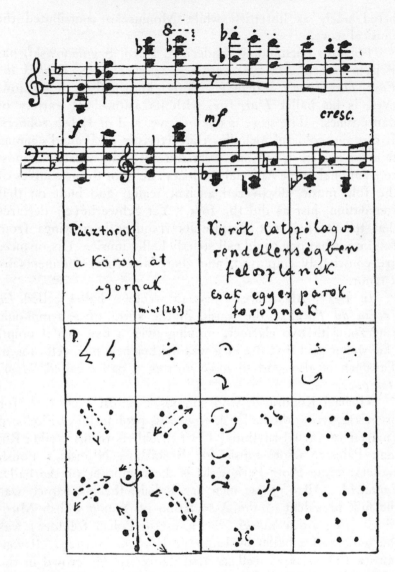

Mrs. Dohninyi's System of Notating Dance Movements along with the Music

(Interpretation of the Symbols: On the left, the Shepherds jump over the circle of girls. On the right, the circle breaks up into seeming disorder and only a few couples continue circling around.)

acted solely as librettist, while Moniuszko contributed the musical score.

Poland's outstanding modernist, Karol Szymanowski, has written several Masques entitled: *Scheherezade, Tantris the Fool, Don Juan's Serenade.* Better known than these, however, is his ballet *Harnasie,* with its astonishing variety of dance tunes. The story is one of love, and of Polish robbers. It contains colorful melodies characteristic of Poland's mountaineers and in it, Szymanowski did not write what was most conventional in the national tendency: he went to the sources of the folk music, discovered ancient scales, and built on that foundation, just as did the folk. Yet Schwerké(2) declares that the score is not, despite its frequent borrowings from folklore, what one could call strictly ballet music. Dissonances are consciously employed, and there are vocal comments by a tenor.

In 1922, Alexandre Tansman wrote a ballet called *Le Jardin du Paradis,* the music in the form of a symphonic scherzo, with two clarinets moving over a bass pedal point. One writer said that the idea was neither new nor well-chosen. Tansman is also said to have written a ballet called *Silversterspuck.*

Michael Kondracki, who composes almost exclusively for orchestra, wrote the ballet *Metropolis;* prolific Jerzy Fitelberg (master of varied rhythms) has two ballets to his credit; Roman Palester wrote music for Bronislava Nijinska's Polish Ballets; while Piotr Perkowski is the composer of the ballet *Santewid.* All of these men are Polish; the last-named was the first president of the Association of Young Polish Musicians. *Pan Twardowski* (the Faust in Polish folklore) was the subject of a ballet by Ludomir Rózycki in 1924. It contains a Polonaise as well as mad dances of the crowd in the marketplace, when the devil's magic music rises to a dramatic climax.

Karaguez, the leading Turkish puppet, was characterized in a ballet by that name written by Michailovitchi (Rumanian) for Adolph Bolm.

Bohuslav Martinu, Czech composer, has composed *The Three Wishes, Istar* and *The Soldier and the Dancer,* ballets. His song-ballet *Spalicek,* in three acts and ten scenes is said to be the most racial and the most characteristic of all his works. His dance music profits by the inclusion of Czech folk melodies. Martinu employs polyrhythms, polyharmonies and many metrical changes. His music, on the whole, tends toward realism, by the road of irony.

The Fates, ballet by Miroslav Ponc, another talented Czech modernist, unifies song, dance and the spoken word. Less successful than this was the three-act ballet, *Princess Hyacinth,* written about 1911 by Oscar Nedbal. When this ballet was produced at the Czech National Theater in 1936, the criticism was that it "had moments of matchless tactlessness by emphasizing the outmoded character of the ballet. Nevertheless, the packed house delighted in all the musical banalities. . . ."

It is not generally known that the Swedish people, having at their disposal gifted and noted choreographers and some fine composers, developed a splendid ballet. This ballet went on tour, astounding key cities in other nations by its excellence. Thus, when we read that Glazounow in 1920 wrote (in Paris) a Swedish ballet called *Derviches,* or that Blasco Ibañez in the same city at the same time wrote a Swedish ballet called *Iberia,* the scenes laid in Granada and Seville, we may presume—not that the subjects, composers or music had suddenly become Swedish—but that the ballets were commissioned by the company from Sweden.

Atterberg wrote a Swedish pantomime called *Les Vierges Folles.* Torjussen wrote a ballet named *Adam and Eve. Maison de Fous,* Viking Dahl's Swedish ballet of 1920, presented a scene in a Paris insane asylum. *Le Porcher* (The Swineherd), also a Swedish ballet, was merely Ferraud's orchestration of Swedish folk tunes to accompany the Hans Andersen tale.

Othmar Schoek, a modern Swiss impressionist, composed *Das Wandbild* in 1921, a pantomime taking place in a Paris antique shop.

Nor has Sibelius been deaf to the lure of this sort of music. His pantomime, *Scaramouche* is fantastic; the music is piquant, rhythmic and mystic. Biondini is a passionate dancer in it; Scaramouche is a diabolic, sensuous fiddler; Leilon a weak-hearted husband. All three die. Sibelius' music, while not directly utilizing Finnish folk themes, is definitely national in character.

The Royal Danish Ballet is also a noted ballet organization, though little is known about it outside of Europe. Several excellent ballets have been composed by Danes. Niels Gade, born in Copenhagen in 1817, wrote music to Bournonville's ballet, *Faedrelandet's Muser* about 1840. August Bournonville was the first great Danish ballet master, the son of French and Danish parents. Emil Reesen's *Gaucho,* a recent Danish ballet, contains Tango and Rhumba rhythms. In 1914, Paul Klenau wrote *Little Ida's Flowers,* a ballet after Hans Christian Andersen. Hakon Borresen wrote the ballet, *Tycho Brahe's Dream* with national dances of the King's Highlanders, dances of the court people, celestial dances and others. In Copenhagen (1910) Fini Henriques wrote a ballet called *The Little Mermaid,* while 1901 saw the completion of August Enna's *Shepherdess and Chimney-Sweep.*

Erik Meyer-Helmund (born in St. Petersburg in 1891) must be mentioned as the composer of the ballet *Rübezahl,* produced in Leipzig in 1893.

CHAPTER 24

NOTES

(1) In an interview with Mrs. Dohnanyi's son, Mr. Huberman, in Los Angeles, California, on March 24, 1936
(2) *Musical Courier,* May 23, 1936, p. 5

THE DANCE IN SILENCE

Often, after a big crescendo of sound, intense silence comes as an unexpected climax. So it is with this chapter. The Dance in Silence is actually a musical rebellion, and has been so through the ages.

Now, by the Dance in Silence one does not mean the dance with percussion accompaniment, simply discarding music, for that is definitely not silent(1). It is here considered as a truly silent art, during which no sound is heard. When one speaks of the *real* Dance in Silence, he encounters distinct surprise. It is so outside the comprehension of most people. It is not, as Marinetti says(2), a result of the influence of cubist research and of Picasso. ("Under the influence of cubist research and of Picasso, a dance of geometric volumes was created which was practically independent of music. The dance became an autonomous art, equivalent to music. It no longer submitted to music, it replaced music.") It is decidedly not an innovation, yet in all cases it has been an isolated thing, not usual with the general run of dancers.

In ancient Greece, when Demetrius the Cynic suggested that dancing owed its entire effect to the music by which it was accompanied, one of the dancers begged him not to condemn the art without seeing *him* perform without the aid of music or song. And, commanding the instrumentalists to cease, he represented in a dance one of the old myths of the gods. Demetrius was convinced of his error.

That the Dance in Silence, or absolute dance, existing solely for itself alone, is not confined to the moderns is further proved by the fact that some simple Yugoslav Kolos are danced without music, even without percussive beats. The great age of these rhythms makes them impossible to describe from a conventional standpoint, though they approximate a ⅔ meter. The Kolos which are danced to a musical accompaniment sometimes approximate a ¾ meter.

The Dance in Silence was in evidence on the English stage in the early eighteenth century. "John Weaver's method," says Avery(3), "was to take a familiar story and to present it without music or dialogue, relying on dancing alone to convey the story to the audience." James Ralph (in *The Taste of the Town*, published in London in 1731) thought the addition of music was a handicap to the pantomime: "Thus by the wrong blending of two arts in one piece; they form alliances which will ruin them, and by joining execrable poetry and vile musick to beautiful scenes of just grotesque dancing, the perfection of one is lost in the stupidity of the other."

Noverre, alive to all that was going on about him, gave a definition of the silent dance as he saw it: "To make bold and brilliant steps, to traverse the stage with speed and lightness to the accompaniment of a cold and dreary melody—that is what I call a dance without music."

As a matter of fact, the Dance in Silence is the only form of the art of movement that has paralleled the development of abstract music and poetry, by developing its own inherent forms. It is the only dance in which dancers have been able to extend or develop a theme as composers have done in music. It marks an epoch in dance history. The Dance in Silence is not primitive, nor is it crude. It is sophisticated: a genuinely creative effort. One who dances in silence must be a complete artist within himself. He must know music, or feel it, thoroughly. This forms his background so that people will not remark, as did Francis Kendig(4), that we become aware of the real significance of music as an accompaniment to the dance when we do not have it.

The dancer in silence must look upon his art with a total disregard of self, must perceive each future development of the art before it arrives, and must be sensitive enough to contact thoughts and dance-forms already in motion. This age is witnessing a disintegration of "schools" of dancing. Every dancer's medium of expression is completely individual, and whether or not the idea is conveyed successfully to the audience depends upon how deeply the artist has delved within.

Now why, one may ask, is the Dance in Silence a musical rebellion?

That is a fair question, and its answer depends upon the degree of creative ability—perhaps also on the degree of temperament and independence—possessed by every dancer.

We have seen how many past composers for the dance wrote little pieces in ²⁄₄, ⁴⁄₄ and ³⁄₄ meters, strung them together and called them ballets. The music was usually pleasant and rhythmic, but not particularly original, and was built to harmonize with the stiffness and artificiality of the classic ballet, in which the feet were of prime importance. Excepting a few geniuses of the ballet, the feet always were more important than any other part of the body. And composers became fascinated with the complicated, involved step combinations. They tried to write suitable music for them. This banal music was the direct cause of the low opinion of dance music held by many musicians, despite the many fine composers who wrote (and wrote well) in that medium. As a result, up to the advent of the modernists, all composers of dance music followed their precedent. Saccharine *Petites Danses* and coy *Airs de Ballet*, all in regular rhythm, glutted the music market. Even today, they write music to fit bygone dance forms while, unknown to them, the dance itself has undergone a radical change. Most of these composers have not tried to know the medium for which they compose as well as a song-writer understands the limitations and possibilities of the human voice. Their pure music may be as modern as the modern dance, but when they consciously set out to write something for that dance, they unconsciously fall into old, regular forms. It was unthinkable to suppose, for instance, that a dancer could retard naturally, as the music does. Those were the days of set steps.

Had the dances done to classical ballet music been choreographed according to phrase, pitch and thematic development, they would have been some of the best of all choreographic creations as far as form and pattern are concerned. Instead of that, traditional ballet steps were combined in new but not unexpected *enchainements*, and the only musical element to be noted was the obvious rhythm and perhaps a banal melody.

Inevitably, the creative dancer rebelled against being forced into such an arbitrary pattern, both as to dance and music, much as a composer would rebel if he were compelled to write songs constantly, and to limit his melodies and his musical expression to a certain sort of verse form and a certain sort of wording. So, some dancers danced to abstract music as a means of escape from the tyranny of obvious music. A storm of protest arose.

Joseph Arnold(5), for one, objected to the pernicious habit in the dance of treating musical compositions of definite meaning and character as pegs on which to hang the ideas of a dancer. Of course, when a dancer dances to a familiar, greatly loved composition, she must be prepared to combat many preconceived ideas on the part of critics, musicians and laymen who comprise her audience, for each of these will have his own opinion as to the meaning and possibilities of the composition. (The writer cannot refrain from wondering why critics worry so much about the disagreements between dancer and audience, when eminent musical authorities themselves *always* disagree on a mere musical interpretation of a master work. Ask any pianist or violinist who has studied the same composition with two different authorities!) Some argumentative music lovers find it necessary to close their ears to the familiar music while they watch the dance. Many insist that a sensitive soloist, rather than a group, is able to realize better the beauties of great music in dance form.

Gradually, when composers began to write good music designed for dancing, the need for using abstract compositions was no longer so desperate. Still the creative dancer found herself in a dilemma. When the musical phrase ended, the movement was incomplete. When the musical phrase was extended, the movement was incapable of being drawn out to an equal length. Rarely was there a true agreement between the musician's preconceived creation and the dancer's new idea. In short, the creative dancer still found herself under the domination of another mind, and she resented it. Fancy a composer yielding to another mind! Why then, should a dancer?

Thus the Dance in Silence, with its possibilities of time and space rhythms independent of music, came into being. It goes without saying that the Dance in Silence needs a greater spiritual awareness on the part of the dancer, though John Martin(6) believes that the dancer's art is much more closely related to the theater than to music. (Although there is no reason why a theater art *cannot* be spiritual, despite the frequent departures from this ideal.) We are told that Martin also believes that dance and music are only externally related; musical patterns existing in sound and dance patterns existing in time. The Dance in Silence quickly bares a dancer's resource, or lack of resource; imagination or lack of imagination, for she is left without a crutch. She must create her own accompaniment. "There is no motion," say the Chinese, "without sound."

Elizabeth Selden(7) is of the opinion that the dance may perhaps lose more than it gains by an isolation from music: Music and the dance have so much in common that the one invariably recalls the other. No good silent dance is ever danced which is not in some way accompanied, on the part of the dancer, by inner music. Music facilitates for the spectator that vicarious sharing of the dancer's experience, and that is probably why the silent dance vanished so quickly from the concert platform, after the first enthusiasm over the new theory subsided. Mary Wigman could very well dance an entire program without musical accompaniment. But Mary Wigman has that rare knack of listening to the music of the body. Doris Humphrey's music is primarily the music of the dancer's body.

As a matter of fact, the Dance in Silence may be (when it occurs) only a passing phase in the development of the individual dancer, so that she may the more easily find herself. Someday there will be dancers who can create their own music, who can record that inner music so that it actually will be audible to less practiced ears. In the words of Novalis(8) : "Rhythmical feeling is genius. Every person has his individual rhythm. All melody is rhythm. He who has control of rhythm has the world in control."

When the musical rebellion first took possession of the dancer, Bertha Wardell, she attributed it to her own inadequate knowledge of music. She had considered her inability to fit her movements to set musical patterns a distinct handicap, and did not realize the equal importance of her own body rhythm. Upon analyzing her problem, she found that the reasons for her departure were more basic than that. The age-old struggle of the true creator for freedom was one of them. Another was her distaste for an incorrect musical interpretation, as well as her desire not to interpret music so correctly from a technical standpoint that she would lose the spirit of the composition as a whole. She knew, then, that she must discard music.

First, she used a percussion accompaniment. Finally, even that was eliminated. Audiences scarcely knew how to look at her dances. They were so different from anything ever seen before! Little by little, their minds began to comprehend the unsounded music that emanated from her movements. They understood it then as (in the words of Isabel Morse Jones) "silent music, created in its own image."

When Wardell danced in silence, there would be a bare salon shaded with mellow lights, and back of those lights a group of intense, earnest faces. Her art, she felt, was for the intimate group, not the packed auditorium. Then the slight figure of the dancer emerged from the shadows. Every gesture was rhythm incarnate, and so great was her intensity that she pulled her audience along until it, too, seemed to be dancing. When she finished there was no applause: only the intaken breath, the silence that is the tribute of intelligence to art. She danced such things as four chapters from Genesis, a difficult subject to approach. Yet, her interpretation gave the breadth and spiritual force that underlie the Scriptures, rather than a literal presentation of the Scriptures themselves. What music could have formed a base for this dance? Where is there a Bach who will compose such a masterpiece in music, one that will also adequately underscore movement?

The foregoing example belies the words of the critic in *Theater Arts Monthly* for August, 1927: Experiments in the dance unaccompanied are interesting in theory, but have so far resulted in the substitution of story-accompaniment for tone-accompaniment.

Of course, Wardell is an introvert, to a certain extent. She withdraws from the flippancies of everyday life to emerge richer, more intense, broader mentally. Her dancing thus coming from within, becomes thought in motion. Hall Johnson, on hearing of her work, declared, "How interesting! She must have a marvelous mind, a great deal to say, and many fine ideas!" She has. But she creates very little, comparatively speaking, since she never begins to create until she has an idea or a rhythm that appears to her to be absolutely fundamental. Those are indeed few! This is the real dancer in silence, as contrasted to those who dance in silence with empty gestures, hands that simply move hither and yon, legs that are placed in various positions: a pseudo, commonplace art.

Many dancers have succeeded in developing independent dance themes without music, but few have managed to achieve an orderly, logical and coherent sequence of movement, no one movement being complete without the movement preceding it, and all ascending toward a climax: the spiral form of creation. The dancer who has absorbed too many forms foreign to herself will be apt never to realize completely that spiral perfection. Smallness of movement is the sacrifice one must make for a certain limited type of technical perfection in the dance, as in the classic ballet. The Dance in Silence demands a greater breadth of movement.

In Benjamin Zemach's classes, music is used for beginners, to help them along. Advanced students are allowed to develop their movements independently of music. "I am not afraid to work on modern technic as such," declared Zemach, "Just as a pianist works on scales."

The Strauss dancers once gave a whole concert in silence. Tina Flade has danced in silence, as has Doris Humphrey, whose *Drama of Motion* was based on abstract movement alone, with neither musical nor dramatic foundation. Her *Water Study* was described by Lucile Marsh as a dance for large group in which the "wave-beat in the body gave a rhythm which suggested design." Humphrey herself avers that "Music is for tone-color and rhythm and for stimulation to the dancer, but we can also dance quite well by our inner emotional rhythm or by the dynamics of natural forces."

Fokine, despite his outstanding choreographic creations, has never been able to conceive of the dance as an independent art, without music or costume. His feeling is that absence of music is only justified at some particular point, so as to emphasize and bring out a definite dramatic meaning. Dancing, he believes, always implies noise, stamping, clapping, singing, drums or percussion of some sort, but today it is no longer interesting to return to such primitive sounds, therefore he prefers to use the more highly developed forms of music. Palucca (9) has taken an intermediate view of the situation: It stands without saying that inspiration is necessary in order to create a masterpiece of dancing. Whether the source of inspiration is music, newly discovered movements or an idea that demands expression seems to be of little importance.

On the other hand, Angna Enters (10) effectively forestalled theories for and against the Dance in Silence when she wrote: "Dancers' notion today seems to be to *avoid* music—if you can. The impulse is not toward a composition which is unconcerned with music but one which can manage without music. Such dance without music is a make-shift, an art-game with artificial obstacles to overcome. Now, there is no more virtue in dancing without music than there is in dancing with. In some instances, music is one of the dancer's tools of composition; in others, it is either superfluous or uncalled for. The natural modern approach is that one uses music or not, as need be." But Enters herself has realized the ideal situation, when she created the music for several of her own compositions in dance form. Hubert Stowitts must envy Enters this accomplishment, for in 1923 he said(11), I wish I could compose music. Then I could conceive a ballet as a complete work and do everything necessary to bring it to a realization . . . a sort of Wagner of the dance, as it were; for Stowitts already understands the arts of scenery and costuming. Said Louis Kalonyme of Angna Enters(12): There is never any "interpretation" of the music, although music may be used as an illustration. For in Enters' dancing the music flows from the dances. . . . Another critic wrote: Miss Enters has the good manners not to "interpret" the music of the defenseless masters (who need no help) save when they specifically wrote music for dancing.

Perhaps the entire situation was most aptly summarized by Ruth St. Denis(13) in 1924, when she wrote: I have been at work for over six years on the principle that dance is an independent art; that it can and should exist independently of music. Dancing has suffered from a sort of arrested development. Holding us back is our utter dependence upon music, upon external and audible rhythm and harmony, to give life and animation to the body. I want to bring home the fact that dancing is essentially a visual art; that we cannot command the attention of the intellect until we dance from the intellect and that we cannot appeal to man's spiritual being until we move also in the spiritual plane.

CHAPTER 25

NOTES

(1) When Serge Lifar composed a ballet called *Icarus* to be presented at the Paris Opéra, it was advertised as a silent ballet, although it had an accompaniment of percussion instruments. He was not bold enough to go completely into the silence, and for the Paris Opéra with all its traditions, it must be admitted that his venture was indeed an adventure.

(2) *Dance Observer*, October, 1935, p. 75

(3) *Studies in Philology*, vol. 31, no. 3

(4) *Saturday Night*, February 1, 1936

(5) *American Dancer*, June, 1934, p. 13

(6) *New York Times*, November 29, 1936

(7) Selden, *The Dancer's Quest*, pp. 45, 46, 71, 77

(8) *The Étude*, March, 1902, p. 109

(9) Stewart, *Modern Dance*, pp. 26-27

(10) *The Drama Magazine*, December, 1930

(11) *Musical America*, May 26, 1923

(12) *The Arts*, May, 1926

(13) *Denishawn Dance Magazine* (now in the collection of Vocha Bertha Fisk), June, 1924

OCCASIONAL DANCE ACCOMPANIMENTS

Every dancer thinks that Dalcroze Eurhythmics are splendid for musicians; every musician thinks them fine for dancers. Both are right. They are wrong who consider Dalcroze's system an end in itself, not a means to an end.

The word "eurhythmics" comes from the Greek eurhythmia. Dalcroze thought that by interpreting literally every chord, every note, every phrase and every nuance in music, he would eventually have exhausted all the possibilities in movement. Also, the body would be given a training so refined and so detailed as to make it sensitive to every rhythmic impulse and able to lose itself in any music. This involves ear-training, transposition, memorization and improvisation on the piano which must be done with infinite thought, and rhythmically. For the accompanist, the mental training is strenuous. Some Dalcroze students have compelled themselves to think of movement only in terms of music and of music only in terms of movement.

Dalcroze may have fostered many theories in his time, but it has always been his belief that the aim of artistic education should not be the production of performers, but the production of musically intelligent human beings. His work is not supposed to be a mere refinement of dancing, nor an improved method of music teaching, but a principle that must have its effect upon every part of life. He has always wished to establish complete harmony between the brain and the body. He has been said to protest periodically against the many travesties of his method which masquerade under his own word "eurhythmics," by people insufficiently trained. He says his own is "not a theory, but an experience."

In 1909, he declared that before teaching the relation of sound and movement, it is wise to undertake the independent study of each of these elements. (In his later years, he was accustomed to tell his students that "A dancer needs no technic," according to two American girls(1) who studied with him.) Because tone has not its origin in ourselves it is secondary, whereas movement is instinctive in man and is primary. Therefore he began the study of music by teaching movement. To teach time measures, he advocated various accentuations of the foot. Pauses in marching indicated the durations of sound. When Dalcroze gives a lesson it is said that he seldom repeats himself, so varied and limitless are the possibilities of his work.

Dalcroze's implication that his method alone will produce superlative dancers is unfortunately not true, since absolute musical perfection (without an understanding of the technic of motion) leads to inaccuracies in movement. No attention is paid to line, or to movement in space in the classes devoted to this work. As to music, pure Dalcrozians are accurate. As to movement, they are often careless, rarely free from sloppiness. Those who have attained a pleasing movement are usually those who have also made a study of other methods and ideas, or who have questing minds of their own.

Dalcroze is known as a composer. Among his larger works, the *Youth of Figaro*, a three-act opera from the play by Sardou, should be mentioned. He has also composed an orchestral *Tanz Suite* in four movements. Today, this dynamic personality that once influenced the trend of the dance so strongly is an enormously humorous, rather satirical, rather crotchety little old man who, with the prerogative of "The Master," loves to single out certain people in his classes for almost constant criticism over a period of months.

More dancers have employed percussion as an accompaniment to their dances than have ever danced in silence. It is easy, inexpensive, comprehensible to most audiences, and it allows the dancer a great deal of freedom. Since the character of the sound has an uncanny way of influencing that of the dance, movements done to percussive accompaniment assume a forced, primitive quality. They become as elemental and as limited as the accompanying sound.

Tamiris is one dancer who turned gradually from modern music to percussive effects, in the belief that the new dance no longer explains music. It speaks for itself; is self-explanatory. If dancing is in any way related to music it is because the movement comes out of the music and music out of the movement. She once used the beating of strings as an accompaniment to a dance. Gluck-Sandor and Sorel did a geometric dance to the beat of a metronome. Jacques Cartier and Charles Teske used barefoot-rhythms, as did Ruth St. Denis and Ted Shawn in their *Trágica*, a group dance, a "fine study in moving masses(2)." Angna Enters allowed the swish of her taffeta dress to form the accompaniment to her *Dance of Death*, thus giving a "half-sinister, half-hopeful sound like the beating of wings against the bars of a cage(3)" and forming a "noise counterpoint to a tragic composition." Doris Humphrey's *Life of the Bee* had a chorus of humming voices as its sole accompaniment. Ruth St. Denis uses primitive percussion instruments to accompany oriental dances. Zemach uses a singer and tambour for his oriental numbers, and a weird rumbling on the strings of the piano for his *Jacob's Dream*. Stuart and Lea used a vocal accompaniment for their *Trees*. Lester Horton uses drums and voice for his Indian dances, purely percussive combinations for his modern work. Mary Wigman uses a small wind instrument for her *Pastorale* and drums for *Face of the Night*. Kreutzberg used a distant phonograph for one of his *Three Mad Dances*. Annia Brey-

mann used voice and harp in her *Ave Marie*, while Helen
March used only a guitar for her Spanish impression. Concert
impressions of old-time dances have been done to fiddle alone.

In Germany, Dorothea Gunther's dance group used for
musical accompaniment a new sound: a high-tension dance
orchestra, consisting of drums and stopped flutes, handled in
a sharply different manner. The accompaniment was contrapuntally interwoven with the dance. Since its inception, this
particular orchestra has been refined. The wild rhythm has
been subdued, and a few more melodic instruments have been
added. Xylophones, metallophones, bells, the spinettino and
the portative have begun to dominate the ensemble and completely to change its tonal aspect.

Elizabeth Selden(4) is of the opinion that the flute,
inasmuch as it uses respiration in the most sensitive way, and
inasmuch as a phrase-length was originally a breath-length, is
destined to play a leading part in the readjustment of music
and dance, in conjunction with percussion instruments, which
may perform the functions of a rhythmic base.

In Wigman's German school of the dance there is a teacher
of primitive percussion instruments, and a teacher of dance
music, while the musicians who accompany in the classes are
called faculty members! Martha Graham's American school
also devotes much thought to the musical training of all who
study.

John Bovingdon's array of gongs to be struck and to re-
sound while he danced on the vibrations, or overtones, was
unique. He achieved moments of great beauty. But he was
not great enough as an artist to make a real contribution in
that form. He later took to the interpretation of recitations
by means of movement, calling them *Portraits of a Changing
World*, mainly on subjects that are yet controversial. It was
said of him that to see him in one number is to get the impression that he has developed a new medium of expression, but to
see him in an entire program is to permit the original serious
regard to disintegrate fast.

Vicente Escudero is apparently the only dancer on the

contemporary concert stage who is able to use fingernail rhythms effectively. They originated with him when he was a child, about to dance in a café. Every other dancer there employed a guitarist, or used castanets. He had neither, and no money to get them. While casting about in his mind for a remedy for this desperate situation, he hit upon the idea of clicking his fingernails together. People liked it, so he was easily persuaded to use it often, since his economical soul approved of the enormous saving of money. When he became able to afford a musician, he allowed himself to forget the old fingernail trick. Years later, the idea suddenly recurred to him. "If they liked it then," thought he, "Why not now?" Thus the café trick found its way to the concert stage.

The sounds of some castanets are repellent. La Argentina's castanets were said by a Spanish critic not to clash, but to caress each other (*que no chocan, sino que se acarician*). La Argentina is another who achieved a musical tone as well as an emotional nuance with the percussion instruments that have heretofore been considered of small importance. She actually managed to translate a melodic line into a rhythmic form! Her castanets often played alone, and one never realized the lack of a musical tone. Strangely enough, in the beginning she hated castanets. But in later years she was able to say that(5) "gradually I have succeeded in making out of the abhorred castanets an instrument that thrills me with its musical possibilities and that seems a perfect collaboration with my choreographic art." Add to this John Martin's statement(6), and the tale is practically complete: "When she lays them (i.e., the castanets) aside, there is still a running accompaniment of rhythmic sounds from her snapping fingers and strangely musical noises made with tongue and teeth. If it is possible to translate music into movement, here is its supreme manifestation."

There are several ways that poetry may be used as an accompaniment for the dance: as rhythmic base, as mood background, or as an outline for a dance pantomime. The poetry may be read offstage, may be sung, may be chanted by one person or recited by a speech choir, with an unobtrusive instrumental accompaniment. The poem may be read beforehand to set the mood, or chanted by the dancer himself. When poetry is used as a rhythmic base, it precludes the use of good music, thereby lessening the emotional appeal of the dance. Further, any poem sufficiently strong in rhythm to suggest itself for dancing is also apt to be rather monotonous rhythmically. There is always a naïve quality about poetry used as an outline for a dance pantomime, according to Melissa Blake (7), since a good dance pantomime needs no words; whereas if the poem relates a story, it should not require dancing to make it clear. One of the most successful methods of combining poetry and dance is as a title for the dance, or as a short quotation immediately following the dance title, to eliminate the necessity of explaining at length the intellectual concept behind the dance, or its emotional mood. Many dancers are too literal in their uses of poetry. They would be wiser simply to dance the mood of the poem, thus retaining its charm and the feeling that something is left to the imagination.

Theodore Stier's early experience as conductor for the Court Theater, when in *Prunella*, a play in which the music was written to fit the rhythm of the verse, he had to keep his eyes fixed on the mouths of the singers to insure exact synchronization, aided him when he at last became musical director for Pavlowa and had to get his cues from her feet. The rhythm of the word and the step guided his music.

One of Isadora Duncan's first dances was to Longfellow's *I shot an arrow into the air*. She used to recite the poem and teach the children to follow its meaning in gesture and movement. Later she danced to Fitzgerald's translation of the Rubáiyát of Omar Khayyám, while someone read it aloud. Such a venture, on a large scale, was more recently made (1939) at the Bennington School, when the drama, dance and music divisions combined to produce *The Bridge*, an epic poem by Hart Crane. The words were spoken by onstage and offstage choruses and leaders, the actions made visible through dance movements, and original music by Gregory Tucker used to accompany both dancers and singers.

Since Miriam Marmein(8) regards the dance and pantomime as a theater art, she employs any oral means at her disposal to induce the emotions she demands from her audiences at certain points. If her accompaniment is music, she demands that it be secondary to the dance. Rarely, there will spring into being a number that needs no sound accompaniment. Miss Marmein once danced Shelley's *Ode to the West Wind* in plastic pantomime with large, lyrical and dramatic movements. Audiences were enthusiastic; critics were not. She has danced to Euripides' poetry in the Gilbert Murray translation, as well as to the accompaniment of wood-block alone. The latter was a dance of pure design. In another instance, she utilized piano, drums, rattle and wood-block in a primitive fantasy. Her *March* is done to drum alone, and would be spoiled by the addition of music, although generally speaking she prefers music as an accompaniment and would rather have music especially composed for each dance, despite her difficulty in finding musicians with sufficient creative talent to stimulate an audience or to meet in emotional content the quality of feeling that the dance demands. Each dance idea, to her way of thinking, dictates its own form, and the form dictates the accompaniment. Any device that will produce an emotional reaction in the audience is legitimate.

Anita Zahn and a company of dancers presented a dance-drama called *Arouse and Beware*. The title was from Walt Whitman, whose *Leaves of Grass* supplied spoken dialogue to accompany the dancing. Orchestral music, composed by Mary Shambaugh, was also used. Blanche Yurka and Richard Hale were the speakers. Lillian Shapero once danced to Langston Hughes' *Good Morning, Revolution*. Hughes' *Air Raid over Harlem*, *Drums of Tragedy* and *Shake Yo' Brown Feet, Honey* have also been danced. Miriam Blecker and James Morrison are two others who have interpreted his poems in dance. Though he had no thought of movement when he wrote these poems, so many of them have been danced that one might almost believe them especially inspired by movement. Teru, young Japanese-American dancer, made a graphic study in this vein when she danced to one of her own poems, spoken by an invisible voice, perfectly synchronized with the actions. The Poetry Playhouse at the University of Southern California has made interesting experiments along this line, under the leadership of Cloyde Dalzell. Valentine de Saint-Point once conceived an abstract dance intended to translate pure thought. Her metachorie consisted of poetry, mimed and danced. This was a series of philosophic rituals with orchestral music written by Dane Rudhyar, then newly-arrived in America. The dance (more introspective and calmer than most dances) and music were equal in that they were both abstract expressions of a poem that was recited in the dark as a prelude to each number. Due to the intervention of the World War, this idea was short-lived. Agnes Boone has made a dance interpretation of Vachel Lindsay's *Congo*, with the poet himself chanting the words. When this happened, Lindsay wrote to her: "I hate jazz, and they call it jazz! Believe me, I wrote the third section with the heart of an early Christian."

Lindsay himself was a unique figure in the world of American dance. From a notebook he kept in 1912(9), we discover that he had the following plan for writing: "Write poems to conform to popular tunes in the outline of their melody, like *A Hot Time, After the Ball*, etc., but with a silk finish. When we consider that half of the popular songs rhyme moon and spoon we need not fear wearing out the theme of the moon as an adjunct of desire." Masters says(10): At the time that Lindsay became famous a new sort of dance music which had been growing up for more than a decade was coming to full tide. Formal dances like the Waltz and the Polka were giving way to any extemporaneous steps in which people with music in their feet could express it to music that was equally spontaneous and unconventional. This freedom in dancing and dance music was a contemporaneous phenomenon of Lindsay's poems. Long before this he had been brooding upon a way to put his own themes into the voice of his time. He resented the epithet of jazz, but blew into his humorous and many-voiced lines the exciting accentuations, pauses and silences that Beethoven nearly one hundred years before had put into the Scherzo of the *B Flat Quartet no. 6*. Lindsay was tremendously affected by the curious, syncopated music that he found among the Negroes of the South. He was very proud that his poems could be danced; yet he said that all poetry is first and last for the inner ear. His *Potatoes' Dance* he used for what he called poem games. He also wrote *The Firemen's Ball*. Into the reading of his poetry, he put a great deal of himself, moving in a sort of dance. He is survived by his voice on several phonograph records, reading *Congo* and two others of his poems.

Sappho always set her poetry to a musical accompaniment on the harp. She was accustomed also to make rhythmic movements in time to the music and gestures expressing the emotions aroused by the subject of the poem. To the girls who were gathered around her she taught the arts in which she excelled: the writing of poetry, music and dancing.

Nietsche included two rhythmic dance-songs in *Thus Spake Zarathustra*, both dedicated to Life, both dramatic as well as philosophic, each with a deeper meaning (that gives strength to the dance element) than appears on the surface. Nietsche himself wrote in his autobiographical sketch (1888) that "It would even be possible to consider all Zarathustra as a musical composition."

Henry Irving had caught the most difficult Shakespearian rhythm, in the opinion of Gordon Craig(11), and was suiting the action to the word. Every now and again the words were natural, but as a rule they were more than natural—they were highly artificial. And thus it came about that Irving positively designed (as M. Fokine has designed) dances which fitted perfectly to the speeches given him by Shakespeare.

When poets compose music, they usually compose in dance-like forms. Sydney Lanier wrote a composition called *Danse des Moucherons*, describing the movement of a swarm of gnats, or the "rhythmic beating of the heart of God." He claimed that rhythm is the basis of music, poetry and physical fact as well as moral living; that it is to be found in all those motions we call nature. Owen Wister, when in his senior year at Harvard, wrote and had published a semi-popular dance. Jean Jacques Rousseau, in his *Émile, or the Education of the Child*, held that a child should not be taught the three R's until its twelfth year; until then all of its knowledge should be gained through music and dancing(12). Rousseau, despite the fact that he owes his reputation to his philosophic and literary ability, owed most of the income necessary for his existence to the composition and practice of music. When he failed in fencing and dancing as professions and resigned his position in the land-survey, he began to teach music and set out for Paris with his own system of musical notation. Once, when he was penniless, he set himself up as a teacher of singing. Unfortunately, M. de Treytorens, professor of law, loved music and insisted that Rousseau give him a proof of his talents. Though he knew little or nothing about it, Rousseau started to compose a symphony for Monsieur's concerts. Fortunately, he ended it with a pretty Menuet, that was then commonly played about the streets. Of course, the rest of the music was a confusion of discords. But the Menuet saved the situation by putting everyone in a good humor. Rousseau was congratulated and told that the Menuet would make him famous. Meanwhile, as his *Confessions* tell us, he was horribly uneasy(13)!

In passing, it is interesting to note that a famous German dance critic (Dr. Artur Michel) began his career by investigating the rhythm of poetry, and grew from that into a study of rhythms in music and dance.

In April of 1936(14), Conrad Aiken thought the idea of dancing to poetry was interesting, with immense possibilities, and was himself considering doing just such a poem, in collaboration with Paul Nash, the English painter, and a composer —possibly Bliss—which would also be danced or mimed. His idea was then uncertain, but intriguing. He thought it would be fun to try and didn't see why it wouldn't be successful, for at bottom it was just a return to ritual poetry, which is at bottom the archetype of all poetry. He found great charm and originality in some of Kreymbourg's *Plays for Poem Mimes* and *Puppet Plays*, which inclined somewhat in that direction.

There are poems enough dealing directly with the dance to make several volumes. At least one anthology has been compiled by Edward R. Dickson. There are these major poems on the subject: *Negro Dancers* by Claude McKay; *Dance Figure* by Ezra Pound ("There is none like thee among the dancers, None with swift feet"); *Iron-Wind Dances* by Lew Sarett, lately set to music by Isadore Freed, with the beat of the tom-tom suggested in the rhythm of the lines; *After Hearing a Waltz by Bartok* by Amy Lowell; *Jazz Fantasia* by Carl Sandburg; *A Cabaret Dancer* by Zoë Akins; *She of the Dancing Feet Sings* by Countee Cullen; *Poem to be Danced* by Helen Hoyt; *The Cakewalk* by Wilfrid Gibson; *Javanese Dancers* by Arthur Symons; *The Dancer* by Mary Carolyn Davies; *Lobster Quadrille* by Lewis Carroll; and *The Dancer* by James Stephens. All of the poems of Sherwood Trask are to be danced as well as sung. Interesting is the venture of C. Day Lewis, whose *A Time to Dance* is a volume in which poetry is approached as a necessity to people, in that it is a "refreshment of emotional life." In this book, *Noah and the Waters* is a choral ballet dramatizing the choice that Noah must make between clinging to his own life and trusting himself to the flood.

Helen March uses spoken lines, wordless sounds, or melodies to accompany her movements. The flexibility of her voice matches that of her body. All aim toward a full and complete expression of the basic idea. Miss March believes that every act in life has its own peculiar rhythm which may be translated into dance. Not only daily acts but good paintings have a rhythm so strong that they can be translated into dance movements and further carried on with words. She brings out the best qualities in her voice not only as an instrument and for a technical satisfaction, but so that at a performance she may clarify the reality behind the words. Sometimes the rhythmic, or dance patterns come first to her and suggest the words to be used as an accompaniment. Then at other times, the actual rhythm and meaning of the words may bring out the gestures, patterns in space, and perhaps necessary foot sounds. To her, a musical accompaniment is not entirely compulsory, but it adds a colorful and dramatic element; nevertheless her music (if she uses it) must be composed to fit the finished movement.

Since rhythm is the basis of all stage art, whether it subtly underlies the make-up of a scene or is stylized as pure dance, a combination of stage arts is inevitable, believes Helen March (15). Dancing is essential to acting, as is pantomime. The voice is essential to movement and movement to the voice, all uniting in a complete expression of the basic idea.

CHAPTER 26

NOTES

(1) Frances and Rosemary Stack
(2) Lucile Marsh in the *Dancing Times,* April, 1930, p. 14
(3) Lucile Marsh in the *Dancing Times,* April, 1930, p. 14
(4) Selden, *The Dancer's Quest,* p. 50
(5) *Theatre Arts Monthly,* January, 1932, p. 44
(6) *New York Times,* later quoted in La Argentina's souvenir program edited by Arnold Meckel in Paris
(7) In a letter to the author from Los Angeles, California
(8) In a letter to the author from New York City, dated December 2, 1935
(9) Masters, *Vachel Lindsay,* p. 221
(10) Masters, *Vachel Lindsay,* p. 289
(11) Craig, *Henry Irving,* pp. 73-74
(12) *Theatre Arts Monthly,* August, 1927, p. 589
(13) *Musical Quarterly,* July, 1931, pp. 346-347
(14) In a letter to the author from England, dated April 21, 1936
(15) In a letter to the author from Los Angeles, California, dated November 21, 1935

THE SIMULTANEOUS CREATION OF DANCE
AND MUSIC

Percussive sound is most satisfactory as an accompaniment to a dance that is primitive in feeling. When the dance approaches a deeper meaning, however, music (in the minds of most dancers) is indispensable. The solution of the problems of both dancers and musicians seemed at first to be in what the musician regarded as a simultaneous creation of dance and music with each creator sharing ideas; and what the dancer complacently regarded as music made to fit her dance. In the words of Massine(1): Choreography has too long followed in the footsteps of music and painting. Now, once again choreography can take the lead and demand a new form of music and painting.

It is not impossible to achieve perfection in such a collaboration, but perfection seldom results. Why? Because in every artistic collaboration there is always one person more positive than the other. In the case of dancer and musician, the dancer is usually the stronger of the two: if she discovers, perchance, that her accompanist has a mind of his own, she changes accompanists. Let us take one example. A young dancer was accustomed to compose his dances, then to bring them to his pianist to have music built around them. He was affronted when the pianist tore his nicely made dances to pieces and cried out, at moments: "That's not so good for the musical pattern. Try another movement!" Yet the dancer had made the same sort of suggestions to the pianist regarding the new music, in even more ruthless fashion, and had thought nothing of the musician's inconvenience nor of the quality of the music as a result of his arbitrary dictation of the musical form and content.

That is only one instance, showing the cause of some of the unpleasant music written today in collaboration with dancers. Sidney Cuttner, himself a composer for the dance, has declared(2) that "The contemporary composer, working continually with the dancer, has accented the obscenity and ugliness of the dance without adding musically to his own stature. This easy path—easy because it makes no real demands of talent upon the composer—is being trodden by a continually larger group of musicians, who apparently are sincere but unfortunate in their choice of inspiration. In fact, they need a much finer sense of values. A few outstanding composers have been able to create for the dance and still remain inviolate, because their preoccupation was primarily with the music, and with the last vital dance tradition. Now there must be a catharsis, a fresh slate and an inquiring, uncompromising systemization of artistic values. It is so carelessly easy to simulate artistic worth with an art which has no set tradition except primitive or sophisticated folk meaning, and grace." (Cuttner has lately composed a new work for mass dance, voice choir and full symphony orchestra.) Thus we see that the composer may be at fault, as well as the dancer.

There are some dancers who create their dances solely to mental music, then expect the musicians who compose for their dances to be psychic enough to record what is in their own (the dancers') minds. "No!" they will shout. "That's not correct. There must be another chord here—plunk! Like that, you see." The result is something that produces nausea in the very souls of all musicians, but the dancers will add with ill-concealed pride, "There! Now we've done practically all the work, but your name will appear on the program as composer. We believe in fairness. We always acknowledge the excellence of our musical accompaniments as factors in our success."

Such are the causes of the percussive quality of most music composed for dances. This musicians decry, because of the lack of form; pattern, and consequently, of musical worth. Dancers seem to be very well satisfied with it. It reminds one of Schumann's comment on a pianoforte Sonata in which the opening theme was repeated four times with but one note varied: "Heavens! It is a little too much to tell a man four times that he has nothing to say(3)!"

When Josef Holbrooke was very young, he wrote *Four Futurist Dances* which he describes as being horrible and hideous, caused by a piano recital. He was irritated, and had to write them to get the taste of Mr. Ornstein out of his mouth. "Yet," he adds(4), "These idiotic dances of mine have been taken seriously by many a Bolshevik in music!" Possibly, by many a Bolshevik in dance also!

Although Clifford Vaughan has composed much music for Ruth St. Denis' oriental impressions, there was evidently no "simultaneous" creation of music and dance in this case. Both music and dance were "impressions" of the arts in oriental lands. (When Sol Cohen wrote the ballet music, *Angkor-Vat*, for St. Denis, he based it on the oriental melodic themes she outlined to him from time to time.) Also "impressions" of the folk are the *Bulerías*, *Alegrías*, *Farruca* and *Zapateado* composed by Francisco Avellan for the dancer Escudero, for he simply wrote the music as the Gypsies play their guitars, with the piano imitating the strumming and plucked rhythms; and since Escudero dances as the Gypsies do, the music and dances invariably fit.

So, to speak of simultaneous creation, one must confine himself to more intimate collaborations. However, the person who believes that this is a purely modern invention is sadly mistaken. Its existence in ancient times has already been mentioned. In the belief that Greek music was undoubtedly very simple and knowing that there exist only fragments of Greek instrumental music, Angna Enters composed music for her own Greek mimes. In doing so she sought to solve the various harmonic modes according to her own ear and for her own purposes, the object being to fit them into the composition as a whole. Meanwhile, she bore in mind her own conclusion: that the Greeks at their cultural apex didn't make distinctions between song and speech; that to them, sung speech was the supreme musical form.

John Weaver, English dancing master, in his *Anatomical and Mechanical Lectures on Dancing*, published in London in 1721, declared that high qualifications were essential in a good dancer: "It is therefore requisite, for such a master in our art, to have, not only an universal knowledge in dancing and to apply himself to the study and consideration of all characters; but also, as much skill in musick, as, at least, to be able to give instructions to a master in musick for the composition of his airs; to judge, whether such musick express well his ideas; be justly apply'd to his design; and well adapted to the characters he would represent."

We find Noverre, in a different country during the same epoch, writing this: "Instead of writing the steps on prescribed airs as is done with the couplets of familiar tunes, I composed, if I may so express myself, the dialogue of my ballet and had the music made for each phrase and each idea. It was just so that I dictated to Gluck the characteristic air of the Ballet of the Savages in *Iphigenia in Tauris*. But, while Noverre worked melodically, our modernists build their movements on a structure of massed tones.

Ballet composers in formal ballet schools were dictated to by ballet-masters, as we have already discovered. These were Dalcroze's views on the subject(5): The art of dancing, if it still insists on union with music, should achieve the transmutation of sound into bodily movement and of movement into sound. It is not enough that movement should be superimposed on music. It should spring from music as a spontaneous growth. Indeed, the arts of music and the dance have been so long dissociated that the public has forgotten that they were originally one. Rhythmic movement is ennobled by melody and harmony. These rouse the organism, stimulate the imagination. Dalcroze looks toward the creation of pure music and plastic music, the latter designed especially for the dance.

An entirely different view of this matter is expressed by Charles Marriott (6) : "Some kinds of music are more obviously danceable than others; diatonic progressions and bold rhythms are easier to dance than chromatic progressions and subtle rhythms. It would be extravagant to say that the only test of music is "Can it be danced?" But . . . given competent performance, it is one test. When music is heard, only the ear is apt to be beguiled by the quality of voice or instrument, and poor stuff will go down, but when music is translated into movement, written large, any weakness of form or slackness of rhythm is immediately betrayed."

Dancers in Germany have made some composers dance-conscious by their evolvement of a new, vital, modern dance form. Certain of these composers, such as Wilckens and Hastings, have written music especially for this new form. It is attractive, exotic and always eminently suitable to the need for which it was invented. Some say it has small value as pure music. However, an examination of some of this music, independent of the movement, shows that it *has* a musical value, though it is not developed as a purist would have it. It manages to achieve the same end as various forms of ancient music. It is, perhaps, "mood" music; but it is pleasant to the ear and not unoriginal. It has the same repetitious quality as various form of oriental music. The fact that it does not adhere to classic European forms should have no effect on its quality. The American variety of this music is more percussive than the European, therefore the foreign music is more pleasing to musicians.

Mary Wigman was studying the Dalcroze system when she made her first tentative efforts to compose. The music for most of her big ensembles is due to Will Götze, predecessor of Hanns Hastings, of whose improvisations to her finished dances Wigman speaks as "inspired." Neither Hastings nor Wigman believe that dance develops independently of music. Declares Hastings(7) : Both dance and music are based on rhythm, there being no difference in music and dance rhythm. Both are related to the rhythms found in breathing and other life processes. Musical rhythm, however, produces melody, whereas dance rhythm produces gesture. Also, space and harmony go together. The actual process of composing dance accompaniments is based entirely on practical experience and work. It is not possible to give a precise formula for composing dance music. Each new dance creates its own form. The new dance music should and can be an integral part of this form. The dance music of the future will no longer accept its motive, then proceed on an entirely independent line to development of already existing musical forms. The motive or theme of dance music today springs from the actual bodily movement.

Hastings has written, among many works, music for Wigman's four cycles: *Shifting Landscapes, Sacrifice, The Way, Dance of Women.* He also conducts in Wigman's school the musicians' courses, consisting of piano improvisation and composition for dance, studies to combine piano and percussion, the use of percussion instruments, accompanying actual dance movement and composition, and lectures on the relation between dance and music. In taking this course of lectures and lessons, the student must attend twenty-four dance classes to observe the musical accompaniment.

Mary Wigman has described the birth of a creation(8) : "I owe everything to music. Never had I a creation born in my mind. It is always born in my blood. Slowly it germinates and takes form; and next it begins to sing within me—not in musical notes, you understand, but there are melodies and harmonies and strong, swinging rhythms that make my whole body feel like a great pulse. The music is evolved by a process of communally intuitive understanding between my pianist and myself. First we go to the piano. Then I steep myself in every possible aspect of the picture or emotion which has formed itself in my consciousness. Gradually the pianist's own intuitive emotions catch the contagion; and then gropingly at first, but presently more and more certainly, a rhythmic music begins to form under his fingers, and he has improvised a colorful scroll of harmonious sound and movement that dovetails perfectly into the self-same creation that filled my consciousness." Thus it is apparent that Wigman's music is created, not by studied plan but by improvisation, and not by a composer, as such, but by an accompanist. And of the dancer's accompanist, Wigman believes that (9) "if he understands anything of the character of the dance, he reads the cues and tempos from the dancer's eye, not from his hands, nor his feet." Really, music should change with every dancer and with every accompanist, because the true artist feels decidedly uncomfortable in fitting his mind into the path of interpretation established by another artistic mind. No two creations are the same, no two interpretations are identical—nor are any two performances given by the same artist. As with native craftsmen, set patterns remove the breath of inspiration.

Wigman has further described the composition of her *Pastorale* (10): "One day in my studio, out of a sense of deepest peace and quietude I began slowly to move my arms and my body. Calling to my assistants, I said, 'I do not know if anything will come of this feeling, but I should like a reed instrument that will play over and over again a simple little tune, not at all important, always the same one.' Then, with the monotonous sound of the little tune, with its gentle lyric suggestion, the whole dance took form. *Afterwards* we found that it was built in ⅝ time."

Palucca has danced to music written for her by Herbert Tranton, and Harald Kreutzberg has collaborated with the composer, Friedrich Wilckens, in whose successful opera, *Don Morte*, Kreutzberg danced the rôle of the Jester. Since then, Wilckens has written these dances for Kreutzberg: *Flag Dance*,

Angel of Annunciation, Rural Dance, Révolte, The Envious Girls, Angel of Last Judgment, Capriccio, Hangman's Dance, Tyl Eulenspiegel. For Yvonne Georgi, he wrote *Kassandra.*

For Tina Flade, also of the German school of the dance, Schwinghammer wrote: *The Sonnambulist, Bolero, Dance in the Spirit of War.*

Gunild Keetman of Germany, a pupil of Orff and Hindemith, has composed for the dancer, Maja Lex. In the *Barbaric Suite,* composed of five parts: Dynamic Rhythms, Dance with Sticks, Dance with Kettledrums, Canon, and Leap Dance, the dance was said to have become music, while the music became dance. This suite, however, was scored for what we would term a percussion orchestra, with various drums and other percussion instruments, plus two large and two small chromatic xylophones. It is interesting to note that, during the performance of this Suite, the composer alternately played in the orchestra and danced! This feat was the result of the training of the Gunther school, where dance and music are one.

Trudi Schoop has given this explanation of the origin of music for her dances(11): "For dances based entirely on an idea there exists almost no music at all. Together with my brother Paul, I hunted for suitable music, we made cuts, arranged pieces, but it was a hopeless task. All at once, my brother sat down at the piano endeavoring to improvise music to what I was dancing. And, lo, I had discovered my composer!" Paul Schoop, then, and Huldreich Frueh, composed Trudi Schoop's *Want Ads* and *Fridolin.* Critics later described this music as being "expert." One wrote(12): "Perfect timing and perfect rhythm is another quality that makes Trudi Schoop's dancing outstanding. The music is apparently created for her and her particular style of dancing and is very definitely subjected to the dancing. And we find in it the same economy we spoke of in connection with her movements."

Since Kurt Jooss began as a musician, he is always trying to bring the dance and music into closer affinity and to eradicate the scorn felt by both dancers and musicians for each other(13). Now he doesn't attempt to compose for the dance, but contents himself with the selection of a collaborator whom he considers expert in that line. Jooss, as an artist, has the good sense to attempt only what he feels he can do well. Though he adores Bach, he considers it impossible for him to create in Bach's style. He cannot "sense" the Orient, so he doesn't try to create an oriental ballet.

The musical score for Jooss' *Ballade*, a story of court life, was written by the pianist, John Colman. It is based on the melody and variations of an old French song, *Le Roi Fait Battre le Tambour*. This music, said one commentator (14), is inconsequential, thin and uninspiring, and detracts from *Ballade's* value as a choreographic composition. Why, asked he, was it necessary to have Colman compose a special piece for *Ballade* when there already exists music on the same theme? Jooss' *The Mirror*, reflecting the confusion and despair of the post-war world, was composed by F. A. Cohen. The latter also wrote a superb musical background for Jooss' *The Green Table*, as for the later edition of Jooss' *Prodigal Son*, first created five years before to a musical score by Prokofieff. Jooss' *Big City* was originally done to Alexandre Tansman's *Sonatine Transatlantique* which, not having been composed especially for ballet, was found to be unadaptable in sections. Then Tansman was commissioned to write a new score, which made possible the inclusion of Jooss' complete final section, impossible to the former music. Musicians disagree on Jooss' musical accompaniments. Some say they are captivating, charming. Others assert they are good for the dance, valueless in themselves. Norma Gould, dancer, said they formed the most satisfying music of any used by dancers. They were colored by sudden changes of tempo and heightened in effect by the use of two pianos. The Jooss group performed *A Spring Tale*, four-act romantic ballet, to music by F. A. Cohen, pleasant because of the fairy-tale character of the theme. The group also danced *Chronica*, subtitled *The Rise and Fall of a Dictator*, to music by Berthold Goldschmidt. This was a dance-drama in prelude and three acts. The music was said to be lacking in variety and in the quality of supplying "body" for the stage action since it was played on two pianos for more than an hour.   (The dictator theme was also used for a ballet by Ernest Krenek, called *Eight-Column Line*.)

Mario Salerno, Italian, was a rather assertive composer when he collaborated with the dancers, Frances and Rosemary Stack.   His strict training had given him well-defined ideas as to what one may or may not do in the composition of music. Eventually, however, an agreement was reached, and he wrote *Momento Fantástico* on rhythmic patterns in a composition to which Michio Ito had previously danced; a suite of five modern dances for the piano utilizing the English Waltz rhythm, jazz motives and Cuban Rhumba rhythms; *Peter Pan*, *Repeated Rhythm* based on the rhythmic pattern of a strange Mexican fox trot subtitled *The Poet and the Typewriter*, *Prisoners*, composed simultaneously with the dance; and *Il Saltarello Anticolano*, a little fantasy on original motives of this dance of Anticoli, as earthy and monotonous as the dance itself.

Highly interesting was a recent conversation(15) between two serious composers: Ernst Toch (European) and William Grant Still (American) on the subject of music created for dancers.   Said Toch: "Nowadays the dance is in the foreground, the composition in the background which I, as a composer, regret.   The idea of dancing whole symphonies doesn't appeal to me at all.   And the very fact that dancers now use such devices as percussion shows how little they think of music."

Still thought both dance and music should be given equal recognition.   As for the modern percussion accompaniments, he considered them different in but one respect from primitive dance accompaniments: they are presented in a way that sophisticates can understand.   "The real reason dancers want music composed to fit their dances," he added, "must be that they are unacquainted with music.   If they knew it really well, they would realize what a great help it could be."

"It would be fine," rejoined Toch, "if all dancers would study music.   Some worked with me in Europe and studied hard. But I believe that if a dancer has a sure, intuitive instinct for music, it might be more satisfactory than a too-intricate knowledge of technicalities." This writer's view is that the trouble arises when dancers take an intuitive feeling for granted and don't study at all! However, to continue Toch's thought: "Music means little when it is composed to fit steps and moods. About ten or twelve years ago, I composed several things for dancers, one of whom gave me a rough outline in advance, and another of whom (Heidi Woog) worked with me in still greater detail. It limited me so much! I am unhappy when I am compelled to follow someone else's thoughts. Dancers don't agree with musical developments. They wish to dictate their own climaxes."

"But have you ever noticed," asked Still, "That dances built to music can be made in a coherent form, while music built to dances is usually both formless and incoherent?"

Martha Graham, who occupies the same place in the American dance field that Mary Wigman holds in Germany, is a very positive person. She likes to control the situation as far as her accompanying music is concerned. She believes that music was long able to cover bad and unauthentic dancing, and that true dancing need not depend upon such a prop. She believes, further, that a dancer should be enough of a musician to be able to read and interpret an already-composed score and to be able to assist any composer who works with her to unify the music and dance patterns. Because she loves the classics, because she believes that they need no additional interpretation to enhance them, and because they have nothing in common with the percussive beat of her dance, only the names of modern composers are found on Martha Graham's programs. The composers who write especially for her attend her rehearsals, note the dance forms and rhythms, discuss matters and then proceed to composition. Her accompaniments have one leading function in the eyes of the writer: the setting of a mood. Either one likes them or one doesn't; either the dance appeals or it does not. Graham's movements have been called grotesque. They are not, really, and her music is often too dissonant and too acrid for her movement. (Louis Horst(16), who most often composes for her, considers strings too luscious and romantic to accompany the modern dance; overuse of percussion is also too romantic and oriental. Brasses give brilliance and vitality; reeds supply a primitive atmosphere.) To Graham's ears, however, this music is not strange. It is the music of modern America and like other music, it helps to make the silence more beautiful(17). It is what she needs to hear while dancing. Her appreciation for this dissonance seems to be more mental than physical, since the lack of balance between ordinary movements and acrid musical sounds is always noticeable in her concerts.

From the depths of his soul, Anton Rolland cried out after a Graham concert: "I liked her enormously, but the music she uses drives me insane. I'm all for tolerance in modern music and form, but an hour and a half of continuous nauseating, empty, raucous, whiney, dissonance! The music definitely distracts the mind from the dance, is ugly without being colorful or interesting, two redeeming qualities."

One cannot help but approve of the remarks of Edwin Denby(18) on the composers who write for Miss Graham: "In general they stick literally to the rhythmic detail of her dance, the way many dancers—inversely—might try to stick to the rhythmic detail of music. It isn't a good method. Especially because Miss Graham's motives are so obvious they need no reiteration in music. . . . For the musicians the result of following her is that, instead of making their piece a whole, they divide it up into a series of brief phrases, each stopping on an accent. . . . One very good kind of dance music is that of Uday Shan-Kar. It sounds as though it made sense without being emphatic, it repeats itself without insistence. The oriental music I have heard always has this independent friendliness toward the dancers."

Louis Horst, who has been called the "perennial pianistic patron saint" of dance, has also been said to know more about dancing than do the dancers. In the old days, he wrote the music as Miss Graham's dance was being created, making suggestions as to the actual movement, costumes and lighting. Now she composes the dances before he is even allowed to see them, so that his composition now arises from her need, not from his own creative powers. Horst also conducts classes in composition in dance form, where the students are first taught form, then told to forget form and compose subjectively, when knowledge will discipline subconsciously without dominating. Horst definitely wishes to write music that will *not* have musical value, because if it is interesting musically it obtrudes upon the dance. After all, declares he(19), the question is not how great a dance composer is, but what he does for the dance. "Music for the dance," he adds, "cannot be judged apart from the dance for which it was written. The body is the most dangerous of all instruments and without the boundary of music and the authority of form, is likely to run riot in emotional expression. Motion is born of emotion, and both must be kept under control. The musical accompaniment provides aural assistance to the audience and gives emphasis to the movement. The composer-accompanist must expect to sacrifice some of his identity as a musician when he writes and plays for the dance, though he is important in his way." Horst's music for Martha Graham (including *Act of Piety* and *Frontier*, with its wind instruments, piano and tambourine alternating between stark religiosity and unrestrained gaiety, and seeming to partake of abstractions of American song) tends toward extremely dissonant simplicity, as does Lehman Engel's dance music.

For Martha Graham, Engel has written *Ceremonials*, *Transitions*, *Ekstasis*, *Sarabande*, *Imperial Gesture*, *Two Lyric Fragments* (scored for wind instruments), *Marching Song*, and *Dance of Greeting*, in which both music and dance had a hard, fibrous character. For Charles Weidman he wrote *Traditions* and *Atavisms*, in three realistic parts: Bargain Counter, Stock Exchange, Lynch Town. For Gluck-Sandor he wrote *Phobias*; for Harry Losee, *Jungle Dance*; *Symphony of a City* and *Songs of the Night*; for Gene Martel, *Anathema* and *Parade*; for Edgar Frank, *Idyll*; and for Tashamira, *Crystal*. Engel believes that some dancers have such an acute feeling for what their particular dance requires in the music that an uncomfortable rhythm, instrumental coloring or melodic line may completely upset them. He looks forward to the time when, with evolution, music for the dancer will change; and with the removal of economic obstacles, the dancers will engage larger groups of musicians to accompany them, thus allowing the composers a wider scope.

In contrast to most of the music (with its nerve-racking unresolved melody-notes) on Miss Graham's programs, the usually dissonant music of Kodály and Wallingford Riegger seems like a welcome respite, and in the latter's *Three Frenetic Rhythms*, an occasional resounding bass gives an effect of stability to the whole. This music, as well as Riegger's *Evocation*, followed his *Bacchanale*, also written for Miss Graham in 1931 and which Adolph Weiss(20) described as a concatenation of heterogeneous two-bar phrases which might be suitable for the dance but are hardly exemplary of good musical form. They are flamboyant, sensational, self-conscious. Weiss, however, anticipated a public approbation. When Riegger first began to write for the dance he was elated, because Martha Graham was like a revelation to him, but also covered with confusion at the necessity of setting to music so many measures of three-four time, so many of two-eight and so many of seven-four. For, when he came to the studio to consult with Miss Graham, he found to his surprise her dance group assembled and ready to perform for him the already-completed dance! His confusion did not prevent his rather welcoming the limitations imposed upon him by a preconceived form and rhythm, because they challenged his skill and ingenuity.

As a result, when Riegger wrote music for Doris Humphrey's and Charles Weidman's long trilogy, including *Theatre Piece* (depicting the injustice of the present system of life); *New Dance* (showing the ideal human existence and including Variations in the form of festive, fugal music); and *With My Red Fires* (showing individuals visited by tragedy); critic Joseph A. Kaye(21) was able to say, "For the first time in modern dance, the music had meaning and musical worth. Riegger's music for Variations can stand apart from the dance, and that should be the test for any music written to go with a dance composition. It has a fascinating rhythmic and melodic pattern, adding tremendously to the choreography." It must be explained here that Mr. Kaye has always been puzzled over how music written to fit a given number of dance passages can possibly have any value as music. John Martin(22) comments further on Riegger's "admirable" music for the trilogy: "He is not afraid to experiment with strange tonalities, and by these means as well as by more orthodox methods he has succeeded in capturing the strange flavor of the choreography. It is perhaps as near as we have yet come to a truly functional dance setting." The music is scored for two pianos and small orchestra.

Norman Lloyd, director of music for the Bennington Festival, composed music for Charles Weidman's *Quest*. For the section called *Transition* in this, Mr. Lloyd hit upon the happy idea of having music composed by someone else (Clair Leonard) so that the difference in style would underline the interlude quality of the section. Martin has said that Mr. Lloyd knows excellently the problem of composing for dancing. His music is admirably simple, direct and unpretentious. Lloyd also composed music to fit Martha Graham's *Panorama*, a dance epic of America with three themes (Puritanism, Southern Imperialism and Popularism) dominating contemporary life. It aimed to present themes that are basically American, part of the national consciousness and part of an inheritance that contributes to the present. Since the choreographer, composer, dancers and scenic designer were also American, it was finally hailed as a significant advance in the art of dance in our own country.

Henry Cowell once made an experiment with Martha Graham in establishing a contrapuntal relation between the high points of interest in dance and music. They worked out the details together, and succeeded in getting a complete dance and musical composition in which the dance rose to its point of interest when the music was quiescent, and then the dance diminished in interest when the music rose. In this way, they believed that neither one of the arts relied on the other, and that neither was a servant of the other, but each was given its time to shine and to hold the audience's attention. For Miss Graham, Cowell also wrote his *Synchrony* for symphony orchestra, and *Heroic Dance*, for piano. At the time that Hanya Holm was teaching and concertizing at Mills College in California, Cowell was directing a class in percussion there. It followed, quite naturally, that he should create some percussion studies (*Drive*, *In Quiet Space* and *Madrigal*) for her group. (This writer has since been informed that in concert, *Drive* was finally performed to music of Harvey Pollins, *Madrigal* to music of Victor Schwinghammer, and *In Quiet Space* to Miss Holm's own percussion accompaniment.) More, Cowell has composed *Two Appositions* for symphony orchestra, for Doris Humphrey; *Three Work Dances* for chamber orchestra, for Charles Weidman and group; *Machine Music* for Elsa Findlay's group and *Woman's Cycle* for Sophie Delza—both percussion studies; and *Morning Dance*, *Fire Cycle* and *Evil Hands*—all three for piano and for Tina Flade.

In the beginning, Cowell believed firmly that adequate dance music can only be achieved by a simultaneous effort on the part of a fine dancer and a fine composer, both artists. He still holds to that belief, but he has somewhat modified his ideas as to the method of obtaining the best results. Now he has advanced the theory that (23) both dancer and musician should leave their creation elastic as to phrase, rhythm and melody and should suggest variants of each incident, so that there will be less arbitrariness on the part of one or the other. It is interesting in theory. How will it work out in practice? What sort of music will result? The *Sarabande* he wrote for Martha Graham was built on that idea, so it should, in itself, answer those questions.

Donald Pond, formerly connected with Dartington Hall and later associated with the Federal Dance Project in New York, has composed the music for Don Oscar Becque's *Young Tramps*. He has strong opinions, and necessarily controversial ones, on dance and music. In a symposium(24), he raised the question of whether the dance really is an independent art. Then he said: "The mutilation of music by dancers is dishonest. Dancers do use music rhythms, but elementary ones, whereas dance should be composed in terms of dance rhythms, music in terms of music. Both arts collaborating, must remain individual arts, the compulsion arising from the dance."

Contrast with this Lester Horton's statement(25): "The making of new music simultaneously with the making of choreography, welding the two elements, movement and sound, makes it possible to achieve a homogeneity which is a stronger entity than either separate one" and with Sara Mildred Strauss' fear(26) that the musician will supplant vision by tone when he works with a choreographer unless he is closely watched, and you have the ingredients of a heated debate. Incidentally, Horton recently produced two ballets to original music by Gerhardt Dorn: *Conquest* and *Something to Please Everybody*.

Dane Rudhyar(27) has been hesitant about writing for the modern dance, since dancers are so eager to subordinate composers to their whims. Usually, dancers are not able to dictate what they want, says he, for they don't *know* what they want. Rudhyar believes that few composers write music with any knowledge of what the completed dance will be. They simply write music. In Rudhyar's own choreographic music, as in his other works, he has tried to present a deeper occult and metaphysical meaning. This makes him much misunderstood. Now, when he has almost given up trying, people are at last beginning to offer him understanding and appreciation.

Rudhyar wrote a suite of dances in the oriental manner for Ruth St. Denis, along with some ritual dramas concerning the symbolism of the lotus. To do this, he first discussed with her the general ideas and then wrote the music without ever seeing the dance or the movements. Doris Humphrey and he worked together on *Dances of Women*, in two parts, of which she now uses only the first. She told him the idea, duration, type of music, form, and showed him the gestures. Then he improvised a little. They agreed on the general style, and then he worked alone, before they worked together in detail. Rudhyar's music is strong and carries a definite meaning of its own. It is not easy to dance to it and dance independently of it!

Carmalita Maracci first danced to simple piano accompaniment, then to two pianos, and now she dances to piano combined with percussion instruments. She creates her dances simultaneously with the composing of the music by Antonio Albanese, and "while they show definitely the result of a thorough painstaking work, she still allows for a consciously free scope in execution, so that her interpretation each time she dances becomes a new emotional experience." Some of Albanese's compositions for her are *Madrigal of Sorrow*, *Canto Hondo*, *Dance of Elegance* and *Tango Introspective*, the essence of the Tango in all its forms.

Joseph Schillinger has been most interested in music for the dance. In his investigations, he devised what he calls the "principles of dance composition in relation to movable settings, lighting, music and speech." From 1930 to 1933 he did experimental work in dance with Sara Mildred Strauss, Sophia Delza and Pauline Koner. He incorporated the results in an article. His *Funeral March* is danced by Zemach who, with his group, also interpreted *The People and the Prophet* in 1931.

An unusual procedure must be noted here, in the case of Hugo Davise, young American composer. Davise was once asked to orchestrate a piano composition by Niemann for a performance. The dance had already been created and learned. Davise, wishing to have his own name appear on the program as composer instead of Niemann's, refused to orchestrate another man's music. The dancers stubbornly refused to change their dance to fit any original music he might write. Davise therefore constructed upon the rhythmic patterns in the Niemann music a *Javanese Dance* of his own. It was cast in a modernistic form, aiming at an oriental atmosphere. Both dancers and composer were eminently satisfied with the result! It must be said in its favor that the music was not so inconsequential as one might expect, judging from its method of construction, and that some of the harmonies are genuinely attractive.

Elizabeth Selden dances a *Hymn to the Day* in three parts (Dawn, Noon and Dusk) to music especially composed for her by Bernard Gabriel and Walter Schoenberg. Ted Shawn calls his new dances "music visualizations" and has the music composed simultaneously with them by his accompanist, Jess Meeker. Two of his dances worked out in this fashion are *Fetish* and *John Brown Sees the Glory*, an American epic. Frank Harling wrote for Michio Ito the music to accompany Ito's dance-drama, *Mary Magdalene*, in three episodes. David Diamond wrote *Praeludium* for Martha Graham. Vladimir Horowitz wrote a *Danse Exotique* for Eleanore Bock. John Haussermann of Cincinnati wrote *Nocturne and Dance* for Blake Scott. Jerome Moross wrote music for Charles Weidman's *Saga*, a ballet based on the legend of Paul Bunyan. Imre Weisshaus composed a *Satyric Festival Song* for flute alone for Martha Graham, during which Miss Graham three times took a series of four steps in silence, on the last of which she left the stage. The audience was convulsed. Herbert Kingsley wrote music for *Tempo* or *Dance Marathon*, a lengthy ballet in three acts. Harvey Pollins composes for dancers in the New York Wigman school. Manuel Galea has composed many dances (among them a group dance, *Marco Polo*) for Myra Kinch. Pasquin Bradfield, pianist, has composed and played for the NYA Dance Group of San Francisco. One of his compositions is *March*, containing dissonant, percussive tone clusters. Norman Cazden works musically in connection with the New Dance League and Paul Creston has written many of the dances for Sophia Delza. Hanya Holm danced to a recording of Edgar Varese's *Ionization*, in her *Trend*; while Martha Graham has danced to his *Integrales*. Neither of these, however, was directly composed for the dances.

A special attempt to compromise the exigencies of musical with dance form was made when Lou Harrison and the Northern California Dance Council collaborated on the suite *Chang-*

ing World—Illusions of a Better Life. In this there were times when the composer was subordinate to dancers (twelve of them), and other times when the dancers had to accustom themselves to strict musical forms: two Sonata-allegros, for example, and a March-Passacaglia. Alex North has composed *Façade-Esposizione Italiana* in three sections (Belle Arti, Giovanezza and Prix Femina) for Anna Sokolow. Henry Clark has written *Danza de la Muerte* in two sections (sarabande for the Dead and Sarabande for the Living) for José Limón. The latter also dances with Esther Junger in the group dance called *Festive Rites* (Processional, Betrothal, Recessional) to music by Morris Mamorsky. Katherine Dunham has danced to original music by Robert Sanders: *L'Ag'ya* and *Sarabande to Madame Christophe, Queen of Haiti.*

So sensible is the procedure adopted by the dancer, Bonnie Bird, and her composers (George Frederick McKay, Henry Cowell, John Cage) that one wonders why other artists do not use similar methods. In the belief that a too-close collaboration between dancer and composer results in a clash of individualities and a series of small compromises destructive to the form of both dance and music, Miss Bird usually gives her composers a written description, or scenario, of her dance-idea. They then play for her approval the themes they've created. She gives them indications of the time elements involved, and they complete the music to their own satisfaction away from her.

After careful consideration of the methods employed by many composers and dancers, and after much personal experimentation, the writer has come to the conclusion that the methods used by Doris Humphrey and Dane Rudhyar, and by Bonnie Bird, are by far the most effective and the most satisfying to both artists as well as to the audiences. No arbitrary theories should be expounded as to the writing of dance music. Dancer and composer should start out with the same basic idea, and with an acquaintance of each other's style and ideals. If there is a literary or historic basis for the dance, both should be familiar with it. Then they should begin to work alone. The composer should recall the dancer's individual style of movement as he works, and should remember how long a human breath can be sustained, how long repetitions of figures will hold audiences, and certain other technicalities. The dancer should refrain from thinking (unconsciously) in terms of music until she again works with the composer. At that time the welding process should take place. Then, if both artists have given themselves leeway, if they are not already too set and too stubborn as regards their own patterns, the joint creation should be a success.

There is good and bad dance music just as there is good and bad music. But dance music can never be judged from the same standpoint as pure music; it cannot be judged apart from its function. If it is sufficiently strong and vital, it will recall its function even when it is played alone. A changing world of the dance is gradually bringing about an improvement in the attitudes of both dancer and composer. Surely more worthy artistic creations will result!

CHAPTER 27

NOTES

(1) Haskell, *Balletomania*, p. 142
(2) In a personal interview in Los Angeles, later published in the *Dance Observer* for November, 1936, and altered somewhat
(3) Schumann, *Music and Musicians, second series*, pp. 237-238
(4) Holbrooke, *Contemporary British Composers*, p. 181
(5) Dalcroze, *Eurhythmics, Art and Education*, the chapters on the Nature of Rhythmic Movement and the Technique of Moving Plastic
(6) *Art and Letters*, July, 1917
(7) Stewart, *Modern Dance*, pp. 38, 40, 41
(8) *Musical West*, October, 1936, an interview by Homer Henley
(9) Souvenir program for Wigman's American concerts, published by Sol Hurok in 1930 (?), p. 19
(10) *Modern Music*, January-February, 1931, p. 22
(11) From a souvenir program prepared by Sol Hurok
(12) Anatole Chujoy in the *American Dancer Magazine*, February, 1936, p. 15

(13) In conversation in Los Angeles on December 6, 1936
(14) Anatole Chujoy in the *American Dancer Magazine,* March, 1936, p. 16
(15) At Dr. Toch's home in the Pacific Palisades, Santa Monica, California, on December 22, 1936
(16) *Christian Science Monitor,* March 3, 1936
(17) In conversation in Los Angeles, California, on April 9, 1936
(18) *Modern Music,* January-February, 1937, pp. 110-111
(19) Excerpt from souvenir program of Martha Graham's 1936 concert tour
(20) Cowell, *American Composers on American Music,* p. 73
(21) *American Dancer Magazine,* March, 1936, p. 12
(22) *New York Times,* August 23, 1936
(23) *Dance Observer,* January, 1937
(24) Reported in the *American Dancer Magazine,* March, 1936
(25) *Theatre Journal,* Los Angeles, California, February, 1936, p. 8
(26) *Los Angeles Times,* October 25, 1936
(27) In an interview in Hollywood, California, on November 6, 1935

PROBLEMS OF THE DANCER

A disgruntled classicist once said, "I think the dance should go back where it was originally and where it still belongs: to the accompaniment of percussion. Why doesn't it keep its place?" There will always be such statements made; there will always be people who criticize. The problem of the dancer is to dance to the music of her choice in such inspired fashion, yet withal correctly and so intelligently that she will win opinionated people over to her point of view.

"The ability to select good music is an essential part of dancing." So wrote Noverre. He added, "It is the time and tone of the music which fix and determine all the dancer's movements. If the playing be expressionless, the ballet, like its model, will be dull and uninteresting. The ballet master who ignores the study of music will ill-phrase the melodies and understand neither their spirit nor their character. Owing to the affinity between music and dancing, a ballet master will derive marked advantage from a knowledge of this art. He will be able to communicate his thoughts to the composer, and . . . perhaps write the music himself, or supply the composer with the principal ideas which should govern his work; these being expressive and varied, the dance cannot fail to be so in

413

its turn. Well-composed music should paint and speak: dancing, in imitating its sounds, will be the echo. . . . The arts go
hand in hand."

The contemporary dancer has all the musical wealth of
the past to choose from. It is not necessary to adhere to any one
phase, or period. Classic music and classic dance were of the
same period of development and were thus similar as to external
characteristics (the music being mostly melodic) so that classic
dancing may be done best to music of the same epoch. Hastings (1) has optimistically advanced the opinion that classic
music, having forms of its own, forced the dancer to respect
those forms. More likely, what the dancer was respecting
was *tradition*, pure and simple. Modern dancing can best be
done to modern music, with its freedom of rhythmic successions
and harmonies, because its rhythm best conforms to movement
phrases of modern dancing. Musical rigidity is now as absent
as formal dance forms. When these are resurrected, music
of the same type should be used as accompaniment.

The fact that contemporary dancers are not content to
dance to the dance music of the masters, but must attempt
to interpret their greater works, greatly scandalizes musical
purists. Richard Buhlig once remarked, "I don't think the
masters would mind if their music were accompanied by dancing
if it were done beautifully and reverently. But the things the
dancers do to the music! Why, if it be true that the masters
turn over in their graves each time some wrong is done their
music, they must all be whirling dervishes by now!" So then,
the dancer who wishes to dance to music should study music
history as the surest way to gain an understanding of the music
she interprets. Each piece of music is merely an infinitesimal
part of a large scheme. No one composition would be as it is
without what has gone before. Only by study can one gain an
adequate conception of the vast panorama of the creation of
all music.

Though many departures from classic forms are made
nowadays, all of them are (or should be) balanced in some way.
Informality does not imply incoherence. A too-metrical musical

construction is often called "squareness" and is avoided by most composers. Some believe that the old musical resources have been exhausted and that it is now necessary to find new ones: hence the strange noises that call themselves music that are frequently heard. Hence the trick key signatures and fractional metrical notations which, at best, are but mechanical devices. (One cannot refrain from commenting on a contemporary venture by Willy Stahl who, in writing music for a string quartet, tuned all of his instruments to different notes so that different sounds would come forth. If Mr. Stahl knew in advance what notes would result from this unorthodox tuning, why was he not able to write them in the ordinary way, with the instruments tuned as everyone tunes them? Of course, if he was simply taking a chance on the outcome and merely wished to see what *would* happen, or if he was experimenting with queer tone qualities, the objections are withdrawn. He succeeded in his purpose.) All these mechanical devices have been discarded by most modern composers who are gifted with truly creative minds. They disprove the theory of the present exhaustion of musical resources.

Dancers often cut music. They would be shocked if someone were to omit a line or a word from a poem, or to remove the climax from their dance, but they have no qualms about mutilating music, and will smile and assure people that it was necessary because the composition was "too long." It is true, for example, that many Sonatas are tempting to dancers, and most of them too long to dance for physical reasons, so that cutting them sometimes seems the only solution. The musician's solution (if he is consulted) is a much simpler one. He would not dance to the Sonata. His decision would be backed by an excellent reason, since the Sonata form itself is so complex and the music so bound up with the form that when a dancer merely dances to part of the composition, she removes from the music its character, its soul, its very life.

Some dancers tie together great strings of excerpts from compositions of every composer they can find. This was done on a large scale by the Philadelphia Opera Company in 1927, when a Russian ballet allegory called *The Red Terror* had its American première. It was founded on a book by Max Marceaux, with music adapted from the scores of Borodin, Saint-Saëns and Tschaikowsky. Only once, in his early career, did Diaghileff make such a potpourri of composers and periods. His *Cléopâtra* contained the Turkish Dance from Glinka's *Russlan and Ludmila*, the Persian Dances from Moussorgsky's *Kowantchina*, the *Bacchanal* from Glazounow's *Seasons*; parts of Rimsky-Korsakow's *Mlada*, and part of Arensky's ballet *Cléopâtra*. Diaghileff quickly realized his mistake and never repeated it.

Musical integrity of this sort won for the Russian impresario many devoted, admiring composers. One of these was Eugene Goossens, who was drafted into immediate service as conductor for Diaghileff's ballets after an impromptu luncheon with the impresario, who had conceived a dislike for the conductor actually in charge. In spite of the hasty invitation, Goossens remained to conduct all the ballets in the repertoire between 1920 and 1926, and was so impressed that he composed a ballet of his own, *L'École en Crinoline*. This was his sole effort in ballet form, and was neither published nor performed because, having dedicated it to Diaghileff, he had set his heart on having Diaghileff produce it. The latter's death forestalled his dream. Goossens withdrew the ballet(2).

Dancers often change the entire character of a piece of music by merely changing the tempo. They retard in impossible spots so that they can execute a difficult movement with ease. They sometimes command that their music be played slowly in rehearsal while they learn their dances. Unconsciously then, they add too much movement, which cannot be included when the music is later danced in tempo. Their simple remedy for such a situation is to play the music too slowly in performance. Stravinsky(3) declares it "undeniably clumsy to slow down the tempo in order to compose complicated steps which cannot be danced in the prescribed tempo. I have never known any choreographer who erred in that respect as much as

Nijinsky." Said Noverre: "A dancer without an ear resembles a madman who talks ceaselessly and at random, with no sequence in his conversation and who articulates disconnected words devoid of common sense. The music which should direct his movements serves only to betray his incapability and imperfections. The study of music can remedy the defect."

The matter of tempo has ever been of the greatest importance. Harald Kreutzberg, for one(4), believes that music should be treated in accordance with inherent musical laws: If, for example, the original tempo of a piece of music is changed by unnatural cutting or arbitrary rhythmic shiftings, which are unscrupulously practiced with the excuse that music has but a secondary significance, it only results in overemphasis of the music. That is the opinion of one of the foremost contemporary dancers. Consider, now, the opinions of some of the world's leading musicians on the matter of tempo in the mere interpretation of music. Mozart thought it the most necessary, the most difficult and the main thing in music. Grieg(5) said that if tempo were not in the blood, one could be sure that the other intentions of the composer would be bungled also. Wagner wrote an essay, "On Conducting(6)," in which he spoke of the spoiling of music by incorrect tempi. "The choice of tempo," he asserted, "tells us at once whether or not the conductor has grasped the true inwardness of the composition." Dancers are not the only ones at fault in this respect, when one reflects upon the way great musicians criticized each other. After hearing Mendelssohn conduct Beethoven's *Ninth*, Wagner(7) wrote to Uhlig that "Mendelssohn's gross errors in the conception of the tempi show clearly his failure to comprehend the content of a composition." In this matter, we may entirely discount Wagner's dislike of Mendelssohn (for real or fancied personal slights) since Wagner's *Life* (8) states clearly that on this one point Schumann agreed with him, as he (Schumann) had been compelled to listen for so many years to Mendelssohn's rushing of the *Ninth*! Yet, Charles Villiers Stanford(9) says that Mendelssohn's conducting even of his own music was fast. Under him, the *Midsummer Night's Dream Overture* was so rapid that he seemed to be whipping cream! His Allegros were very fast and his Adagios very slow.

There is not only the matter of the initial, or correct tempo, for the dancer to consider. There is also the matter of acceleration and retarding. Some composers simply mark "accelerando" or "ritardando" on their scores, whence the utmost intelligence must be shown in interpreting their wishes properly. Once in a while, there will appear a composer who painstakingly writes metronome indications over every two measure phrase of the music. In an accelerando, for example, he will write 72, then 76, then 80, and so on. Such a composer will be very exact, very particular in every way, and woe betide the dancer who fails to regard him with respect!

Montagu-Nathan(10) brings to light the obvious fact that the ballet audience cannot always be expected to know whether the composer is still alive and has been consulted as to the uses of his music, and many blame him if the music is not appropriate. (Most music for dancers depends for its use on its appeal to individual dancers, else they would not have selected it. They should never, however, force music to fit a dance idea of different character or meaning. Schumann(11) was opposed to all such remoulding as being an offense against the divine first inspiration.) Montagu-Nathan goes further when he declares that the dancer is too often convinced that he is the artistic compeer of the composer and therefore has the right to dictate and change. Edwin Evans(12) continues along this line by saying that the fact that some composers are dead should not prevent their being treated as collaborators if their music is used for the dance. Musicians like Tschaikowsky and Delibes would have written more or less in the same regular patterns if no ballet master had imposed his wishes on them. Rhythmic emancipation is a modern development (or revival) in music. In choreographing a piece of music, every bit of construction and texture should be noticed. Too often the dancer looks to music, not as a partner, but as a servant. Music is not so easily shackled to themes outside itself.

This brings up the matter of interpretation which, in one sense, includes correct tempo. As a matter of fact, every piece of music contains within itself a multitude of suggestions which the sensitive choreographer may use to advantage, so that "the gestures of the limbs will keep time with the musical instruments, and not the foot speak of one thing and the music of another," as Arbeau has it. Henry Cowell (13) used to laugh at the interpretive dance, because in no case was the music really interpreted—simply the same movements to different music.

The dancer's problem, then, is to avoid flagrant misinterpretations for, strangely enough, there can be two musical interpretations of the same composition, and both of them can be correct! Dancers who are angered when new accompanists do not play their music exactly as they are accustomed to hearing it, must remember that, in music as in dance, there is such a thing as an individual interpretation. Alexander Brailowsky (14) tells us that the *B Minor Sonata* of Liszt is susceptible to an infinite variety of treatment. Mr. Paderewski very probably plays it in a manner quite different from that of Liszt, yet I am certain that Mr. Paderewski left nothing undone to secure all available information relating to Liszt's ideas about his own work. This is a duty which every sincere interpreter owes to the composer or creator.

Introductions are sometimes a preamble to what is to come. At other times they contain some germs or atmosphere of the approaching music. It is possible for a dancer to dance an introduction as it appears in the music, and to embody in her dance the identical qualities of the musical prologue. Too often, dancers simply stay off the stage during the introduction, or dance it as if it contained thematic material. It is also possible to dance codas as they appear in the music, giving a simple summary, a more emphatic finish, or a lingering farewell to what has gone before.

Some dancers have difficulty in recognizing the fundamental motif of a composition in feeling and in structure. Once they understand it, in terms of phrasing, melody, dynamics and rhythm, the dance creation becomes fairly simple, for the sensitive dancer may then forget technicalities and operate intuitively. Recognition of theme or motif is simply a matter of ear-training, of keen powers of observation. Most composers state their themes very definitely at the beginnings of their compositions. There is a reason for this: it is impossible to develop or expound a theme until that theme is there to develop. A debate is impossible when the subject is not known at the outset. (Schumann wrote (15) vehemently about a certain Fantasia without a theme: "A key without a ward, a riddle without a solution, Paganini without a violin, a piece in itself —a ruin, if you will, for which no critic can lay down a rule— almost nothing but observations on scales.") Most composers state their themes immediately, clearly, simply and definitely. The simplest way is the best; the fireworks can come later.

Not all of music is thematic. There are also episodes, cadenzas, modulatory passages or transitions. These should be recognized as such in dance movement. Musical sequences and their discontinuances are important. Dancers should not continue to develop an effective movement-theme long after the corresponding music has changed its character. They should not carry movements over phrase-endings. (In this respect, Stravinsky (16) has written that "the defect of forced, artificial composition frequently arises, as choreographers are fond of cutting up a rhythmic episode of the music into fragments, of working up each fragment separately, and then putting them all together. Thus the choreographic line rarely coincides with that of the music, and the results are deplorable.") One might suggest also that dancers give the greater part of their attention to the dynamic line of the music as a whole, not to scattered changes in dynamics. Dancers should not accent inner melodies for forceful gestures, thus spoiling the line of those melodies and their relation to the principal one. Deliberate counterpoint is often splendid, but ignorant or erratic counterpoint is lamentable. When one recalls that most spontaneous primitive or folk dances accompany definite musical characteristics with similarly definite movements, one cannot help but wonder why cerebral dances differ from their accompaniments in so many instances.

There is one case where it is possible for the dancer to move while the music is static: when the music is played on some instrument capable of sustaining the tones, so that the vibrations form a basis for continued movement. It is sometimes extremely funny to be aware that the musical accompaniment has paused and to see the dancer doggedly continue to move about; conversely, it is strange to see a dancer standing motionless while the music rises around her. It is also disheartening to see imperfect cadences danced with final gestures, and perfect cadences treated as though they were the beginning of a new thought.

Any intelligent dancer can recognize certain musical facts for herself, without having to depend on an accompanist's prodding. She may, if she does not understand expression marks, consult either one of two books, or both: a musical dictionary, or an Italian dictionary, for the musical meanings are usually the word meanings. If she is unable to read music, she can readily see by looking at the score that when the printed notes go upward, they rise in pitch. If they go down, they descend in pitch. If they are massed on the page, they will sound that way. The eye is thus a splendid guide for the ear, and choreography should take all those details into account. One of the most successful of all interpretations of Bach's music was that of a Fugue in which four girls danced to the four different voices, moving directionally as the voices moved. The effect was at once satisfying musically and choreographically.

Orchestral instruments and their varied tone qualities will have a relation to dance movement for the choreographer who intends to dance to an orchestral accompaniment, for the best of themes can change character when played by different instruments. Picture the dancer's amazement when, after setting a suave movement to what was apparently a lyric passage when it was played on the piano, she finds that the composer has scored it for martial horns!

The inner ears of most dancers demand the accompaniment

of a large orchestra which, in our day, is economically impossible for most performers to have. Nevertheless, the dancers are then dissatisfied with a mere piano accompaniment and they set out to employ a trio, no member of which is experienced as to the ways of dancers and, since the dances are usually not built on trio music, the music must be *arranged* for trio. This is not a simple matter, even for the most experienced of arrangers—and so often those employed for this sort of makeshift are not experienced. The result, even if the performance were perfect (and it seldom is!) is bad from a musical standpoint. The same is true of presenting great symphonic works with small orchestra, omitting many of the instrumental parts from necessity. There is no substitute for an orchestra! Most reductions of orchestral scores and amplifications of piano scores are equally abominable. It is necessary in the beginning to select music written for the instrument or combination of instruments to be used as accompaniment.

There is, too, the matter of the accompanist. Read this scathing criticism of a dance concert by Francis Kendig(17), and judge the accompanist's importance for yourself: "The effectiveness of the entire program suffered immeasurably from the piano accompaniment to the dances. The music is so extremely vital that only concert pianists, or at least those who can imbue their renditions of dance rhythms with point and artistry should be employed, for the effect of motion depends so much on the mood which the composer generates in the minds of the hearers. Many of the musical compositions used were difficult; it is too much to give them to just one who plays the piano and expect him to present outstanding interpretations."

The new cult of loudness for dancers' accompaniments must not pass unnoticed. They often sacrifice beauty of tone for volume, and deceive themselves by thinking that it adds force, much as the singer who practices to a loud accompaniment under the delusion that she is preparing for a future orchestral background and that she is producing lovely tones. The very opposite is true. Forcing leads to harshness. No one would wish to have an accompaniment without body. In either case, extremes are bad. The dancer who belongs to this new cult is thoroughly convinced that he cannot hear the music when he dances to an ordinary accompaniment. Another camouflage dancers use for their desire to hear crashing accompaniments is the delusion that all such music is "inspired" and that soft music is meaningless. Nothing could be farther from the truth.

Doubtless, dancers who have been courageous enough to read this chapter will feel that the points discussed are too technical, especially since the remark was made that, after recognizing the initial theme, one may work intuitively. They will feel that they would like to be more carried away with the emotional quality of the music. However, there comes a time in the creation of any really artistic thing when the creator's analytical powers function clearly and distinctly. Why cannot these powers be applied to bare musical facts as well as to the basic elements in the dance?

After all, the important thing in dancing to music is to dance to the music. All that is necessary then is to recognize clearly what is in the music. Intuition will do the rest.

CHAPTER 28

NOTES

(1) Stewart, *Modern Dance*, p. 37
(2) In a letter to the author from Cincinnati, Ohio, dated February 7, 1936
(3) Stravinsky, *An Autobiography*, p. 75
(4) Stewart, *Modern Dance*, p. 30
(5) *Étude*, January, 1931, p. 15
(6) *Étude*, November, 1916, pp. 777-778
(7) Wagner, *Letters to Uhlig*, p. 191
(8) Wagner, *My Life*, p. 329
(9) Stanford, *Pages from an Unwritten Diary*, p. 31
(10) *Dancing Times*, February, 1931, p. 570
(11) Schumann, *Music and Musicians, second series*, p. 222

(12) See Edwin Evans' articles on the function of music for the dance in the *Dancing Times* for December, 1925, December, 1926, January, 1927

(13) *Dance Observer,* January, 1937

(14) *Étude,* June, 1925, p. 389

(15) Schumann, *Music and Musicians, second series,* p. 436

(16) Stravinsky, *An Autobiography,* p. 144

(17) *Saturday Night,* June 27, 1936

PROBLEMS OF THE COMPOSER

"No sculptor is obliged to create a model. If he accepts the commission, he is in duty bound to see that his model is executable. So it is with composers who undertake to write music for dancing. . . ."

To most dancers who use music, it is the most powerful of all choreographic suggestions. If the music is strong enough, the dancer's creation will conform, at least in part, to the original intention of the composer. Baudelaire thought the dance could do more than that: that it could reveal all that the music hides.

More than ever, the composer who wishes to write for the dance today is at a loss. In addition to the arguments and problems already mentioned, there is always the fact that there is today very little adequate criticism of dance music. Few critics are capable of judging choreographic music as such, and their sometimes superficial comments betray their lack of interest and knowledge of the subject. Perhaps they do not realize the great value that such intelligent criticism would have for a composer. Perhaps they do not realize how it would raise the standard of dance music on the whole. True, there *are* a few critics who are eminently competent in this respect: only a few.

What is left, then, for the composer? He, too, should study the dance. He need not dance if he does not enjoy it, but by diligent reading and observation he should be able to know the medium for which he composes. For years, composers have wished that dancers would study music. Why should they not learn something of the dance in return? Both composers and dancers should be fair. What's sauce for the goose is sauce for the gander, said our pioneering grandparents, and how very right they were!

In view of the mental state in which many composers find themselves in relation to dance, one is justified in saying that it is ridiculous to limit a dancer's choice of music to that which composers intend for dance music, for that would completely stop the belated development of the dance in the abstract. Moreover, as Angna Enters puts it(1): "The fact that a composer calls his composition a ballet does not automatically make it music which can be used by a dancer, whereas music which is without dance itself can be vested with that element by a dancer who uses it as part of his composition. When the dancer tries to use most music for the dance, the result is the negative one of two positives. There may be *so much dance* in the music that anything the dancer does is anticlimax. Furthermore, interpretive dancers are at a disadvantage when the composer doesn't provide the scenario, for no one can know as well as the composer what was in his mind."

It is true that many dancers massacre their music. Everyone sympathizes with the poor composer then. There is, nevertheless, a good deal to be said for the dancer, whose physical limitations and whose own creative faculties make it impossible for her to bow her head under absolute musical tyranny. There is, for instance, no excuse for such tyranny as shown by composer Ernest Schelling, in a dance production of his *Victory Ball*, when he wished to have most of the costumes re-made because he feared that *the cellophane skirts would drown out his martial music* in the Hollywood Bowl!

Long years ago, Noverre urged composers for the dance to learn their medium and to gauge their music by the requirements of the dance: "A musical composer must have a knowledge of dancing; but, so far from taking the pains to acquire the first elements of this art and to learn the theory of it, he avoids the ballet master, he imagines that it is his art which elevates and gives him superiority over dancing. I shall not dispute with him, although it is only the superiority of a man's art and not the nature of the art which merits such priority and distinction." Noverre also said, "The dance of our time is new, it is imperative that the music shall be so also . . ."

Let us review briefly the different phases of the dance, for those musicians who have not studied them before. There are many sorts of dancing: folk, athletic, ritual, religious and theatrical. Under the latter heading comes ballet dancing, which Arnold Haskell has called "organized beauty." It would be difficult to dance abstractly in the formula so rigidly prescribed by the classic ballet. It strove for beauty of line, for style and charm. The music most acceptable to it was that which aided in the realization of such beauty. Bolm says of the music for this dance form: "One cannot write a ballet on an illogical sequence of events. A ballet is essentially of the theater and depends on much more than good music, which in itself is vague. When the curtain rises, the audience should know where it is and what is happening. There should be no doubt. Yes, certain pieces of music are interesting. But if they do not convey anything, of what use are they to the ballet?" So closely was a certain type of regular-rhythmed dance music allied to the formal ballet in the minds of the public that when music of Chopin was orchestrated for the Russian ballet's production of *Les Sylphides*, it occasioned such hot discussion in the press that one would infer that it was the boldest of all possible steps in relation to choreographic music!

Nijinsky, product of the formal Russian ballet school, was flagrantly ignorant of the most elementary notions about the music he was called upon to interpret, according to Stravinsky(2). He required a fantastic number of rehearsals. Even Fokine, product of the same school of dancing, claimed that when Nijinsky choreographed Debussy's *Afternoon of a Faun*, the music and choreography were not only unsympathetic, but were definitely hostile.

Walford Hyden(3), accompanist for Pavlowa, deplored the insignificant music to which she used to dance, such as Drigo's charming, but ineffectual *Sérénade*. But under her charm and artistry, the music itself became remarkable. In 1916, Pavlowa herself wrote: "The great musical classics of past centuries have treated dance as an insignificant side issue, thereby putting a label of inferiority upon this loftiest of arts. All the dance music of the great classics sounds naïve and lacking in choreographic images. Yet dance and music are like light and shadow, each depending upon the other. As canvas is to a painter, so is music to a dancer the essential element upon which he can draw his picture. The fact that the art of dancing has not evolved into its normal state of equality with the other arts is wholly due to the lack of musical leadership." One cannot help but wonder whether Pavlowa did not know—or did not want to know—or was prevented from knowing—what was happening outside of her own little world. Stravinsky had appeared long before 1916! So had interpretive dancers, the forerunners of those who later made such an advance in the dance as an independent art.

Isadora Duncan thought the Bacchanale from Wagner's *Tannhäuser* one of the most beautiful expressions of Bacchic and sensuous love ever written. She was shocked—and rightly so—when she saw it danced at Bayreuth by three ballet dancers in stiff skirts, on the toes of their ballet slippers(4)!

Yet all ballet dancers were not and are not remiss in the matter of musical interpretation. January 21, 1852 found Hans von Bülow(5) writing to his father: "Really and truly, Lucille Grahn, who has been dancing here this week, has more music in her little toe than Sontag [a famous singer] and I much prefer her as a musician." M. Fokine(6) has said that "music is not a mere accompaniment to a rhythmic step, but an organic part of the dance. The quality of choreographic inspiration is determined by the quality of the music." Musicians have said that he treats the intention of the composer with reverent understanding, and that he can work out the musical counterpoint in a dance with great exactitude. Balanchine is said to be musically educated far in advance of anyone else in ballet, and to be an excellent pianist who might easily have adopted that career. Whereas Irving Deakin(7) tells us that certain music critics are prone to use the word "presumptuous" when they speak of Massine's preoccupation with the choreographic translation of symphonic works, the eminent Ernest Newman(8) saw parallels in the music of Tschaikowsky's *Fifth Symphony* and the movements of Massine's *Les Presages* (danced to it) and acclaimed the choreographer's genius and common sense. Of this composition, Haskell(9) has written: "The music is still close to conventional ballet music and suggests a definite programme, so that it is still possible to conceive of a theme and to coördinate that theme logically with the development of the music. Choreographically, the weakest portion (the third) coincides with the weakest in the music, but throughout, the two are so close together that it seems possible to see the music and to hear the dancers."

A transitory period in the history of dance and music was that of Loie Fuller(10), predecessor of Isadora Duncan. Fuller, before 1913, wrote in a manner for which she would be severely condemned today: A given motion is produced by such and such music . . . a Polka or a Waltz to which we listen informs us as to the motions of the dance and blends its variations. Slow music calls for a slow dance just as fast music requires a fast dance. Dancing means a conventional motion, accompanied by music, and the motion, it is unnecessary to say, is regulated rather by the time than by the spirit of the dance. In general, music ought to follow the dance. The best musician is he who can permit the dancer to direct the music instead of the music inspiring the dance. To dance to new music, the dancer has to learn the conventional steps adapted to that music. Music, however, ought to indicate a form of harmony, or an idea with instinctive passion, and this instinct ought to incite the dancer to follow the harmony without special preparation. This is the true dance.

Then came Isadora, who demanded stimulation from her music; who declared that "Music is very much more than an accompaniment to the dance. Its function is to give the keynote and sustain the whole mood of the dance" and who would not rehearse with her accompanists because, said she (11), "You are an artist and I am an artist. There is but one truth in art, and we will both express that truth." Only in one instance did she disagree with Rabinowitch when he accompanied for her, as to interpretation: the Schubert Waltzes. She wanted some places faster, some slower.

When Isador Duncan first did her "Greek" dancing to the music of Schubert, Chopin and others, she was criticized because the music was not Greek! Adrian Stokes' (12) comment on her dancing is typical: "In less inspired moments, Isadora Duncan followed the music as a bear might pursue a mouse. This interpretative dancing does not make the music itself unforgettable." There were many more who said kind things of her, like the poet Joel Elias Spingarn, that she was "Human motion married to immortal music." After all, she had a great rôle to play in the world of dance, and she played it well. She was the first dancer to use great music. She improvised, perhaps, but her improvisations brought out the very soul of the music. Rabinowitch says her understanding of music was deep, and that she could explain hidden meanings of phrases better than most musicians. It was as an interpreter of music that she won her fame. No one had ever regarded Pavlowa in such a light!

The term "music visualizations," now used by Ted Shawn, was evidently invented by Ruth St. Denis, an American dancer as was Isadora Duncan, and Loie Fuller. Though Miss St. Denis has always been more sensitive to lights than to music, an investigation reveals that she pioneered in many things relating to music and the dance. Her Synchoric Orchestra was a group of dancers who identified themselves with different instrumental groups in an orchestra (really a dancer to correspond to every musician) in order to give literal group translations of large symphonic scores. These were the first "music visualizations" and they were presented in concert. The Synchoric Orchestra was first formed because it seemed obvious to Miss St. Denis that one dancer could no more visualize a symphony than one violin could play it. In following the actual architectural construction of the music, there was also an attempt at a close relation between the written page of music and its dance rendition, while also giving dramatic expression to the emotional content of the composition. This was a true pioneer effort toward an orchestration of movement. Kendig(13) has perhaps best expressed Miss St. Denis' contribution to the dance when he said that she brought in new ideas, accented natural and habitual motions, gave characterizations. Mentally, she has always been one of the most alert and progressive of dancers.

La Argentina graduated from a conservatory of music. When she began to create a dance, she was able to study the music thoroughly—as thoroughly, in fact, as would a musician who intended to add it to his repertoire. When she danced, she emphasized certain parts of the music and added significance to them by a sudden gesture, a glance, a mere movement of a finger, or the slight bending of a knee. Naturally, she thought that all dancers should be thorough musicians. As for herself, she never stopped studying.

In the field of untrammeled, rhythmic modern dance, Mary Wigman dances frankly for the sake of the dance. Martha Graham thinks too much of the dance as a separate and complete art to allow herself or her pupils to interpret music in the dance. Yet she reads scores and makes graphs from them before she ever hears the music played, and requires her company to study with Louis Horst, her official composer.

Fokine finds the association of modern German dancers with percussion and undeveloped music wretched, and "highly significant"—of what? Doubtless of the downfall of the dance as an art. Massine thinks Wigman's whole connection between dancing and music is weak, especially in the abuse of percussion.

The modern dance may be defined in several ways. Most

effective is by contrasting it with what has gone before. Whereas the classic dance was concerned with floor patterns, the modern dance is concerned with space patterns. While the classic choreographer was anxious over the technical perfection and precision of his company, the modern choreographer is careful of his groupings, his massed actions, the contrapuntal movements in his creations. The classic dance was a series of transitions from pose to pose, while modern dancing is a continuous flow in which the poses are but incidents, just as music does not jump from chord to chord, but is created on a large pattern in which the chords are only a part. One secret of the modern dance which few of its participants will disclose is that many of the most rabid in the ranks have built their revolutionary technic on pure ballet principles. So, if the composer studies these thoroughly, he will have a working knowledge of some kinds of modern movement also, for these will be found to be ballet movements with but a single alteration, or distortion.

Today, too, as Wardell remarks(14), we speak of the dance in terms of personalities. Pavlowa and Genée of the classic era could be compared, but how to compare Yvonne Georgi and Angna Enters, Harald Kreutzberg and Ted Shawn? Each has a peculiar idiom in which, as a dancer, he or she speaks unchallenged. This is the keynote of the modern dance; something that cannot be classified as "ballet," "interpretive," or "theatrical" in the manner of a few years ago.

For these individuals, there is no single standard of perfection as there is in music. The dance must always be a contemporary expression. In music it is possible to interpret the works of great masters, whereas in the dance, the dancer must also be creator. While pupils of a certain famed dancer are always being roundly criticized for dancing the compositions that reviewers have previously seen him do to perfection, scores of musicians nightly stand upon stages and pour forth their souls in the compositions of others, being then criticized for their interpretations only, not for their deed.

One of the best contrasts between two schools of dancing was afforded by two famous, different interpretations of the

same, rather obvious music. Pavlowa once danced Delibes'
Pizzicato Polka on her toes exquisitely for Michio Ito. Then
she asked if he would not like to dance for her. He had no
music with him, so he asked the pianist to repeat Delibes' music,
whereupon he planted his feet firmly on the floor and danced
the entire dance with only his arms and hands. Later, Pavlowa
attended Ito's recital in London, and at the end of the program
shouted her request for this dance. Ever since, he has used
it to conclude his programs. A more decided contrast in movement cannot be imagined: Pavlowa with her precision and Ito
with his dynamic movements belonging to a modern age.

There is one requirement in the dance, as in music: that it
shall have form, design, coherence. Some dancers build their
dance-plans on the structure of the music, a wise procedure,
when they are dancing to music that is pre-composed.

A good accompanist for the dance will play the music just
a little differently from the way a pedant would have it. That
is, there is a lift: a rise and fall in each phrase that is almost
indescribable. At least, it is not possible of description with
ordinary crescendo and diminuendo marks. A curve of the
hand or a rising gesture will occasion this "lift." It follows
that a successful composer for the dance will have in his music
that indescribable something that gives to choreographic music,
on the whole, that strange, unrigid, rhythmic, living character!

CHAPTER 29

NOTES

(1) *The Drama Magazine,* December, 1930, p. 6
(2) Stravinsky, *An Autobiography,* p. 63
(3) From a review in the *Theatre Arts Monthly,* January, 1932, p. 86;
        or p. 146 of the book itself, *Pavlowa,* by Walford Hyden, pub-
        lished by Little Brown and Company, Boston, 1931
(4) *Theatre Arts Monthly,* August, 1927, p. 593
(5) von Bülow, *Letters of Hans von Bülow,* p. 108
(6) *Dancing Times,* April, 1930, p. 49
(7) Deakin, *To the Ballet,* p. 125

(8) Haskell, *Balletomania*, pp. 245-246

(9) Haskell, *Balletomania*, p. 242

(10) Fuller, *Fifteen Years of a Dancer's Life*, pp. 67, 68, 69

(11) In an interview with Max Rabinowitch in Hollywood, California, on June 8, 1931

(12) Stokes, *Tonight the Ballet*, p. 15

(13) *Saturday Night*, February 1, 1936

(14) *The American Dancer Magazine*, May, 1931, p. 13

*

CHAPTER 30

*

APPENDICES

A. Explanatory Note
B. Bibliography
C. Musical Examples
D. Ballet Terms
E. Miscellaneous Dance Music

A. EXPLANATORY NOTE

For much of the material in this book, I am indebted to Conrad Aiken, George Antheil, Joseph Achron, Renzo Bossi, Adolph Bolm, Robert Russell Bennett, John Alden Carpenter, James Francis Cooke, Henry Cowell, Jesús Castillo, Carolyn Cummings, Melissa Blake, Mrs. Dohnanyi, Luisa Espinel, Nathan Emanuel, Arthur Farwell, Eleanore Flaig, Eugène Goossens, Gabriel Grovlez, Ruth Eleanor Howard, Howard Hanson, Dr. Hsiao, Reynaldo Hahn, W. C. Handy, Jessmin Howarth, John Herat, Langston Hughes, Mme. Kimiyo Ito, Jaap Kool, Erich Wolfgang Korngold, Darius Milhaud, Harl MacDonald, Miriam Marmein, Modupe Paris, Helen March, Vittorio Rieti, Dane Rudhyar, Cyril Scott, Joseph Schillinger, William Grant Still, Arnold Schoenberg, Hubert Stowitts, Joaquín Turina, Vincenzo Tommasini, Alexandre Tcherepnine, Ernst Toch, Edgar Varese, Bertha Wardell, Emerson Whithorne, Tom Youngplant—all of whom responded to requests for information, and whose assistance in those particular fields in which their individual knowledge is outstanding, was invaluable. I am also indebted to Ernest Belcher, Vocha Bertha Fiske, Norma Gould, Wm. Manger (Counsellor of the Pan-American Union) and to the Henry E. Huntington Library for the use of rare books and clippings. The bulk of research was done at the Los Angeles Public Library. To Dale Arvey I owe many fine translations from the French books graciously lent by Frances and Rosemary Stack.

My appreciation of this assistance is all the greater, since many composers failed to respond to requests for information about their work

435

in this field. A case of this kind is Louis Horst. After failing to receive a reply to my letter, I approached him backstage after a concert. Perhaps, I suggested, he had not received my letter, since I had not had the pleasure of an answer. "Oh yes," said he, looking off into space. "I did receive your letter, but the answers to your questions would fill a book, so when I get around to answering all of them, I'll submit the manuscript to a publisher on my own." It is doubtless just such incidents that cause so many inaccurate things to be written. Authors, unable to secure cooperation, in desperation write what they believe to be true, afterwards to be heatedly attacked by those who did not cooperate when they were invited to do so.

Needless to say, every attempt has been made to make this book accurate. Errors may have crept in despite this effort. If so, that is for the reader to discover. Not all of the scores mentioned in the text were available for study, therefore some descriptions were reconstructed from the writings of others. Then, there is always the fact that the more one learns, the more one finds to learn. I venture to say that the studious investigator will discover as much more material on this subject as is included in this book. I am only sorry that the confines of a single volume are not broad enough to include every available fact on choreographic music.

It was also instructive to learn how few historians agree on important details, and how few pay their readers the compliment of presenting both sides of controversial questions. This I have endeavored to do not only in historical matters, but in critical views on certain pieces of music, for a criticism, in the final analysis, narrows itself down to the individual. That is, it is a product of individual taste. Critics are too often prone to condemn the opinions and the likes and dislikes of others without considering the fact that they are themselves listening to the voices of their own private preferences. A rabid modernist will bitterly decry a contemporary composition that has a melody, or is otherwise pleasing to the ear, while a pedant will be bitter against modernism on the grounds that it is contrary to the rules he has learned. The same modern music will also be damned by the casual listener for the simple reason that he cannot understand a new idiom, and that it is therefore displeasing to him. It has, then, been impossible for me to quote a single authority in most instances.

The use of the word "choreography" seems to be a purely American idiosyncrasy. According to the Funk and Wagnalls New Standard Dictionary of the English Language, published in 1933, "choreography" and "choregraphy" are presumably interchangeable, although most British writers use the latter term for some subtle reason. I have used the former, since it is the one that comes more familiarly to my pen.

When the names of dances are used as nouns throughout the book I have capitalized them. I have also capitalized the words Sonata, Symphony, Concerto—all this to emphasize the words. The names of all musical compositions have been italicized, but *excerpts* from compositions are merely capitalized.

THE AUTHOR

B. BIBLIOGRAPHY

In the preparation of this volume, complete files of these periodicals were consulted:

The American Dancer Magazine, published monthly in New York City by Ruth Eleanor Howard

Archives Internationales de la Danse, Revue Trimestrielle, published at 6, rue Vital, (16e) Paris, France

The Dance Observer, published monthly in New York City

The Dancing Times, published monthly in London, edited by P. J. S. Richardson

Diario del Sureste, published in Mérida, Yucatan, Mexico

The Étude Music Magazine, published monthly in Philadelphia, Pa., by the Presser Company, edited by Dr. James Francis Cooke

Mexican Folkways, published quarterly in Mexico City, edited by Frances Toor

Modern Music, published quarterly by the League of Composers in New York City

The Musical Courier, published weekly in New York City

The Musical Quarterly, published by G. Schirmer in New York City

Saturday Night, published weekly in Los Angeles, California

Theatre Arts Monthly, published in New York City

The Times, published daily in Los Angeles, California

The Times, published daily in New York City

Single issues of the following periodicals were consulted:

The American Weekly, published in New York City, for December 1, 1935

Asia Magazine, published monthly in New York City, for January 1922

The Arts, edited by Mr. Forbes Watson, for May 1926

Art and Letters, for July 1917

Chesterian, published in London, for March-April 1939 and January-February 1939

Christian Science Monitor, published in Boston, Mass., for March 3, 1936

Denishawn Dance Magazine, now discontinued, but published by Ruth St. Denis and Ted Shawn

The Drama Magazine, published in Chicago, Illinois, by the Dramatic Publishing Company, for December 1930

Esquire, published monthly in Chicago, Illinois, for February 1936
The Moscow News, for February 19, 1936
Musical America, published in New York City, for May 26, 1923
Musical West, published in San Francisco, California, for October 1936
The Pacific, published in Berkeley, California, for October 1935
Pro Musica Quarterly, published in New York City, for October 1928
Rivista Musicale Italiana, Vol. 39 (1932) printed in Turin, Italy, by
    Fratelli Bocca Editori
The Theosophist, for December 1922
Travel, published in New York City, for January 1933

    These books were consulted:

Abraham, Gerald H., *Borodin, the Composer and His Music,* published
    by William Reeves, London
Arbeau, Thoinet, *Orchésography,* translated by Cyril W. Beaumont, in
    the Henry E. Huntington Library collection
Avery, Emmett Langdon, "Dancing and Pantomime on the English Stage
    1700-1737" in studies in *Philology,* Vol. 31, no. 3, 1934
Bath, Hubert, an article in the *London Musical Herald,* in the collec-
    tion of Vocha Bertha Fiske
Bauer, Marion, *Twentieth Century Music,* G. P. Putnam's Sons, New
    York City, 1933
Bauer and Peyser, *Music Through the Ages,* G. P. Putnam's Sons, New
    York City, 1932
Berlioz, Hector, *Autobiography,* Macmillan and Company, London,
    1884
Berlioz, Hector, *Memoirs, 1803-1865,* Alfred A. Knopf, New York City,
    1932
Berwick-Sayers, W. C., *Samuel Coleridge-Taylor, His Life and Letters,*
    Funk & Wagnalls, 1927
Blümner, Prof. H., *Home Life of the Ancient Greeks,* published in 1893
Boughton, Rutland, *The Reality of Music,* Kegan Paul, Trench, Trub-
    ner and Company Ltd., London, 1934
Bourman, Anatole and D. Lyman, *The Tragedy of Nijinsky,* Whittlesey
    House, New York City, 1936
Broadbent, R. J., *A Masque at Knowsley* (in the Huntington Library
    collection)
Brown, Irving, *Deep Song,* Harper & Brothers, New York, 1929
Burney, Charles, *A General History of Music* (re-issue) Harcourt,
    Brace and Company, New York. First published in 1789

Calvocoressi, M. D., *Music and Ballet,* Faber, London, 1934

Casella, Alfredo, *L'Evoluzione della Musica,* published in London by Chester, 1924

Chaliapin, Feodor, *Pages from My Life,* Harper & Brothers, New York City, 1927

Chao-Mei-Pa, *The Yellow Bell,* published in English in 1934 at Barberry Hill, Baldwin, Md.

Chopin, *Collected Letters,* Alfred A. Knopf, New York, 1931

Clavigero, *History of Mexico,* translated by Charles Cullen and published in London in 1787

Coleridge-Taylor, Samuel, *Twenty-Four Negro Melodies Transcribed for Piano,* Oliver Ditson Company, New York and Boston, 1905

Cooke, James Francis, *Great Men and Famous Musicians on the Art of Music,* the Presser Company, Philadelphia, Pa., 1925

Coomaraswamy, Ananda, and Gopala Kristnayya Duggirala, *The Mirror of Gesture,* Harvard University Press, Cambridge, Mass., 1917

Cooper, Martin, *Gluck,* Chatto and Windus, London, 1935

Cowell, Henry, *American Composers on American Music,* Stanford University Press, 1933

Craig, Gordon, *Henry Irving,* Longmans, Green and Company, New York, 1930

Cuney-Hare, Maud, *Negro Musicians and Their Music,* Associated Publishers, Inc., Washington, D. C., 1936

Curtis, Natalie, *Songs and Tales from the Dark Continent,* G. Schirmer, New York and Boston, 1920

de Leeuw, Hendrik, *Crossroads of the Java Sea,* Jonathan Cape and Harrison Smith, New York, 1931

de Staël, Mme., *Corinne,* translated by Holstein, A. L. Burt, New York, 1892 (?)

Deakin, Irving, *To the Ballet,* published in America, 1935

Debussy, Claude, *Letters of Debussy to His Editor,* Jacques Durand, Paris, 1927

Debussy, Claude, *M. Croche, the Dilettante-Hater,* Whitefriars Press, Ltd., London, 1927

Derwent, Lord, *Rossini,* Duckworth, London, 1934

Dickinson, *The Study of the History of Music,* Charles Scribner's Sons, New York, 1925

Draper, Muriel, *Music at Midnight,* Harper & Brothers, New York, 1929

Ekman, Karl, *Jean Sibelius, His Life and Personality,* Alan Wilmer, Ltd., London, 1936

Engel, Carl, *Music of the Most Ancient Nations,* William Reeves, London

Evans, Herbert Arthur, *Introduction to "English Masques,"* published in London by Blackie and Son, London, 1818

Ewen, David, *Wine, Women and Waltz,* Sears Publishing Company, New York City, 1933

Farwell, Arthur, *American Indian Melodies,* op. 11, G. Schirmer, New York, copyright 1901 by the Wa-Wan Press and in 1914 by G. Schirmer.

Fellowes, E. H., *English Madrigal Composers,* The Clarendon Press, Oxford, 1921

Fergusson, Erna, *Dancing Gods,* Alfred A. Knopf, New York, 1931

Finck, Henry T., *Grieg and His Music,* John Lane Company, New York, 1909

Flaig, Eleanore, *The Dance Divine,* running serially in the *American Dancer Magazine*

Fleischer, Edwin A., *Catalogue of the Music Collection,* privately printed in Philadelphia, Pa., 1933

Fletcher, Alice, *The Pawnee Hako,* American Bureau of Ethnology, Washington, D. C., 1900-1901, vol. 2, no. 22

Flood, Grattan, *A History of Irish Music,* Browne and Nolan, Dublin, Ireland, 1927

Fox-Strangways, *The Music of Hindostan,* The Clarendon Press, Oxford, 1914

Fuller, Loie, *Fifteen Years of a Dancer's Life,* Small, Maynard and Company, Boston, 1913

Fuller-Maitland, J. A., *The Keyboard Suites of J. S. Bach,* The Oxford University Press, London, 1925

Glyn, Margaret, *Elizabethan Virginal Music and Its Composers,* William Reeves, London

Gorer, Geoffrey, *Bali and Angkor,* Little, Brown and Company, Boston, 1936

Gorer, Geoffrey, *Africa Dances,* Alfred A. Knopf, New York, 1935

Gounod, *Gounod,* William Heinemann, London, 1896

Gjerset, Knut, *History of Iceland,* The Macmillan Company, New York, 1924

Grove, *Dictionary of Music and Musicians,* The Macmillan Company, New York, 1904

Grove, Mrs. Lilly, *Dancing,* from the Badminton Library of Sports and Pastimes published in England, 1895

Hadden, J. Cuthbert, *Haydn,* J. M. Dent and Company, London, 1902

Hague, Eleanor, *Latin American Music,* The Fine Arts Press, Santa Ana, California, 1934

Hague, Eleanor, *Music in Ancient Arabia and Spain,* Stanford University Press, Palo Alto, California, 1929

Havemeyer, Loomis, *The Drama of Savage People,* Yale University Press, New Haven, Conn., 1916

Haskell, Arnold, *Balletomania,* Simon and Schuster, New York, 1934

Haskell, Arnold and Walter Nouvel, *Diaghileff,* Simon and Schuster, New York, 1935

Henderson, *Some Forerunners of Italian Opera,* Henry Holt and Company, New York, 1911

Herskovits, Melville J., *Life in a Haitian Valley,* Alfred A. Knopf, New York, 1937

Heseltine, Philip, *Frederick Delius,* John Lane, London, 1923

Hill, Edward Burlingame, *Modern French Music,* Houghton Mifflin and Company, Boston, 1924

Hoffmeister, Karel, *Antonin Dvorak,* John Lane, the Bodley Head, London, 1928

Holbrooke, *Contemporary British Composers,* Cecil Palmer, London, 1925

Howard, John Tasker, *Our American Music,* Thomas Y. Crowell Company, New York, 1930

Howard, John Tasker, "Studies of Contemporary Composers" pamphlet devoted to Emerson Whithorne, published by Carl Fischer Inc., New York City, 1929

Idelsohn, A. Z., *Jewish Music,* Henry Holt and Company, New York, 1929

James, E. O., *Primitive Belief and Ritual,* Methuen and Company, London, 1917

Jaques-Dalcroze, Émil, *Eurhythmics, Art and Education,* Chatto and Windus, London, 1930

Jacques-Dalcroze, Émil, *Rhythm, Music and Education,* G. P. Putnam's Sons, New York, 1921

Karsavina, *Theatre Street,* E. P. Dutton & Co., Inc., New York, 1930

Kenney, *A Memoir of Michael William Balfe,* published in London in 1875 and in New York in 1893

Kidson, *The Beggar's Opera,* The Cambridge University Press, 1922

Kinney, Troy and Margaret, *The Dance,* Tudor Publishing Company, New York, 1936

Kirstein, Lincoln, *Dance,* G. P. Putnam's Sons, New York, 1935

Lacroix, Paul, *The Arts in the Middle Ages and at the Period of the Renaissance,* Chapman and Hall, London, 1875

Lawrence, Arthur, *Sir Arthur Sullivan,* Herbert S. Stone and Company, Chicago and New York, 1899

Lawson, Mary, *Paderewski's Life Story,* running serially in the *Saturday Evening Post,* Philadelphia, Pa., 1937

Levinson, André, *La Danse d'Aujourd'hui,* Duchartre et Van Buggenhoudt, Paris, 1929

Lieven, Prince Peter, *The Birth of Ballets-Russes,* George Allen and Unwin, Ltd., London, 1936

Liszt, Franz, *The Gypsies and Their Music,* translated by Edwin Evans, published by William Reeves in London

Liszt, Franz, *Letters of Franz Liszt,* Scribner, New York, 1894

MacDowell, Edward, *Critical and Historical Essays,* published by Arthur P. Schmidt, Boston, 1912

Mahaffey, J. P., *Rambles and Studies in Greece,* Macmillan, London, 1887

Martens, Frederick H., *A Thousand and One Nights at the Opera,* D. Appleton and Company, New York, 1926

Massenet, Jules, *My Recollections,* Small, Maynard and Company, Boston, 1919

Masters, Edgar Lee, *Vachel Lindsay,* Charles Scribner's Sons, New York, 1935

Mendieta, *Ecclesiastical Indian History,* written at the end of the sixteenth century and published in Mexico in 1869

Montagu-Nathan, *A History of Russian Music,* William Reeves, London, 1918

Mozart, *Mozart's Letters,* J. M. Dent and Sons, Ltd., London, 1928

Narodny, Ivan, *The Art of Music,* vol. 10, National Society of Music, New York, 1916

Newman, Ernest, *A Musical Motley,* John Lane and Company, New York, 1919

Osgood, Henry O., *So This Is Jazz,* Little, Brown and Company, Boston, 1926

Otero, José, *Tratado de Bailes,* Tipografía de la Guia Oficial de Sevilla, Spain, 1912

Parker, D. C., *Georges Bizet*, Harper & Brothers, New York, 1926

Parry, Hubert H., *Studies of Great Composers,* George Routledge and Sons, London, 1894

Pedrell, Felipe, *Lírica Nacionalizada,* published by the Librería Paul Ollendorff, Paris, 1909

Piggott, Sir Francis, *Music and Musical Instruments of Japan,* Kelly and Walsh, Yokohama, 1909

Powell, Hickman, *The Last Paradise,* Jonathan Cape and Harrison Smith, Inc., New York, 1930

Propert, W. A., *The Russian Ballot in Western Europe, 1909-1920,* John Lane, London, 1921

Prunières, Henry, *Monteverdi,* J. M. Dent and Sons, Ltd., London and Toronto, 1926

Puccini, *Letters of Giacomo Puccini,* J. B. Lippincott Company, Philadelphia, 1931

Ragini, Sri, *Hindu Dancing,* Hari G. Govil, Inc., New York, 1928

Rahamin, Atiya Begum Fyzee, *The Music of India,* Luzac and Company, London, 1925

Rameau, Pierre, *The Dancing Master,* in Henry E. Huntington Library Collection

Rameau, Jean Phillippe, *Treatise on Harmony,* in Henry E. Huntington Collection

Rawlinson, George, *History of Ancient Egypt,* A. L. Burt, New York, 1876

Ribera, Julian, *Music in Ancient Arabia and Spain* (*La Música de las Cantigas*)—see this listed under *Hague, Eleanor.*

Riesemann, Oskar, *Moussorgsky,* Alfred A. Knopf, New York, 1929

Riesemann, Oskar, *Rachmaninoff's Recollections,* George Allen and Unwin, Ltd., London, 1934

Rimsky-Korsakow, *My Musical Life,* Tudor Publishing Company, New York, 1935

Roberts, *Ancient Hawaiian Music,* published by the Museum in Honolulu, 1926

Rockstro, *General History of Music,* Sampson Low, Marston and Company, London, 1886

Rosenfeld, Paul, *An Hour with American Music,* J. B. Lippincott Company, Philadelphia, 1929

Rosenthal, Ethel, *The Story of Indian Music and Its Instruments,* William Reeves, London, 1929

Saint-Saëns, Camille, *Outspoken Essays on Music,* E. P. Dutton and
    Company, New York, 1922
Saint-Saëns, Camille, *Musical Memories,* Small, Maynard and Com-
    pany, Boston, 1919
Saminsky, Lazare, *Music of the Ghetto and the Bible,* Bloch Publish-
    ing Company, New York, 1934
Schauffler, Robert Haven, *The Unknown Brahms,* Dodd, Mead and
    Company, New York, 1934
Schumann, Robert, *Music and Musicians, second series,* Reeves, London,
    1876-1880
Scott, Cyril, *Influence of Music on History and Morals,* Theosophical
    Publishing House, Ltd., London, 1927
Seabrook, William, *Jungle Ways,* Harcourt, Brace and Company,
    New York, 1931
Searchinger, César, *The Art of Music,* vol. 9, National Society of Music,
    New York, 1916
Selden, Elizabeth, *The Dancer's Quest,* University of California Press,
    Berkeley, California, 1935
Sharp, Cecil, *The Dance, an Historical Survey of Dancing in Europe*
    (in collaboration with A. P. Oppé), H. and T. Smith Ltd., London,
    1924
Sharp, Cecil, *English Folksong, Some Conclusions,* Simpkin and Com-
    pany, Ltd., London, 1907
Shaw, Bernard, *Music in London 1890-94* (three volumes), R. and R.
    Clark, Edinburgh, 1932
Smyth, Ethel, *Beecham and Pharaoh,* Chapman and Hall, Ltd., Lon-
    don, 1935
Solvay, Lucien, *La Musique,* Van Oest, Brussels, 1922
Stanford, Sir Charles Villiers, *Pages from an Unwritten Diary,* Edward
    Arnold, London, 1914
Stewart, Virginia, *Modern Dance,* published in the United States in
    1935
Stier, Theodore, *With Pavlowa around the World,* Hurst and Blackett,
    Ltd., Great Britain
Stokes, Adrian, *Tonight the Ballet,* E. P. Dutton & Co., Inc., New
    York, 1935
Strauss, Richard and Hugo von Hofmannsthal, *Correspondence,* Alfred
    A. Knopf, New York, 1936
Stravinsky, Igor, *An Autobiography,* Simon and Schuster, New York,
    1936

Sullivan, Herbert and Newman Flower, *Sir Arthur Sullivan, His Life, Letters and Diaries,* George H. Doran Company, New York, 1927

Sunaga, Katsumi, *Japanese Music,* The Board of Tourist Industry, Japan Government Railways, 1936

Thayer, *Life of Beethoven,* The Beethoven Association, New York, 1921

Toye, Francis, *Giuseppe Verdi,* Alfred A. Knopf, New York, 1931

Travaglia, Silvio, *Riccardo Drigo, l'Uomo e l'Artista,* Guglielmo Zanibon, Padua, 1928

Trend, J. B., *Alfonso the Sage and Other Spanish Essays,* Houghton Mifflin and Company, Boston, 1926

Trend, J. B., *Music of Spanish History to 1600,* Milford, London, 1926

Trend, J. B., *Manuel de Falla and Spanish Music,* Alfred A. Knopf, New York, 1929

Tschaikowsky, *Life and Letters of Peter Ilyich Tschaikowsky,* John Lane and Company, London, 1906

Tucker, Dr. A. N., *Tribal Music and Dancing in the Southern Sudan,* William Reeves, London

Upton, George P., *The Standard Symphonies,* A. C. McClurg Company, Chicago, 1911

Urlin, *Dancing, Ancient and Modern,* Simpkin, Marshall, Hamilton, Kent and Company, London

von Bülow, *Letters of Hans von Bülow,* D. Appleton and Company, New York, 1896

Vaughan-Williams, Ralph, *National Music,* Oxford University Press, London, 1934

Wagner, Richard, *Letters,* Scribner and Welford, New York, 1890

Wagner, Richard, *My Life,* Dodd, Mead and Company, New York, 1929

Wallaschek, *Primitive Music,* Longmans, Green and Company, London and New York, 1893

Walker, Conway, *Folksong and Dance,* vol. 2 of Fundamentals of Musical Art, Caxton Inst., Inc., New York, 1926-1928

Weighall, Arthur, *Sappho of Lesbos,* Butterworth, London, 1932

White, Eric Walter, *Stravinsky's Sacrifice to Apollo,* Leonard and Virginia Woolf, The Hogarth Press, London, 1930

Whiteman, Paul, *Jazz,* J. H. Sears and Company, Inc., New York, 1926

Williams, W. S. Gwynn, *Welsh National Music and Dance,* J. Curwen and Sons, Ltd., London, 1932

C. MUSICAL EXAMPLES

CHAPTER 1. Dance-melody of the Urobai and Timminni people in Africa, as sung by Prince Modupe.

CHAPTER 2. Ex. a. Ancient oriental melody danced today by Benjamin Zemach.

Ex. b. Samisen prelude to the Japanese dance, *Kappore.*

CHAPTER 3. *Ad Mortem Festinamus,* the medieval Dance of Death music, as quoted by one writer, although another has quoted an almost identical melody as an early Carol with a dance rhythm.

CHAPTER 4. *A Halling,* one of the Norse Folkdance tunes harmonized by Halfdan Kjerulf.

CHAPTER 5. Ex. a. An example of the regular-rhythmed music common to early ballets. This is the Cracovienne as danced in the ballet *La Gypsy* by Fanny Elssler.

Ex. b. Excerpt from the ballet *Les Deux Pigeons* by André Messager.

All'tto ben moderato.

CHAPTER 6. The Ball Scene in Mozart's *Don Giovanni*, with its simultaneous Minuet and Country Dance.

CHAPTER 7. Monteverdi's Entrée for the *Ballo del Ingrate* (as quoted by Prunières). Most of the dances in the ballet were done to this same theme, with its rhythm slightly altered in each instance.

CHAPTER 8. Dance of the Reed Pipes, from Tschaikowsky's *Nutcracker* Ballet.

CHAPTER 9. Ex. a. Gigue from Bach's *Second English Suite* (classic).

Ex. b. Gigue from Ernst von Dohnanyi's contemporary *Suite in the Olden Style,* published by N. Simrock, Leipzig. Note the composer's subtlety in conveying the modern idiom, while adhering strictly to the form of the classicists. (Reprinted by permission of Associated Music Publishers, Inc., American representatives.)

CHAPTER 10.   Minuet from Mozart's *Jupiter Symphony,* no. 551 in A Major.

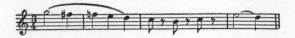

CHAPTER 11.   Two ways of writing choreographic music into modern operas.

Ex. a. Opening of the third act of Wagner's *Flying Dutchman,* when the sailors sing and dance on the deck of their ship.

Ex. b. The Seguidilla sung by *Carmen* in Bizet's opera, both melody and accompaniment typical of the Spanish dance that the song represents.

CHAPTER 12.   Chabrier's notes on the heel rhythms of Spanish dancers, later utilized in his own creations are, in part, as follows (as quoted in the *Musical Quarterly*).

CHAPTER 13. Ex. a *Rigaudon* by Jean Philippe Rameau (1683-1764).

Ex. b. The same *Rigaudon*, as idealized by Godowsky in 1906 and published by Schlesinger in Berlin. It is no. 2 of Godowsky's Renaissance pieces.

CHAPTER 14. Ex. a. Schubert's Viennese Waltz as included in Liszt's *Soirée de Vienne*, no. 6.

Ex. b. The Viennese Waltz as Schumann wrote it into his *Papillons*, op. 2.

Ex. c. Waltz from Johann Strauss' *Die Fledermaus*, op. 367.

CHAPTER 15. Ex. a. Stravinsky's use of unusual rhythmic combinations in the fantastic music describing the capture of Ivan Tsarevitch in *L'Oiseau de Feu*, published by Chester in London, in 1920. (Reprinted by permission of the publisher.)

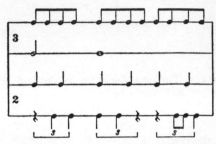

Ex. b. Stravinsky's famous polyharmonies in his *Petrouchka* (excerpt from the piano score).

CHAPTER 16. Vigorous Bacchanale theme from Glazounow's ballet, *The Seasons*, op. 67 (published by G. Schirmer in New York and reprinted by permission of the publisher and copyright owner).

CHAPTER 17: The Rhythmic Evolution of Jazz in America.

Ex. a. Typical American barn dance melodic rhythmic figure.

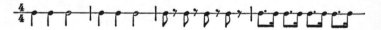

Ex. b. Schottische—1890.

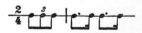

CHAPTER 17—*Continued*

Ex. c. Cakewalk—1899   or   in 1903.

Ex. d. American Polka in 1910, also designated as a two-step.

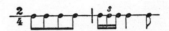

Ex. e. Mattchiche, danced to a two-step with a Spanish flavor.

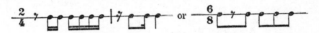

Ex. f. Ragtime two-step—1908   or   March and two-step in 1908.

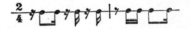

Ex. g. Slow Drag—1908.

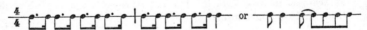

Ex. h. Rag—1911.

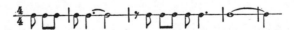

Ex. i. St. Louis Blues—1914.

Ex. j. Hesitation Waltz—1914.

CHAPTER 17—*Continued*

Ex. k. Two Fox Trots (1922 and 1926) with Jazz effects left to the players'
improvisation.

Ex. l. Fox Trot (1930) and comedy Fox Trot, similar to the old March and
Two-step rhythm as in Ex. f.

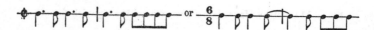

Ex. m. Charleston:

Ex. n. American Rumba.

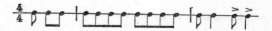

CHAPTER 18.   Ex. a. One form of the theme of Carpenter's *Skyscrapers,* published
by Schirmer in New York in 1926 and reprinted by permission of the publisher and copyright owner.

Ex. b. Negro scene in Carpenter's *Skyscrapers,* with melodic cadences reminiscent
of an ecstatic Spiritual. (Reprinted by permission of the publisher and copyright owner.)

CHAPTER 18—*Continued*

Ex. c. Flirtation scene from the ballet version of *Lenox Avenue* by William Grant Still. Reprinted here by permission of the publishers, J. Fischer and Bro.

Ex. c. Choral church scene from the ballet version of *Lenox Avenue* by William Grant Still. Reprinted here by permission of the publishers, J. Fischer and Bro. In this the composer has created an original Negro Spiritual of the rhythmic type, in contrast to the slower type used by John Alden Carpenter in *Skyscrapers.*

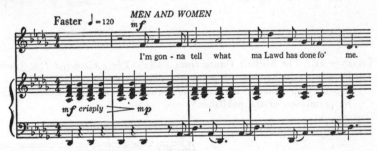

CHAPTER 19. Emerson Whithorne's unusual use of the "dance feeling" in his *Saturday's Child* scored for tenor, mezzo-soprano and chamber orchestra, on a series of poems by Countee Cullen. Reprinted by permission of the publisher, C. C. Birchard.

CHAPTER 20. Ex. a. The Scherzando theme appearing near the outset of Debussy's *Jeux*, to set the playful mood. (Copyright 1913—by permission Durand et Cie., Paris, and Elkan-Vogel Co., Inc., Philadelphia, Pa., copyright owners.)

Ex. b. Music immediately preceding the woman's dance without music in Satie's *Relâche*. (Copyright 1926—by permission Rouart, Lerolle et Cie., Paris, and Elkan-Vogel Co., Inc., Philadephia, Pa., copyright owners.)

CHAPTER 21. The Miller's Dance from Falla's *Three-Cornered Hat* (published by Chester in London) showing his effective use of Gypsy rhythms. This appears throughout his music, but is intensified in his ballet scores. (Reprinted by permission of the publisher.)

CHAPTER 23. Opening of a Fanfare from Lord Berners' *Triumph of Neptune,* published by Chester in London. (Reprinted by permission of the publisher.)

CHAPTER 26. A percussion accompaniment created by Henry Cowell for one of Hanya Holm's dances. (Reprinted by permission of the composer.)

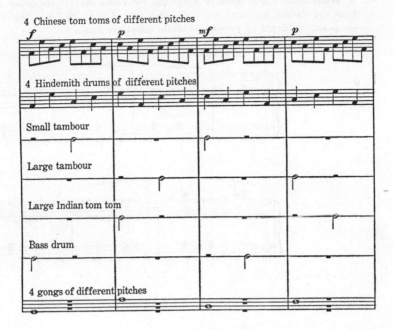

CHAPTER 27. Ex. a. The Nocturne from *Three Spanish Epigrams* by Verna Arvey, created simultaneously with the dance. (Printed by permission of the copyright owner.)

Chapter 27—*Continued*

Ex. b. Waltz from *Three Spanish Epigrams* by Verna Arvey, composed away from the dancer, but upon the basic idea agreed upon by both dancer and composer. (Printed by permission of the copyright owner.)

D. BALLET TERMS

Ballet Terms, as clarified by Eleanore Flaig

Arabesque—An attitude on one foot, with the free leg extended horizontally in back. The arabesque has a wide range of variations by reason of the different arm positions that distinguish it.

Attitude—Also an attitude on one foot, the free leg being lifted in back, but with a bent, open knee position. The arm corresponding to the free leg is in a high, circular position, while the other is extended at shoulder level. The two forms of the attitude are simple, and croisée, corresponding to the position of the body.

Plié—A flexing of the knees. The position preceding and following every jump.

Jeté—A jump to one foot, usually ending with the knees in an open position, as in the petit jeté. The jeté ouvert finishes in an arabesque; while in the tour jeté, sometimes called grand jeté, the dancer turns in the air while executing the jump.

Bourrée—A native of Auvergne, it has a great variety of forms. Its prototype was a Branle favored by the peasantry. The ballet so modified it that its original form is no longer recognizable. There is a bourrée in the form of a simple running step on toe, the bourrée crossing, bourrées executed in place, bourrées from side to side, and many others.

Rond de Jambe—A circle of the leg, ending in an extension to the side.

Battement—The battement family is large. The petit battement is a point on the floor, while the grand battement is a kick. Both may be done to front, side, back or in intermediate positions. The battement tendu is a grand battement which proceeds by degrees, rising higher by prolonged tension. Battement cloche is a movement of the leg, swinging forward and back from the hip, a pendulum-like action. Battement frappé is the small beat done on the ankle.

Sissonne—A jump from both feet to one, beginning in a closed position and ending in an open one, i.e., sometimes in arabesque with the supporting leg bent.

Pirouette—The union of the French words pied (foot) and rouet (wheel) describing the wheel-like movement, or turn, on one foot. It was highly developed among the Italians. There are many kinds of pirouette: inside and outside pirouettes, fouetté (whipped turns) and pirouettes in the air.

Renversé—A twisting movement which varies according to the type of composition being danced. In classic ballet, it is executed in an attitude position, during which the dancer turns backward, bringing the arms overhead at the same time. Its name means, literally, "upset."

Relevé—An abrupt rising to the toe or half-toe from a plié position, as opposed to the elevé, a gradual rising to the half-toe. The latter cannot be employed in rising to the toe-tips.

Changement de Pieds—Changing of the feet from one to the other, with a jump.

Port de Bras—A series of arm movements.

Supersole—A jerk, or a leap. A term differently understood among authorities. Ostensibly a step on one foot while the other is brushed into a forward position, after which the body is turned toward the opposite direction with a sudden movement. It may be done in the air or on the floor. Some authorities also use the term to designate any movement performed in the air.

Brisé—A beaten step executed by pointing one foot near the floor and, from a plié position, bringing the supporting leg to beat on the calf of the extended one.

Entrechat—A cross-caper, invented by the danseuse Camargo in 1730. The dancer jumps into the air and crosses the legs from the hip, the knees being straight. Among accomplished technicians, and particularly among male dancers, the crossings sometimes reach eight, and even ten.

Cabriole—A cousin of the brisé, but a much broader movement, and always ending in an open position, with the free leg rebounding upward after the beat.

Dégagé or *Dévelopé*—An unfolding of the leg from knee and hip joints. A slow movement.

Balancé—A step or jump to the side on one foot, while the free foot either points or steps into fourth position behind, sometimes taking the weight, while the front foot is lifted preparatory to resuming it.

Glissade or *Glissé*—A gliding step, often the step used to precede an arabesque or tour jeté.

Ménage—A term used to designate any series of steps executed in a circle.

Chassé—Also a gliding movement, widely used in such dances as the Mazurka. The dancer hops, or slides, on one foot, while bringing the free foot forward to alternate the movement. It has a skating quality.

Enchaînement—A choreographic sentence.

Assemblé—A jump in the air with a battement in second position, after which the feet end in the fifth position.

Pas de Chat—A cat-step, or jump in the air, with both knees open in a bent position.

Pas de Poisson—A fish-step, always preceded by an assemblé. The dancer jumps into the air with both legs together, curving the body backward, the arms being overhead in a circle. The position is sustained in the air as long as possible.

Pas de Basque—A Basque step. The classical variety begins in fifth position, passes into second, thence into fourth forward, while the back foot closes in the opposite fifth position.

Déboulé or *Tour de Force*—A series of single outside turns on one foot.

Croisé—The arms and feet used in opposition.

Balloné—Frequently used in character dancing, but also used by the classicists. The dancer jumps into the air with a battement in second position and finishes with the supporting leg bent and the free foot at the ankle.

Coupé—The cutting of the foot from an open position to a closed position, sometimes taking the weight.

E. MISCELLANEOUS DANCE MUSIC

This includes only music not mentioned in the preceding text, and no apology is made for the fact that the list is incomplete, since it is as impossible to make a complete list of all music available for dancing as to catalogue all the music ever written.

This is offered merely as a suggestion to those dancers and teachers who wish to enlarge their musical repertoire.

BALLETS AND BALLET-OPERAS

Auber . . . . *Le Dieu et la Bayadère,* 1830
Aubert . . . . *La Momie*
                                            Chrysothémis
Borowski, Felix . . . . *Boudour,* an oriental ballet
                                            Pierrot in Arcady
Becker, John J. . . . . *Dance-Figuer,* duo-drama for singer
                                            and dancer
Berckman, Evelyn . . . . *From the Odyssey*
Bucharoff . . . . *Sakarah*
Carter, Ernest . . . . *Namba* or *The Third Statue*
Crist, Bainbridge . . . . *Le Pied de la Momie*
                                            Pregiwa's Marriage, a Javanese ballet
                                            The Sorceress, on a Hindu legend
Cutler, Murray . . . . *The Snow Queen*
Carter, Elliott . . . . *Pocahontas*
Casadesus . . . . *Esterelle*
Casavola, F. . . . . *L'Alba di Don Giovanni*
                                            Castello Nel Bosco
Ducasse, Roger . . . . *Orphée*
Delannoy, Marcel . . . . *Le Fou de la Dame*
Fairchild, Blair . . . . *Dame Libellule*
Farwell, Arthur . . . . *The Grail Song*
Freed, Isidore . . . . *Vibrations*
Guiraud, Ernest . . . . *Gretna Green,* 1872
Gaubert . . . . *Philotis, Danseuse de Corinth,* 1914
Ganne, Louis . . . . *The Princess at the Witches' Revels*
Gerhard, Ariel . . . . *Ariel*

Hess, Ludvig ....*Abu und Nu*
Hammond, Richard ....*Fiesta*
Carnival
Hill, Edward Burlingame ......*Pan and the Star,* the end of the mythological age
Hue, Georges ....*Siang-Sin,* 1924
Huré, Jean ....*Au Bois Sacre*
James, Philip ....*Judith,* ballet for narrator and chamber orchestra
Konstantinoff ....*Port Said*
Lully ....*Fêtes de Bacchus et de l'Amour,* 1677
Lahusen ....*Wedding of the Shepherds and the Wood*
Loder, James ....*The Night Dancers*
Monsigny ....*Aline, Reine de Golconda,* 1766, Paris
Mirande, Hippolyte ....*Une Fête Directoire,* 1895
Maganini, Quinto ....*Even Hours*
Mattfield, Julius ....*Virgins of the Sun,* on a Peruvian legend
Mathé ....*Mallika,* 1911
Menier ....*Djali,* 1913
Monti, V. ....*The Birth of Pierrot*
Nielsen ....*Lackschmi*
Nogués, Jean ....*Narkissa,* on an Egyptian tale *La Danseuse de Pompeii*
Perrot ....*Catarina, ou la Fille du Bandit,* 1846
Porter, Cole ....*Within the Quota,* 1923, Paris
Pougin ....*Les Princesses de Rana,* 1913
Polignac, Armande ....*Les Mille et Une Nuits,* 1914 *La Source Lointaine,* 1912
Rosenthal, Manuel ....*Un Baiser pour Rien*
Reger, Ernest ....*Sacountala,* 1858, oriental in character
Rousseau, Samuel ....*Le Hulla,* 1923
Reiter, Joseph ....*Der Totentanz,* 1906, the medieval dance of death
Sommers, Hans ....*Rübezahl* (wherein German peasants dance madly to magic pipes)
Sommi, Guido ....*The Chinese Screen*
Swift, Kay ....*Alma Mater*

Tweedy, Donald Nicholas ......*Alice in Wonderland*
Tomasi ....*La Rosière de Village*
Thomas, Ambroise ....*La Tempête,* 1889
Urgel, Louis ....*Le Loup et l'Agneau,* 1921
Venth, Carl ....*Pan in America*
Wormser, André ....*L'Enfant Prodigue,* modernizing the
     Biblical tale
Zuelli, Guglielmo ....*Mokanna,* on the Lalla Rookh theme
Zador, Eugene ....*The Machine Man*

MISCELLANEOUS

Arnold, Maurice ....an orchestral *Plantation Dance*
Achron, Joseph ....*Hebrew Dance* for violin and piano
     or orchestra
     Dance Improvisation for violin and
     piano or orchestra
     Scher (Dance) for violin and piano
     or clarinet and orchestra
     Dance from the orchestral music to
     The Fiddle's Soul
     Salome's Dance for vocal orchestra,
     piano and percussion
     Dance Overture for orchestra
     Little Dance Fantasy for orchestra
     Dance of the Tsadikim for orchestra
     First and Second *Suites in the Olden
     Style* for violin and piano
     Stempenyu Suite for violin and piano
Arensky, Anton ....Dances in *Suite III,* op. 33
Aulin, Tor ....*Three Gottland Dances* for orchestra
     op. 28
     Four Swedish Dances for orchestra
     op. 32
Arends, H. ....*Salammbó,* an orchestral ballet suite
Alimento, Feodor Stepanovitch ..*Orchestral Ballet Suite*
Atterberg, Kurt ....*Barocco,* a dance suite for small or-
     chestra

Auber . . . . Guarache, Bolero and Tarantella in the opera *La Muta de Portici*
Tarantella in the opera *Fra Diavolo*
A Negro Dance in the Louisiana act of the opera *Manon*
Old Spanish Bolero in the opera *Masaniello*
Cachucha in the opera *Le Domino Noir*

Alfano, Franco . . . . Dances in the opera *Sakuntala*

Aerov . . . . Dances in the opera *Judith*

Abert, Joseph . . . . Oriental dances in the opera *Die Almohaden*

Alexandroff, Anatol Nicolaevitch . *Classic Suite* for Orchestra, op. 33

Bordier, Jules . . . . *Habanera* for flute and chamber orchestra

Bartok, Bela . . . . *Rhapsodies I and II* for violin and orchestra, with dance parts

Bull, John . . . . *Dr. Bull's Myselfe,* Gigge for harpsichord

Boccherini . . . . *Minuets* in E Flat Major and D Major

Bliss, Arthur . . . . *Purcell Suite,* containing Hornpipe and Minuet

Beon, Alexandre . . . . *Suite Louis XV* for string orchestra

Bizet, Georges . . . . Dances in incidental music to Daudet's play *L'Arlesienne*

Boyce, William . . . . Dance movements in sonatas (18th century) later scored for strings and piano by James Brown

Bossi, Marco Enrico . . . . *Siciliana e Giga* for orchestra, op. 73

Balfour, Henry . . . . *Shepherd Fennel's Dance* for orchestra

Bauer, Marion . . . . *Dance Sonata,* for chamber orchestra

Branscombe, Gena . . . . *The Dancer of Fjaard* for women's voices and chamber orchestra

Burleigh, Cecil . . . . *The Village Dance* for chamber orchestra

Bloch, Ernest . . . . Rustic Dance in the quarter, *In the Mountains*

Bloch, Ernest .... Pastorale and Rustic Dance (Movt.
                                III) in the *Concerto Grosso* for
                                piano and strings
Bridges, Frank .... *Dance Rhapsody* for orchestra
Busoni .... *Song of the Spirits' Dance* for or-
                                chestra, from the second book of
                                his op. 47 (Indian Diary) com-
                                posed in 1915
                                Danza alla Turca in the opera
                                Turandot
                                Garden Festival and Sarabande in the
                                opera *Doktor Faustus*
                                Ghostly Midnight Dances in the opera
                                Die Brautwahl
Braunfels, Walter .... Bohemian and Spanish dances in the
                                opera *Don Giles of the Green
                                Breeches* and
                                Turtledove Wedding Scene in the
                                opera *The Birds*
Blaramberg, Paul .... Greek dances in the opera *Volna*
Bruneau .... Legend of the Gold, a ballet in the
                                opera *Messidor*
Bittner, Julius .... Dionysiac Ballet and Waltz in the
                                opera *Kohlheimer's Widow*
                                Dances from Austria for orchestra
Boero, Felipe .... Argentine folk dances in the opera
                                Raquela
Bretón, Tomás .... Aragonese Jota in the opera *La
                                Dolores*
Blecht, Leo .... Waltz in the opera *Versiegelt*
Boito .... Dances in the opera *Mefistofele*
Berners, Lord .... *Valses Bourgeoises* for four hands on
                                the piano
                                "Valse Sentimentale" and "Cossack
                                Dance" in his *Three Orchestral
                                Pieces*
                                "Fandango" and "Pasodoble" in his
                                Fantasie Espagnole
Behm .... A Masked Ball in the opera *Der
                                Schelm von Bergen*

Caplet, André Simon . . . . Dance of the Little Negroes, the third
episode in *Epiphanie*, a fresco for
'cello and orchestra

Coleridge-Taylor, Samuel . . . . . . *Three-Fours*
Four Characteristic Waltzes for or-
chestra op. 22
Hemo Dance-Scherzo op. 47 no. 2 for
orchestra
Scenes from an Imaginary Ballet
Dance in F Sharp for violin
Moorish Dance for piano
Four Danses Nègres
Minuet in G
Dance in G for string quartet
Dances in the incidental music to
Stephen Phillipps' *Nero*, to *Othello*
and to *Herod*, as well as to Phil-
lipps' *Faust*

Chausson, Ernest . . . . "Air de Danse" and "Danse Rustique" in incidental music to
Shakespeare's *Tempest*

Carse, Adam . . . . *The Merry Milkmaids* for orchestra,
on an old English dance tune
Three Dances for string orchestra:
Dainty Dance, Languid Dance,
Waltz
"Northern Dance" in the *Two
Sketches for string orchestra*
The Nursery, an orchestral dance
fantasy

Caldara, Antonio . . . . *Suonata da Camera* for two violins
and piano (17th century)

Corelli, Arcangelo . . . . *Gavotta*, of the 17th century

Cowen, Sir Frederick . . . . *Two sets of Four English Dances in
the olden style* for orchestra

Chabrier . . . . Rustic Dance and Waltz in the *Pastoral Suite*
Bourrée Fantasque, originally for
piano

Chabrier .... *Habanera* for orchestra
                            Danse Slav
Cadman, Charles Wakefield .... Ballet of Poison Elementals in the
                            opera *The Garden of Mystery*
                            Dark Dancers of the Mardi Gras for
                            orchestra
                            Indian Tribal Dances in the opera
                            Shanewis
Carpenter, John Alden .... *Danza* for orchestra
Casella, Alfredo .... *Suite, to Jean Huré* op. 13 for orches-
                            tra, with dances
                            Minuetto in *Scarlatianna* for piano
                            and orchestra
                            Passacaglia in *Partita* for piano and
                            orchestra
                            Two dance movements in the *Sere-
                            nata* in the olden style
                            Valse Diatonique
Crist, Bainbridge .... *Vienna,* for orchestra
                            Chinese Dance for orchestra
                            Nautch Dance for orchestra
                            Arabian Dance for orchestra
Cole, Rossetter Gleason .... Dances in the opera *The Maypole
                            Lovers*
Casadesus .... Dances in the folk style in the opera
                            La Chanson de Paris
Cilea .... Dances in the opera *Adriana Le-
                            couvreur*
                            Saltarello in the opera *Tilda*
Coronaro, Gellio .... Dances in the opera *Festa a Marina*
Clapisson .... Bamboula in the opera *Le Code Noir*
Chvala, Emanuel .... *Sousedski,* folk dances in chamber
                            style
Claassen, Arthur .... *Sansouci* for strings, a Minuet on a
                            theme by Quantz
Cowell, Henry .... *The Irishman Dances*
                            Reel, for orchestra
Chaminade .... *Danse Créole* for piano, op. 94
Coppola, Piero .... *Deux Danses Symphoniques: Haba-
                            nera and Blues*

Conus, George E. . . . . *Carmagnole,* song and dance of the
French Revolution, for orchestra
Chavarri, Eduardo L. . . . . Dance in the *Acuarelas Valencianas*
for strings
Caturla, Alejandro García . . . . . . *Three Cuban Dances* for orchestra
Bembé, an orchestral Afro-Cuban
movement
Dances in the *Primera Suite Cubana*
for wind instruments and piano
d'Indy, Vincent . . . . Rustic Waltz in the *Wallenstein
Trilogy* op. 12 for orchestra
Sarabande and Menuet in the *Suite*
op. 24 for trumpet, two flutes and
string quartet
Songs and Dances for wind instru-
ments op. 50
"Danses Rhythmiques" in *Poème des
Montagnes*
Ducasse, Roger . . . . *Prélude d'un Ballet,* for orchestra
Bourrée and Menuet in the orchestral
French Suite
Dubensky, Arcady . . . . *Passacaglia* for violin and 'cello
Dvorak . . . . "Polka" in the *Pianoforte Trio* op.
21
Mazurek in E Minor op. 49 for vio-
lin and orchestra
Dances in the orchestral *Suite in D
Major* op. 39
Delamarter, Eric . . . . *The Dance of Life,* suite for ballet
Delius . . . . *Tanz for Harpsichord*
Mazurka and Waltz in *Five Little
Piano Pieces*
Dances in the opera *Koanga*
Debussy . . . . "Cortége" and "Air de Danse" from
the cantata *L'Enfant Prodigue*
Gigues in the orchestral *Images*
"Danseuses de Delphes" in the *First
Book of Préludes*
"La Danse de Puck" in the *First
Book of Préludes*

Debussy ....*Danse Sacrée et Danse Profane* for chromatic harp and strings

Dance on the Burning Brazier in the opera *Le Martyr de Saint-Sébastien*

Dohnanyi ....*Pavane mit Variationen* for piano

Dopper ....*Gothic Chaconne*

Dupont, Gabriel ....Arabian Ballet in the opera *Antar*

Spanish Folk dance in the opera *La Cabrera*

de Beriot, Charles ....*Scène de Ballet*

de Manen, J. ....Dances in the opera *Acté*

David ....Dances in the opera *Herculanéum*

d'Albert, Eugen ....Dutch folk dance themes in the opera *Mareike von Nynwegen*

Minuet and Tyrolean Waltz in the opera *Flauto Solo*

Dances in the *Aschenputtle Suite* (Cinderella) for orchestra, op. 33

d'Ambrosio..................Tarantella in *Four Pieces for Orchestra* op. 3

Gavotte-Musette and Waltz in *Scattered Leaves* for orchestra, op. 33

Dutréze, Jean ....*Air à Danser* for string orchestra with flute and clarinet

Dunhill, Thomas ....*Sailor Dance* for string orchestra op. 46 no. 2

Dance in the *Chiddingfold Suite* for strings

Dalcroze, Emil Jaques- ....*Seven Dances for Strings* (Quartet or Orchestra)

de Greef, Arthur ....*Menuet Varié* for piano and strings

Diaz, E. ....A Jail Ballet in the opera *Benvenuto Cellini*

Deffés.....................Dances in the opera *Jessica*

de Leone, F. B. ....Choral Ballet in the opera *Alglala*

Eyman, Henry ....*Air à Danser* for string orchestra

Erlebach, Philipp Heinrich .....Six Overtures for string orchestra (Similar to the dance suites of his contemporaries in the 17th century)

Eppert, Carl .... *The Awakening,* a symphonic Waltz Suite

Eilenberg, Richard .... *May I have the Pleasure of This Waltz* for strings, op. 143

Enesco, Georges .... *Three Dances,* for orchestra

Elgar, Sir Edward .... Dances in the incidental music to the child's play, *The Wand of Youth* Nautch Dance and Menuetto in *The Crown of India,* an orchestral suite op. 66

Franchetti, Alberto .... Indian Ballet in the opera *Cristoforo Colombo* Dances in the opera *Giove a Pompeii*

Foerster, Joseph Bohuslav ...... Ballet of Angels in the opera *Bloud*

Franck, Maurice .... *Suite à Danser* for orchestra in five movements

Franck, Cesar .... *Danse Lente*

Farwell, Arthur .... *Dance of Idleness* and *Rustic Dance* for seventeen instruments *Navajo War Dance* for sixteen instruments

Fuentes, Laureano .... *Two Cuban Dances* for orchestra *Gavotte* for orchestra

Fux, Johann Joseph .... *Overture Suite* for Students' String Orchestra of olden dance tunes (Seventeenth Century)

Foster, Arnold .... *Suite on English Folk Airs* (dance tunes) for strings

Fletcher, Percy E. .... *Folk Tunes and Fiddle Dance,* a suite for strings

Forchheim, Johann Wilhelm .... *Dance Suite* for five strings (17th century)

Förster, Cristoph .... Dances in the *Suite for Strings* (17th century)

Friedman, Ignace .... *Les Révérences,* a Minuet for strings

Fraser, Norman .... *Chilean Dances,* for orchestra

Fibich, Zdenko .... Waltz in the *Bagatelles* for strings, op. 10

Forni, Oreste .... *Valse des Chasseurs* for strings

Fairchild, Blair .... *Twelve Indian Songs and Dances*

Guiraud, Ernest ....*Danse Persane* for orchestra

Grosz, Wilhelm ....*Symphonischer Tanz* op. 24, a piano concerto

Godard ....Danse Rustique in *En Plain Air,* a suite op. 145 for violin and orchestra

Gatty, Nicholas Comyn ....*Haslemere Suite* for strings, containing dances

Giorni, Aurelio ....*Minuet* for orchestra

Gniessen, Michael ....*Danses Funèbres* for orchestra

German, Edward ....Four characteristic dances in the orchestral *Gypsy Suite*

Gossec ....*Gavotte*
Tambourins in D and F Major

Guarnieri, Antonio de ....*Habanera* in his orchestral impressions of Spain

Glinka ....*Minuett und Trio* in Quartet in F Major
Valse Fantaisie for orchestra

Grainger, Percy ....*English Dance* for orchestra and organ
Green Bushes, a Passacaglia for chamber ensemble
Handel in the Strand, clog dance for piano and strings
Spoon River for orchestra and piano
The Warriors, imaginary ballet for orchestra and 3 pianos

Gruenberg, Louis ....Orchestral *Music to an Imaginary Ballet*
Waltz, op. 25 no. 3

Glazounow ....*Valse de Concert* op. 47 for orchestra
Orchestral *Dance of Salome* to Wilde's drama
Three Dances in the *Suite Caractéristique* for orchestra op. 9
Dance of the Young Folk in *Vostochnaya Rapsodia* op. 29 for orchestra
Baletnaya Stsena (Ballet Scene) for orchestra op. 81

Glazounow .... *Grand Pas Espagnole* with dance rhythms

Goossens, Eugène .... *Rhythmic Dance* for orchestra
Three Greek Dances for orchestra
Clockwork Dance in *Kaleidoscope*
Dance Memories in *Four Conceits*

Gomez, Carlos .... Dances in the opera *Il Guarany*

Goldmark .... The Dance of the Bee in the opera *Queen of Sheba*
Dance of the Will-o'-the-Wisps in the opera *Merlin*
Dances in *A Winter's Tale*

Gerlach .... Tarantelle in the opera *Matteo Falcone*

Giordano, Umberto .... Waltz in the opera *Fedora*
Italian Minuet for piano

Guimet, Emile .... Dances in the opera *Tai-Tsoung*

Grovlez .... Dances in the opera *Nabuchodonozer*

Gaillard, M. F. .... Fandango in the opera *The Dance during the Banquet*

Graener, Paul .... Bacchanale in the opera *Byzanz*

Haarklou, Johannes .... *Springdans* for orchestra, op. 14 no 1

Holbrooke, Joseph .... Dance in the *Dreamland Suite* op. 38

Holst, Gustav .... Jig in the *St. Paul's Suite* for strings
Dances in the oriental *Beni Mora Suite*
Dances in the orchestral *Suite de Ballet* op. 10
Dances in the opera, *The Perfect Fool*

Halévy .... Dances in the opera *La Juive*
Bee Ballet in the opera *Le Juif Errant*
Tropical Ballet in the opera *Jaguarita l'Indienne*

Halvorsen, Johann .... Dances in the incidental music to a gnome play, *Fossegrimen*
Bacchanals in the incidental music to an old Indian play, *Vasantasena*
Ancient Suite in Memory of Holberg for orchestra op. 31

Ilyinsky .... "Dance of Gnomes" in the *Nour and Anitra Suite*

Ippolitov-Ivanov .... Lesghinka, a dance in *Iverija,* the second series of *Caucasian Sketches*

Jongen, Joseph .... *Prélude et Danse* for orchestra

Jacob, Gordon .... Dance movements in the *Denbigh Suite* for string orchestra

Josten, Werner .... Dance, in the *Serenade*

Joucieres, Victorin de .... Dances in the opera *Dimitri*

Jacobi, Frederick .... *Orchestral suite of Indian Dances*

Kullman .... Alsatian folk dances in the opera *Satan Overcome*

Korestchenko, Arseny .... Dances in the *Armenian Suite* for orchestra

Karel, Rudolf .... *Slavic Dance Tunes* for orchestra

Knipper, Lev .... *Symphonic Suite* based on folk songs and dances of Turkestan
Dances (The Man's Lament and The God's Dance) in the orchestral suite: *Stories of a Plaster God*

King, Arnold .... *Five Romanesque Dances* for orchestra

Kodály, Zoltán .... *Dances of Marosszék* for orchestra

Konjovic, Peter .... Jugoslav Folk Dances in the opera *Koshtana*

Kienzl, Wilhelm .... Lanner Waltz in the opera *Der Evangelimann*
Classic Minuet in the opera *Der Kuhreigen*
Tanzfest, three suites for orchestra

Krieger, Johann Philipp .... Dances in the *Lustige Feldmusic* for small instrumental ensemble (17th century)

Klaas, Julius .... *From Gallant Times,* a dance suite for chamber orchestra op. 10

Kaiser, Alfred .... Breton Folk Dances in the opera *Stella Maris*

Laparra, Raoul .... *Four Basque Dances* for orchestra

Liadov .... *Dance of the Amazons*
I Danced with a Mosquito

476 CHOREOGRAPHIC MUSIC

Mazellier, J. ....Neapolitan Saltarello in the opera
    Graziella

Massé, Victor ....Bamboula and Minuet in the opera
    Paul et Virginie

Milhul ....Old Spanish Bolero in the opera *Les*
    Deux Avenglis

Mule, Giuseppe ....Dances in the opera *Dafni*
    Satirical Dances for orchestra
    Dance pieces in his incidental music
    for old Greek dramas

Merikante, Aarre ....*Dance Suite* for orchestra

Moskowski ....Malaguena and Scherzo-Valse in the
    opera *Boabdil*

Marschner, Heinrich ....Village Dances in the opera *Der*
    Vampir

Mattausch, Albert ....Choral Ballet in the opera *Esther*

Mercadante ....Sacred Dances in the opera *La*
    Vestale

Medtner, Nicolai ....*Dances and Dithyrambs,* for piano

Moussorgsky ....Dance in *Pictures at an Exhibition*
    Ensign's Polka for piano
    Menuet Monstre (now lost)

Mraczek, Karl ....Slavic Dances for orchestra

Mascagni, Pietro ....*La Gavotta delle Bambole*

MacDowell ....*Witches' Dance*
    Rigaudon

McPhee, Colin ....*Sarabande* for orchestra

Massenet ....*Gavotte Royal*
    Dances in the following orchestral
    works: *Scènes Hongroises, Scènes*
    Pittoresques, Scènes Napolitaines,
    Scènes de Féerie

Maganini, Quinto ....*La Rumba,* a Cuban rhapsody for
    orchestra

Martucci, Giuseppe ....Tempo di Gavotta and Giga in the
    four *Piccoli Pezzi* for orchestra

Malipiero ....Tarantella in Capri and Rustic Fes-
    tival in the *Impressioni dal Vero*

Nachèz, Tivadar ....*Danses Tziganes* for violin and or-
    chestra op. 14

Prokofieff ....Dance in the orchestral *Egyptian Nights*

Paganini ....*Le Stregghe,* a witches' dance for violin and orchestra op. 8

Palester, Roman ....*Danse d'Osmoloda* for orchestra

Parry, Sir Hubert ....*Lady Radnor's Suite* in F, for strings *English Suite* for strings

Pachelbel, Johann ....Dances in the *Partie in G Major* for five strings and thorough bass (Seventeenth Century)

Paderewski ....*Fantaisie-Polonaise* for piano and orchestra op. 19

Powell, John ....*Natchez on the Hill,* three Virginia country dances

Puccini, Giacomo ....*Minuet* in A Major

Pierné ....*Farandole* for small orchestra op. 14 no. 2

Praus, Arnost ....Slavic Dance in *The Linden Tree* for voice and small orchestra

Penerl, Paul ....Padouan, Intrada, Dantz and Galliarda in the five Variationensuiten and two Canzonen for strings (Seventeenth Century)

Pezel, Johann ....*Delitae Musicales oder Lust-Music* from which a dance suite was made for strings and piano (Seventeenth Century)

Pizzetti, Ildebrando ....Gagliarda e Finale in the *Concerto dell'Estate* *Rondo Veneziano* *Dance Movement for Trio*

Riegger, Wallingford ....*American Polonaise*

Röntgen, Julius ....*Old Netherland Dances* for orchestra op. 46

Roldan, Amadeo ....*Danza Negra,* poem for voice and seven instruments

Rogers, Bernard ....*Three Japanese Dances* for orchestra; Dance with Pennons, Mourning Dance, Dance with Swords

Reznicek .... Tanzsymphonie

Dances in the opera *Holofernes*

Rosenmüller, Johann .... *Studenten Music* for strings and piano
(Seventeenth Century)

Ravel .... *Pantoum,* an Eastern dance

Passacaille in the Trio in a Minor

Rhapsody Espagnole (including the
Habanera written for 2 pianos in
1895)

Mout de Menuet in the Sonatine for
piano

Raff .... *Cachoucha Caprice* op. 79

Two Minuets and Gavotte in the
Suite in E Flat Major for piano
and strings op. 200

Dances in the orchestral *From Thuringia* suite

Dance movements in the *Suite for
violin and orchestra* op. 180

Dance of the Dryads in *Im Walde,*
symphony no. 3 in F Major op. 153

Rathaus, Karl .... *Tanzsuite* for orchestra

Rubinstein, Anton .... Andalusian dance rhythms in *Bal
Costumé*

Waltz Caprice

Polonaise and Waltz de Concert in
Le Bal for piano, op. 14

German Waltz op. 82 no. 5

Boheme Polka op. 82 no. 7

Trepak

Le Menuet

Valse

Cracovienne

Roussel, Albert .... Sarabande and Gigue in the *Suite in
F Major* op. 33 for orchestra

Reutter, Herman .... *Tanzsuite* for piano op. 29

Rameau .... Dance movements in nos. 2, 3, 4 and
6 of the *Six Concerts en Sextuor*
for strings

Respighi .... *Balletto* for piano
Ballata delle Gnomidi (Dance-Song of the Gnomes)

Reinecke, Carl .... *Old and New Dances* for piano, op. 228
Dances in the opera *Princess Glückskind*
Dances in the opera *King Manfred*

Reger, Max .... *Bacchanals,* one of the four tone poems for orchestra op. 128

Rebikov .... Three Dances in the second *Suite Miniature* for small orchestra
Harlequin's Dance and Dance of the Chinese Dolls in op. 21, a fairy play called *The Christmas Tree*
Hindustani Nautch, from op. 9 for piano
Waltz

Rodrigo, Joaquin .... *Distant Sarabande* for piano

Reinworth, R. .... *She Dances in Her Dream,* waltz for strings

Rachmaninoff .... *Waltz* in the second *Suite for two pianos,* op. 17

Randegger, Alberto .... Grotesque Contra Dance in the opera *Maria de Bréval*

Rocca, Ludovico .... Spectral Dance in the opera *Il Dibuk*

Stearns, Theodore .... Dances in the opera *Snowbird*
Dances in the opera *Atlantis*
Dances in the eurhythmic oratorio *Song of Solomon*

Silver, Charles .... Dances in the opera *Taming of the Shrew*

Schnittelbach, Nathaniel .... Five Dance Movements in the *Suite for strings and cémbalo,* (Seventeenth Century)

Scheiffelhut, Jakob .... Dances in the eight suites comprising *The Awakening of Spring* for strings and cembalo (Seventeenth Century)

Salzedo, Carlos . . . . Four dance movements in the *Concerto* for Harp and Seven Wind Instruments

Saint-George, George . . . . Six dance movements in the olden style in each of the two petite suites in D and G Major comprising *L'Ancien Régime* op. 60

Stanford, Sir Charles Villiers . . . Dance movements in the *Suite in D Major* for violin and orchestra op. 32
Suite of Ancient Dances op. 58
Irish Jigs in opera *Shamus O'Brien*

Spohr . . . . Portuguese Military Polonaise in the opera *Jessonda*
Ballet "Witches' Sabbath" in the opera *Faust*

Sanchez-Fuentes, Eduardo . . . . . . Danza Epitalamica (Sacred Indian Tribal Rites) in the opera *Doreya*

Spontini, Gasparo . . . . Dances in the opera *Ferdinando Cortez*

Schmidt, Franz . . . . Witch's Dance in the opera *Fredegundis*

Strauss, Oscar . . . . *Old Vienna Round Dance* for strings, op. 45

Strauss, Johann . . . . *Neue Pizzicato Polka* for strings op. 44

Samper, Balthasar . . . . *Danses Mallorquines* for strings and piano

Šebek, Gabriel . . . . *Bulgarian Dances* for orchestra op. 7

Scott, Cyril . . . . *Valse Caprice* op. 74 no. 7
Trois Danses Tristes
Danse Nègre
Three Dances for four hands on the piano
"Elephant Dance" in *Jungle Book Impressions*

Schillinger . . . . Dance music in that for the play, *Deeds of Hercules*

Schillinger .... Dance music in that for the Japanese
pantomime play op. 16, *Merry
Ghost*
Dance Suite for 'cello
Valse, for piano

Spendiarov .... *Valse de Concert* for orchestra
Danse Ancienne

Stoessel, Albert .... *Minuet Crinoline* for orchestra

Stringham, Edwin John .... *Danses Exotiques* for orchestra

Stenhammer, Wilhelm .... Old dance tunes in the orchestral
Midwinter op. 24 (This also calls
for a chorus)

Stcherbatcheff .... *Chœur Danse* for piano

Scriabine .... *Danse Languide*

Shostakovitch .... *Trois Danses Fantastiques* for piano

Salvayre, Gervais (1847-1916) .. *Air de Danse Variée* for strings

Satie, Erik .... *Danses Gothiques*
"Danse Cuirassée" in *Vieux Sequins
et Vielles Cuirasses*

Saint-Saëns .... *Sarabande et Rigaudon* for orchestra
op. 93
Dances in the *orchestral suite* op. 49
Étude en Forme de Waltz

Sibelius .... *Tanz-Intermezzo* for orchestra op.
45 no. 2
Pan und Echo an orchestral Dance-
Intermezzo op. 53
Polka in the *Suite Mignonne* in G
for strings and flute op. 98a
Dance in the *Suite Champêtre* op. 98b

Scharwenka .... *Two Polish Dances for orchestra,* op.
20
Polish Dance Tunes for piano duet,
op. 38

Slavenski, Josip .... *Jugoslav Song and Dance* for violin

Smetana .... *Bohemian Dances*

Strickland, Lily .... Oriental dances on native themes

Saminsky, Lazare .... *La Danse Amerique* for orchestra

Sanders, Robert I. .... Barn Dances for chamber orchestra
Skilton, Charles Sanford .... *Two Indian Dances* (Deer and War
  Dances) for orchestra
  Shawnee Indian Hunting Dances for
  orchestra
Sowerby, Leo .... *Passacaglia, Interlude and Fugue* for
  orchestra
Strauss, Richard .... *Dance Suite* for orchestra
Salmhofer, Franz .... Sarabande and Minuet in *Chamber
  Suite* op. 19 in C Major
Szeligowski, Tadenz .... Polish Dances in the orchestral suite
  Kaziuki
Shepherd, Arthur .... *Choreographic Suite* for orchestra
Shreker, Franz .... Orchestral Dance Suite
Sarasate .... *Muneira* with variations for violin
  and orchestra op. 32
  Peteneral, op. 35
  Jota de San Fermin, op. 36
  Danse Espagnole on a Zortzico
  theme by Joaquin Larregla op. 37
  Introduction et Caprice (Jota) op. 41
  Miramar (Zortzico) op. 42
  Introduction et Tarantelle op. 43
  Jota de Pamplona op. 50
  Jota de Pablo op. 52
Tiedemann .... *Tanzweisen* for strings, op. 1 and 2
Taneiev, Sergei .... Gavotte and Tarantella in *Konzert-
  Suite* for violin and orchestra op. 28
Tiessen, Hans .... "Totentanz Suite" for small orches-
  tra from his incidental music to
  Hauptmann's *The Poor Broom-
  Makers*
Telemann, George Philipp ..... German, Danish and Swedish Dances
  in the six suites for strings and
  piano (Seventeenth Century)
Tuma, Franz .... *Tanz Suite* in A Major for strings
  (Eighteenth Century)
Thomson, Virgil .... *Two Sentimental Tangos* for twenty
  five instruments
  Valse Gregoriane

White, Paul .... Hippo Dance and Mosquito Dance in the *Five Miniatures* for piano or for orchestra

White, Clarence Cameron ...... "Meringüe" in the music of Matheus' play *Tambour*

Weinberger, Jaromir .... *Six Bohemian and Dances* for orchestra

Whithorne, Emerson .... *Valse de Concert* for piano op 9 no. 1
Fandango for orchestra

Whyte, Ian .... *Three Scottish Dances*

Winterling, William .... *Die Beiden Schwarzdrosseln,* a fantasy Polka for two piccolas and orchestra

Woods, Francis Cunningham ... Jig and Finale in the *Gressenhall,* a suite in F Major for strings and piano

Weprik, Alexander .... *Dances and Songs of the Ghetto* for orchestra

Wolf-Ferrari .... *English Dance Suite* for strings, op. 12
Apache Dance in the opera *Jewels of the Madonna*
Dance of the Angels in the opera *La Vita Nuova*

Wald, Max .... *The Dancer Dead* for orchestra

Wetzler, Hermann Hans .... *Dances in Basque Style* for orchestra (Probably excerpts from the opera *The Basque Venus*)

Weisman, Julius .... *A Dance Fantasy* for orchestra, op. 35

Weill, Kurt .... *Fantasy, Passacaglia and Hymn* for orchestra

Weiss, Karl .... Slavic Dance themes in the opera *The Polish Jew*
Six Dramatic Dances for small orchestra

Weinberg, Jacob .... Arabian Dance on authentic themes in the opera *The Pioneers*

Youferoff, Serge .... *Suite de Ballet* for orchestra, op. 49

Zarzycki, Alexander .... Dances in the *Polish Suite* for orchestra, op. 37

Zelenski, Wladislaw .... *Suite of Polish Dances,* for orchestra, op. 47

Zandonai, Riccardo .... Torch Dance in the opera *Romeo and Juliet*

Dances in the opera *I Cavalieri di Ekebu*

Zepler .... Dances in the opera *Der Vicomte de Létorières*

GENERAL INDEX

A

Abraham, Gerald H. (quoted), 249, 259

Achron, Joseph (composer), 183, 208, 209

Adam, Adolphe (composer), 89, 90, 92, 109, 116, 230

Adami, G. (librettist) 341

Adenès, the Trouvere, 137

Adlington, Fred, 213

Aeschylus, 31

Africa, dance music of, 15, 16, 17, 18, 19, 24

African Pas (a dance), 276

Aiken, Conrad (poet), 388

Air, 135, 141, 214

Akins, Zoë (poet), 389

Alarcon, 334

Albanese, Antonio (pianist), 408

Albeniz (composer), 206, 336

Alcman (composer), 31

Alexander II of Russia, 127

Alfane, France (composer), 340

Alfonse the Wise, 50

Allan, Maude (dancer), 316, 318

Allemande (a dance), 56, 135, 136, 144, 145 185, 222

Allende, Humberto (composer), 45

Alter, Martha (composer), 307

Altschuler, Modeste (conductor), 122

Amaterasu, the Sun Goddess, 28

Ambrosio, Alfredo d' (composer), 341

Amé-no-Uzumé (legendary character), 28

Ames, Winthrop (scenarist), 308

Anatomy of Abuses, by Master Stubbs, 55

Anderson, Hans Christian (author), 216, 319, 367, 368

Anderson, Walter (quoted), 286

Angelico, Fra, 50

Angiolini Gaspare (choreographer), 87, 88, 89, 115

Angkor Vat, 30, 393

Anne, Empress of Russia, 123

Annunzio, Gabriele d' (poet), 163, 179

Antheil, George (composer), 242, 243, 249, 254, 259, 273, 285, 302, 303, 311

Anti-masques, 54

Apollo, hymn to, 33

Apponyi, Count Sandor (quoted), 228

Arabia, dance music of, 44

Araucanians of Chile, 45

Arbeau, Thoinet, 50, 53, 136, 222, 419

Arends (composer), 271

Arensky, Anton (composer), 234, 265, 416

Argentina, dance music in, 341

Argentina, La (dancer), 333, 334, 383, 390, 431

Aristides, 32

Aristophanes, 32

Arnaöut (a dance), 33

Arnold, Joseph (quoted), 212, 372

Asafiew, Boris (or Igor Glebov: composer), 269

Aspelmayer (composer), 87

Aspla, Oscar (composer), 334

Assyria, musicians of, 42

Atabales (kettledrums), 47

Athanasius, on religious dance, 49

Atterberg (composer), 367

Auber (composer), 89, 208

Aubert, Louis (composer), 210

Auric (composer), 243, 261, 281, 322, 325

Austin, Mary (quoted), 274

Australia, dance music of, 22

Avellan, Francisco (composer), 206, 393

Avery (quoted), 370

INDEX OF MUSICAL COMPOSITIONS

A

Acante et Céphisse, *Rameau*, 102
Achille à Scyros, *Gardel*, 81
Achille à Scyros, *Cherubini*, 106
Achille auf Skyros, *Wellesz*, 352
Acis and Galatea, *Handel*, 101
Ada et Lolly, *Prokofieff*, 263
Adam and Eve, *Torjussen*, 367
Adèle de Foix, *Reissiger*, 225
Adieu, New York, *Auric*, 281
Adonis, *Severac*, 329
Africaine, L', *Meyerbeer*, 108
African Dances, *Villa-Lobos*, 217
African Suite, *Coleridge-Taylor*, 217
Afro-American Symphony, *Still*, 299-300
Aïda, *Verdi*, 162
Airs de Danse, *Rameau*, 96
Alceste, *Gluck*, 103-104
Alcina, *Handel*, 101
Alegrías, *Avellan*, 393
Aleko, *Rachmaninoff*, 170
Alexander the Great, *Gaubert*, 329
Alla Polacca, *Taubert*, 194
Allegretto (Minuet of Congratulations), *Beethoven*, 214
Alma, *Costa*, 118
Almira, *Handel*, 100
Alt Wien, *Castelnuovo-Tedesco*, 208, 233
Alt Wien, *Godowsky*, 233
Amancay, *Villoud*, 341
Amants Eternels, *Messager*, 94
Amaryllis, *Ghys*, 80
Amazonas, *Villa-Lobos*, 342
Amor Brujo, El, *Falla*, 335
Amphion, *Honnegger*, 324
Anacréon, *Cherubini*, 106
Andrea Chenier, *Giordano*, 163
Andalucía, *Lecuona*, 206

Angel of Annunciation, *Wilckens*, 398
Angel of Last Judgement, *Wilckens*, 398
Angelique, *Ibert*, 329
Angkor-Vat, *Cohen*, 393
Anna-Anna, *Weill*, 352
Années de Pélerinage, *Liszt*, 208
Anthony and Cleopatra, *Youferoff*, 169
Anthony Comstock, *Alter*, 307
Aphrodite, *Nabokoff*, 270
Apollon Musagète, *Stravinsky*, 257
Arabella, *Strauss*, 159
Arabesques, *Debussy*, 190
Ariadne, *Handel*, 101
Ariodante, *Handel*, 101
Arkansas Traveller, *Guion*, 219
Arlequin, *Lalo*, 189
Arlesienne, L', *Bizet*, 173
Armide, *Gluck*, 103-104
Armide et Renaud, *Lully*, 99
Ascanio, *Saint-Saëns*, 171
Aschenbrödel, *Strauss*, 229
Astuzie Femminile, Le, *Cimarosa*, 336
At the Boar's Head, *Holst*, 213
At the Foot of Krivan Mountain, *Móry*, 202
Atlanta, *Handel*, 101
Atlantis, *Cowell*, 309
Aubade, *Poulenc*, 325
Aucassin and Nicolette, *Holbrooke*, 361
Auf der Alm, *Egk*, 352
Aventure de la Guinard, Une-*André Messager*, 94
Aventures de Mercure, Les-*Satie*, 314
Aventures du Serail, Les-*Scarlatti*, 115

B

Bacchanal, *Glazounow*, 416
Bacchanale, *Riegger*, 404
Bacchantes, Les, *Bruneau*, 329

509